MULTICULTURAL EUROPE: EFFECTS OF THE GLOBAL LISBON PROCESS. MUSLIM POPULATION SHARES AND GLOBAL DEVELOPMENT PATTERNS 1990-2003 IN 134 COUNTRIES

MULTICULTURAL EUROPE: EFFECTS OF THE GLOBAL LISBON PROCESS. MUSLIM POPULATION SHARES AND GLOBAL DEVELOPMENT PATTERNS 1990-2003 IN 134 COUNTRIES

ARNO TAUSCH

Nova Science Publishers, Inc.
New York

Copyright © 2008 by Nova Science Publishers, Inc.

All rights reserved. No part of this book may be reproduced, stored in a retrieval system or transmitted in any form or by any means: electronic, electrostatic, magnetic, tape, mechanical photocopying, recording or otherwise without the written permission of the Publisher.

For permission to use material from this book please contact us:
Telephone 631-231-7269; Fax 631-231-8175
Web Site: http://www.novapublishers.com

NOTICE TO THE READER

The Publisher has taken reasonable care in the preparation of this book, but makes no expressed or implied warranty of any kind and assumes no responsibility for any errors or omissions. No liability is assumed for incidental or consequential damages in connection with or arising out of information contained in this book. The Publisher shall not be liable for any special, consequential, or exemplary damages resulting, in whole or in part, from the readers' use of, or reliance upon, this material. Any parts of this book based on government reports are so indicated and copyright is claimed for those parts to the extent applicable to compilations of such works.

Independent verification should be sought for any data, advice or recommendations contained in this book. In addition, no responsibility is assumed by the publisher for any injury and/or damage to persons or property arising from any methods, products, instructions, ideas or otherwise contained in this publication.

This publication is designed to provide accurate and authoritative information with regard to the subject matter covered herein. It is sold with the clear understanding that the Publisher is not engaged in rendering legal or any other professional services. If legal or any other expert assistance is required, the services of a competent person should be sought. FROM A DECLARATION OF PARTICIPANTS JOINTLY ADOPTED BY A COMMITTEE OF THE AMERICAN BAR ASSOCIATION AND A COMMITTEE OF PUBLISHERS.

LIBRARY OF CONGRESS CATALOGING-IN-PUBLICATION DATA

Multicultural Europe : effects of the global Lisbon process / Arno Tausch.
   p. cm.
 ISBN 978-1-60456-806-6 (hardcover)
 1. Europe--Social conditions--21st century. 2. Social indicators--Europe. 3. Europe--Ethnic relations. I. Tausch, Arno, 1951-
 HN374.M85 2008
 305.80094--dc22
                         2008023093

Published by Nova Science Publishers, Inc. ✦ *New York*

Contents

Preface		vii
Chapter 1	Introduction	1
Chapter 2	Developing a Theory	5
Chapter 3	Looking Back on Earlier Research	25
Chapter 4	The Variables	27
Chapter 5	The Research Design	31
Chapter 6	The Results for the Fourteen Core Dependent Variables	53
Chapter 7	Discussion on the Results so far	63
Chapter 8	Life Satisfaction, Unequal Exchange, Unemployment and Muslim Population Shares	71
Chapter 9	The Gender Dimension	83
Chapter 10	The Dimension of Human Rights	89
Chapter 11	Concluding Final Tests and Theoretical Surveys	103
Chapter 12	General Conclusions for the "Global Lisbon Index" and its Components	131
Appendix		139
References		219
Index		291

PREFACE

In this publication, the first of its kind to develop a quantitative assessment of the *"global Lisbon process"* of the convergence or divergence of living conditions across the globe since the 1990s, we draw some optimistic, socio-liberal conclusions about Islam in the world system, while we show at the same time that membership in the EU-15, by comparative standards, has dire long-term consequences in the world economy, and globalization does not fulfill many of its promises. The European political class thus should concentrate on reforming the EU, and not on blocking the accession of Turkey or not even thinking about an increased partnership with the Euromediterranean Southern neighbors because of the alleged "Muslim" or even "alien" "character" of their culuture.

9 key conclusions are drawn:

1) First of all, Islam is hardly to blame for global development problems, let alone, Muslim migration is to blame for the failure of the European Lisbon process
2) it emerges that the European Union, the way it is constructed, is not the answer, but part of the very problem of stagnation and deficient development
3) in particular, the Lisbon target "low comparative price levels" contradicts the other Lisbon targets
4) Europe is characterized by an aging society and the pension crisis. But World Bank pension models will not propel economic growth and sustainable development
5) Opening up to global markets and unfettered globalization will not provide sustainable development to the European political economy
6) Many of the ills of the Muslim world are in reality caused by the crisis of modernization ("things get worse, before they get better")
7) The "Limits to Growth" in the richest countries create serious social and ecological tensions
8) Urbanization negatively affects development in many ways
9) The positive effects of globalization are very limited

Countering some alarmist voices in the West, Muslim culture is not to be blamed for the contemporary European crisis, but the very nature of dependent capitalist accumulation that is at the core of the present European "construction".

This study replicates earlier results by Tausch, 2003 with a new research design, using new data and new variables. Instead of using membership in the Organization of the Islamic Conference (OIC) as a dummy variable to measure the societal weight of "Muslim culture", the present author uses a new data series about the percentage of people adhering to the Muslim faith (Nationmaster, 2007) as a direct estimate of the influence of "Muslim culture" in a given society.

While the analysis on world development 1990 – 2003, which contradicts in many ways Huntingtons famous book (1996), shows the detrimental effects of dependency, low comparative price levels and membership in the EU-15 on the social and ecological balances of countries of the world, we also tested the effects of our new data on Muslims per cent of total population on a comprehensive number of dependent variables of socio-economic development in 134 countries of the world, namely

1) economic growth, 1990-2003 (UNDP HDR, 2005)
2) freedom from political rights violations, 1998, and 2006 (Easterly, 2000-2002, and Freedom House, 2007)
3) Happy Planet Index (Happy Planet Organization)
4) Human development Index, 2005 (UNDP HDR 2005)
5) Gender development index 2004 (UNDP HDR, 2006)
6) Gender empowerment index, 2004 (UNDP HDR, 2006)
7) life expectancy, 1995-2000 (UNDP HDR 2000)
8) Life Satisfaction (Happy Planet Organization)
9) freedom from unemployment (UN statistical system website, social indicators)
10) eco-social market economy (GDP output per kg energy use) (UNDP HDR 2000)
11) the Yale/Columbia environmental sustainability index (ESI-Index), 2005
12) female economic activity rate as % of male economic activity rate (UNDP HDR 2000)
13) freedom from % people not expected to survive age 60 (UNDP HDR 2000)
14) freedom from a high ecological Footprint (Happy Planet Organization)
15) freedom from a high quintile ratio (share of income/consumption richest 20% to poorest 20%) (UNDP HDR 2005)
16) freedom from civil liberty violations, 1998, and 2006 (Easterly, 2002, and Freedom House, 2007)
17) freedom from high CO_2 emissions per capita (UNDP HDR 2000)

Ceteris paribus, **Muslim culture** even **significantly** and **positively affects** the **human rights record, human development, gender development,** and the **ecological balances,** and in general terms **alleviates** the **problem** of **"structural violence",** measured in terms proposed by Galtung (1971). But there is a **significant negative relationship** between the percentages of **Muslims per total population** and the indicator: **life satisfaction**. Also it emerges that Muslim nations and countries with large Muslim population shares suffer dispropotrionately from heavy **unemployment**; which is closely connected to the problem of unequal exchange (low comparative international price levels).

As to the causal directions of these relationships, the article argues in favor of cautious interpretations, and no final verdict is reached. In many ways, **Muslim communities** are to be regarded as **socially stabilizing** and **growth enhancing factors**. But the negative relationship between life satisfaction and Muslim population shares invites for a more thorough debate on happiness, based on classic Muslim philosophy or hanafist Euro-Islam, and against tendencies of a salafist reading of the scriptures. Our work also argues in favor of taking the problem of unequal exchange (low comparative price levels) more seriously as in the past. It is an underlying causal mechanism, creating unemployment in the Muslim world. At any rate, a liberal, tolerant and spiritual reading of the Holy Scriptures is recommended – much in the spirit of major religious Muslim figures as Professor Smail Balic from Bosnia and Professor Ali Bardakoglu from Turkey.

We also discard the thesis, offered by Inglehart and Norris, who maintained that Muslim societies and the West differ especially on issues of gender. But the UNDP **gender development index** is neatly, positively and significantly influenced by the share of Muslims per total population, once we properly control for development levels and other relevant, intervening variables. **Urbanization** significantly **improves** the chances for **gender development**, while two **globalization indicators: low comparative international price levels** and **World Bank three pillar pension reforms, significantly reduce the chances for an equitable gender development**, which *per se* would significantly **rise with rising levels of economic maturity** (ln GDP PPP per capita ^2). Our equation explains more than 9/10 of gender development. Our equation for **gender empowerment**, which explains 4/5 of this variable, however, shows the limits of the **urbanization process**. It is **not Islam**, but the **urbanization process**, which reduces the chances for women for a more equitable share of the power in society, while the historical conquests of *"socialism"* in the **transition economies** and in countries, which even today practice **state interventionism**, significantly **improve** the gender empowerment index. In addition, capitalist globalization – here in the form of high foreign savings – significantly diminishes the power sharing by women, while Muslim population shares even have a slightly positive effect on gender empowerment, once you properly control for the influence of the other variables.

We also reject empirically the thesis that Muslim population shares are related in a linear (or non-linear way) to **conflict. There is also no robust relationship of the Muslim population share with outward migration**.

We also replicate our optimistic findings about human rights with the latest **Freedom House** indicator series about political and civil rights 2003 – 2006.

By using the well-established UNDP indicator construction method, a final analysis combines the 17 indicators of the model into one single and combined **"global Lisbon process"** indicator. Again it is shown that globalization, especially lowering the comparative price level, negatively affects the "Lisbon process", while the presence of a larger Muslim population among the total population is positively related to the global Lisbon performance. Switzerland, Iceland and Austria lead the world league of "Lisbon achievements", while the "Lisbon reference country" United States is only ranked 38th among 134 countries. We also show the determinants of the sub-components of the new global Lisbon index, i.e. growth, cohesion and jobs; the environment, gender equality, basic human needs satisfaction, and human rights. Nowhere Muslim population has a significant negative influence.

JEL classification: C21 - Cross-Sectional Models; Spatial Models; Treatment Effect Models; **C43** - Index Numbers and Aggregation; **Z12** – Religion; **F59** - International Relations and International Political Economy: Other

Chapter 1

INTRODUCTION

Is "Islam" really to blame for many of the ills of the world, like stagnation, gender inequality, social inequality, human rights violations and ecologically unsustainable development?

In this book I'll present a Barro-type of cross-national development accounting framework for the weight that the variable "Muslims per total population" has in comparison to standard world economic openness, political geography and political history indicators for 17 key economic, political, social and environmental variables in 134 countries[1]

1. economic growth, 1990-2003 (UNDP HDR, 2005)
2. eco-social market economy (GDP output per kg energy use) (UNDP HDR 2000)
3. female economic activity rate as % of male economic activity rate (UNDP HDR 2000)
4. freedom from % people not expected to survive age 60 (UNDP HDR 2000)
5. freedom from a high ecological Footprint (Happy Planet Organization)
6. freedom from a high quintile ratio (share of income/consumption richest 20% to poorest 20%) (UNDP HDR 2005)
7. freedom from civil liberty violations, 1998, and 2006 (Easterly, 2000 - 2002, and Freedom House, 2007)
8. freedom from high CO_2 emissions per capita (UNDP HDR 2000)
9. freedom from political rights violations, 1998 (Easterly, 2000 - 2002)
10. freedom from unemployment (UN statistical system website, social indicators)
11. Gender development index 2004 (UNDP HDR, 2006)
12. Gender empowerment index, 2004 (UNDP HDR, 2006)
13. Happy Planet Index (Happy Planet Organization)
14. Human development Index, 2005 (UNDP HDR 2005)
15. life expectancy, 1995-2000 (UNDP HDR 2000)
16. Life Satisfaction (Happy Planet Organization)
17. the Yale/Columbia environmental sustainability index (ESI-Index), 2005

---

[1] For the year 2000 or later, if available. As to the sources, see Chapter 4 and 5.

The choice of the independent variables well corresponds to the published literature on the subject, "pitting", so to speak, the predictive power of the "Huntington factor" against:

- foreign saving [(I-S)/GNP]
- low comparative international price level [(ERD, exchange rate deviation index)]
- penetration by core-capital [(MNC PEN 1995)]
- state interventionism (absence of ec. freedom)
- world bank pension reforms

under proper control for the well-known world geographic and world economic and world historic determinants of the development chances of a nation:

- Development level [ln(GDP PPP pc)]
- Development level squared [ln (GDP PPP pc)^2]
- Dummy for being landlocked
- Dummy for transition economy
- EU-membership (EU-15)
- Urbanization ratio, 1990

Much has been written during recent years about the triumph of globalization and the free markets, and considerable empirical evidence in favor of economic openness and economic freedom has been made available [Barro R. J. (1991), Barro R. J. (1994), Barro R. J. (1996a), Barro R. J. (1996b), Barro R. J. (2000), Barro R. J. (2001), Barro R. J. (2003), Barro R. J. (2004a), Barro R. J. (2004b), Barro R. J. and Grilli V. (1994), Barro R. J. and McCleary R. M. (2003a), Barro R. J. and McCleary R. M. (2003b), Barro R. J. and McCleary R. M. (2004), Barro R. J. and Sala-i-Martin X. (1991), Barro R. J. and Sala-i-Martin X. (1995/98), Barro, R. J. and Sala-i-Martin X. (1992), Becker G. (1993), Betcherman G. (2002), Bhagwati J.N. (1989), Carroll E. (2000), Dollar D. (2005), Dollar D. and Kraay A. (2000), Dollar D. and Kraay A. (2001a), Fukuyama F. (1991), Gholami R., Lee S. Y. T and Heshmati A. (2003), Haouas I; Yagoubi, M; and Heshmati A (2002a), Haouas I; Yagoubi, M; and Heshmati, A. (2002b), Harss C. and Maier K. (1998) Heshmati A. (2003a), Heshmati A. (2003b), Heshmati A. and Addison T. (2003), Kearny A.T. (2001), Klein M. et al. (2001), Moore M. (2003), Nederveen-Pieterse J. (1997), Olson M. (1982), Olson M. (1986), Olson M. (1987), Weede E. (1990), Weede E. (1992), Weede E. (1993a), Weede E. (1993b), Weede E. (1996a), Weede E. (1996b), Weede E. (1997), Weede E. (1999a), Weede E. (2002) Weede E. (2003), Weede E. (2004a), Weede E. (2004b), Weede E. (2004c), Weede E. (2004d), Weede E. (2005), Weede E. and Muller E. N. (1998)]. Save some exceptions, hard cross-national evidence in favor of the "Huntington thesis" has been rather scarce, while quantitative dependency and world systems theory by and large has neglected the "Huntington challenge".

Yet, world systems theory, going back to its four "founding fathers" Samir Amin, Giovanni Arrighi, Andre Gunder Frank and Immanuel Wallerstein, would contain lots of "building blocs" for such a renewed world systems paradigm of dependency and underdevelopment, properly integrating the "Muslim factor". For the Egyptian "founding father" of the world systems paradigm, Samir Amin, (1997), ascent and decline is largely being determined in our age by the following 'five monopolies'

- the monopoly of technology, supported by military expenditures of the dominant nations
- the monopoly of control over global finances and a strong position in the hierarchy of current account balances
- the monopoly of access to natural resources
- the monopoly over international communication and the media
- the monopoly of the military means of mass destruction

Let us also recall, that for Amin (1975), there are four main characteristics of the peripheral societal formation

- the predominance of agrarian capitalism in the 'national' sector
- the formation of a local bourgeoisie, which is dependent from foreign capital, especially in the trading sector
- the tendency of bureaucratization
- specific and incomplete forms of proletarization of the labor force

In partial accordance with liberal thought, (i) and (iii) explain the tendency towards low savings; thus there will be

- huge state sector deficits and, in addition, their 'twin':
- chronic current account balance deficits

in the peripheral countries. High imports of the periphery, and hence, in the long run, capital imports, are the consequence of the already existing structural deformations of the role of peripheries in the world system, namely by

- rapid urbanization, combined with an insufficient local production of food
- excessive expenditures of the local bureaucracies
- changes in income distribution to the benefit of the local elites (demonstration effects)
- insufficient growth of and structural imbalances in the industrial sector
- and the following reliance on foreign assistance

The history of periphery capitalism, Amin argues, is full of short-term 'miracles' and long-term blocks, stagnation and even regression.
While mass demand and reforms in the agricultural structures (Elsenhans, 1983, a disciple of Amin) were responsible for the transition from the tributary mode of production in Western Europe to capitalism from the Long 16th Century onwards, periphery capitalism was and is characterized by the following main tendencies (Amin, 1973 - 1997):

- regression in both agriculture and small scale industry characterizes the period after the onslaught of foreign domination and colonialism
- unequal international specialization of the periphery leads to the concentration of activities in export oriented agriculture and or mining. Some industrialization of the periphery is possible under the condition of low wages, which, together with rising productivity, determine that unequal exchange sets in (double factorial terms of trade < 1.0; see Raffer, 1987)
- these structures determine in the long run a rapidly growing tertiary sector with hidden unemployment and the rising importance of rent in the overall social and economic system
- the development blocks of peripheral capitalism (chronic current account balance deficits, re-exported profits of foreign investments, deficient business cycles of the periphery, which provide important markets for the centers during world economic upswings)
- structural imbalances in the political and social relationships, inter alia a strong 'compradore' element and the rising importance of state capitalism and an indebted state class.

These factors, described by Amin, are highly relevant in the Muslim world. They, and not "Muslim culture", would explain the trajectory of this part of our globe according to world systems theory.

Chapter 2

DEVELOPING A THEORY

In the following, we will present a fairly comprehensive theoretical survey of earlier research on the subject of the causes of cross-national differences in international development and growth, and try to present the amazing and often contradictory quantitative research findings, presented thus far in the literature.

SURVEYING THE "GRAND THEORIES"

Today, a truly massive cross-national research literature exists, whose results are often diametrically opposed to one another, with dependency scholars claiming that dependency has adverse affects on the 'human condition' (economic growth, income equality, human well-being, gender and ecological relationships), while neo-liberal scholars claiming the opposite. We try to do justice to some 240 quantitative studies that are contained in our bibliography, and try to present in this theoretical overview those determinants of the "human condition" that are sufficiently available for more than 120 nations [see Ahluwalia M. S. (1974), Ahulwalia M. S. (1976), Alderson A. and Nielsen F. (1999), Alderson A. S., Beckfield J. and Nielsen F. (2005), Babones S. J. (2002), Barro R. J. (1991), Barro R. J. (1994), Barro R. J. (1996a), Barro R. J. (1996b), Barro R. J. (2000), Barro R. J. (2001), Barro R. J. (2003), Barro R. J. (2004a), Barro R. J. (2004b), Barro R. J. and Grilli V. (1994), Barro R. J. and McCleary R. M. (2003a), Barro R. J. and McCleary R. M. (2003b), Barro R. J. and McCleary R. M. (2004), Barro R. J. and Sala-i-Martin X. (1991), Barro R. J. and Sala-i-Martin X. (1995/98), Barro, R. J. and Sala-i-Martin X. (1992), Becker G. (1993), Beckerman W. (1992), Beer L. (1999), Beer L. and Boswell T. (2002), Bergesen A. and Fernandez R. (1999), Betcherman G. (2002), Bhagwati J.N. (1989), Bornschier V. and Ballmer-Cao, T. H. (1979), Bornschier V. and Chase-Dunn Ch. K (1985), Bornschier V. and Heintz P., reworked and enlarged by Th. H. Ballmer - Cao and J. Scheidegger (1979), Bornschier V. and Nollert M. (1994), Bornschier V. et al. (1980), Bornschier V., Chase-Dunn Ch. and Rubinson R. (1977), Boswell T. and Dixon W. J. (1993), Boswell T. and Dixon W.J. (1990), Bradshaw Y. (1987), Bradshaw Y. and Huang J. (1991), Bradshaw Y. W. and Schafer M. J. (2000), Bradshaw Y. W., Noonan R; and Gash L. (1993), Breedlove W. L. and Armer J. M. (1996), Breedlove W. L. and Armer J. M. (1997), Bullock B. and Firebaugh G. (1990), Burns T. J. et al. (1994), Burns T. J., Kentor J. D. and Jorgenson, A. (2002), Burns T. J., Kick E. L. and

Davis B. L. (2003), Caporaso J. A. (1978), Carroll E. (2000), Chan St. and Mintz A. (1992), Chase-Dunn Ch. K. (1975), Chase-Dunn Ch. K. (2005), Clark R. (1992), Clark R. et al. (1991), Crenshaw E. M. (1991), Crenshaw E. M. (1992), Crenshaw E. M. (1993), Crenshaw E. M. (1995), Crenshaw E. M. and Ansari A. (1994), Crenshaw E. M. and Jenkins J. C. (1996), Crenshaw E. M. and Oakey, D. R. (1998), Crenshaw E. M.; Ameen A. Z.; and Christenson. M. (1997), Crenshaw E. M.; Christenson M.; Oakey D. R. (2000), Delacroix J. and Ragin Ch. (1981), Dixon C. J., Drakakis-Smith D. and Watts H. D. (1986), Dixon W. J. (1984), Dixon W. J. and Boswell T. (1996b), Dollar D. (2005), Dollar D. and Kraay A. (2000), Dollar D. and Kraay A. (2001a), Easterly W. (2001), Easterly W. (2002), Ehrhardt-Martinez K.; Crenshaw E. M.; and Jenkins J. C. (2002), Evans P. B. and Timberlake M. (1980), Fain H. D. et al. (1997), Fiala R. (1992), Firebaugh G. (1992), Firebaugh G. (1996), Firebaugh G. and Beck F. D. (1994), Frey R. S. and Field C. (2000), Fukuyama F. (1991), Galtung J. (1971), Galtung J., Chase-Dunn, Ch. K. et al. (1985), Gartner R. (1990), Ghobarah H. et al. (2001), Gholami R., Lee S. Y. T and Heshmati A. (2003), Gissinger R. and Gleditsch N. P. (1999), Goldfrank W. L. (1999), Gore A. (1994), Grimes P. and Kentor J. (2003), Hadden K. and London B. (1996), Haouas I; Yagoubi, M; and Heshmati A (2002a), Haouas I; Yagoubi, M; and Heshmati, A. (2002b), Hertz E. et al. (1994), Heshmati A. (2003a), Heshmati A. (2003b), Heshmati A. and Addison T. (2003), Huang J. (1995), Roberts J. T., Grimes P. E. and Jodie L. Manale J. L. (2003), Jenkins J. C. and Scanlan S. J. (2001), Johnson R. B. (1986), Jorgenson A. K. and Rice J. (2005), Kasarda J.D. and Crenshaw E.M. (1991), Kearny A.T. (2001), Kent G. (1995), Kentor J. D. (1998), Kentor J. D. (2001), Kentor J. D. (2005), Kentor J. D. and Boswell T. (2003), Kentor J. D. and Jang J. S. (2004), Kick E. L. and Davis B. L. (2001), Kick E. L. et al. (1990), Kick E. L. et al. (1995), Kick E. L., Davis B. L. and Burns T. J. (1998), Kick E. L., Davis B. L. and Burns T. J. (2000), Klein M. et al. (2001), Klitgaard R. and Fedderke J. (1995), Köhler G. (1976a), Köhler G. and Tausch A. (2002), Kohli A. et al. (1984), Krahn H. and Gartrell J. W. (1985), Lena H. F. and London B. (1993), London B. (1987), London B. (1988), London B. (1990), London B. and Robinson T. (1989), London B. and Ross R. J. S. (1995), London B. and Smith D. A. (1988), London B. and Williams B. A. (1988), London B. and Williams B. A. (1990), Lopez G. A. and Stohl M. (1989), Meyer W. H. (1996), Miller C. D. (1999), Mittelman J. (1994), Moaddel M. (1994), Moon B.E. and Dixon W.J. (1992), Moore M. (2003), Muller E. N. (1988), Muller E. N. (1993), Muller E. N. (1995), Muller E. N. and Seligson M. A. (1987), Munasinghe M., Miguel: de and Sunkel O. (2001), Neapolitan J. L. and Schmalleger F. (1997), Nederveen-Pieterse J. (1997), Nielsen F. (1995), Nolan P. D. (1983), Nollert M. (1994a), Nollert M. (1994b), O'Loughlin J.; Ward M. D.; and Shin M. (1998), Olson M. (1982), Olson M. (1986), Olson M. (1987), Prechel H. (1985), Ragin C. C. and Bradshaw Y. W. (1992), Ram R. (1992), Robinson T.D. and London B. (1991), Rothgeb J. M. Jr. (1993a), Rothgeb J. M. Jr. (1993b), Rothgeb J. M. Jr. (1996a), Rothgeb J. M. Jr. (1996b), Rothgeb J. M. Jr. (1999), Rothgeb J. M. Jr. (2002), Rothgeb, J. M. Jr. (1995), Rubinson R. (1976), Russett B. (1983a), Russett B. (1983b), Sawada Y. and Yotopoulos P. A. (1999), Sawada Y. and Yotopoulos P. A. (2002), Shafik N. and Bandyopadhyay S. (1992), Shandra J. M., London B. and Williamson J. B. (2003), Shandra J. M., Ross R. J. S., London B. (2003), Shandra J. M.; London B.; Whooley O. P; Williamson J. B. (2004), Shandra J. M.; London B.; Williamson J. B. (2003), Shandra J. M.; Nobles J.; London B.; Williamson J. B. (2004), Shandra J. M.; Nobles, J. E.; London B.; Williamson, J. B. (2005), Shandra J., London B, Whooley O. P., et al. (2004), Shen C. and Williamson J. B. (2001), Shin M. E. (1975), Shin M. E. (2002),

Simpson M. (1990), Smith D. A and London B. (1990), Smith D. A. (1994), Smith D. A. (1996), So A. Y. (1990), Soysa I. de (2002), Soysa I. de (2003), Soysa I. de and Gleditsch N. P. (2002), Soysa I. de and John R. Oneal, J. R. (2000), Soysa I. de and Neumayer E. (2005), Spar D. (1999), Stack St. (1998), Stokes R. and Anderson A. (1990), Sunkel O. (1990), Suter Ch. (2005), Tausch A. (1986), Tausch A. (1989a), Tausch A. (1989b), Tausch A. (1990), Tausch A. (1991), Tausch A. (1998a), Tausch A. (1998b), Tausch A. (2003b), Tausch A. (2005b), Tausch A. (2005d), Tausch A. and Prager F. (1993), Timberlake M. and Kantor J. (1983), Timberlake M. and Williams K.R. (1984), Timberlake M. and Williams K.R. (1987), Trezzini B. and Bornschier V. (2001), Tsai P-L. (1995), Van Rossem R. (1996), Wagstaff A. and Watanabe N. (2002), Ward K. B. (1984), Weede E. (1985), Weede E. (1990), Weede E. (1992), Weede E. (1993a), Weede E. (1993b), Weede E. (1996a), Weede E. (1996b), Weede E. (1997), Weede E. (1999a), Weede E. (2002), Weede E. (2003), Weede E. (2004a), Weede E. (2004b), Weede E. (2004c), Weede E. (2004d), Weede E. (2005), Weede E. and Muller E. N. (1998), Weede E. and Tiefenbach H. (1981), Wickrama K. A. S. and Mulford Ch. L. (1996), Wimberley D. W. (1990), Wimberley D. W. (1991), Wimberley D. W. and Bello R. (1992), Wimmer A. (2002), Yotopoulos P. A. (1996), Yotopoulos P. A. (1997a), Yotopoulos P. A. (1997b), Yotopoulos P. A. and Floro S. L. (1992), Yotopoulos P. A. and Lin J. Y. (1993), Yotopoulos P. A., Nugent J. B. (1976), Yotopoulos P. and Sawada Y. (2005)].

Cultural theories of development tend to stress that at present development perspectives for the large Muslim region between Morocco in the West and Iran in the East are not good. Their principal spokesperson today is Huntington, but also such diverse sources as the UNDP's *Arab Human Development Report* (2002) or the World Bank's *MENA Report* (2002) tend to highlight the various development constraints in that region. While the UNDP stresses lack of democracy, human resource development and gender equality as the main development blocks, the World Bank highlights the negative heritage of "Arab Socialism" or past state sector influence. Several authors, among them Noland[1] and Tausch, explicitly contradicted Huntington with empirical, cross-national evidence, however. With all the global interest being expressed nowadays on Islam after the 9/11 terrorist attacks, the negligence of the issue of Muslim culture as a variable in cross-national comparative social science is surprising. For an informed debate, *inter alia* the following cross-national-research-relevant background literature on the trajectory of Muslim nations is available [for a very small and selective bibliography, see, among others Abdullah M. S. and Khoury A. Th. (1984), Garcia de Cortázar F. and Gonzáles Vesga J. M. (1995, on *"Al Andalus"), S. P. (1993), Huntington S. P. (1996), Jabber P. (2001), Khoury A. Th. (1980), Khoury A. Th. (1981), Khoury A. Th. (1991), Moaddel M. (1996), Moaddel M. (1998), Moaddel M. (2004), Raffer K. and Salih M. A. M. (Ed.)(1992), Tausch A. (2003b), Tausch A. (2005c), Tausch A. (2005d), Tibi B. (1973), Tibi B. (1981), Tibi B. (1985), Tibi B. (1990), Tibi B. (1992), Tibi B. (1997a), Tibi B. (1997b), Tibi B. (1997c), Tibi B. (1998a), Tibi B. (1998b), Tibi B. (2001a), and Tibi B. (2001b)].

---

[1] See especially: Marcus Noland and associates: http://www.iie.com/publications/pb/pb04-4.pdf and http://www.iie.com/publications/wp/2003/03-8.pdf. Arno Tausch: (2005) 'Is Islam really a development blockade? 12 predictors of development, including membership in the Organization of Islamic Conference, and their influence on 14 indicators of development in 109 countries of the world with completely available data'. Ankara Center for Turkish Policy Studies, ANKAM, Insight Turkey, 7, 1, 2005: 124 - 135. Full PDF version available at http://www.insightturkey.com/tausch2005_multivariate_analysis_world_dev.pdf

Without question, one of the issues dominating the social scientific debate over recent years has been **globalization**. A recent very thorough liberal globalist flagship synopsis of the quantitative peace- and development research evidence over the last decades by de Soysa and Gleditsch (2002) maintains that **globalization**, especially **openness to trade and foreign direct investment**, leads towards

a) increased democracy
b) development
c) less inequality
d) a better environment
e) peace.

De Soysa and Gleditsch would say: the *banlieues* in France and countries like Madagascar in Africa or Myanmar in Asia remained so poor because France – or Madagascar and Myanmar – did not sufficiently open up to the world economy, while countries like Singapore did. **World market open capitalism is compatible with social cohesion**, indeed it would be one if it's main preconditions.

The **"Washington Consensus"** has been summarized by Raffer (pp. 305 - 323 in Tausch, 2003) as to represent the following policy priorities:

1. Fiscal discipline: a primary budget surplus of several percent of GDP
2. Public expenditure priorities: defined as re-directions of public expenditures towards fields with high economic returns such as primary health and education
3. Tax reform: cutting marginal tax rates
4. Financial liberalization: moderately positive real interest rates and the abolition of preferential interest rates (such as for developmentally useful or socially demanded projects)
5. Exchange rates: unified and competitive
6. Trade liberalization: abolishing quotas (replacing them by tariffs) and reducing tariffs to a uniform low level within three to ten years.
7. Foreign direct investment: equal treatment with domestic firms. The World Bank calls this the elimination of barriers. This principle is also enshrined in the WTO treaties.
8. Privatization
9. Deregulation: abolishing regulations aiming at achieving developmental or social aims
10. Property rights: must be guaranteed.

Literature, supporting the **"Washington Consensus"** now abounds, highlighting **pro-market policies and world economic openness as strategies for social and economic well-being, social justice and economic growth, and a peaceful world** [Barro R. J. (1991), Barro R. J. (1994), Barro R. J. (1996a), Barro R. J. (1996b), Barro R. J. (2000), Barro R. J. (2001), Barro R. J. (2003), Barro R. J. (2004a), Barro R. J. (2004b), Barro R. J. and Grilli V. (1994), Barro R. J. and McCleary R. M. (2003a), Barro R. J. and McCleary R. M. (2003b), Barro R.

J. and McCleary R. M. (2004), Barro R. J. and Sala-i-Martin X. (1991), Barro R. J. and Sala-i-Martin X. (1995/98), Barro, R. J. and Sala-i-Martin X. (1992), Becker G. (1993), Betcherman G. (2002), Bhagwati J.N. (1989), Carroll E. (2000), Dollar D. (2005), Dollar D. and Kraay A. (2000), Dollar D. and Kraay A. (2001a), Fukuyama F. (1991), Gholami R., Lee S. Y. T and Heshmati A. (2003), Haouas I; Yagoubi, M; and Heshmati A (2002a), Haouas I; Yagoubi, M; and Heshmati, A. (2002b), Harss C. and Maier K. (1998) Heshmati A. (2003a), Heshmati A. (2003b), Heshmati A. and Addison T. (2003), Kearny A.T. (2001), Klein M. et al. (2001), Moore M. (2003), Nederveen-Pieterse J. (1997), Olson M. (1982), Olson M. (1986), Olson M. (1987), Weede E. (1990), Weede E. (1992), Weede E. (1993a), Weede E. (1993b), Weede E. (1996a), Weede E. (1996b), Weede E. (1997), Weede E. (1999a), Weede E. (2002) Weede E. (2003), Weede E. (2004a), Weede E. (2004b), Weede E. (2004c), Weede E. (2004d), Weede E. (2005), Weede E. and Muller E. N. (1998)].

The counter-position, advanced by **globalization critics, environmentalists, liberation theologians of all denominations,** and - most recently - **dissidents from the once homogeneous neo-liberal camp** would hold that unfettered globalization increases the social gaps between rich and poor both within countries as well as on a global scale. Most of the adherents of this camp would share the view proposed by Cornia and Kiiski that income distribution in the world system has worsened during the period of globalization. Indeed, the challenge by dependency theory to the neo-classical consensus is a real one – especially in a time of relative stagnation in the centers and social polarization in many countries of the periphery. The massive literature on dependency is still influential in the countries of the world periphery and semi-periphery, the recent wave of neo-liberal globalization notwithstanding [Addo H. (1986), Amin S. (1973), Amin S. (1976), Amin S. (1980) Amin S. (1984), Amin S. (1989), Amin S. (1992), Amin S. (1994a), Amin S. (1994b), Amin S. (1994c), Amin S. (1997a) Amin S. (1997b), Avery W. P. and Rapkin D. P. (1989), Bello W. (1989), Bello W.; with Shea Cunningham and Bill Rau (1999), Cardoso F. H. (1969), Cardoso F. H. (1972), Cardoso F. H. (1973), Cardoso F. H. (1977), Cardoso F. H. (1979), Cardoso F. H. and Faletto E. (1971), Cordova A. (1973), Cordova A. and Silva - Michelena H. (1972), Dubiel I. (1983), Dubiel I. (1993), Falk and Szentes (1997), Feder E. (1972), Flechsig St. (1987), Flechsig St. (1994), Flechsig St. (2000), Froebel F. et al. (1977a), Froebel F. et al. (1977b), Froebel F. et al. (1984), Froebel F. et al. (1986), Furtado C. (1970), Gonzales Casanova P. (1973), Griffin K. and Gurley J. (1985), Hettne B. (1983), Kay C. (1989), Kay C. (1991), Kent G. (1984), Kirby P. (2003a), Kirby P. (2003b), Köhler G. (1975), Köhler G. (1976b), Köhler G. (1978b), Köhler G. (1995), Prebisch R. (1981), Prebisch R. (1983), Prebisch R. (1984), Prebisch R. (1986), Prebisch R. (1988a), Prebisch R. (1988b) Raffer K. (1987a), Russett B. (1978), Singer P. I. (1971), Singer P. I. (1971), Singer P. I. (1972), Singer P. I. (1973), Singer P. I. (1974) Singer P. I. (1976), Singer P. I. (1977), Singer P. I. (1981a), Singer P. I. (1981b), Singer P. I. (1986), Singer P. I. (1987), Singer P. I. (1988), Singer P. I. (1991), Singer P. I. (1998), Singer P. I. (1999a), Singer P. I. (1999b), Singer P. I. et al. (1977), So A. Y. (1990), Sunkel O. (1966), Sunkel O. (1973a), Sunkel O. (1973b), Sunkel O. (1978a), Sunkel O. (1978b), Sunkel O. (1980), Sunkel O. (1984), Sunkel O. (1991), Sunkel O. (1994), Szentes T. (1988), Szentes T. (1989), Szentes T. (2002), Szentes T. (2003a), and Szentes T. (2003b)].

Dependency authors generally explain backwardness and stagnation by the ever-growing dependent insertion of these countries into the world economy. Starting with the writings of Perroux, Prebisch and Rothschild in the 1930s, their leading spokespersons all would stress the unequal and socially imbalanced nature of development in regions that are highly dependent on investment from the highly developed countries, even in the richer countries of the European Union. **Short-term spurts of growth notwithstanding, long-term growth will be imbalanced and unequal, and will tend towards high negative current account balances.**

Later world system analyses – that started with the writings of the Austro-Hungarian socialist Karl Polanyi after the First World War - tended to confirm and expand this dependency argument. Capitalism in the periphery, like in the center, is characterized by strong **cyclical fluctuations**, and there are centers, semi-peripheries and peripheries. **The rise of one group of semi-peripheries tends to be at the cost of another group, but the unequal structure of the world economy based on unequal transfer tends to remain stable.**

So is, then, the poverty, in say, the "*banlieues*" in today's France an immediate consequence of **industrial restructuring**, which takes place, and transfers jobs in an increasing number to the new member countries of the European East? Authors from the world system approach tended to discard the "culturalist" explanations of the malaise in the "*banlieues*," offered by Huntington, and rather would support the argument that **world economic position, and not culture, determines conflict.** The massive world systems literature continues to be a stream of the scientific debate subsisting at the major Universities, publishing houses and scholarly journals around the world, the near complete global triumph of the neo-liberal theory notwithstanding [Arrighi G. (1989), Beaud M. (1990), Chase-Dunn Ch. (1999), Chase-Dunn Ch. K. (1991), Chase-Dunn Ch. K. (1992a), Chase-Dunn Ch. K. (2000), Chase-Dunn Ch. K. and Grimes P. (1995), Denemark R. A., Modelski G., Gills B. K. and Friedman J. (2000), Dunaway W. A. and Wallerstein I. (Eds.)(2003), Frank A. G. (1978a), Frank A. G. (1978b), Frank A. G. (1980), Frank A. G. (1981), Frank A. G. (1983), Frank A. G. (1992), Frank A. G. (1994), Frank A. G. (1998), Frank A. G. and Frank - Fuentes M. (1990), Frank A. G. and Gills B. (Eds.)(1993), Goldfrank W. L. (1978), Goldfrank W. L. (1990), Hettne B. (1989), Hettne B. (1995a), Hopkins T. K. (1982), Hopkins T. K. and Wallerstein I. et al. (1982), Oddone and associates, 2004 – 2005; Polanyi, K. (1979), Polanyi K. (1957), Ray J. L. (1983), Ross R. J. S. and Trachte K.C. (1990), Wallerstein I. (1974), Wallerstein I. (1976), Wallerstein I. (1978), Wallerstein I. (1979a), Wallerstein I. (1979b), Wallerstein I. (1980), Wallerstein I. (1982), Wallerstein I. (1983a), Wallerstein I. (1983b), Wallerstein I. (1984), Wallerstein I. (1986), Wallerstein I. (1989a), Wallerstein I. (1989b), Wallerstein I. (1990), Wallerstein I. (1991a), Wallerstein I. (1991b), Wallerstein I. (1997), Wallerstein I. (1998), and Wallerstein I. (2000)]

Dependency and world system theory generally hold that poverty and backwardness in poor countries and in poor regions of rich countries are caused by the peripheral or quasi-position that these nations or regions have in the **international division of labor**. Ever since the capitalist world system evolved, there is a stark distinction between the nations of the center and the nations of the periphery. Fernando Henrique Cardoso summarized the quantifiable essence of dependency theories as follows:

- there is a financial and technological penetration by the developed capitalist centers of the countries of the periphery and semi-periphery
- this produces an unbalanced economic structure both within the peripheral societies and between them and the centers

- this leads to limitations on self-sustained growth in the periphery
- this favors the appearance of specific patterns of class relations
- these require modifications in the role of the state to guarantee both the functioning of the economy and the political articulation of a society, which contains, within itself, foci of inarticulateness and structural imbalance (Cardoso, 1979)

A rising degree of monopolization in the leading center countries over time determines that, in order to keep the share of wages at least constant, a rising exploitation of the raw material producers sets in to offset the balance. There is massive, internationally published evidence that speaks in favor of dependency theory. However, it would be wrong to portray dependency simply in terms of MNC penetration, and to neglect other aspects of that relationship. Such authors as Singer and Tausch from the dependency camp and Hollis B. Chenery from the World Bank have put emphasis on the **resource balance** as an indicator of the weight of **foreign saving**. The work of the Brazilian economist Paul Israel Singer, which is particularly neglected in the English speaking world, must be especially mentioned here, because his "dependency theory" specifically integrated foreign saving.

Other formulations of dependency insisted that **low international comparative price levels** – one of the fourteen main structural Lisbon indicators designed by the EU-member governments and the European Commission , or as the dependency school calls the phenomenon, **'unequal exchange'**, hampers development. In the literature, we encounter various statistical or empirical concepts to measure this process, one is the Lisbon low comparative price level indicator series, another concept are double factorial terms of trade of the respective country, which are below < 1.0 [see Raffer, 1987, Amin, 1975 furthermore, Kohler/Tausch, 2002, for further literature on unequal exchange as a development bloc includes today Emmanuel, A. (1972), Köhler G. (1998a), Köhler G. (1998a), Köhler G. (1999a), Köhler G. (1999b), Raffer K. (1987b), Raffer K. (1995), Raffer K. and Murshed S. M. (1993), Raffer K. and Singer H. W. (1996), Raffer K. and Singer H. W. (2001), Sawada Y. and Yotopoulos P. A. (1999), Sawada Y. and Yotopoulos P. A. (2002), Yotopoulos P. A. (1996), Yotopoulos P. A. (1997a), Yotopoulos P. A. (1997b), Yotopoulos P. A. and Floro S. L. (1992), Yotopoulos P. A. and Lin J. Y. (1993), Yotopoulos P. A., Nugent J. B. (1976), and Yotopoulos P. and Sawada Y. (2005)]?

Comparative "price levels" are, the Eurostat definition goes, the ratio between GDP at purchasing power parities (PPPs) and GDP at market exchange rates for each country. To quote Eurostat:

"Comparative price levels are the ratio between Purchasing power parities (PPPs) and market exchange rate for each country. PPPs are currency conversion rates that convert economic indicators expressed in national currencies to a common currency, called Purchasing Power Standard (PPS), which equalises the purchasing power of different national currencies and thus allows meaningful comparison. The ratio is shown in relation to the EU average (EU-25 = 100). If the index of the comparative price levels shown for a country is higher/ lower than 100, the country concerned is relatively expensive/cheap as compared with the EU average." (Quotation from Eurostat website, April 6, 2005, at: http://epp.eurostat.cec.eu.int/portal/ age?_pageid=1133, 1406352, 1133_1406373&_dad=portal&_schema=PORTAL

"Comparative price levels" do measure nothing else but the reciprocal value of our variable "unequal exchange" (ERDI). A country, following the Commission's price reform strategy, is a country with a low international price level and a high ERDI.

It seems to be important at this point to emphasize that our three indicators of dependency measure three different types of "dependent development":

- **MNC penetration** measures the different degrees of weight that foreign capital investments have in the host countries, i.e. the UNCTAD percentages of the stocks of multinational corporation investments per total host country GDP
- **Unequal exchange** (ERD or ERDI) measures the degree, to which globalization has contributed to lowering the international price level of a country; i.e. it is an indicator about the openness of the price system *vis-à-vis* the pressures of globalization. The result of this is an unequal transfer from the peripheries to the centers, which used to be high-price countries until very recently. ERD is calculated by the ratio between GDP at purchasing power parities, divided by GDP at current exchange rates
- For dependency authors, **foreign savings** show the weight that foreign savings, mostly from the centers and richer semi-peripheries, have in the accumulation process of the host countries in the periphery and semi-periphery. It is calculated by the difference between the share of investments per GDP and the share of savings per GDP.

Neo-liberal authors, by contrast, interpret the world in a complete different direction from the explanations, offered by dependency theory. For them, **foreign investments** are a solid **pre-condition of growth**. A **reliance on foreign savings** would **not necessarily exclude rapid economic growth and income redistribution** in a world of liberalized financial markets (for an overview of these debates, see Kendall P., 2000; for a dependency-theory oriented counter-position Ghose A. K., 2005, see furthermore Shaw (1973) and McKinnon (1973), as well as the studies by Roubini and Sala-i-Martin (1992) as well as Barro (1991)).

Price levels have risen faster than world price levels for the rich countries while the reverse has been the case for the poor countries. Evidence over several decades thus fails to sustain, Rao, 1998, says, the expectation of **growing price convergence from growing globalization**. However, neo-liberals would argue that the leveling of world price levels is beneficial for world system and country economic growth rates.

An onslaught against the dependency theory consensus [i.e. that dependency leads to stagnation and inequality], was presented by arguments put forward by neo-liberal authors that world economic openness leads to high growth and to a redistribution of incomes. Their preferred measure of world economic openness is the share of foreign trade in total GDP, i.e. countries should re-orient their economic policies towards external markets and unfettered competition. On a global economy level, **neo-liberal authors** like Barro; Barro and associates; Crafts; Dadush and Brahmbatt; Dollar and Kraay and Weede generally tend to think that with the establishment of **"economic freedom"** positive patterns of development will prevail in practically all countries of the globe, irrespective of their development level. As could be easily predicted, such reasoning did not go uncontested.

Especially the **painful experience of the neo-liberal transformation process in Eastern Europe** after the end of Communism is interpreted by many as a warning sign to decision-makers and scholars alike that "economic freedom" plus "world economic openness" alone cannot be for themselves the only necessary, let alone the sufficient condition for a successful capitalist development [Amsden A. H. et al. (1994), Angresano J. (1994), Barta V. and Richter S. (1996), Bauer P. (1998), Bhaduri A. and Laski K. (1996), Borocz J. (1996), Borocz J. (1999), Borocz J. and Kovacz M. (Eds.) (2001), Borocz J. and Sarkar M. (2005), Borocz J. and Smith D. A. (1995), Chase-Dunn Ch. K. (1992b), Chase-Dunn Ch. K. (Ed.), Cornia G. A. (Ed.)(1993), Cornia G. A. (Ed.)(1994), Cornia G. A. and Paniccia R. (Eds.)(2000), Deacon B. (1992a), Deacon B. (1992b), Frank A. G. (1990), Gierus J. (1998), Goldfrank W. L. (1982), Havlik P. (1996), Hettne B. (1994), Hickmann Th. (1994), Hofbauer H and Komlosy A. (1994), Hofbauer H and Komlosy A. (2000), Holmes L. (1999), Holtbruecke D. (1996), Huber P. (1999), Huber P. (1999), Huebner K. (1994), Inotai A. (2001a), Inotai A. (2001b), Inotai A. and Hettne B. (1999), Inotai A. and Hettne B. (2000), Inotai A. and Hettne B. (2001), Inotai A. and Sander H. (2002), Juchler J. (1986), Juchler J. (1992a), Juchler J. (1992b), Juchler J. (1992c), Juchler J. (1992d), Juchler J. (1994), Juchler J. (1995), Juchler J. (2001), Juchler J. (2003), Juchler J. (2004), Linnemann H. and Sarma A. (1991), Morawetz R. (1991), Nolte H. H. (1989), Orenstein M. A. (1996), Orlowski L. T. (1996), Spiesberger M. (1998), Srubar I. (1994), Tausch A. (1991), United Nations Development Programme, Regional Bureau for Europe and the CIS (1999)]. **Thus, selective intervention by the state seems to be the most important development lesson of East and South-East Asia as well as Scandinavia during the last decades.** The ample literature about these aspects of **selective government intervention** as the best strategy to fulfill international growth and social inclusion targets should be more widely known in cross-national research.

"Industrial policy", and **"active adoption to the changing structures of the international division of labor",** and not pure economic freedom seemed at times to be the catchword of the day [Chan St. (1989), Chan St. and Clark C. (1992), Chow P. C. Y. (2002), Cox R.W. (1994), Gereffi G. and Miguel Korzeniewicz M. (1994), Haddad M. (2002), Kiljunen K. (1987), Kiljunen K. (1988), Kiljunen K. (1992), Kiljunen K. (Ed.)(1989), Kiljunen K. (Ed.)(1990), Kiljunen K. and Avakov R. M. (Eds.)(1991), Landesmann M. (1996), Landesmann M. and Burgstaller J. (1997), Landesmann M. and Rosati D. (Eds.)(2004), Landesmann M. and Székely I. (Eds.)(1995), Landesmann M. et al. (Eds.)(2003), Liemt G. van (1992), McCallum C. (1999), Piore M. (1990), Raffer K. (1996), Tausch A. (2002b), Tausch A. (2003), and Tausch A. (2005a)].

In addition, the **"Keynesian"** legacy should not be under-estimated. "Keynesians" would expect **positive trade-offs** to hold between **"government intervention" and the human condition**, and not the other way around. Major Keynesian analyses include nowadays Baran P. A. (1957), Corden W. M. (1987), Cornwall J. and Cornwall W. (2001), Galbraith J. K. (1995), Kalecki M. (1972), Kalecki M. (1979), Modigliani F. (1987), Schmidt M. G. (1983), Schmidt M. G. (1986), Schwartz H. (2000), Stack St and Zimmerman D. (1982), Stack St. (1978), Stack St. (1980), Therborn G. (1985), Therborn G. (1986), and Vickrey W. (1996). Apart from that, current literature, formulating counter-positions to the neo-liberal dogma, suggests that the state is not or not always a "villain", with only some neo-liberally inspired studies postulating a general negative trade-off between age of democracy, state sector strength and economic performance, most notably in the works of the German sociologist

Erich Weede [for a survey of the debate, see also Almond G. (1991), Apter D. (1987), Axtmann R (2004), Balibar E. (1991), Barnes S. H. et al. (1979), Bollen K. A. and Jackman R. W. (1985), Dixon W. J. (1994), Esping - Andersen G. (1985), Gwartney J. et al. (1998), Jackman R.W. (1975), Korpi W. (1985), Korpi W. (1996), Korpi W. and Palme J. (2000), Kothari R. (1986), Lipset S.M. (1994), London B., Bradshaw Y. and Kim Y. J. (1993), Midgal J. S. (2001), Moeller St. et al. (2003), Weede E. (1986a), Weede E. (1986b), and Weede E. (1989)].

Our geographical presentation of our own variables used in the analysis will be kept to a minimum. Among the dependent variables, we just mention **MNC penetration**, **unequal transfer** and the **resource balance** as the three "master variables" of dependency. **Unequal transfer** is strongest in the periphery, and weakest in the centers, with the semi-periphery showing medium levels of exposure to unequal transfer. Our map might be even termed to be an update of this Wallersteinean concept to the realities of the turn of the last Century and Millennium, with the centers having values that correspond to the zones of lighter color, the semi-peripheries in grey colors, and the peripheries in dark colors.

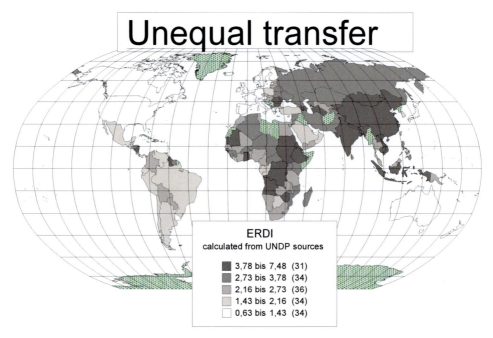

Legend: "bis" is the shorthand for "ranging from" "to". Countries marked in green color: missing values.

Map 2.1. Unequal transfer in the world system.

The abundant research literature on the semi-periphery highlights the non-permanent character of the semi-peripheral position, with historic strong upward and downward movements, but a stability of the structure as such. While some semi-peripheries rise, the others stagnate, almost suggesting that one semi-periphery rises at the cost of the other [Arrighi G. et al. (1991), Arrighi G. et al. (1996c), Arrighi G., Hamashita T. and Selden M. (Eds.)(2003), Chase-Dunn Ch. K. and Hall Th. D. (1997), Inglehart R. and Carballo M. (1997), Martin W. and Wallerstein I. (Eds.)(1990), Tausch A. (1993), Vaeyrynen R. (1997)].

In general terms, we observe today high levels of MNC penetration in the "dominion economies" like Australia and Canada, in Western Europe, in some parts of Eastern Europe, in Central Asia, other parts of the former USSR, in many parts of Latin America, Southern and Western Africa, in Egypt, in Tunisia, and in China and Southeast Asia:

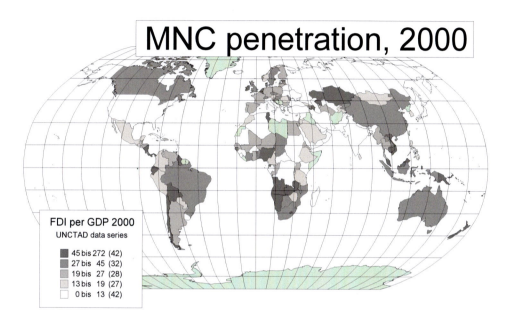

Legend: missing values for Greenland, Suriname, French Guyana, West Sahara, Bosnia/Herzegovina, Serbia, Montenegro, Libya, Iraq, Somalia, Afghanistan and North Korea. "bis" is the shorthand for "ranging from" "to". Countries marked in green color: missing values.

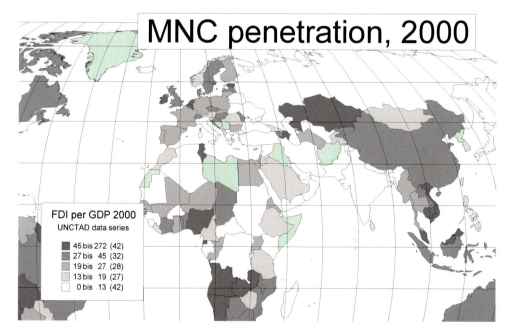

Map 2.2. MNC penetration in the world system.

MNC penetration received a vast attention in the published titles of the comparative research literature of the last 3 decades, among them Bailey P.; Parisotto A. and Renshaw G. (1993), Bornschier V. (1976), Bornschier V. and Heintz P., reworked and enlarged by Th. H. Ballmer - Cao and J. Scheidegger (1979), Bornschier V. et al. (1980), Dixon C. J., Drakakis-Smith D. and Watts H. D. (1986), Gosh P. K. (1984), International Labor Office and United Nations Centre on Transnational Corporations (1988), International Labour Office (2000), Jenkins R. (1987), Nollert M. (2005), Robinson R. D. (1987), Twomey M. J. (1993), United Nations Centre on Transnational Corporations (1983), United Nations Conference on Trade and Development (current issues), and Wheelwright T. (2001). While different authors disagree on the direction of the influence of MNC penetration on the human condition, they'd all underline the **strong influence** of MNC penetration on employment, economic growth, income distribution and overall development.

Foreign saving, for its turn, is strongest in many parts of Latin America, Southern Africa, in the "new Europe" and in China and in several countries of Southeast Asia:

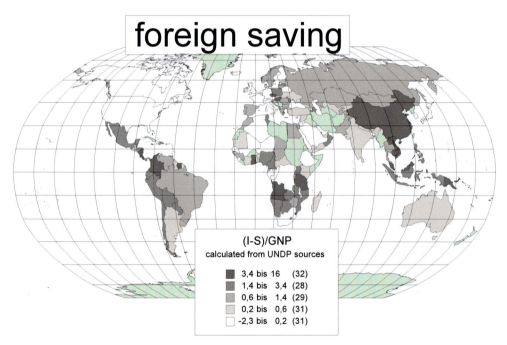

Legend: "bis" is the shorthand for "ranging from" "to". Countries marked in green color: missing values.

Map 2.3. Foreign saving in the world system.

During the 1990s, penetration by transnational capital dramatically increased in many parts of Europe (especially in what was described by Donald Rumsfeld[2], former US Secretary of Defense as "the new Europe"); in eastern Latin America, in Southern Africa, in Central Asia and in South and Southeast Asia. However, there was a **dramatic decrease of MNC penetration in most countries of the Arab world** during the second half of the 1990s:

---

[2] See also: http://www.rferl.org/nca/features/2003/01/24012003172118.asp

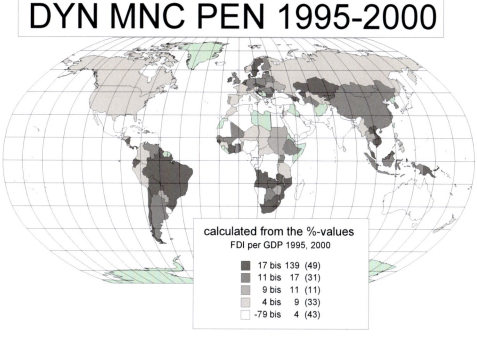

Legend: "bis" is the shorthand for "ranging from" "to". Countries marked in green color: missing values.

Map 2.4. The increase/decrease of MNC penetration in the world system.

As to the **causality** of the **dependency/underdevelopment connection**, perhaps one of the clearest paragraphs to be found in the current literature is to be encountered in the essay written by L. Beer in 1999:

> "As opposed to Modernization theory's emphasis on the internal dynamics of economic growth, World-System and Dependency theories are neo-Marxist perspectives that focus on the global structure of the capitalist world economy.
> (…) This approach argues that national economic growth, inequality and sociopolitical change can only be understood through the analysis of a nation's relative position in the spacioeconomic hierarchy of the world system. That is, the relationship between economic growth and income inequality within any single nation is dependent on that society's relational position in the world division of labor and global power structure. It is asserted that the dynamics of capitalist accumulation in developing countries are different than the processes observable in core nations.
> (…) The issue that World-System/Dependency analyses point our attention to is not the lack of economic growth in developing nations, but the type of growth their dependent status affords them and it's consequences.
> (…) In the World-System/Dependency perspective, capitalist development is dependent on social and material inequality and this inequality is in turn a result of incorporation into the world system. National economic growth and income distribution are in large part determined by growth potentials of productive activities in the larger global structure. Therefore, this approach hypothesizes that stratification of income will correspond with the world division of labor and position in the world economy.

(...) There are variants to the World-System/Dependency approach regarding the creation of income inequality, some of which emphasize concentration of land ownership (...) or national export-structure. (...) Many empirical studies of this relationship have confirmed a significant association between foreign corporate penetration.

(...) In the World-System/Dependency perspective there are three mechanisms that are hypothesized to link foreign investment and social inequality.

(...) . First, foreign investment in developing countries generates large sectoral disparities in the national economy, creates labor aristocracies and results in the underutilization of indigenous labor. Second, transnational corporations operating in developing nations accrue a disproportionate share of local sources of credit and repatriate profits rather than reinvesting them in the local economy. Finally, the governments of these nations, motivated by the necessity (generated by their incorporation into the capitalist world economy) of attracting and maintaining foreign investment, implement policies and strategies that decrease the power of labor and inhibit vertical mobility. These include tax concessions, guarantees of profit repatriation, and labor laws unfavorable to workers.

(...) Scholars in the World-System/Dependency tradition argue that the relationship between foreign investment and internal income inequality has different effects on various sectors of the economy, but in all segments it creates and sustains income inequality in the national population.

(...) Foreign capital investment in the agricultural sector destroys traditional production processes and leads to unemployment and overurbanization through its capital intensive means of organization (i.e. labor shedding, land enclosure). In the extractive sector of the economy, foreign investment benefits only a small portion of the national population and thereby increases income inequality. This is because TNC penetration in this sector creates only a small well-paid labor force and because ownership of natural resources is typically concentrated.

(...) World-System theorists argue that foreign investment in the manufacturing sector has the most harmful effect on national income distribution. National economies in non-core nations with large manufacturing sectors have high levels of income inequality because profits in this sector are increased by the maintenance of a large, surplus low-wage labor force. Therefore, high rates of income inequality are in the interest of transnational corporations and national elites who benefit from foreign investment; they have little incentive to take action to distribute income more equitably. Contrary to the hypotheses of Modernization theorists, the World-System perspective argues that the uneven development of highly penetrated developing economies benefits transnational corporations in that the only segment of the population which can afford to buy these manufactured goods is the wealthy elite.

(...) Domestic demand for these goods depends on the concentration of wealth and high levels of income inequality. Although redistribution of wealth and the resultant expansion of markets may be in the long term interest of foreign corporations, they are driven primarily by the short-term profit logic of capitalism.

(...) Furthermore, there is a convergence of interests between transnational corporations and the wealthy elite segments of the national population in maintaining income inequality which creates barriers to the "trickle-down" effect of industrialization predicted by Modernization theories. In addition to the incentives for inequity for foreign investors discussed above, the national elite strive to maintain their power and higher income so as to maintain privileged consumption patterns and access to status symbols. A common international class interest in the persistence of high levels of inequality thus link foreign investors and indigenous elites, leading these powerful groups to support (and in some cases attempt to increase) the existing unequal income distribution and to coopt and repress opposition from other segments of the population (...) (Beer, 1999: 4 - 7)

Due to its insignificant results in earlier studies, we excluded educational expenditures or mean years of schooling from the research design. Ever since the writings of Colemann (1965), **education** was mentioned among the determining variables of the development performance of a country. Education and human capital formation figure prominently in the *"Human Development Reports"* of the United Nations Development Programme as variables, which determine positively the development outcome. For the UNDP it has been self-evident over the last decade that gender empowerment and the re-direction of public expenditures away from defense will positively contribute to a positive development outcome. However, neo-liberal thought would caution against such premature conclusions. Erich Weede (2002) has shown that standard indicators of human capital endowment - like literacy, school enrollment ratios or years of schooling - suffer from a number of defects. They are crude. Mostly, they refer to input rather than output measures of human capital formation. Occasionally, Weede and Kaempf believe, they produce implausible effects. They are not robustly significant determinants of growth. Weede and associates replaced them by average intelligence. This variable consistently outperforms the other human capital indicators in spite of suffering from severe defects of its own. In earlier studies, most notably by Weede, 2002 and by Tausch, 2003 and 2005, there were some surprising and negative results, which suggested that **public education expenditures** sometimes negatively affect the development chances of a society. For such a theoretical understanding, University reform and University privatization would be important political steps to achieve a more viable development. The UNDP devoted considerable energies into developing its own kind of human capital and human development approach that quoted large amounts of statistics how much different countries devoted to their "unproductive" military efforts and how little they devoted to the "good" public education expenditures. Such number games, however much they were linked to the generally laudable effort to document world poverty and the lack of basic human needs satisfaction, suffered from a major scientific handicap by evading the vital question to statistically show that – development levels constant – high shares of public education expenditures contribute uniformly to a good development performance, measured by indicators of growth, human rights, social justice, gender empowerment and ecological well-being, while the "bad" military expenditures contribute to the opposite. Surprisingly, such a clear-cut evidence does not exist at the cross-national level [see Dasgupta P. (1995), Griffin K. (1987), Griffin K. and Knight J. (Eds.)(1990), O'Neill H. (1997), United Nations Development Programme (1998a); United Nations Development Programme (1998b), United Nations Development Programme (2004), United Nations Development Programme (2005a), United Nations Development Programme (2005b), United Nations Development Programme (current issues), United Nations Development Programme, Arab Fund for Economic and Social Development (2002), and Yunker J. A. (2000)].

Our theoretical survey should include two processes, being of great importance especially to the European continent and the amount of social cohesion or social exclusion, with which Europe is confronted. One is the obvious argument about the **European Union** as a determining factor of European development patterns, for good or for bad. There are very diverse views nowadays on the European Union. As a research paper, published in the journal *"Parameters"* of the US Army, maintains (Wilkie, 2003):

"Still, there are those on both sides of the Atlantic who believe that the European Union, as an old-fashioned socialist bureaucracy, is "fundamentally unreformable" and also culturally hostile to the United States" (Wilkie, 2003: 46)[3]

Is, at the end of the day, the poverty, in say, the *"banlieues"*, the consequence of the political economy of the adverse long-term effects of EU-membership? There is a wide range of literature now available that highlights also the negative effects of European integration in a globalized world economy [for a survey of the literature and politometric evidence, see Tausch and Herrmann, 2001, furthermore Botsford D. (1997), Chiti V. (1998), Friedman M. (1997), Fuest C. (1996), Giering C. (1998), Haller M. (Ed.)(2001), Haller M. and Richter R. (Ed.)(1994), Haller M. and Schachner-Blazizek P. (Ed.)(1999), Haller M. and Schachner-Blazizek P. (Eds.)(1994), Heidenreich M (1997), Heidenreich M (1998a), Heidenreich M (1998b), Heidenreich M. (1999), Heidenreich M. (2001a), Heidenreich M. (2001b), Heidenreich M. (2003a), Heidenreich M. (2003b), Heidenreich M. (2004a), Heidenreich M. (2004b), Heidenreich M. (2004c), Heidenreich M. and Töpsch K. (1998), Hilferding R. (1915), Holzmann R. (Ed.)(1996), Malcolm N. (1995), Nollert M. (1996), Nollert M. and Fielder N. (1997), Portillo M. (1999), Rothschild K. W. (1997), Seers D. (Ed.)(1978), Tausch A. (2004a), Van Apeldoom B. (2002), Woods A. (2000), Woodward A. and Kohli M. (2001)]. The voice of "euro-optimists" is small, but influential, including later works by Volker Bornschier, and the writings by economics Nobel laureate Robert Mundell and Stanford Professor emeritus Pan Yotopoulos. [Bornschier V. (1992), Bornschier V. (1999), Mundell R. A. and Clesse A. (Eds.)(2000), Mundell R. A. et. al. (Eds.)(2005), and Yotopoulos P. A. (2004)].

The well-known **acceleration** and **maturity** effects of development have to be qualified in an important way. Ever since the days of Simon **Kuznets**, development researchers have applied curve-linear formulations in order to capture these effects. The curve-linear function of **growth**, being regressed on the natural logarithm of development level and its square, is sometimes called the 'Matthew's effect' following Matthew's (13, 12):

'For whosoever hath, to him shall be given, and he shall have more abundance: but whosoever hath not, for him shall be taken away even that he hath'

Social scientists interpreted this effect mainly in view of an acceleration of economic growth in middle-income countries *vis-à-vis* the poor countries and in view of the still widening gap between the poorest periphery nations *('have-nots')* and the *'haves'* among the semi-periphery countries (Jackman, 1982). Kuznets was the first to introduce a "light at the end of the tunnel" vision on the development of inequality: first things get worse, before they become better at later "stages" of development.

We also should mention here the variable **"pension reform."** Proponents and critics of fully funded, three-pillar pension models alike agree on the fact that pension reform policy is one of the biggest challenges that especially advanced democracies with their age structure are facing in world society. To neglect pension funds in investigations about the capitalist world economy would be misleading. Private pension funds already amount to 44 % of current world GDP, with countries like the United States; Japan; United Kingdom;

---

[3] http://carlisle-www. army. mil/usawc/Parameters/02winter/wilkie. htm

Netherlands; Canada; Switzerland; Australia; Sweden; Ireland; Finland; and Denmark taking the lead in fund development either via the introduction of a "World Bank" three pillar pension model or simply via a strong element of private pensions ("the third pillar") besides the first, traditional PAYGO pillar (like presently in the United States of America). Slow pension fund development in most countries of the €-zone determines that the overall share of private pension funds from the €-zone is just over 2 % of world GDP. If Europe wants to fulfill its Lisbon agenda of catching up with the United States, it must, the argument runs, overhaul its pension systems and introduce some form or other of private pension funds, which are a major force in financing technological advance in the capitalist world economy today.

Not only in Latin America, where Chile under the generals paved the way, but also in East Central Europe after the end of communism, and even in some former advanced welfare democracies like Australia, Denmark, the Netherlands, Switzerland and the United Kingdom, far-reaching measures to reform the PAYGO-pension systems were introduced. The list of countries with privatization or pre-funding of the pension system grows longer and longer, and even in Sweden, the classic example of a Keynesian social welfare state from the 1930s onwards, the pension system has been drastically reformed in the direction of World Bank reforms. There are 18 countries[4], according to the World Bank study Brooks and James, which fully introduced a three pillar, funded model, and many of them in addition introduced notional pension accounts following the Swedish model at the turn of the millennium. The Bank is now active in reforming pensions in 60 countries, 25 of them in the region Europe and Central Asia. Programs to reform pensions make up 19.4 % of all World Bank credits (Holzmann, 2004). The World Bank starts from the assumption that the following countries have reformed their pension systems in the direction of a three-pillar model:

Argentina	Australia
Bolivia	Chile
Colombia	Croatia
Denmark	El Salvador
Hungary	Kazakhstan
Mexico	Netherlands
Peru	Poland
Sweden	Switzerland
United Kingdom	Uruguay

Tausch (2004) thought that there was evidence that World Bank pension reforms are associated in a positive way with the rates of change of a country's performance to the better [see also Barr N. (2001), Boersch-Suppan A., Ludwig A., and Winter J. (2003), Brooks S.

---

[4] Italy was excluded from the James/Brooks list, because it does not have a second pillar, and only the first pillar was reformed. See: Brooks S. and Estelle J. (1999), 'The Political Economy of Pension Reform' Paper, presented at the World Bank Conference New Ideas about Old-Age Security, September 14-15, Washington D.C., available at: http://www.worldbank.org/knowledge/chiefecon/conferen/papers/polecon.htm. In general terms, we start from the assumption that the World Bank's proposals (pension systems should be based on three pillars, where pillar one is a public (statutory) system (generally financed on the PAYGO principle), funded occupational or other funded systems constitute the second pillar and personal pension arrangements the third pillar) will have an unambiguously positive impact on economic development, spanning benefits such as increased saving and investment, higher growth, the devolution of power from the state to individuals and an improved work ethic.

and James E. J. (1999), Cadette W. (1999), Clark G. L. (2001a), Clark G. L. (2001b), Dahlmanns G. (2000), European Commission (2000a), European Commission (2000b), European Roundtable of Industrialists, ERT (2001), Ferrera M. (2005), Fink M. and Schuh U. (2005), Fox L. and Palmer E. (2000), Gray C. and Weig D. (1999), Hagfors R. (2000), Hausner J. (1999), Holzmann R. (2000a), Holzmann R. (2000b), Holzmann R. (2004), Holzmann R. (2005), Holzmann R. (Ed.)(2001), Holzmann R. (Ed.)(2002), Holzmann R. et al. (1999), Kay St. J. (1999), Lindemann D. (2000), Mackelar L. et al. (2000), Modigliani F. (1985), Modigliani F. and Muralidhar A. (2004), Modigliani F., Ceprini M.L., and Muralidhar A. (2000), Normann G. and Mitchell D. J. (2000), Orenstein M. A. (2001), Orlowski L. T. (1995), Orszag P. R. and Stiglitz J. E. (1999), Paul S. S. and Paul J. A. (1996), Quiggin J. (1998), Raffer K. (2003), Roos J. P. (2000), Rothenbacher F. (2000), Rother P. C., Catenaro M. and Schwab G. (2003), Rutkowski M. (1998), Rutkowski M. (1999), Scherman C. G. (2000), Siebert H. (2000), St. John S. (1999), Tausch A. (2004b), Tausch A. (Ed.)(2003), The World Bank Group (2000), and Turner J. (2000)]. Opponents of the three pillar model were quick to point out the "social contradictions" inherent, according to them, in the "model". Let us quote here a statement by the Pauls, written in 1996:

> "The World Bank and the IMF, advocates and orchestrators of the pension crises, share primary responsibility with corrupt and irresponsible national politicians for the pension debacle. The banks' "conditionalities" never took aim at military profligacy, or ministerial self-indulgence, or vast and growing inequalities of income, or the smuggling by corrupt officials of huge sums abroad for deposit in foreign banks, not to mention gigantic and wasteful public works projects that the Bank itself promoted. Critics could well wonder why the World Bank, if it were truly interested in "equity," never addressed the enormous "pensions" salted away in foreign banks by corrupt politicians and deposed dictators.
>
> None of those at the top, it seems, gave much thought to the human costs of the pension-cutting policies, as they crashed into the lives of ordinary people. When asked about the wave of elder suicides, Argentine President Carlos Menem insisted that "the index of suicides for pensioners is normal." And when pressed to explain why older people were taking their lives, he answered grandly, "I am the President of the Republic, not a psychologist or sociologist."
>
> As a solution to the elder income crisis, Menem urged destitute pensioners to go back to work--at a time when unemployment stood at record levels. Economy Minister Domingo Carvallo cavalierly insisted that families step in with support. Reporters discovered that Carvallo was earning $10,000 a month under questionable circumstances in the midst of the crisis, but he protested he could not live on less (...)
>
> The World Bank's numerous reports on pensions pass in silence over these facts. They also fail to consider the elderly as human beings, whose livelihood and decent treatment should be a litmus test of social policy. Instead, the Bank discusses pensions in arcane, abstract and dehumanized language, full of terms like "information asymmetries," "capital market failures," and "moral hazard." The Bank refers to older people mainly as economic burdens--dependents who no longer have anything further to contribute to the economic machine.
>
> Trade unions, powerful forces in most Latin American countries, denounced the pension reforms and the simultaneous wage cuts brought on by the adjustment programs. At a 1992 ILO conference in Caracas, trade union delegates accused their countries of breaking the rules of the ILO Conventions to which they were signatories. A union leader from Chile said his country's new plan was "not a good example to be followed" and the union delegate from Uruguay insisted that the reforms were a great step backwards away from justice and social solidarity, an ill-disguised means to lower workers' pensions. Journalists, priests, legislators

all joined the chorus of protest; in 1993 the Catholic bishops in Argentina denounced the new elder poverty.

The economic crisis in Latin America was so deep and the international financial pressure so intense, that struggles by the trade unions, political parties and elderly movements did not succeed in preventing major pension cuts, though strikes and demonstrations rocked the capital cities. Elderly Argentines even fought pitched battles with the police, winning eventually minor victories. In one concession, the government agreed to sell the country's richest asset, the state petroleum company, and fund pensions with part of the proceeds. After President Menem vetoed a congressional bill giving retirees direct proceeds of the selloff, the government eventually agreed to give pensioners a partial settlement with government bonds.

In June 1993, the government completed its privatization of the company, but rather than paying off the bonds, it offered company shares to the retirees--shares that had to be held for at least one year. Unable to wait, many impoverished elderly sold their bonds or stock rights to speculators at only a fraction of the face value. In the end, pensioners will get only a small part of what they were due. Speculators and bankers have already taken by far the biggest share. New York-based Citibank and its local partners walked away with more than $1 billion in profits from the privatization moves, raising eyebrows even in the U.S. financial press over the brash and sordid dealmaking.

Government ministers, facing widespread sympathy for the dispossessed elderly, made dramatic gestures to appease public opinion. Argentina's Carvallo wept on television ("crocodile tears" countered Norma Pla, leader of the elderly protest movement). And Ministers of Labor from across the continent, assembled at a conference in the fall of 1992, condemned the neo-liberal policies of the Bank and the Fund and called for a more humane approach to development and for new efforts to protect those hardest hit by the crisis. But the new policies remained intact." (Paul and Paul, 1996).

The solutions, proposed by the Pauls, would consist in advocating:

"Pension-cutting is outrageous. But pensions and other income-security systems have a fatal flaw. They tend to legitimate the concept of "old age" and the expulsion of people from wage work, irrespective of physical abilities, personal preferences and capacities for productive social contribution. Pensions create dependency that can lead to blaming and victimization. Far from providing security, they have all too often proven terribly insecure.

The challenge is how to combine basic income security with the right to stay productive in wage work or be rewarded for productive but unpaid work (like taking care of grandchildren). Remunerated work not only would benefit the elderly, but also would put their talent and labor more fully at the service of society. Full-employment (in a new and expanded sense, for all those who can and wish to work) must become the foremost priority for aging advocates. In a world of great prosperity, wealth and productivity, nothing less should be acceptable.

But what about those who are too infirm to work, or who cannot find productive and paid labor? In an increasingly global economy, where the fates of all are closely intertwined, and where individual nation-states are often too weak to protect their own citizens, a global solution to income security is needed, including support for people in frail old age. Arthur H. Westing, in a book published by SIPRI in 1988, was one of the first to propose a international social security system, based on a world-wide tax. As the global economy becomes more and more productive--and less and less dependent on labor--the need to distribute the social wealth in radically new ways becomes ever more pressing. And the claims of the impoverished elderly become ever more urgent and compelling. " (Paul and Paul, 1996)

Chapter 3

LOOKING BACK ON EARLIER RESEARCH

The almost unlimited number of empirical studies on **peripheral capitalism and development** on a world level in the B-phase of the Kondratieff cycle from 1965 onwards go back, in a way, to the classic essay published by Johan Galtung in the *Journal of Peace Research* (Galtung, 1971). For Galtung, income inequality, and hence, relative poverty in the nations of the world system is linked to trade partner concentration of the peripheral country and a trade structure that relies on the exports of raw materials and the imports of finished products. Bornschier, Chase-Dunn, and their school later on reformulated the argument: not only income inequality, but also long term economic growth are being negatively determined by dependency from transnational capital, to be measured by a weighted share of transnational investment penetration per the economic and demographic size of a nation. Later essays extended the argument to other indicators of human well-being, the environment as well as democratic stability.

Macroquantitative analyses modeled around the **dependency/world system school** generally claimed to have confirmed dependency arguments. According to these quantitative data analyses, there are powerful influences at work, which cause inequality and external imbalances in the periphery and in the underprivileged regions of the centers. Flagship essays and book publications of this school include nowadays over 50 studies, published internationally, dealing with dependency, economic growth and or income inequality [Alderson A. and Nielsen F. (1999), Alderson A. S., Beckfield J. and Nielsen F. (2005), Babones S. J. (2002), Beer L. (1999), Beer L. and Boswell T. (2002), Bergesen A. and Fernandez R. (1999), Bornschier V. and Ballmer-Cao, T. H. (1979), Bornschier V. and Chase-Dunn Ch. K (1985), Bornschier V., Chase-Dunn Ch. and Rubinson R. (1977), Boswell T. and Dixon W.J. (1990), Bradshaw Y. and Huang J. (1991), Breedlove W. L. and Armer J. M. (1996), Caporaso J. A. (1978), Chase-Dunn Ch. K. (1975), Crenshaw E. M. (1991), Crenshaw E. M. (1992), Crenshaw E. M. (1993), Crenshaw E. M. and Ansari A. (1994), Delacroix J. and Ragin Ch. (1981), Dixon W. J. and Boswell T. (1996b), Evans P. B. and Timberlake M. (1980), Fiala R. (1992), Galtung J. (1971), Galtung J., Chase-Dunn, Ch. K. et al. (1985), Johnson R. B. (1986), Kentor J. D. (1998), Kentor J. D. (2005), Kentor J. D. and Boswell T. (2003), Kick E. L. and Davis B. L. (2001), Kohli A. et al. (1984), Krahn H. and Gartrell J. W. (1985), London B. (1987), London B. and Ross R. J. S. (1995), London B. and Smith D. A. (1988), Moaddel M. (1994), Muller E. N. (1988), Muller E. N. (1993), Nielsen F. (1995), Nolan P. D. (1983), Prechel H. (1985), Rubinson R. (1976), Russett B. (1983a),

Russett B. (1983b), Shandra J. M., Ross R. J. S., London B. (2003), Shandra J. M.; London B.; Whooley O. P; Williamson J. B. (2004), Shandra J. M.; Nobles, J. E.; London B.; Williamson, J. B. (2005), Shandra J., London B, Whooley O. P., et al. (2004), Suter Ch. (2005), Tausch A. (1998a), Tausch A. (1998b), Tausch A. (2005b), Timberlake M. and Kantor J. (1983), Trezzini B. and Bornschier V. (2001), Tsai P-L. (1995), and Wimberley D. W. and Bello R. (1992)].

There has been a tendency in more recent cross-national dependency and world system research to focus not only on such variables as economic growth, income inequality and a few other indicators of social well-being, but to interpret "well-being" more widely to include also democracy, demographic transition, freedom from crime, freedom from structural imbalances in the economy, gender equality, political stability, respect for human rights, the environment. Research results by these scholars in general terms indicate that there is reason to believe that the march of global capitalism not only negatively affects the distribution of economic values in the world system, but also of democracy, human development, gender equality and the quality of the environment. These 70 or more studies were published, as their counterparts on the detrimental effects of dependence on economic growth and income inequality, with leading scholarly journals or publishing houses, thus publicizing a scholarly well-founded **"globalization critique"** [Bradshaw Y. (1987), Bradshaw Y. W. and Schafer M. J. (2000), Bradshaw Y. W., Noonan R; and Gash L. (1993), Breedlove W. L. and Armer J. M. (1997), Burns T. J. et al. (1994), Burns T. J., Kentor J. D. and Jorgenson, A. (2002), Burns T. J., Kick E. L. and Davis B. L. (2003), Chase-Dunn Ch. K. (2005), Clark R. (1992), Clark R. et al. (1991), Crenshaw E. M. (1995), Crenshaw E. M. and Jenkins J. C. (1996), Crenshaw E. M. and Oakey, D. R. (1998), Crenshaw E. M.; Ameen A. Z.; and Christenson. M. (1997), Crenshaw E. M.; Christenson M.; Oakey D. R. (2000), Dixon W. J. (1984), Ehrhardt-Martinez K.; Crenshaw E. M.; and Jenkins J. C. (2002), Fain H. D. et al. (1997), Frey R. S. and Field C. (2000), Gartner R. (1990), Ghobarah H. et al. (2001), Gissinger R. and Gleditsch N. P. (1999), Goldfrank W. L. (1999), Gore A. (1994), Grimes P. and Kentor J. (2003), Hadden K. and London B. (1996), Hertz E. et al. (1994), Huang J. (1995), J. Timmons Roberts J. T., Grimes P. E. and Jodie L. Manale J. L. (2003), Jenkins J. C. and Scanlan S. J. (2001), Jorgenson A. K. and Rice J. (2005), Kasarda J. D. and Crenshaw E.M. (1991), Kent G. (1991); Kentor J. D. (2001), Kentor J. D. and Jang J. S. (2004), Kick E. L. et al. (1995), Kick E. L., Davis B. L. and Burns T. J. (1998), Kick E. L., Davis B. L. and Burns T. J. (2000), Lena H. F. and London B. (1993), London B. (1988), London B. (1990), London B. and Robinson T. (1989), London B. and Williams B. A. (1988), London B. and Williams B. A. (1990), Miller C. D. (1999), Miller M. A. L. (1995), Mittelman J. (1994), Moon B.E. and Dixon W.J. (1992), Munasinghe M., Miguel: de and Sunkel O. (2001), Neapolitan J. L. and Schmalleger F. (1997), Nollert M. (1994a), Ragin C. C. and Bradshaw Y. W. (1992), Ram R. (1992), Robinson T.D. and London B. (1991), Shandra J. M., London B. and Williamson J. B. (2003), Shandra J. M.; London B.; Williamson J. B. (2003), Shandra J. M.; Nobles J.; London B.; Williamson J. B. (2004), Shen C. and Williamson J. B. (2001), Shin M. E. (1975), Shin M. E. (2002), Smith D. A and London B. (1990), Smith D. A. (1994), Smith D. A. (1996), Stack St. (1998), Stokes R. and Anderson A.. (1990), Tausch and Prager, 1993, Ward K. B. (1984), Wickrama K. A. S. and Mulford Ch. L. (1996), Wimberley D. W. (1990), and Wimberley D. W. (1991)].

Chapter 4

THE VARIABLES

The **independent** variables of our model for around the year 2000 or later comprise the following list:

- development level ln (GDP PPP pc). This variable should control for the effects of rising incomes on development (UNDP HDR, 2000)
- development level, square (maturity effects) ln (GDP PPP pc)^2. This variable should control for the effects of economic maturity on development (UNDP HDR, 2000)
- Dummy: landlocked country[1] (Easterly, 2000)
- Dummy: transition country[2] (Easterly, 2000 - 2002)
- EU-15-membership (EU member by the year 2000, dummy variable)
- Foreign saving (I-S)/GNP (calculated from UNDP 2000)
- MNC PEN 1995 (UNCTAD World Investment Report, current issues)
- Percentage of Muslims per total population (Nationmaster[3])
- state interventionism (absence of economic freedom; Heritage Foundation and Wall Street Journal website for economic freedom[4], by around 2000)

---

[1] Taken from William Easterly, EXCEL data file freely available at http://www.cgdev.org/doc/expert%20pages/easterly/easterly_consensusdata.xls . Readers are advised to enter the URL and then to disregard three messages, which might appear on the screen, speaking about "missing" linkages to the file etc. "Clicking your way" through these messages, the Easterly file opens at the end of the day, nevertheless. I made all the relevant data available at website, which includes the Easterly "Consensus data" (octet stream format), and my own main data set, which is called "easterly_dependency_Muslim%.xls" (in Excel format, containing all the relevant data for the present analysis) at: http://classic.lalisio.com/members/m_TAUSCH/publications/117707277078/117707376908/

[2] Taken from William Easterly, EXCEL data file freely available at http://www.cgdev.org/doc/expert%20pages/easterly/easterly_consensusdata.xls

[3] See nationmaster.com at http://www.nationmaster.com/graph/rel_isl_per_mus-religion-islam-percentage-muslim

[4] These data are contained in http://www.freetheworld.com/; also: http://www.heritage.org/research/features/index/. We used the latter website as the source of our data. It has to be kept in mind that the "worst" countries on the economic freedom scale have the numerically highest values, while the best countries have the numerically lowest values. Lao People's Dem. Rep. – the economically "unfreest" country in our sample, has the numerical value 4.6, while the economically freest country, Singapore, scores 1.45. We thus decided to call our indicator "state interventionism".

- unequal transfer (calculated from UNDP, concept: ERDI, reciprocal value of comparative "price levels" (developed on the basis of the ERD-Index Yotopoulos et al.)[5] (the Commission maintaining that a low value is good result) (UNDP HDR, 2000)
- Urbanisation[6] (Easterly 2002)
- World Bank pension reform[7] (World Bank sources, quoted in Tausch (Ed.), 2003)

The **dependent variables** for this analysis correspond to standard knowledge in comparative political science and sociology. Although we presume the indicators as to be known generally, we present for our readers a brief summary of the Happy Planet Indicators, available from http://www.happyplanetindex.org/list.htm, the UNDP indicators and the Yale/Columbia environmental data series.

The dependent variables were measured, if not specified otherwise, by around 2000. The list of the dependent variables comprises

1. economic growth, 1990-2003 (UNDP HDR, 2005)
2. eco-social market economy (GDP output per kg energy use) (UNDP HDR 2000)
3. female economic activity rate as % of male economic activity rate (UNDP HDR 2000)
4. freedom from % people not expected to survive age 60 (UNDP HDR 2000)
5. freedom from a high ecological Footprint, 204 (Happy Planet Organization)
6. freedom from a high quintile ratio (share of income/consumption richest 20% to poorest 20%) (UNDP HDR 2005)
7. freedom from civil liberty violations, 1998, and 2006 (Easterly, 2000 - 2002, and Freedom House, 2007)
8. freedom from high CO_2 emissions per capita (UNDP HDR 2000)
9. freedom from political rights violations, 1998, and 2006 (Easterly, 2000 - 2002, and Freedom House, 2007)
10. freedom from unemployment, 2003 (UN statistical system website, social indicators)
11. Gender development index 2004 (UNDP HDR, 2006)
12. Gender empowerment index, 2004 (UNDP HDR, 2006)
13. Happy Planet Index, 2004 (Happy Planet Organization)
14. Human development Index, 2005 (UNDP HDR 2005)
15. life expectancy, 1995-2000 (UNDP HDR 2000)
16. Life Satisfaction, 2004 (Happy Planet Organization)
17. the Yale/Columbia[8] environmental sustainability index (ESI-Index), 2005

---

[5] It can be shown that the Eurostat data series GDP PPP per capita/GDP exchange rate per capita (EU-25=100), used for the "price level", in reality measure GDP exchange rate per capita/GDP PPP per capita (EU-25=100).

[6] Taken from William Easterly, EXCEL data file freely available at http://www.cgdev.org/doc/expert%20pages/easterly/easterly_consensusdata.xls

[7] Argentina; Australia; Bolivia; Chile; Colombia; Croatia; Denmark; El Salvador; Hungary; Kazakhstan; Mexico; Netherlands; Peru; Poland; Sweden; Switzerland; United Kingdom; Uruguay.

[8] http://sedac.ciesin.columbia.edu/es/esi/. The EXCEL spreadsheet for 2005 is freely available from this site

In Chapters 8 and 9 of this work, we expandeded the original series of the 14 core indicators (indicators 1 to 12, indicator 15 and 16) and introduced **unemployment** by around 2003 or 2004 (from the United Nations statistical system website[9]) and **gender development** and **gender empowerment** by around 2004 as additional dependent variables (United Nations Human Development Report, 2006). In Chapter 10, we look at the combined effects of explantory variables on the fourteen core dependent indicators.

The dependent variables are also well-known variables in cross-national development research and really do not need much further comments. The data as well as data descriptions are documented in the appendix.

---

[9] Available from United Nations social statistics at http://unstats.un.org/unsd/demographic/products/socind/default.htm

Chapter 5

THE RESEARCH DESIGN

The present publication is well within the tradition of cross-national, macro-political and macro-sociological research. The fundamental literature on the subject and recent highlights in the relevant methodological debate are assumed to be known here [Achen Ch. H. (1982), Berry W. D. and Feldman S. (1985), Bollen K. A. (1980), Clauss G. and Ebner H. (1978), Davis B. L., Kick E. L. and Burns T. J. (2004), Deininger K. and Squire L. (1996), Deutsch K. W. (1960), Deutsch K. W. (1966), Deutsch K. W. (1978), Deutsch K. W. (1979), Deutsch K. W. (1982), Dixon W. J. and Boswell T. (1996a), Goldstein J. S. (1985a), Haller M. (2003), Haller M. (Ed.)(1990), Kriz J. (1978), Krzysztofiak M. and Luszniewicz A. (1979), Kuznets S. (1955), Lewis - Beck M. S. (1980), Lundberg M. and Squire L. (2001), Nielsen F. and Alderson A. (1997), Opp K.D. and Schmidt P. (1976), Paukert F. (1973), Puchala D. J. (2003), Russett B. (1967), Tellis A. J. et al. (2001), and Whitehouse E. (2000)].

Our publication goes a long way to meet the requirements of *"ceteris paribus"* type of hypotheses. For example, Muslim countries might be performing "badly" not because they are Muslim countries, but because they are, say, at middle income levels. At this point and in view of the results confirmed in this work, it seems appropriate to recall here that Galtung's original 1969 essay was all connected to his theory of "structural violence"[1]. Galtung at that time was not interested in economic growth, but in "structural violence", and what Peadar Kirby today calls "vulnerability", which is occurring when life conditions of a partner in a systematic interaction are below levels, which might be potentially experienced in a different, and more just global social order (i.e. the large majority segments of population living in poverty in the periphery, referred to in "critical peace research" as the "periphery of the periphery", are subjected to a relationship of domination, wielded by the small and powerful elites in the Third World, which is part and parcel of the domination structure, commanded by the elites of the center over the entire global structure).

The term *"potential realizations"*, introduced by "critical peace research" in the late 1960s and early 1970s is also important here, for it links life conditions to the level of development of the productive forces in society. We interpret this as nothing else but the residuals from the "plateau curve of basic human needs", introduced by Joshua Goldstein in

---

[1] See also the article by Professor George Kent from the University of Hawaii at Manoa at http://www2.hawaii.edu/~kent/ANALYZ3.html

his article in "World Development", 1985. Let us re-analyze in this context Galtung's famous definition:

> "(…) the basic idea is that there is such a concept as "premature death." This we know, because we know that with some changes in social structure, in general and health structure in particular, life expectancy can be improved considerably. More particularly, it may be possible to give to the whole population the life expectancy of the class enjoying appropriate health standards, that is, the "upper classes." The level enjoyed by them would be an indicator of the potential possibility to "stay alive" in that society; for all but the upper classes that would be above the actual possibility to stay alive. The difference when avoidable, is structural violence". (Galtung, 1969)
>
> "Violence is present when human beings are being influenced so that their actual somatic and mental realizations are below their potential realizations (…) Violence is here defined as the cause of the difference between the potential and the actual, and that which impedes the decrease of this distance" (Galtung, 1969)
>
> "The structural violence is the sum total of all the clashes built into the social and world structures and cemented, solidified so that unjust, inequitable outcomes are almost unchangeable". (Professor Johan Galtung, on his website at http://www.transcend.org/TRRECBAS.HTM)
>
> "violence as avoidable insults to basic human needs, and more generally to life, lowering the real level of needs satisfaction below what is potentially possible" (Wikepdia, the free Encyclopedia, article on "Structural violence" http://en.wikipedia.org/wiki/Structural_violence)

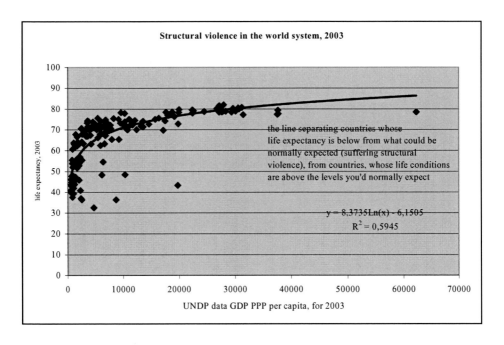

The Research Design

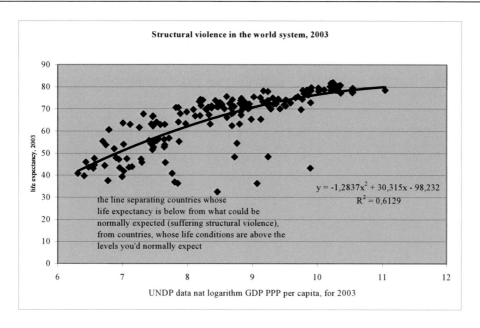

Graph 5.1. Structural violence in the world system and the plateau curve of basic human needs – the actual somatic and mental realizations of the citizens of the countries of the world are below their potential realizations.

The gaps in life expectancy development in relation to the non-linear trade-off with the level of productive forces are distributed in the following fashion in the countries of the world system:

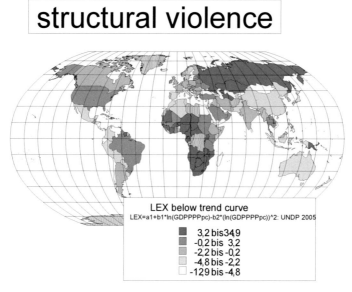

Legend: "bis" is the shorthand for "ranging from" "to". Countries marked in green color: missing values.

Map 5.1. (Continued)

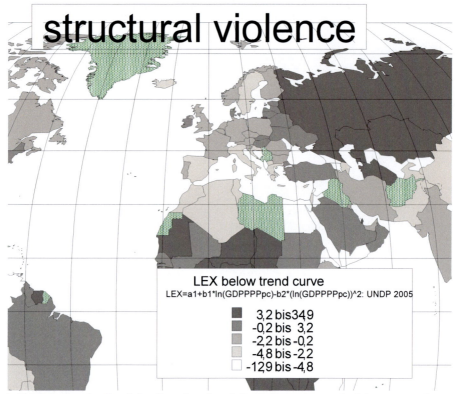

Legend: "bis" is the shorthand for "ranging from" "to". Countries marked in green color: missing values

Map 5.1. Structural violence in the world system.

The choice of a country to be included in the final analysis (134 countries[2]) was determined by the availability of a complete data series for these independent variables (if not mentioned otherwise, UNDP data).

These variables correspond to the following dimensions:

---

[2] Albania; Algeria; Angola; Argentina; Armenia; Australia; Austria; Azerbaijan; Bahrain; Bangladesh; Belarus; Belgium; Belize; Benin; Bolivia; Botswana; Brazil; Bulgaria; Burkina Faso; Burundi; Cambodia; Cameroon; Canada; Chad; Chile; China; Colombia; Congo; Congo, Dem. Rep. of the; Costa Rica; Côte d'Ivoire; Croatia; Cyprus; Czech Republic; Denmark; Dominican Republic; Ecuador; Egypt; Estonia; Ethiopia; Fiji; Finland; France; Gabon; Gambia; Georgia; Germany; Ghana; Greece; Guatemala; Guinea; Guinea-Bissau; Guyana; Haiti; Honduras; Hungary; Iceland; India; Indonesia; Iran, Islamic Rep. of; Ireland; Israel; Italy; Jamaica; Japan; Jordan; Kazakhstan; Kenya; Korea, Rep. of; Kyrgyzstan; Lao People's Dem. Rep.; Latvia; Lebanon; Lesotho; Lithuania; Luxembourg; Madagascar; Malawi; Malaysia; Mali; Mauritania; Mauritius; Mexico; Moldova, Rep. of; Mongolia; Morocco; Mozambique; Namibia; Nepal; Netherlands; New Zealand; Niger; Nigeria; Norway; Pakistan; Panama; Papua New Guinea; Paraguay; Peru; Philippines; Poland; Portugal; Romania; Russian Federation; Rwanda; Saudi Arabia; Senegal; Singapore; Slovakia; Slovenia; South Africa; Spain; Sri Lanka; Swaziland; Sweden; Switzerland; Syrian Arab Republic; Tajikistan; Tanzania, U. Rep. of; Thailand; Togo; Trinidad and Tobago; Tunisia; Turkey; Uganda; United Kingdom; United States; Uruguay; Uzbekistan; Venezuela; Viet Nam; Yemen; Zambia; Zimbabwe.

World economic openness and globalization

foreign saving [(I-S)/GNP]
low comparative international price level [ERD]
state interventionism (absence of economic. freedom)
transnational capital penetration [MNC PEN 1995]

Percentage of the population adhering to the Muslim faith

Membership in the European Union

Geography

Dummy for being landlocked
Urbanization ratio, 1990

Recent world economic history

Dummy for transition economy
Development level and development level squared [ln(GDP PPP pc) and ln (GDP PPP pc)^2]

Pension Reform efforts

World Bank pension reform

The list of our fourteen core dependent variables is multidimensional.

We proceeded in each multiple regression with list wise deletion of missing data from the list of dependent variables.

Democracy and human rights

Absence of democracy: political rights and civil rights violations (based on Freedom House, 2000, reported in Easterly, 2000 - 2002 and Freedom House, 2007)

Environment

CO_2 emissions per capita
ESI-Index ((Yale/Columbia environment sustainability index project website)
GDP output per kg energy use *("eco-social market economy"[3])*
Ecological Footprint[4]
Happy Planet Index[5]

---

[3] This term is most probably an Austrian invention. The governing Conservative People's Party – to be precise, its former Chairman Dr. Josef Riegler – seems to have invented this term in the late 1980s. For more on that debate: http://www.nachhaltigkeit.at/bibliothek/pdf/Factsheet11OekosozMarktw.pdf; and Michael Rösch, Tubingen University at http://tiss.zdv.uni-tuebingen.de/webroot/sp/spsba01_W98_1/germany1b.htm. As an indicator of the reconciliation between the price mechanism and the environment we propose the indicator GDP output per kg energy use; the term 'eco-social market economy' neatly grasps all the aspects of this empirical formulation.

[4] http://www.happyplanetindex.org/list.htm

[5] http://www.happyplanetindex.org/list.htm

Human development and basic human needs satisfaction % people not expected to survive age 60 human development index life expectancy, 1995-2000 Life Satisfaction[6] **Gender justice** Gender development index 2004 (UNDP HDR, 2006) Gender empowerment index, 2004 (UNDP HDR, 2006) female economic activity rate as % of male economic activity rate (UNDP HDR 2000) **Redistribution, growth and employment policies** economic growth 1990-2003 share of income/consumption richest 20% to poorest 20% unemployment 2003 (from United Nations statistical website)

Thus, we use the following regression equation:

(Equation 2) development performance $_{1990 - \text{end } 1990s}$ = a_1 +- b_1*first part curvilinear function of development level +- b_2*second part curvilinear function of development level +- b_3 *stock of transnational investment per GDP (UNCTAD) $_{\text{mid } 1990s}$ +- b_4 * comparative price levels (ERDI) +- b_5 * foreign saving +- b_6 * dummy transition economy +-b_7 * percentage of the population adhering to the Muslim faith +- b_8 * European Union membership +- b_9 * state interventionism +- b_{10} * urbanisation +- b_{11} * dummy landlocked country +- b_{12} * dummy World Bank pension reform +- b_{13}* net migration rate per total population, 1950 - 2000

The trade-off between development level and the dependent variables is the following:

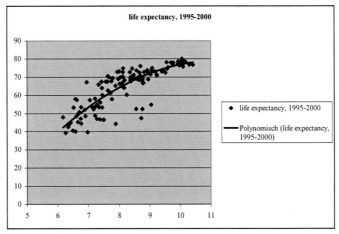

x-axis: n-log GDP PPP per capita.

---

[6] http://www.happyplanetindex.org/list.htm

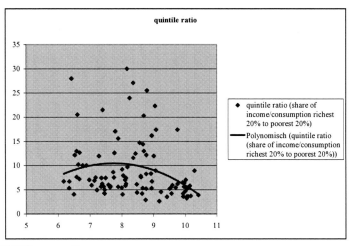

x-axis: n-log GDP PPP per capita.

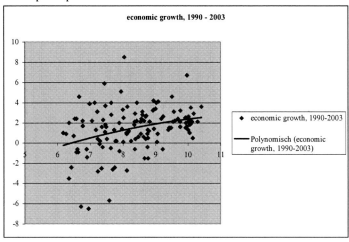

x-axis: n-log GDP PPP per capita.

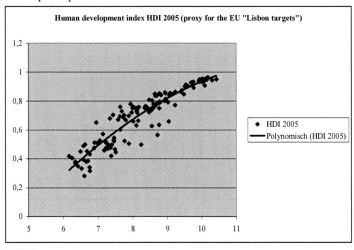

x-axis: n-log GDP PPP per capita.

Graph 5.2. (Continued)

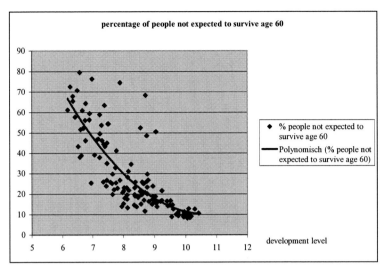

x-axis: n-log GDP PPP per capita.

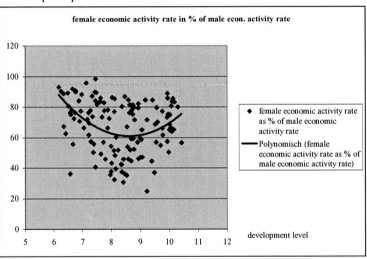

x-axis: n-log GDP PPP per capita.

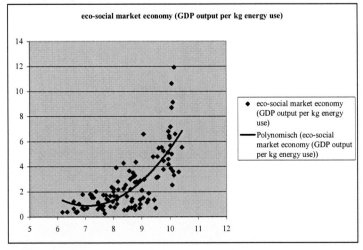

x-axis: n-log GDP PPP per capita.

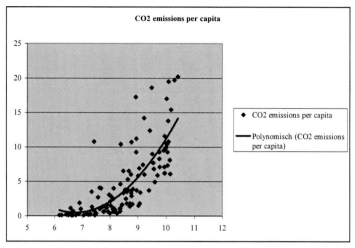

x-axis: n-log GDP PPP per capita.

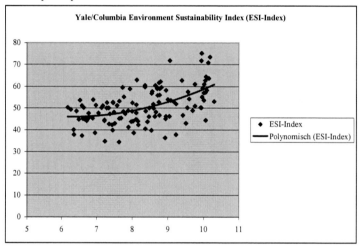

x-axis: n-log GDP PPP per capita.

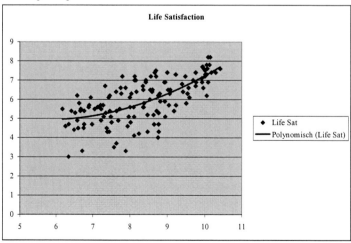

x-axis: n-log GDP PPP per capita.

Graph 5.2. (Continued)

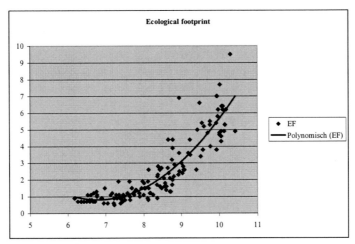

x-axis: n-log GDP PPP per capita.

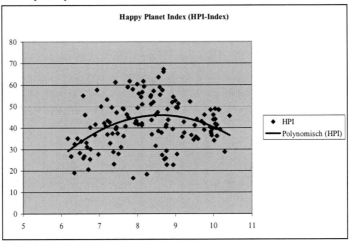

x-axis: n-log GDP PPP per capita.

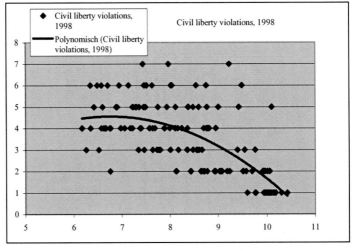

x-axis: n-log GDP PPP per capita.

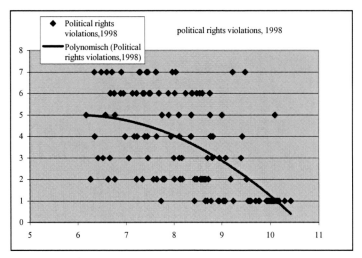

x-axis: n-log GDP PPP per capita.

Graph 5.2. Specifications for development performance $_{1990 - end\ 1990s}$ = a_1 +- b_1*first part curvilinear function of development level +- b_2*second part curvilinear function of development level.

We also introduce here our methdology to estimate what we call the "global Lisbon process". As it is well known, in March 2000, the EU Heads of States and Governments agreed to make the EU *"the most competitive and dynamic knowledge-driven economy by 2010"*. Although some progress was made on innovating Europe's economy, there is growing concern that the reform process is not going fast enough and that the ambitious targets will not be reached[7]. As it is also widely known, the 14 main structural "Lisbon" agenda indicators, created to measure progress in meeting the Lisbon targets, play an important role in European policy making[8]. The Lisbon lists of indicators, apart from the highly publicized debt-related Maastricht criteria of the European Monetary Union, are perhaps the most important checklists for government success or failure in Europe today. They are omnipresent in the public political as well as scientific debate and are defined by Eurostat as:

List of Lisbon indicators:

GDP per capita in PPS
Labor productivity
Employment rate
Employment rate of older workers
Educational attainment (20-24)
Research and Development expenditure
Comparative "price levels" (developed on the basis of the ERD-Index Yotopoulos et al.)[9]
    (the Commission maintaining that a low value is a good result)

---

[7] For a short survey of the Lisbon process, see also: http://www.euractiv.com/Article?tcmuri=tcm:29-117510-16&type=LinksDossier
[8] http://epp.eurostat.cec.eu.int/portal/page?_pageid=1133,1403427,1133_1403432&_dad=portal&_schema=PORTAL
[9] It can be shown that the Eurostat data series GDP PPP per capita/GDP exchange rate per capita (EU-25=100), used for the "price level", in reality measure GDP exchange rate per capita/GDP PPP per capita (EU-25=100). For more on that, see Appendix A of the full Internet version of our paper at http://www.insightturkey.com/

Business investment
At risk-of-poverty rate (low value = good result)
Long-term unemployment rate (low value = good result)
Dispersion of regional employment rates (low value = good result)
Greenhouse gas emissions (low value = good result)
Energy intensity of the economy (low value = good result)
Volume of freight transport (low value = good result)

It is assumed that a good performance on one indicator is causally linked to a good performance on the other indicators. Or in the words of Professor Romano Prodi, the former Commission President:

> "The Lisbon Strategy remains the right course for an enlarged European Union. It is the best way of delivering what concerns our citizens most - prosperity, more and better jobs, greater social cohesion and a cleaner environment - and making sure that they are achieved sustainably for future generations." (*http://www.socialdialogue.net/en/en_lib_068.htm*)

But a recent study by the European Commission (2005, Literature survey) warns that it is very difficult to quantify the impact of the reforms because of the "heterogeneity" of individual reform measures, time lags in implementation and complementarities and trade-offs between reforms. The Commission classifies the Lisbon reforms into five categories:

18. product and capital market reforms;
19. investments in the knowledge-based economy;
20. labor market reforms;
21. social policy reforms;
22. environmental policy reforms.

In Graph 5.3, we summarize our vision of the **"global Lisbon process"** from what is known from the international indicators. The dimension of human rights and gender equality is conspicuously absent from the original Lisbon 14 list. Our list, by contrast, integrates the five dimensions growth, environment, human rights, basic human needs, and gender equality.

To evaluate the global Lisbon indicators at once, we constructed a UNDP-type index from the data, contained in the appendix.

The UNDP type indicators are based on a simple principle, designed in the 1990s by Nobel laureate Amartya Sen: if you want to combine 2 or more variables to an indicator, calculate for each of the variables a dimension index, using the formula (UNDP, 2005):

(2) Dimension index = (actual value − minimum value) / (maximum value − minimum value)

The Research Design 43

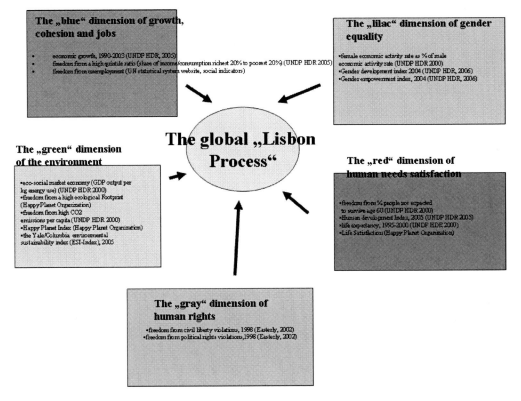

Graph 5.3a. The "global Lisbon process".

Calculating the famous **"Human Development Index"** of the United Nations Human Development Programme, one is supposed to proceed in the following way. According to formula (1), one first has to calculate a **life expectancy component**, called **"life expectancy index"**. Then, the same formula is used for an **"education index"**, based on the figures for adult literacy and gross enrollment (the weight for adult literacy is 2/3, and 1/3 for gross enrollment). The **"GDP index"** is now based on a small alteration of formula (1), working with the log GDP. In earlier years, the UNDP worked exactly with formula (1). Today, the UNDP calculates according to the following formula:

(2a) **GDP index** = (log (actual value GDP PPP per capita) minus log (100))/(log (maximum value GDP PPP per capita) minus log (100))

The UNDP HDI then will be the combined result of

(3) **Human development index** = 1/3 * (life expectancy index) + 1/3 * (education index) + 1/3 * (GDP index)

In our case, we calculated, using formula (1) the 17 different dimension indices for the global Lisbon process:

- economic growth, 1990-2003 (UNDP HDR, 2005)
- eco-social market economy (GDP output per kg energy use) (UNDP HDR 2000)

- female economic activity rate as % of male economic activity rate (UNDP HDR 2000)
- freedom from % people not expected to survive age 60 (UNDP HDR 2000)
- freedom from a high ecological Footprint, 204 (Happy Planet Organization)
- freedom from a high quintile ratio (share of income/consumption richest 20% to poorest 20%) (UNDP HDR 2005)
- freedom from civil liberty violations, 1998 (Easterly, 2000 - 2002)
- freedom from high CO_2 emissions per capita (UNDP HDR 2000)
- freedom from political rights violations, 1998 (Easterly, 2000 - 2002)
- freedom from unemployment, 2003 (UN statistical system website, social indicators)
- Gender development index 2004 (UNDP HDR, 2006)
- Gender empowerment index, 2004 (UNDP HDR, 2006)
- Happy Planet Index, 2004 (Happy Planet Organization)
- Human development Index, 2005 (UNDP HDR 2005)
- life expectancy, 1995-2000 (UNDP HDR 2000)
- Life Satisfaction, 2004 (Happy Planet Organization)
- the Yale/Columbia environmental sustainability index (ESI-Index), 2005

Due to missing values, **we were satisfied with simply calculating the means from the 17 available different components:**

- **(4a) Global Lisbon Index** = the means from
  - component index for the dimension economic growth, 1990-2003 (UNDP HDR, 2005)
  - component index for the dimension eco-social market economy (GDP output per kg energy use) (UNDP HDR 2000)
  - component index for the dimension female economic activity rate as % of male economic activity rate (UNDP HDR 2000)
  - component index for the dimension freedom from % people not expected to survive age 60 (UNDP HDR 2000)
  - component index for the dimension freedom from a high ecological Footprint, 204 (Happy Planet Organization)
  - component index for the dimension freedom from a high quintile ratio (share of income/consumption richest 20% to poorest 20%) (UNDP HDR 2005)
  - component index for the dimension freedom from civil liberty violations, 1998 (Easterly, 2000 - 2002)
  - component index for the dimension freedom from high CO_2 emissions per capita (UNDP HDR 2000)
  - component index for the dimension freedom from political rights violations, 1998 (Easterly, 2000 - 2002)
  - component index for the dimension freedom from unemployment, 2003 (UN statistical system website, social indicators)

- component index for the dimension Gender development index 2004 (UNDP HDR, 2006)
- component index for the dimension Gender empowerment index, 2004 (UNDP HDR, 2006)
- component index for the dimension Happy Planet Index, 2004 (Happy Planet Organization)
- component index for the dimension Human development Index, 2005 (UNDP HDR 2005)
- component index for the dimension life expectancy, 1995-2000 (UNDP HDR 2000)
- component index for the dimension Life Satisfaction, 2004 (Happy Planet Organization)
- component index for the dimension the Yale/Columbia environmental sustainability index (ESI-Index), 2005

We also undertook to calculate the "Global Lisbon Index" as an equally weighted combination of the five dimensions growth, environment, human rights, basic human needs, and gender equality. The scheme of graph 5.3 now is adapted accordingly: instead of 134 countries (as before), only 133 countries can be entered into the analysis. Since there are now data for the growth dimension for Chad, this country had to be dropped for the final analysis.

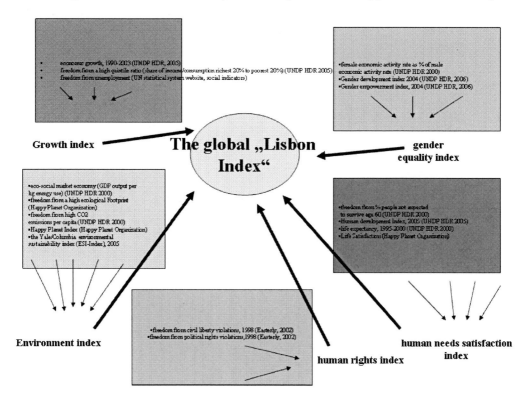

Graph 5.3b. an alternative method to calculate the "global Lisbon Index":

Table 5.1a. The global Lisbon process

Country code	UNDP type component index: % people not expected to survive age 60	UNDP type component index: CO2 emissions per capita	UNDP type component index: female economic activity rate as % of male economic activity rate	UNDP type component index: eco-social market economy (GDP output per kg energy use)	UNDP type component index: life expectancy, 1995-2000	UNDP type component index: quintile ratio (share of income/Consumption richest 20% to poorest 20%)	UNDP type component index: economic growth, 1990-2003	UNDP type component index: HDI 2005	UNDP type component index: ESI-Index	UNDP type component index: EF ecological footprint	UNDP type component index: HPI Happy Planet Index	UNDP type component index: Life Satisfaction	UNDP type component index: Civil liberty violation, 1998	UNDP type component index: Political rights violations, 1998	UNDP type component index: GDI 2006	UNDP type component index: GEM 2006	UNDP type component index: unemployment	Country code	Global Lisbon Index ↓
Switzerland	0,978	0,701	0,549	1,000	0,968	0,883	0,467	0,977	0,720	0,467	0,626	1,000	1,000	1,000	0,973	0,832	0,921	Switzerland	0,827
Iceland	0,997	0,602	0,823	0,261	0,977		0,573	0,990	0,894	0,511	0,628	0,923	1,000	1,000	0,994	0,918	0,947	Iceland	0,815
Austria	0,962	0,642	0,537	0,724	0,928	0,978	0,553	0,960	0,695	0,544	0,636	0,923	1,000	1,000	0,963	0,854	0,895	Austria	0,811
Sweden	0,993	0,697	0,870	0,371	0,965	0,964	0,567	0,979	0,916	0,278	0,427	0,904	1,000	1,000	0,981	0,939	0,868	Sweden	0,807
Norway	0,987	0,239	0,792	0,544	0,955	0,960	0,627	1,000	0,958	0,367	0,447	0,846	1,000	1,000	1,000	1,000	0,895	Norway	0,801
Denmark	0,935	0,468	0,800	0,761	0,894	0,964	0,560	0,968	0,585	0,344	0,490	1,000	1,000	1,000	0,967	0,912	0,895	Denmark	0,797
Finland	0,957	0,428	0,827	0,336	0,923	0,964	0,600	0,968	1,000	0,278	0,411	0,904	1,000	1,000	0,972	0,902	0,789	Finland	0,780
Netherlands	0,985	0,507	0,549	0,465	0,950	0,894	0,573	0,971	0,474	0,533	0,581	0,865	1,000	1,000	0,975	0,891	0,921	Netherlands	0,773
Ireland	0,975	0,517	0,349	0,517	0,911	0,861	0,880	0,975	0,609	0,367	0,451	0,885	1,000	1,000	0,984	0,777	0,921	Ireland	0,763
Japan	1,000	0,542	0,565	0,889	1,000	0,971	0,500	0,971	0,563	0,578	0,496	0,615	0,833	1,000	0,970	0,534	0,895	Japan	0,760
Costa Rica	0,952	0,935	0,268	0,277	0,903	0,620	0,607	0,817	0,619	0,822	0,976	0,865	0,833	1,000	0,804	0,680	0,842	Costa Rica	0,754
Mauritius	0,853	0,930	0,303		0,789		0,700	0,748		0,789	0,652	0,673	0,833	1,000	0,746		0,789	Mauritius	0,754
Canada	0,985	0,318	0,759	0,195	0,976	0,905	0,587	0,979	0,737	0,344	0,458	0,885	1,000	1,000	0,978	0,848	0,842	Canada	0,753
Cyprus	0,975	0,652	0,500	0,359	0,946		0,647	0,894		0,611	0,581	0,750	1,000	1,000	0,907	0,567	0,895	Cyprus	0,752
Germany	0,965	0,483	0,596	0,592	0,932	0,923	0,520	0,952	0,555	0,522	0,538	0,808	0,833	1,000	0,949	0,856	0,737	Germany	0,751
Luxem-bourg	0,966	0,000	0,431	0,453	0,919	0,953	0,673	0,979		0,511	0,573	0,885	1,000	1,000	0,981		0,895	Luxem-bourg	0,748
Italy	0,989	0,652	0,442	0,561	0,956	0,942	0,533	0,957	0,386	0,633	0,626	0,750	0,833	1,000	0,958	0,653	0,789	Italy	0,745
New Zealand	0,959	0,592	0,712	0,300	0,925	0,460	0,573	0,956	0,654	0,444	0,500	0,846	1,000	1,000	0,955	0,832	0,921	New Zealand	0,743
Slovenia	0,910	0,667	0,744	0,250	0,865	0,942	0,640	0,913	0,568	0,633	0,542	0,692	0,833	1,000	0,919	0,591	0,868	Slovenia	0,740
Guyana	0,719	0,950	0,320		0,618	0,825	0,673	0,644	0,700	0,889	0,791	0,808	0,833	0,833	0,907			Guyana	0,739
France	0,957	0,697	0,685	0,530	0,955	0,891	0,540	0,963	0,511	0,411	0,391	0,692	0,833	1,000	0,967	0,479	0,763	France	0,737
Uruguay	0,898	0,915	0,546	0,542	0,852	0,770	0,493	0,820	0,919	0,767	0,646	0,635	0,833	1,000	0,828		0,579	Uruguay	0,737

Country	1	2	3	4	5	6	7	8	9	10	11	12	13	14	15	16	17	Value	Country
United Kingdom	0,978	0,532	0,658	0,418	0,932	0,858	0,600	0,965	0,388	0,456	0,468	0,788	0,833	1,000	0,964	0,780	0,895	0,736	United Kingdom
Belgium	0,973	0,483	0,539	0,406	0,932	0,964	0,553	0,974	0,246	0,511	0,542	0,827	0,833	1,000	0,972	0,904	0,789	0,732	Belgium
Spain	0,973	0,711	0,409	0,452	0,952	0,898	0,593	0,949	0,354	0,522	0,522	0,769	0,833	1,000	0,957	0,806	0,737	0,732	Spain
Portugal	0,938	0,761	0,615	0,448	0,885	0,880	0,580	0,913	0,486	0,478	0,360	0,596	1,000	1,000	0,910	0,688	0,868	0,730	Portugal
Australia	0,990	0,159	0,681	0,307	0,958	0,839	0,607	0,988	0,654	0,200	0,346	0,827	1,000	1,000	0,991	0,877	0,895	0,725	Australia
Belize	0,923	0,925	0,080		0,870		0,580	0,692		0,767	0,700	0,750	0,833	1,000		0,456	0,763	0,718	Belize
Fiji	0,910	0,955	0,239		0,821		0,553	0,691		0,867	0,749	0,712	0,667	0,500			0,895	0,713	Fiji
Jamaica	0,928	0,806	0,822	0,065	0,874	0,869	0,593	0,670	0,253	0,767	0,680	0,769	0,833	0,833	0,640		0,737	0,703	Jamaica
Panama	0,903	0,881	0,395	0,291	0,844	0,558	0,540	0,767	0,572	0,856	0,927	0,808	0,667	0,833	0,767	0,547	0,711	0,701	Panama
Israel	0,985	0,542	0,560	0,427	0,946	0,869	0,540	0,930	0,405	0,467	0,445	0,712	0,667	1,000	0,945	0,657	0,789	0,699	Israel
Thailand	0,753	0,831	0,813	0,166	0,726	0,818	0,620	0,729	0,378	0,878	0,767	0,673	0,667	0,833	0,730	0,445	0,974	0,694	Thailand
Greece	0,990	0,622	0,435	0,389	0,955	0,898	0,573	0,925	0,386	0,456	0,377	0,635	0,667	1,000	0,933	0,604	0,789	0,684	Greece
Argentina	0,884	0,821	0,266	0,387	0,826		0,520	0,853	0,695	0,767	0,704	0,731	0,667	0,667	0,846	0,708	0,605	0,684	Argentina
Hungary	0,812	0,706	0,635	0,138	0,777	0,931	0,607	0,852	0,432	0,667	0,415	0,519	0,833	1,000	0,858	0,537	0,842	0,680	Hungary
Korea, Rep. of	0,881	0,557	0,595	0,244	0,815	0,905	0,740	0,909	0,211	0,678	0,484	0,538	0,833	0,833	0,915	0,465	0,921	0,678	Korea, Rep. of
United States	0,938	0,025	0,749	0,284	0,920	0,770	0,573	0,972	0,457	0,000	0,241	0,846	1,000	1,000	0,976	0,846	0,895	0,676	United States
Chile	0,921	0,836	0,302	0,233	0,877	0,460	0,707	0,840	0,472	0,767	0,686	0,673	0,833	0,667	0,833	0,470	0,842	0,672	Chile
Mongolia	0,752	0,831	0,846	0,195	0,653	0,891	0,267	0,584	0,383	0,844	0,652	0,712	0,667	0,833	0,587	0,323	0,921	0,672	Mongolia
Dominican Republic	0,849	0,925	0,285		0,770	0,639	0,700	0,686	0,229	0,878	0,800	0,769	0,833	0,833	0,676		0,553	0,664	Dominican Republic
Poland	0,872	0,542	0,741	0,094	0,817	0,901	0,713	0,846	0,260	0,656	0,449	0,558	0,833	1,000	0,846	0,600	0,526	0,662	Poland
Slovakia	0,885	0,637	0,812	0,076	0,828	1,000	0,593	0,833	0,452	0,656	0,379	0,462	0,833	0,833	0,837	0,586	0,553	0,662	Slovakia
Latvia	0,764	0,821	0,770	0,084	0,716	0,901	0,580	0,814	0,639	0,567	0,211	0,327	0,833	1,000	0,822	0,613	0,789	0,662	Latvia
Sri Lanka	0,900	0,985	0,402	0,150	0,832	0,898	0,653	0,689	0,346	0,933	0,864	0,596	0,500	0,667	0,682	0,303	0,789	0,658	Sri Lanka
Colombia	0,825	0,915	0,466	0,251	0,766	0,354	0,460	0,739	0,602	0,911	1,000	0,808	0,500	0,667	0,739	0,470	0,711	0,658	Colombia
Lithuania	0,788	0,821	0,741	0,053	0,753	0,905	0,467	0,837	0,602	0,622	0,251	0,327	0,833	1,000	0,842	0,631	0,684	0,656	Lithuania
Philippines	0,809	0,960	0,481	0,163	0,713	0,741	0,513	0,699	0,194	0,922	0,842	0,654	0,667	0,833	0,700	0,504	0,737	0,655	Philippines
Croatia	0,885	0,811	0,636	0,216	0,820		0,573	0,821	0,617	0,733	0,536	0,558	0,500	0,500	0,824	0,590	0,658	0,642	Croatia
Trinidad and Tobago	0,905	0,149	0,438	0,037	0,849	0,792	0,647	0,762	0,047	0,800	0,698	0,750	0,833	1,000	0,766	0,662	0,763	0,641	Trinidad and Tobago
Romania	0,825	0,741	0,698	0,040	0,754	0,942	0,473	0,833	0,290	0,756	0,417	0,423	0,833	0,833	0,764	0,453	0,816	0,641	Romania
Mexico	0,850	0,821	0,289	0,225	0,809	0,504	0,527	0,782	0,290	0,778	0,747	0,750	0,500	0,667	0,776	0,583	0,947	0,638	Mexico
Albania	0,920	0,975	0,649	0,179	0,823		0,773	0,732	0,600	0,889	0,504	0,308	0,333	0,500	0,728		0,632	0,636	Albania
Bolivia	0,655	0,940	0,438	0,125	0,544	0,781	0,520	0,595	0,617	0,922	0,585	0,481	0,667	1,000	0,590	0,461	0,895	0,636	Bolivia

Table 5.1a. Continued

Country																			Country	
Papua New Guinea	0,537	0,975	0,716			0,457	0,635	0,447	0,355	0,511	0,911	0,557	0,635	0,667	0,833	0,342		0,947		Papua New Guinea	0,635
Honduras	0,795	0,970	0,284	0,094	0,740	0,471	0,447	0,566	0,319	0,900	0,893	0,808	0,667	0,833	0,573		0,921		Honduras	0,634
China	0,863	0,866	0,834	0,042	0,751	0,807	1,000	0,695	0,103	0,889	0,779	0,635	0,167	0,000	0,706	0,500	0,921		China	0,629
Malaysia	0,889	0,716	0,474	0,158	0,804	0,657	0,660	0,755	0,482	0,722	0,713	0,846	0,333	0,333	0,751	0,463	0,921		Malaysia	0,628
Peru	0,792	0,950	0,236	0,344	0,714	0,672	0,573	0,705	0,639	0,956	0,761	0,500	0,500	0,333	0,697	0,562	0,737		Peru	0,628
Bulgaria	0,858	0,682	0,842	0,023	0,781	0,934	0,473	0,773	0,383	0,756	0,296	0,250	0,667	0,833	0,779	0,581	0,711		Bulgaria	0,625
Venezuela	0,877	0,682	0,368	0,100	0,814	0,569	0,333	0,720	0,337	0,789	0,808	0,846	0,667	0,833	0,728	0,502	0,605		Venezuela	0,622
Ecuador	0,813	0,900	0,175	0,168	0,743	0,759	0,440	0,701	0,442	0,856	0,646	0,500	0,667	0,833		0,515	0,789		Ecuador	0,622
Estonia	0,781	0,448	0,780	0,063	0,723	0,850	0,653	0,839	0,585	0,289	0,121	0,404	0,833	1,000	0,842	0,597	0,763		Estonia	0,622
Indonesia	0,741	0,945	0,563	0,119	0,636	0,891	0,567	0,610	0,354	0,922	0,816	0,692	0,500	0,167	0,615		0,789		Indonesia	0,620
Ghana	0,626	0,995	1,000	0,065	0,509	0,912	0,553	0,350	0,452	0,933	0,601	0,615	0,667	0,667	0,352				Ghana	0,620
Armenia	0,837	0,955	0,830	0,128	0,767		0,620	0,701	0,462	0,944	0,385	0,135	0,500	0,500	0,706		0,816		Armenia	0,619
India	0,698	0,950	0,332	0,054	0,573	0,887	0,700	0,471	0,265	0,967	0,634	0,462	0,667	0,833	0,446		0,921		India	0,616
Tunisia	0,840	0,915	0,287	0,234	0,743	0,810	0,640	0,692	0,428	0,900	0,836	0,654	0,333	0,167	0,675		0,658		Tunisia	0,613
Czech Republic	0,916	0,388	0,811	0,092	0,851	0,967	0,533	0,870	0,300	0,500	0,395	0,654	0,333	0,500	0,879	0,606	0,816		Czech Republic	0,612
Madagascar	0,571	1,000	0,721		0,448	0,723	0,373	0,320	0,388	0,967	0,581	0,538	0,500	0,833	0,321		0,895		Madagascar	0,612
Brazil	0,739	0,920	0,374	0,350	0,676	0,164	0,513	0,749	0,683	0,811	0,632	0,635	0,500	0,667	0,742	0,445	0,789		Brazil	0,611
Kyrgyzstan	0,759	0,935	0,788	0,098	0,697	0,821	0,273	0,617	0,344	0,933	0,838	0,692	0,333	0,333	0,610		0,684		Kyrgyzstan	0,610
Bangladesh	0,583	0,995	0,698	0,124	0,464	0,916	0,640	0,350	0,238	0,989	0,723	0,519	0,500	0,833	0,346	0,306	0,921		Bangladesh	0,597
Paraguay	0,839	0,970	0,237	0,169	0,746	0,106	0,393	0,695	0,622	0,811	0,682	0,673	0,667	0,500			0,816		Paraguay	0,595
Morocco	0,792	0,955	0,362	0,312	0,673	0,839	0,500	0,513	0,256	0,956	0,747	0,500	0,500	0,333	0,482		0,711		Morocco	0,589
Viet Nam	0,780	0,468	0,880	0,030	0,691	0,891	0,827	0,620	0,194	0,967	0,881	0,596	0,000	0,000	0,621		0,974		Viet Nam	0,589
Singapore	0,966	0,035	0,531	0,287	0,930		0,667	0,918		0,367	0,385	0,750	0,333	0,333		0,720	0,895		Singapore	0,580
Georgia	0,870	0,975	0,708	0,117	0,822		0,253	0,661	0,420	0,967	0,486	0,212	0,500	0,667		0,347	0,684		Georgia	0,579
Guatemala	0,679	0,975	0,200	0,217	0,609	0,000	0,507	0,560	0,236	0,922	0,891	0,769	0,500	0,667	0,548		0,947		Guatemala	0,577
Turkey	0,833	0,861	0,470	0,213	0,731	0,796	0,520	0,688	0,300	0,833	0,490	0,442	0,333	0,500	0,676	0,200	0,763		Turkey	0,568
Moldova, Rep. of	0,755	0,871	0,789	0,034	0,694	0,876	0,053	0,572	0,413	0,922	0,287	0,096	0,500	0,833	0,597	0,517	0,816		Moldova, Rep. of	0,566
Nepal	0,567	1,000	0,565	0,036	0,444	0,880	0,580	0,359	0,327	0,989	0,660	0,481	0,500	0,667	0,330				Nepal	0,559
Jordan	0,842	0,881	0,103	0,097	0,759	0,883	0,493	0,692	0,329	0,844	0,502	0,404	0,333	0,500	0,679				Jordan	0,556
Azerbaijan	0,805	0,806	0,661	0,000	0,752		0,260	0,657	0,270	0,889	0,476	0,365	0,500	0,167	0,658		1,000		Azerbaijan	0,551
Belarus	0,749	0,706	0,768	0,049	0,706	0,989	0,493	0,740	0,452	0,700	0,182	0,192	0,167	0,167	0,748		0,974		Belarus	0,549

Benin	0,467	1,000	0,884	0,066	0,348		0,580	0,220	0,322	0,944	0,464	0,462	0,833	0,833	0,179			Benin	0,543
Botswana	0,157	0,935	0,718		0,200		0,613	0,416	0,528	0,911	0,174	0,462	0,833	0,833	0,393	0,464	0,500	Botswana	0,543
Cambodia	0,461		0,963		0,346	0,843	0,700	0,425	0,386	0,933	0,506	0,500	0,167	0,167	0,427	0,305	0,974	Cambodia	0,540
Namibia	0,380		0,574		0,323		0,493	0,507	0,550	0,878	0,431	0,673	0,667	0,833	0,493	0,616	0,132	Namibia	0,539
Lao People's Dem. Rep.	0,485	1,000	0,805		0,343	0,942	0,680	0,387	0,442	0,944	0,468	0,462	0,167	0,000	0,378			Lao People's Dem. Rep.	0,536
Algeria	0,856	0,841	0,155	0,118	0,728	0,872	0,473	0,647	0,285	0,889	0,579	0,423	0,333	0,167	0,628		0,553	Algeria	0,534
Tajikistan	0,760	0,955	0,714	0,027	0,686		0,000	0,544	0,103	0,989	0,812	0,596	0,167	0,167	0,531		0,947	Tajikistan	0,533
Gabon	0,433	0,841	0,685	0,259	0,323		0,407	0,519	0,671	0,867	0,472	0,615	0,500	0,333				Gabon	0,533
Kazakhstan	0,753	0,488	0,753	0,023	0,697		0,460	0,704	0,349	0,744	0,401	0,538	0,333	0,167	0,716		0,816	Kazakhstan	0,530
Uzbekistan	0,763	0,801	0,799	0,025	0,694	0,894	0,400	0,606	0,000	0,844	0,644	0,654	0,167	0,000	0,600			Uzbekistan	0,526
Russian Federation	0,698	0,473	0,761	0,026	0,671	0,650	0,333	0,754	0,533	0,567	0,123	0,250	0,500	0,500	0,751	0,440	0,816	Russian Federation	0,520
Senegal	0,456	0,985	0,638	0,131	0,321	0,821	0,520	0,260	0,410	0,922	0,478	0,500	0,500	0,500	0,237			Senegal	0,512
Tanzania, U. Rep. of	0,258	1,000	0,926	0,010	0,213	0,850	0,500	0,201	0,391	0,956	0,366	0,481	0,500	0,333	0,200	0,583	0,895	Tanzania, U. Rep. of	0,510
Egypt	0,792	0,930	0,249	0,122	0,664	0,949	0,600	0,554	0,236	0,889	0,494	0,346	0,167	0,167		0,167	0,737	Egypt	0,504
Lebanon	0,849	0,776	0,172	0,174	0,753		0,627	0,701	0,150	0,800	0,534	0,500	0,333	0,167				Lebanon	0,503
Pakistan	0,741	0,970	0,214	0,076	0,607	0,938	0,507	0,361	0,135	0,978	0,451	0,250	0,333	0,500	0,330	0,310	0,816	Pakistan	0,501
Mali	0,509		0,757		0,345	0,650	0,593	0,076	0,474	0,933	0,338	0,442	0,667	0,667	0,055			Mali	0,501
Uganda	0,045		0,861		0,009	0,839	0,693	0,333	0,415	0,889	0,219	0,327	0,500	0,500	0,307		0,947	Uganda	0,492
Mozambique	0,261	1,000	0,911	0,010	0,146	0,832	0,740	0,144	0,256	0,978	0,324	0,462	0,500	0,667	0,142			Mozambique	0,491
Mauritania	0,492	0,940	0,664		0,350	0,825	0,540	0,287	0,201	0,933	0,409	0,442	0,333	0,167	0,278			Mauritania	0,490
Guinea	0,352	0,995	0,878		0,178	0,825	0,540	0,271	0,337	0,944	0,411	0,404	0,333	0,167	0,212			Guinea	0,489
Gambia	0,362	0,995	0,720		0,190	0,657	0,427	0,277	0,383	0,933	0,512	0,519	0,333	0,000				Gambia	0,485
South Africa	0,407	0,662	0,461	0,107	0,380	0,281	0,440	0,553	0,290	0,744	0,221	0,519	0,833	1,000	0,528		0,316	South Africa	0,484
Iran, Islamic Rep. of	0,816	0,816	0,141	0,039	0,736		0,573	0,667	0,133	0,822	0,605	0,577	0,167	0,167	0,663	0,246		Iran, Islamic Rep. of	0,478
Syrian Arab Republic	0,825	0,851	0,146	0,081	0,728		0,527	0,645	0,231	0,844	0,526	0,404	0,000	0,000	0,612		0,711	Syrian Arab Republic	0,475
Malawi	0,098	1,000	0,890		0,000		0,493	0,180	0,366	0,978	0,200	0,308	0,667	0,833	0,152			Malawi	0,474
Yemen	0,582	0,950	0,155	0,082	0,460	0,818	0,593	0,305	0,071	0,978	0,759	0,615	0,167	0,333	0,254	0,000	0,711	Yemen	0,461
Rwanda	0,123	1,000	0,873		0,030	0,949	0,480	0,248	0,256	0,978	0,231	0,269	0,167	0,000	0,234		1,000	Rwanda	0,456

Table 5.1a. Continued

Kenya	0,325	0,990	0,805	0,036	0,314	0,730	0,393	0,283	0,268	0,956	0,397	0,500	0,333	0,167	0,291		Kenya	0,453
Haiti	0,419	0,995	0,607	0,110	0,356		0,247	0,284	0,010	1,000	0,528	0,481	0,333	0,500			Haiti	0,452
Bahrain	0,910	0,080	0,165	0,037	0,826		0,533	0,828		0,322	0,352	0,808	0,167	0,000	0,831		Bahrain	0,451
Cameroon	0,467	0,990	0,442	0,109	0,380		0,447	0,317	0,445	0,956	0,320	0,404	0,333	0,000	0,306	0,816	Cameroon	0,449
Burkina Faso	0,213	1,000	0,894		0,126	0,730	0,547	0,053	0,278	0,933	0,267	0,327	0,500	0,333	0,064		Burkina Faso	0,447
Swaziland	0,631	0,985	0,367		0,515	0,223	0,447	0,318		0,933	0,036	0,231	0,500	0,167	0,279		Swaziland	0,433
Saudi Arabia	0,879	0,299	0,000	0,093	0,790		0,393	0,720	0,084	0,567	0,516	0,827	0,000	0,000	0,675	0,142	Saudi Arabia	0,430
Togo	0,289	0,995	0,501		0,235		0,460	0,339	0,248	0,956	0,401	0,365	0,333	0,167	0,275		Togo	0,428
Guinea-Bissau	0,306	0,995	0,514		0,140	0,073	0,273	0,098	0,349	0,978	0,366	0,462	0,333	0,667			Guinea-Bissau	0,427
Congo	0,282	0,910	0,623	0,130	0,228		0,340	0,339	0,477	0,956	0,494	0,519	0,333	0,000	0,339		Congo	0,426
Nigeria	0,383	0,970	0,419	0,007	0,266	0,631		0,252	0,270	0,922	0,287	0,481	0,500	0,167	0,225		Nigeria	0,413
Zambia	0,000	0,990	0,698	0,033	0,020	0,620	0,373	0,166	0,410	0,967	0,184	0,365	0,500	0,333	0,155	0,711	Zambia	0,408
Lesotho	0,508		0,421		0,412	0,310	0,587	0,317		0,989	0,128	0,250	0,500	0,500	0,290		Lesotho	0,401
Côte d'Ivoire	0,226	0,960	0,346	0,151	0,183	0,869	0,407	0,204	0,317	0,956	0,241	0,288	0,500	0,167	0,163	0,000	Côte d'Ivoire	0,398
Ethiopia	0,196		0,577	0,012	0,100	0,850	0,567	0,126	0,084	0,978	0,314	0,327	0,500	0,500		0,421	Ethiopia	0,397
Zimbabwe	0,070	0,925	0,723	0,047	0,119	0,526	0,380	0,328	0,167	0,944	0,000	0,058	0,500	0,333	0,285	0,868	Zimbabwe	0,392
Angola	0,352	0,985	0,774	0,053	0,177		0,460	0,240	0,209	0,967	0,223	0,346	0,167	0,167	0,207		Angola	0,381
Niger	0,391	1,000	0,682		0,227	0,347	0,393	0,000	0,260	0,933	0,202	0,288	0,333	0,000	0,000		Niger	0,361
Chad	0,328		0,698		0,195			0,088	0,260	0,911	0,174	0,288	0,500	0,167	0,087		Chad	0,336
Burundi	0,164		0,868		0,078	0,901	0,200	0,142	0,138	0,978	0,047	0,000	0,167	0,000	0,131	0,658	Burundi	0,319
Congo, Dem. Rep. of the	0,380		0,646	0,013	0,283		0,013	0,152	0,238	0,978	0,081	0,058	0,167	0,000	0,128		Congo, Dem. Rep. of the	0,241

Due to missing values, **we were satisfied with simply calculating the means from the available different components.**

- **(4b) Growth Dimension Index** = the means from
  - component index for the dimension economic growth, 1990-2003 (UNDP HDR, 2005)
  - component index for the dimension freedom from a high quintile ratio (share of income/consumption richest 20% to poorest 20%) (UNDP HDR 2005)
  - component index for the dimension freedom from unemployment, 2003 (UN statistical system website, social indicators)
- **(4c) Environment Dimension Index** = the means from
  - component index for the dimension eco-social market economy (GDP output per kg energy use) (UNDP HDR 2000)
  - component index for the dimension freedom from a high ecological Footprint, 204 (Happy Planet Organization)
  - component index for the dimension freedom from high CO_2 emissions per capita (UNDP HDR 2000)
  - component index for the dimension Happy Planet Index, 2004 (Happy Planet Organization)
  - component index for the dimension the Yale/Columbia environmental sustainability index (ESI-Index), 2005
- **(4d) human rights index** = the means from
  - component index for the dimension freedom from civil liberty violations, 1998 (Easterly, 2000 - 2002)
  - component index for the dimension freedom from political rights violations, 1998 (Easterly, 2000 - 2002)
- **(4e) the basic human needs satisfaction index** = the means from
  - component index for the dimension freedom from % people not expected to survive age 60 (UNDP HDR 2000)
  - component index for the dimension Human development Index, 2005 (UNDP HDR 2005)
  - component index for the dimension life expectancy, 1995-2000 (UNDP HDR 2000)
  - component index for the dimension Life Satisfaction, 2004 (Happy Planet Organization)
- **(4f) the gender equality index** = the means from
  - component index for the dimension female economic activity rate as % of male economic activity rate (UNDP HDR 2000)
  - component index for the dimension Gender development index 2004 (UNDP HDR, 2006)
  - component index for the dimension Gender empowerment index, 2004 (UNDP HDR, 2006)

- **(4g) The Global Lisbon Process Index (2)** = the means from
  - **Growth Dimension Index**
  - **Environment Dimension Index**
  - **Human Rights Index**
  - **Basic Human Needs Satisfaction Index**
  - **Gender equality index**

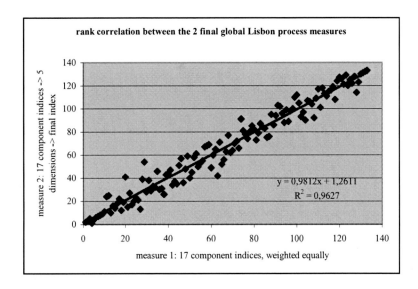

Graph 5.4. the correlation between the two Lisbon process measures.

The results of this exercise are documented in the Appendix. The two measures correlate very closely with each other. The Global Lisbon Process Index (1) is more reactive towards data concerning basic needs and the environment, the Global Lisbon Process Index (2) is more reactive towards data concerning growth and gender issues.

Chapter 6

THE RESULTS FOR THE FOURTEEN CORE DEPENDENT VARIABLES

We now will present t-values and the direction of influence, significant at least at the 10 % level, for the 14 core predictors of our model:

- absence of % people not expected to survive age 60
- absence of Civil liberty violations, 1998
- absence of CO_2 emissions per capita
- absence of high ecological footprint
- absence of high quintile ratio (share of income/consumption richest 20% to poorest 20%)
- absence of political rights violations,1998
- economic growth, 1990-2003
- eco-social market economy (GDP output per kg energy use)
- ESI-Index
- female economic activity rate as % of male economic activity rate
- HDI 2005
- HPI-Index
- life expectancy, 1995-2000
- Life Satisfaction

Our first results concern the effects of **Muslim culture** on development. The empirical test reveals that – *ceteris paribus* – there is lot of reason for optimism for the future of inter-cultural relations, with the percentage of Muslims per total population **positively** affecting life expectancy, human rights, the human development index, longtitivity, CO_2 emissions reduction and the eco-social market economy of a country. The negative trade-off between the presence of the "Muslim factor" in a country and life satisfaction however shows the relevanmce of liberal Muslim thought ever since the writings of Abu Nasr Mohammed Ibn Tarkhan al Farabi (870 – 950) with his central theme of the necessity to focus Muslim thought on the issue of **happiness**, developed in his classic *"Kitab tahsil al-sa'ada"*. Some further summaries about the importance of the thinking of Muslim philosophers from the Middle Ages for this problem are presented in the appendix. They all show that classic Muslim philosophy reflected on the issue of human happiness, and in many ways formulated thoughts that were path-breaking for the Age of Enlightment (see especially Tibi, 1999, and Bloch, 1952).

dependent variable	Political rights violations, 1998	Civil liberty violations, 1998	quintile ratio (share of income/consumption richest 20% to poorest 20%)	% people not expected to survive age 60	life expectancy, 1995-2000	HDI 2005	female economic activity rate as % of male economic activity rate	CO_2 emissions per capita	eco-social market economy (GDP output per kg energy use)	ESI-Index	economic growth, 1990-2003
Predictor: Muslims as % of total population	-4,075	-2,786		-2,321	2,523	2,072		-2,019	1,943		
dependent variable ->	Life Satisfaction	Ecological footprint	Happy Planet Index								
Predictor: Muslims as % of total population	-1,823										

We will not shy away from a debate on these issues, and we will include in Chapters 8 and 9 also a discussion of the results for unemployment and the gender dimension.

Geography, as William Easterly correctly observes, also plays an important part among today's cross-national development determinants. Paradoxically enough, the status of a country as a **landlocked country** significantly and positively affects two of the four environment variables under scrutiny here, CO2 emissions reduction and the eco-social market economy.

dependent variable ->	Political rights violations, 1998	Civil liberty violations, 1998	quintile ratio (share of income/consumption richest 20% to poorest 20%)	% people not expected to survive age 60	life expectancy, 1995-2000	HDI 2005	female economic activity rate as % of male economic activity rate	CO_2 emissions per capita	eco-social market economy (GDP output per kg energy use)	ESI-Index	economic growth, 1990-2003
Predictor: landlocked country								-1,943	2,522		
dependent variable ->	Life Satisfaction	Ecological footprint	Happy Planet Index								
Predictor: landlocked country											

Urbanization also plays a major role. In the vast quantitative literature on globalization and development, there is recurrent reference to the issues of "structural disarticulation", i.e. the imbalance between the different economic sectors. Although highly urbanised, and often prematurely urbanized societies especially in Africa, Asia and Latin American can manage better than their less urbanised counterparts the problem of CO2 emissions (with population density making environmental investments, public transport and energy saving less costly), and ecological footprint, and although they tend to have a very positive human development record and a high value on the Happy Planet Index, their main structural deficits are income polarization and a very high social exclusion of women from employment, thus supporting earlier literature, which tended to analyze structural disarticulation on such terms [see the results, reported by Breedlove W. L. and Armer J. M. (1997), Huang J. (1995), Stokes R. and Anderson A.. (1990), Wickrama K. A. S. and Mulford Ch. L. (1996)]. The same applies to the interesting studies on premature and "inflated" urbanization that is well compatible with the original writings of dependency theory [see: Bradshaw Y. (1987), Bradshaw Y. W. and Schafer M. J. (2000), Crenshaw E. M. and Oakey, D. R. (1998), Kasarda J.D. and Crenshaw E.M. (1991), Smith D. A and London B. (1990), Smith D. A. (1996)]. So, *ceteris paribus,* the net effects of urbanization are, somewhat paradoxically, good for the environment but bad for distribution and female employment:

dependent variable ->	Political rights violations, 1998	Civil liberty violations, 1998	quintile ratio (share of income/consumption richest 20% to poorest 20%)	% people not expected to survive age 60	life expectancy, 1995-2000	HDI 2005	female economic activity rate as % of male economic activity rate	CO2 emissions per capita	eco-social market economy (GDP output per kg energy use)	ESI-Index	economic growth, 1990-2003
Predictor: Urbanization ratio, 1990			2,400	-3,260	3,317	3,624	-6,119	-5,989			
dependent variable ->		Life Satisfaction	Ecological footprint	Happy Planet Index							
Predictor: Urbanization ratio, 1990			-7,307	+4,320							

Easterly also correctly pointed out that what we call here **development history** plays an important role in the determination of development. **Transition economies** ever since the times of Communist rule still tend to be characterized by comparatively lower rates of economic inequalities and higher shares of women in the labor force, and notably enough they tended to increase their eco-market efficiency in recent years, but still they are characterized by very high rates of CO2-emissions, a bad human development performance, a low life expectancy, a high rate of early death at age 60, a high ecological footprint index and a bad performance on the Happy Planet Index.

dependent variable ->	Political rights violations, 1998	Civil liberty violations, 1998	quintile ratio (share of income/consumption richest 20% to poorest 20%)	% people not expected to survive age 60	life expectancy, 1995-2000	HDI 2005	female economic activity rate as % of male economic activity rate	CO2 emissions per capita	eco-social market economy (GDP output per kg energy use)	ESI-Index	economic growth, 1990-2003
Predictor: Dummy for transition economy			-2,584	2,342	-2,290	-1,918	5,959	6,576	2,115		
dependent variable ->	Life Satisfaction	Ecological footprint	Happy Planet Index								
Predictor: Dummy for transition economy		+8,195	-4.,163								

Next, we look into the well-known curve-linear effects of development levels on development performance. Critics of Western civilization and of capitalist globalization, as well as social scientists, who looked into the more negative sides of the "modernization process", would all agree on the empirically measurable effect of *"things getting worse with higher development levels"*. The first expression in the well-known **acceleration and maturity effects of development** - + b1* ln (PCI*tn*) – yields the following results. The immediate **effects** of rising **development levels** on world development are **deteriorating human rights records**, increasing **marginalization** of women on the labor market, rising **environmental strains** and **sinking rates of economic growth**, thus contradicting the optimistic views of the development process. Much of the ills of the Middle Eastern region, often attributed to Islam, are in reality nothing else but the expression of this **"modernization crisis"** of all poorer countries in the world system, already described in great detail by the classics of political science. Most notably enough, several of these ills seem to disappear with rising levels of per capita incomes, but not all of them (see below).

dependent variable ->	Political rights violations, 1998	Civil liberty violations, 1998	quintile ratio (share of income/consumption richest 20% to poorest 20%)	% people not expected to survive age 60	life expectancy, 1995-2000	HDI 2005	female economic activity rate as % of male economic activity rate	CO2 emissions per capita	eco-social market economy (GDP output per kg energy use)	ESI-Index	economic growth, 1990-2003
Predictor: ln(GDP PPP pc)	2,294	2,447					-2,793	2,947	-1,854		-3,666
dependent variable ->	Life Satisfaction	Ecological footprint	Happy Planet Index								

The Results for the Fourteen Core Dependent Variables

dependent variable ->	Political rights violations, 1998	Civil liberty violations, 1998	quintile ratio (share of income/consumption richest 20% to poorest 20%)	% people not expected to survive age 60	life expectancy, 1995-2000	HDI 2005	female economic activity rate as % of male economic activity rate	CO2 emissions per capita	eco-social market economy (GDP output per kg energy use)	ESI-Index	economic growth, 1990-2003
Predictor: ln(GDP PPP pc)											

Ever since the days of Nobel laureate Simon Kuznets, there were social scientists, who held the view that at least after reaching certain development levels, there are then the **"lights at the end of tunnel"**. The **second part of the so-called "Kuznets-curve"** - b2* (ln (PCItn))2 - has the following empirical **results** for the "maturity effects" of development: life expectancy, longevity and the gender specific employment record of a society dramatically improve, and indeed social cohesion makes good progress after certain levels of development are being reached. But modernization and ecological or religious or other western civilization pessimsits alike would expect that there are just no lights at the end of the tunnel. Whatever lights there are, these are just *"headlamps of an approaching train"*. There are deteriorating ecological balances on the GDP output per kg energy use indicator, as ln GDP per capita squared reaches very high values, and there are lamentable effects on the ecological footprint indicator and CO2 emissions. Life satisfaction and the performance on the Happy Planet Index plummet as very high incomes are being reached. These very pessimistic results are a warning signal that there are indeed contradictory processes at work in global capitalism, which provide a fertile ground for the kind of pessimism inherent in the works of green critics of Western society. Needless to say that the modernization pessimism, inherent in the early works of Samuel Huntington, also receives strong support from these pessimistic results:

dependent variable ->	Political rights violations, 1998	Civil liberty violations, 1998	quintile ratio (share of income/consumption richest 20% to poorest 20%)	% people not expected to survive age 60	life expectancy, 1995-2000	HDI 2005	female economic activity rate as % of male economic activity rate	CO2 emissions per capita	eco-social market economy (GDP output per kg energy use)	ESI-Index	economic growth, 1990-2003
Predictor: ln (GDP PPP pc)^2			-3,188	-1,988	2,381	4,699	6,046	3,182	-3,692		
dependent variable ->	Life Satisfaction	Ecological footprint	Happy Planet Index								
Predictor: ln (GDP PPP pc)^2	-1,898	+4,525	-2,218								

We stated above that Muslim culture is **not an impediment against human rights, human development and ecological development**, but *ceteris paribus* the **European Union** is. Our results again clearly support many of the expectations inherent in the writings of EU pessimists. Three dimensions of development – human rights, human development and ecological development, are *ceteris paribus* positively and significantly determined by the percentage share of Muslims per total population, while the old member countries of the EU (EU-15) have – *ceteris paribus* – a very **negative human rights balance, slow economic growth** and **a low environment sustainability index** (ESI index).

dependent variable ->	Political rights violations, 1998	Civil liberty violations, 1998	quintile ratio (share of income/consumption richest 20% to poorest 20%)	% people not expected to survive age 60	life expectancy, 1995-2000	HDI 2005	female economic activity rate as % of male economic activity rate	CO2 emissions per capita	eco-social market economy (GDP output per kg energy use)	ESI-Index	economic growth, 1990-2003
Predictor: EU-membership (EU-15)	4,801	5,384								-1,787	-2,477
dependent variable ->	Life Satisfaction	Ecological footprint	Happy Planet Index								
Predictor: EU-membership (EU-15)											

Our results about the effects of **globalization** are not as clear-cut as one might expect from the literature. By introducing five predictors of a "pro-globalization" economic policy, we avoid the problems of the consequences of measurement errors and mis-specification and present rather a very broad picture of the realities of globalization, described by the effects of

- foreign saving [(I-S)/GNP]
- low comparative international price levels [ERD]
- state interventionism (absence of economic. freedom)
- transnational capital penetration [MNC PEN 1995]
- world bank pension reforms

As one of the three main indicators of dependency, the **reliance on foreign savings** eases the distribution burden against the poorer segments of society during the accumulation process and it positively affects the longitivity record in society, but it hampers environmental sustainability and it has a negative effect on female employment, and it is to be considered as one of the main negative determinants of the human rights record of a country:

The Results for the Fourteen Core Dependent Variables

dependent variable ->	Political rights violations, 1998	Civil liberty violations, 1998	quintile ratio (share of income/consumption richest 20% to poorest 20%)	% people not expected to survive age 60	life expectancy, 1995-2000	HDI 2005	female economic activity rate as % of male economic activity rate	CO2 emissions per capita	eco-social market economy (GDP output per kg energy use)	ESI-Index	economic growth, 1990-2003
Predictor: (I-S)/GNP	5,404	4,847	-2,167	-2,816	1,768		-3,556			-2,556	
dependent variable ->	Life Satisfaction	Ecological footprint	Happy Planet Index								
Predictor: (I-S)/GNP											

MNC penetration contributes to a negative balance of a country on the eco-social market economy indicator, while other, often well-known effects on economic growth, human survival and life expectancy cannot be maintained any longer under the specifications of the present research design.

dependent variable ->	Political rights violations, 1998	Civil liberty violations, 1998	quintile ratio (share of income/consumption richest 20% to poorest 20%)	% people not expected to survive age 60	life expectancy, 1995-2000	HDI 2005	female economic activity rate as % of male economic activity rate	CO2 emissions per capita	eco-social market economy (GDP output per kg energy use)	ESI-Index	economic growth, 1990-2003
Predictor: MNC PEN 1995									-2,241		
dependent variable ->	Life Satisfaction	Ecological footprint	Happy Planet Index								
Predictor: MNC PEN 1995											

dependent variable -->	Political rights violations, 1998	Civil liberty violations, 1998	quintile ratio (small)/ income/consumption richest 20% to poorest 20%	% people not expected to survive age 60	life expectancy, 1995-2000	HDI 2005	female economic activity rate as % of male economic activity rate	CO2 emissions per capita	eco-social market economy (GDP output per kg energy use)	ESI-Index	economic growth, 1990-2003
Predictor: world bank pension model	2,658			2,351	-2,087	-2,599					-2,719
dependent variable -->	Life Satisfaction	Ecological footprint	Happy Planet Index								
Predictor: world bank pension model	-1,773	-1,866	-1,957								

Pension reform emerges as a major new variable of dependency theory and capitalist globalization. The only good effects of **World Bank three pillar pension reforms** are the reductions of economic footprint, which seem to be connected with them. This is an interesting effect, which would need further study. One possible explanation might be that World Bank policies in general imply a liberalization of prices across the board, so that the prices of energy go up sharply, thus reducing the economic footprint. Maybe. The costs of these **World Bank pension reforms** in social terms seem to be very high. In many ways, the pension reform variable takes over the negative weight of globalization variables for the development process, reported in earlier studies. Our cross-national design confirms the scepticism, voiced by such authors as Raffer (2003), thus also contradicting earlier findings reported in Tausch, 2003. Pension reforms, World Bank type, are very negatively associated with the life satisfaction indicator and the Happy Planet Index, and World Bank pension reforms negatively and significantly affect the human development index, the economic growth rate, the political rights performance, and longevity, thus confirming the early apprehensions against the three pillar pension models, voiced by Paul and Paul.

State interventions do have a variety of very positive effects. **Contrary to the neo-liberal credo,** a policy of stae interventions has good effects on social cohesion (it reduces income polarization), on CO_2 emissions reduction and on the eco-social efficiency of a country:

The Results for the Fourteen Core Dependent Variables

dependent variable ->	Political rights violations, 1998	Civil liberty violations, 1998	quintile ratio (share of income/consumption richest 20% to poorest 20%)	% people not expected to survive age 60	life expectancy, 1995-2000	HDI 2005	female economic activity rate as % of male economic activity rate	CO2 emissions per capita	eco-social market economy (GDP output per kg energy use)	ESI-Index	economic growth, 1990-2003
Predictor: state interventionism (absence of ec. freedom)			-1,758					-2,498	2,166		
dependent variable ->	Life Satisfaction	Ecological footprint	Happy Planet Index								
Predictor: state interventionism (absence of ec. freedom)											

The crown jewel of neo-liberal European Union policies, the **lowering of comparative international price levels**, or, if you wish, **unequal exchange,** which is part and parcel even of the 14 structural indicators of the so-called Lisbon process, initiated by EU-member governments in 2000 to catch up with the US by 2010, has very negative significant effects on the human rights record, on the human development index, and on two of the four ecological indicators presented here:

dependent variable ->	Political rights violations, 1998	Civil liberty violations, 1998	quintile ratio (share of income/consumption richest 20% to poorest 20%)	% people not expected to survive age 60	life expectancy, 1995-2000	HDI 2005	female economic activity rate as % of male economic activity rate	CO2 emissions per capita	eco-social market economy (GDP output per kg energy use)	ESI-Index	economic growth, 1990-2003
Predictor: low comparative international price level (ERD)	3,061	2,007				-1,794		3,226	-2,032		
dependent variable ->	Life Satisfaction	Ecological footprint	Happy Planet Index								
Predictor: low comparative international price level (ERD)											

This process – just as the contradictory effects of modernity described above - , well explains the crisis in many parts of the Middle East. Several Muslim countries are not in crisis, because they are Muslim, but because they suffer from the general contradictions of the modernization process, and because they have a low comparative international price level or – if you wish – they suffer from unequal exchange. At this point, our readers should be reminded of the fact – as Brolin (2007) so neatly explains, classic Muslim thought already discovered the issue of unequal exchange. In the legal terminology of Islam, *'riba'* has been defined as "an increment, which, in an exchange or sale of a commodity, accumulates to the owner or lender without giving in return an equivalent counter-value or recompense *('Iwad)* to the other party." (Sarakhsi 1906-07, VII: 109, cit. doc. in Brolin, 2007). It would be one of the challenges of future research to look into the Arabic debate on *riba al-fadl* and *riba al-buyu* in the framework of contemporary debates initiated by the theories of unequal exchange (see Sarakhsi, M. ibn A., 1906-07 (orig. 1324-1331). Kitab al-Mabsut. Vol. 1-30, Misr. 1906/07-1912/13, cit. doc. in Brolin, 2007.)

Chapter 7

DISCUSSION ON THE RESULTS SO FAR

In order to look into the combined effects of our independent variables on the dependent ones, we took the positive or negative directions of the different indicators into account and somewhat heroically lumped together the t-values of our multiple regressions to arrive at a very crude, rule of the thumb first estimate of the combined effects:

Dependent variable	Category
economic growth, 1990-2003, R^2 = 31.9 %, F = 4.61	economy
absence of CO2 emissions per capita, R^2 = 74.7 %, F = 27.6	environment
absence of high ecological footprint, R^2 = 85.2 %, F = 58.2	environment
eco-social market economy (GDP output per kg energy use), R^2 = 71.4 %, F = 19.8	environment
ESI-Index, R^2 = 39.6 %, F = 6.1	environment
HPI-Index R^2 = 27.6 %, F = 3.8	happiness
Life Satisfaction, R^2 = 58.5 %, F = 14.2	happiness
absence of Civil liberty violations, 1998, R^2 = 28.6 %, F = 19.6	human rights
absence of Political rights violations,1998, R^2 = 64.1 %, F = 18.0	human rights
absence of % people not expected to survive age 60, R^2 = 73.2 %, F = 27.6	social effects
absence of high quintile ratio (share of income/consumption richest 20% to poorest 20%), R^2 = 31.6 %, F = 3.5	social effects
female economic activity rate as % of male economic activity rate, R^2 = 49.2 %, F = 9.8	social effects
life expectancy, 1995-2000, R^2 = 78.4 %, F = 36.5	social effects
HDI 2005, R^2 = 91.2 %, F = 104.9	social effects

The average effects of our independent variables on the four indicators of the environment are:

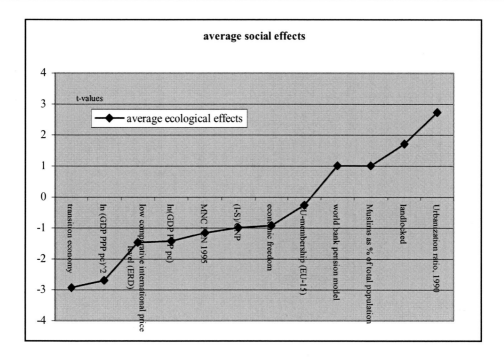

Graph 7.1a. The average effects on the environment.

To this, one might add that the neo-liberal policy framework of the European Union also negatively affects the human rights record of a country. The average effects are:

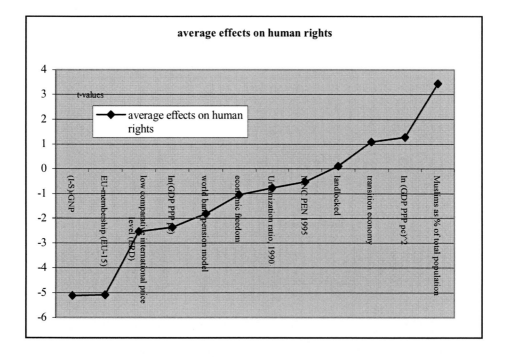

Graph 7.1b. The average effects on human rights.

The combined effects on all the social indicators are:

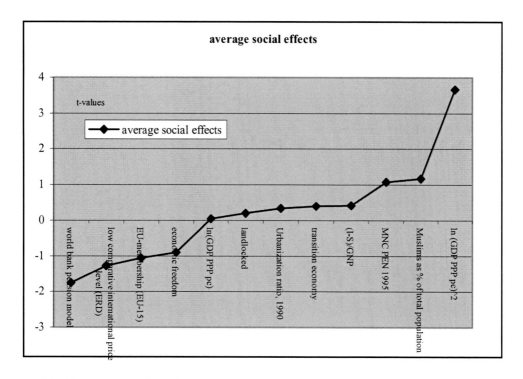

Graph 7.1c. The average social effects.

The vast dependency and world systems research literature on **globalization and the decaying environment** receives qualified support. (I-S)/Y, i.e. foreign savings, negatively affects the environment sustainability index, state interventions in reality are helpful in achieving a better environmental balance, and MNC penetration negatively affects the capaibility of a country to achieve a better eco-social economy balance. Low comparative price levels desastrously affect the environment, thus replicating earlier findings about the negative effects of globalization on the environment [see Beckerman W. (1992), Burns T. J. et al. (1994), Burns T. J., Kick E. L. and Davis B. L. (2003), Crenshaw E. M. and Jenkins J. C. (1996), Ehrhardt-Martinez K.; Crenshaw E. M.; and Jenkins J. C. (2002), Fain H. D. et al. (1997), Goldfrank W. L. (1999), Grimes P. and Kentor J. (2003), J. Timmons Roberts J. T., Grimes P. E. and Jodie L. Manale J. L. (2003), Jorgenson A. K. and Rice J. (2005), Munasinghe M., Miguel: de and Sunkel O. (2001), Shafik N. and Bandyopadhyay S. (1992), Shandra J. M., and London B. and Williamson J. B. (2000)].

The literature on **dependency as a reason of repression, political and social conflict** also receives **confirmation**. Pro-globalization policies that increase foreign savings, price reform or World Bank inspired pension reforms, or the two or three mentioned indicators at once, all negatively affect the human rights record of a country, thus again replicating many of the earlier research findings by cross-national, world-systems oriented development research [Lopez G. A. and Stohl M. (1989), Meyer W. H. (1996), Muller E. N. (1995), O'Loughlin J.; Ward M. D.; and Shin M. (1998), Simpson M. (1990), Spar D. (1999), Timberlake M. and Williams K.R. (1984), Timberlake M. and Williams K.R. (1987)]. But no significant negative effects can be reported for the other repression, political and social conflict variables under scrutiny here, thus only allowing a rather cautious confirmation of the earlier quantitative research literature [Gartner R. (1990), Gissinger R. and Gleditsch N. P. (1999), Kick E. L., Davis B. L. and Burns T. J. (2000), London B. and Robinson T. (1989), London B. and Williams B. A. (1988), Mittelman J. (1994), Neapolitan J. L. and Schmalleger F. (1997), Nollert M. (1994a), and Robinson T.D. and London B. (1991)].

Support for a **gender-oriented world systems theory** is to be found in the multiple regression that shows the strong negative trade-off between foreign savings and **female employment**. **State interventions** alleviate **social injustices,** and furthermore, variables of **neo-liberal globalization negatively** affect the **basic human needs** record of a society, to be measured by life expectancy, early death or the human development index.

But there are also results, which render support to neo-liberal thinking and are against the mainstream of world-systems theory. High **foreign savings** have **good effects for the freedom of a society from a high income concentration** – [again measured by the ratio of the share of income/consumption richest 20% to poorest 20%]. High foreign savings also positively affect the basic human needs record (=avoiding a high mortality before the age 60 is reached). The reaction to the quantitative evidence on dependency, **income distribution and economic growth** was massive indeed in the macro-quantitative research literature. After the pioneering studies by Volker Bornschier and his school in Zurich [based on the famous compendium of data by Bornschier V. and Heintz P., reworked and enlarged by Th. H. Ballmer - Cao and J. Scheidegger (1979), with the first research results published among others in Bornschier V. et al. (1980)], this debate never really ended, and grew to hundreds of titles in the major journals of social sciences, especially published in the United States of America. That dependency in the short term might lead towards spurts of growth, but to long-term stagnation and an unequal distribution of incomes, was among the early consensuses of this kind of theory. Needless to say that Latin American dependency theory – especially in the works of Fernando Henrique Cardoso – never accepted such a stagnation oriented implications of dependency "economic growth theory", while in the macro-quantitative research literature this theme received an enormous attention. Only some of the most important titles can be mentioned here [see Alderson A. and Nielsen F. (1999), Alderson A. S., Beckfield J. and Nielsen F. (2005), Babones S. J. (2002), Beer L. (1999), Beer L. and Boswell T. (2002), Bergesen A. and Fernandez R. (1999), Bornschier V. and Ballmer-Cao, T. H. (1979), Bornschier V. and Chase-Dunn Ch. K (1985), Bornschier V., Chase-Dunn Ch. and Rubinson R. (1977), Boswell T. and Dixon W.J. (1990), Bradshaw Y. and Huang J. (1991), Breedlove W. L. and Armer J. M. (1996), Caporaso J. A. (1978), Chase-Dunn Ch. K. (1975), Crenshaw E. M. (1991), Crenshaw E. M. (1992), Crenshaw E. M. (1993), Crenshaw E. M. and Ansari A. (1994), Delacroix J. and Ragin Ch. (1981), Dixon W. J. and Boswell T. (1996b), Evans P. B. and Timberlake M. (1980), Fiala R. (1992), Galtung J. (1971), Galtung J., Chase-Dunn, Ch. K. et al. (1985), Johnson R. B. (1986), Kentor J. D. (1998), Kentor J. D. (2005), Kentor J. D. and Boswell T. (2003), Kick E. L. and Davis B. L. (2001), Kohli A. et al. (1984), Krahn H. and Gartrell J. W. (1985), London B. (1987), London B. and Ross R. J. S. (1995), London B. and Smith D. A. (1988), Moaddel M. (1994), Muller E. N. (1988), Muller E. N. (1993), Nielsen F. (1995), Nolan P. D. (1983), Prechel H. (1985), Rubinson R. (1976), Russett B. (1983a), Russett B. (1983b), Shandra J. M., Ross R. J. S., London B. (2003), Shandra J. M.; London B.; Whooley O. P; Williamson J. B. (2004), Shandra J. M.; Nobles, J. E.; London B.; Williamson, J. B. (2005), Shandra J., London B, Whooley O. P., et al. (2004),

Suter Ch. (2005), Tausch A. (1998a), Tausch A. (1998b), Tausch A. (2005b), Timberlake M. and Kantor J. (1983), Trezzini B. and Bornschier V. (2001), Tsai P-L. (1995), and Wimberley D. W. and Bello R. (1992)].

True enough, this literature received an unusual attention also from neo-liberal authors. The uncomfortable facts (with or without "") of globalization and dependence, leading towards poverty and stagnation, could not go uncontested, because such facts contradict the very basic neo-liberal assumptions of how our global system works and should work. Writers were quick to point out several of the methodological difficulties of the dependency + stagnation + income inequality paradigm, and as the numbers of published articles supporting dependency theory grew, so did the methodological critiques in tandem [Firebaugh G. (1992), Firebaugh G. (1996), Firebaugh G. and Beck F. D. (1994), Rothgeb J. M. Jr. (1993a), Rothgeb J. M. Jr. (1993b), Rothgeb J. M. Jr. (1996a), Rothgeb J. M. Jr. (1996b), Rothgeb J. M. Jr. (1999), Rothgeb J. M. Jr. (2002), Rothgeb, J. M. Jr. (1995), Soysa I. de (2002), Soysa I. de (2003), Soysa I. de and Gleditsch N. P. (2002), Soysa I. de and John R. Oneal, J. R. (2000), Soysa I. de and Neumayer E. (2005), Van Rossem R. (1996), Weede E. (1985), Weede E. and Tiefenbach H. (1981)].

Neo-liberal authors, writing mostly in the 1990s, went further by trying to prove that the opposite of dependency theory holds true – not dependency, but the very lack of world economic openness and state sector influence are to blame for Third World stagnation and indeed for global economic ills. In the neo-liberal 1990s, this approach became the dominant paradigm [Barro R. J. (1991), Barro R. J. (1994), Barro R. J. (1996a), Barro R. J. (1996b), Barro R. J. (2000), Barro R. J. (2001), Barro R. J. (2003), Barro R. J. (2004a), Barro R. J. (2004b), Barro R. J. and Grilli V. (1994), Barro R. J. and McCleary R. M. (2003a), Barro R. J. and McCleary R. M. (2003b), Barro R. J. and McCleary R. M. (2004), Barro R. J. and Sala-i-Martin X. (1991), Barro R. J. and Sala-i-Martin X. (1995/98), Barro, R. J. and Sala-i-Martin X. (1992), Becker G. (1993), Betcherman G. (2002), Bhagwati J.N. (1989), Carroll E. (2000), Dollar D. (2005), Dollar D. and Kraay A. (2000), Dollar D. and Kraay A. (2001a), Fukuyama F. (1991), Gholami R., Lee S. Y. T and Heshmati A. (2003), Haouas I; Yagoubi, M; and Heshmati A (2002a), Haouas I; Yagoubi, M; and Heshmati, A. (2002b), Harss C. and Maier K. (1998), Heshmati A. (2003a), Heshmati A. (2003b), Heshmati A. and Addison T. (2003), Kearny A.T. (2001), Moore M. (2003), Nederveen-Pieterse J. (1997), Olson M. (1982), Olson M. (1986), Olson M. (1987), Weede E. (1990), Weede E. (1992), Weede E. (1993a), Weede E. (1993b), Weede E. (1996a), Weede E. (1996b), Weede E. (1997), Weede E. (1999a), Weede E. (2002), Weede E. (2003), Weede E. (2004a), Weede E. (2004b), Weede E. (2004c), Weede E. (2004d), Weede E. (2005), Weede E. and Muller E. N. (1998)].

But our final cross-national evidence regarding economic growth and income redistribution is rather mixed: while foreign savings alleviate social inequalities (as already predicted by the dependency author Paul Israel Singer) economic growth is negatively affected by neo-liberal World Bank pension reforms. Most determinants of growth and redistribution however belong to the institutional sphere – EU membership, the transition process, and the urbanization process.

The **most promising research direction for future dependency and world system research** will deal with **vulnerability (Kirby, 2006), social conditions and structural violence**. The earlier more than two dozen studies, which receive ample confirmation here, are, among others Bradshaw Y. W., Noonan R; and Gash L. (1993), Burns T. J., Kentor J. D. and Jorgenson, A. (2002), Chase-Dunn Ch. K. (2005), Dixon W. J. (1984), Frey R. S. and

Field C. (2000), Ghobarah H. et al. (2001), Jenkins J. C. and Scanlan S. J. (2001), Kick E. L. et al. (1995), Kick E. L., Davis B. L. and Burns T. J. (1998), Klitgaard R. and Fedderke J. (1995), Lena H. F. and London B. (1993), London B. (1990), London B. and Williams B. A. (1990), Moon B.E. and Dixon W.J. (1992), Ragin C. C. and Bradshaw Y. W. (1992), Ram R. (1992), Shandra J. M.; Nobles J.; London B.; Williamson J. B. (2004), Shen C. and Williamson J. B. (2001), Shin M. E. (1975), Shin M. E. (2002), Tausch A. (1989b), Tausch A. (1990), Tausch A. (1991), Tausch A. and Prager F. (1993), Wimberley D. W. (1990), and Wimberley D. W. (1991).

Scholars and policy-makers alike would be well advised to study the **"dissidents"** (in one way or the other) of the **not at all so homogeneous camp of neo-classical economics**, often coinciding with a continuation of debates begun by classical development economics of the 1940s, 1950s and the early 1960s. The contradictions and inefficiencies of the "neo-liberal model" are too obvious, and critical assumptions are hardly met in the oligopolistic environment of a periphery or semi-periphery country, characterized by centuries of colonization [Abbott J. P. and Worth O. (2002), Aghion Ph. and Williamson J. G. (1998), Alexandratos N., Bruinsma J. and Yotopoulos P. A. (1983), Chenery H. and Syrquin M. (1975), Dadush U. and Brahmbhatt M. (1995), Easterly W. (2001), Easterly W. (2002), Floro S. L. and Yotopoulos P. A. (1991), Gurr T. R. (1991), Holzmann R. (1999), Kanbur R. (2001), Kanbur R. (2005), Kanbur R. and Squire L. (2001), Lewis Sir W.A. (1978), Meier G.M. and Seers D. (Eds.)(1984), Milanovic B. and Squire L. (2005), Mills J. (2002), Myrdal G. (1972), Myrdal G. (1974), Myrdal G. (1984), O'Hara P. A. (2000), O'Hara P. A. (2003a), O'Hara P. A. (2005b), O'Hara P. A. (Ed.)(2001), O'Hara P. A. (Ed.)(2004), Pepelasis A. and Yotopoulos P. A. (1962), Perroux F. (1961), Rodrik D. (1997), Rostow W. W. (1980), Rothschild K. W. (1993a), Rothschild K. W. (1993b), Schumpeter J. A. (1950), Schumpeter J. A. (1969), Schumpeter J. A. (1980), Schumpeter J. A. (1982), Stiglitz J. (1998), Streissler E. (2002), United Nations Economic Commission for Latin America, ECLAC/CEPAL, (2002), Wood A. (1994), Yotopoulos P. A. (1966), Yotopoulos P. A. (1967), Yotopoulos P. A. (1977), Yotopoulos P. A. (1984), Yotopoulos P. A. (1989a), Yotopoulos P. A. (1989b), and Yotopoulos P. A. (1989c)]. In view of the current *"fundamentalism"* **of the Washington Consensus** and neo-liberalism, it seems appropriate here to recall one of the last articles by the late **Sir Karl Raimund Popper** (Popper, 1991), who quite explicitly warned against a type of market economy totalitarianism, substituting the ideological dominance of the socialist planned economy in the East.

A certainly promising direction of future research is the **basic human needs** and **growth-for-the-poor** approach that is so prominent nowadays also in the publications influenced by the UNDP. The cross-national quantitative studies about poverty reduction, basic needs and economic growth all suggest that the basic Myrdalian argument about poverty reduction as an engine of growth is correct. In view of the existing research results, future world system scholars, studying the relationship between dependency and development, would be well advised to think about poverty, basic human needs, life expectancy, infant mortality, survival probability at age 40 or 60 etc. and not so much on phenomena relating to "the sphere of production" like economic growth or the distribution of money incomes [see Ahluwalia M. S. (1974), Ahulwalia M. S. (1976), Bradshaw Y. W., Noonan R; and Gash L. (1993), Burns T. J., Kentor J. D. and Jorgenson, A. (2002), Chase-Dunn Ch. K. (2005), Crenshaw E. M. (1995), Crenshaw E. M.; Ameen A. Z.; and Christenson. M. (1997), Crenshaw E. M.; Christenson M.; Oakey D. R. (2000), Dixon W. J. (1984), Frey R. S. and Field C. (2000),

Ghobarah H. et al. (2001), Jenkins J. C. and Scanlan S. J. (2001), Kentor J. D. (2001), Kick E. L. et al. (1995), Kick E. L., Davis B. L. and Burns T. J. (1998), Klitgaard R. and Fedderke J. (1995), Lena H. F. and London B. (1993), London B. (1988), London B. (1990), Lopez G. A. and Stohl M. (1989), Meyer W. H. (1996), Moon B.E. and Dixon W.J. (1992), Muller E. N. (1995), O'Loughlin J.; Ward M. D.; and Shin M. (1998), Ragin C. C. and Bradshaw Y. W. (1992), Ram R. (1992), Shandra J. M.; Nobles J.; London B.; Williamson J. B. (2004), Shen C. and Williamson J. B. (2001), Shin M. E. (1975), Shin M. E. (2002), Simpson M. (1990), Spar D. (1999), Stack St. (1998), Tausch A. (1989b), Tausch A. (1990), Tausch A. (1991), Tausch A. (2003b), Tausch A. (2005c), Tausch A. (2005d), Tausch A. and Prager F. (1993), Timberlake M. and Williams K.R. (1984), Timberlake M. and Williams K.R. (1987), Wimberley D. W. (1990), and Wimberley D. W. (1991)].

Chapter 8

LIFE SATISFACTION, UNEQUAL EXCHANGE, UNEMPLOYMENT AND MUSLIM POPULATION SHARES

The picture presented up to now about Muslim civilization in world society contradicted one of the two central pillars of Huntington's argument, i.e. that sustainable economic development does not go along very well with Muslim or, for that matter, Orthodox culture (the other pillar was that Muslim culture and especially the West are in increasing conflict). As we have noted already in Chapter 6, the story would not be complete, if we were to skip over the emerging evidence, which highlights a negative relationship between the share of Muslim population per total population and indicators of life satisfaction and human happiness.

This interesting relationship however does not necessarily have to be interpreted in a Huntingtonian way. It might just indicate to us that Muslims are very unhappy,

1. perhaps because of what they (and not only they) predominantly see as Western disrespect of their culture, religion, or history.
2. Another explanation might be dealing with culture, but using the dependency frame of reference: since world culture is so dominated by the West, especially by the Anglo-American film industry, the media and science, this might cause a deep feeling of unhappiness, which might be combined with the deep knowledge and memory of days full of past glories, when the *"Dar al Islam"* indeed was the world's leading civilization –in terms of world economics, health standards, medicine, world political power, astronomy, navigation, science, philosophy etc.

3. A third very plausible explanation might rest on the tendency, that a *"salafist"* reading of the Muslim Holy Scriptures[1] nowadays seems to be gaining ground and that this Salafism eliminates Muslim liberalism and – in the end – also the feeling of happiness among Muslims around the globe. While many arguments might speak in favor of that explanation of the negative trade-off between Muslim population and indicators of happiness, solid cross-national opinion research, especially by the Washington-based PEW institute[2], seems to discount the idea that Salafism has such a mass following throughout the Muslim world. At best, Islamist, salafist radicalism is a minority phenomenon, while Muslim *"alter-mondialization"* (anti-globalization counter culture) seems to be increasingly successful, culminating in the world-wide launching of *Al Jazeera's* English language global news program, etc. etc. Thus, the socio-liberal optimistic expectation will be that not Salafism, but Muslim entrepreneural ingenuity will find its proper place in the world "cultural market". An absolute imperative for policy-makers would be to favor all manifestations of hanafist, liberal and spiritual expressions of the Muslim faith, as is evident in the works of such writers as Smail Balic from Bosnia or Ali Bardakoglu from Turkey

4. Another explanation might be much more simplistic, and down-to-earth, starting from the fact that unemployment in the Muslim world is one of the highest around the globe, and that especially in the Arab countries, unemployment increased over the last decades. This kind of analysis, which also uses the

---

[1] As for Salafism, see especially „MIDDLE EAST SALAFISM'S INFLUENCE AND THE RADICALIZATION OF MUSLIM COMMUNITIES IN EUROPE" by Juan José Escobar Stemmann, available from the MERIA Institute in Israel at: http://meria.idc.ac.il/journal/2006/issue3/jv10no3a1.html. Let us quote the author's definition

„*Jihadi ideology is based today on what is commonly known as Salafism, an ambiguous concept that has served to designate various and very different movements throughout the years. The term is derived from the word Salaf, which means "to precede." In Islamic vocabulary, it is used to describe the followers of al Salaf al salih, the virtuous fathers of the faith who were the companions of the Prophet. The group includes the first three generations of Muslims.Since they learned Islam directly from the Prophet, they understood the true meaning of the religion. Salafis aim to eradicate the impurities introduced during centuries of religious practice. (...) Lastly, Salafis consider the division of Muslims into separate schools to be unacceptable, because there can only be one correct interpretation or opinion. One of the main problems the Muslim community is experiencing is precisely this blind adherence or imitation (taqlid) of a particular school. Salafis insist, therefore, that the truth is to be found in the sources, not in the texts written by jurists. Salafism is thus a path and a method to search for religious truth, a desire to practice Islam exactly as it was revealed by the Prophet. The Salafi mission is grounded on avoidance of bid'a and shirk, strict adherence to the principle of tawhid and a desire to transcend the differences between the various schools, as well as the quest for religious truth in the original sources of Islam. (...)During the 1960s and 1970s, Salafism enjoyed at best a marginal and largely local presence in the majority of Arab countries. It had become a form of apolitical pietism along very similar lines to the Hanbali school, which was based on a literal reading of the Koran and excluded all use of reason in interpreting the holy scriptures. The concept of Salafism once again became associated with the puritan reformism advocated, among others, by Ibn Taymiyya and Ibn Abd al-Wahhab. During this period, doctrine was produced largely in Saudi Arabia, where authors such as Ibn Otheimin, Nasr Al Din al-Albani, Ali Hassan al-Halabi, and the Grand Mufti of Saudi Arabia, Ibn Baz, laid the ideological foundations of modern Salafism, bringing its content more into line with the ideas propounded by the founder of Wahhabism. The Salafi movement benefited from Saudi Arabia's designs to spread Wahhabi Islam, and its development came to be tied closely to events in the country. Funding Salafi schools and publications and offering a strict vision of Islam very similar to Wahhabism became the best way to promote the peculiar vision of Wahhabi Islam while also enhancing the influence of Salafi sheikh and fostering Salafi thinking in the majority of Islamist movements throughout the Arab world.*"

[2] See also Tausch A. (2006, with Christian Bischof, Tomaz Kastrun and Karl Mueller), and The PEW Research Center for the People and the Press (2006).

arguments of the theories of unequal exchange, was first developed by Gernot Köhler (2005). Needless to say that the present author much more was originally inclined towards this "materialistic" explanation, stressing also the desastrous role, which unemployment played in the rise of authoritarianism in Europe in the interwar period.

5. Also the trade-off between low comparative price levels (unequal exchange) and human unhappiness is evident – and not only in the Muslim world, but also in Eastern Europe. In many ways, obscurantism could possibly thrive, where unemployment is high and where local currencies do not offer market exchange values, especially when citizens in countries with low comparative price levels want to buy imported "Western" products from "high price countries" or when citizens from low price countries travel to the "West", or when citizens, enterprises or governments from high-price countries command over disproportionate resources from low price countries. The low value of their local currencies suggests to them that they are "citizens of a second category" on the globe and also in United Europe. This effect alone explains 38 % of life satisfaction in the world.

Our empirical data first show the spread of unemployment over the last two decades in the Muslim world, in Latin America and in Eastern Europe. In this context, it should be added that Latin America's political development over the last years also showed a decisive swing away from the neo-liberal tide:

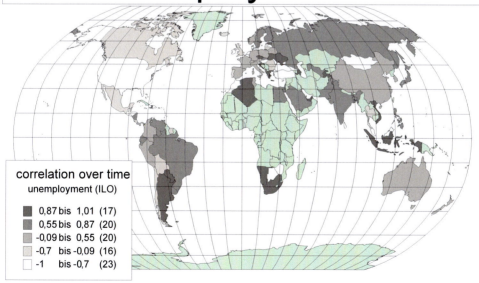

Legend: "bis" is the shorthand for "ranging from" "to". Countries marked in green color: missing values. Our own compilations from Laborsta (ILO). No data for wide parts of Africa and West Asia.

Map 8.1. (Continued)

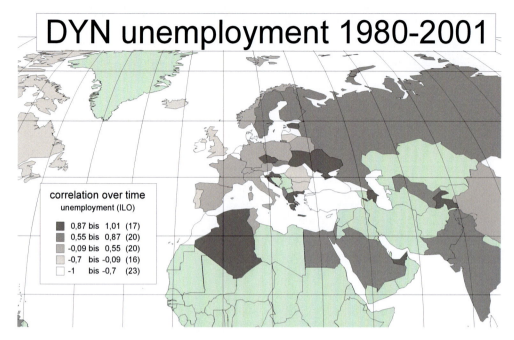

Map 8.1. The changing structure of unemployment in the world system.

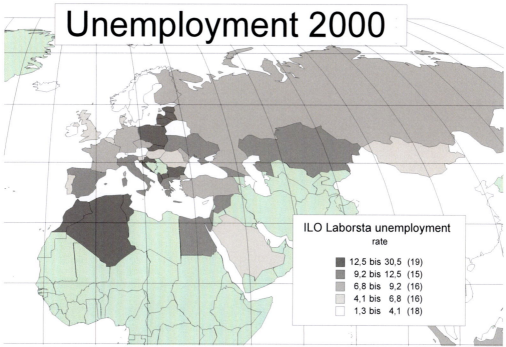

Legend: "bis" is the shorthand for "ranging from" "to". Countries marked in green color: missing values. Our own compilations from Laborsta (ILO). No data for wide parts of Africa and West Asia.

Map 8.2. Unemployment in the world system.

Graph 8.1. now shows the trade-off between development level and unemployment (figures from the United Nations Statistical Office).

Graph 8.2. shows the trade-off between life satisfaction and "unequal exchange".

Indeed, Muslims per total population and low comparative price levels explain the **unemployment rates** in **more than 100 countries of the world**. The data from Table 8.1 support the thesis, first developed by Gernot Kohler, according to which **unequal exchange, which hits the Muslim world especially hard, is to be blamed for unemployment in the periphery and the semi-periphery.**

However, **life satisfaction is not sufficiently well enough explained by unemployment**, so we dropped that variable again in our multivariate research design. Now, the following relationships hold: with **rising income levels**, and with the long-term **negative** effects of **pension reforms, life satisfaction diminishes**. The variable: **"percentage of Muslims"** is also connected in **a negative way to life satisfaction**, but however, **this effect is being shared with the negative effects of pension reforms and rising income levels** (Table 8.2).

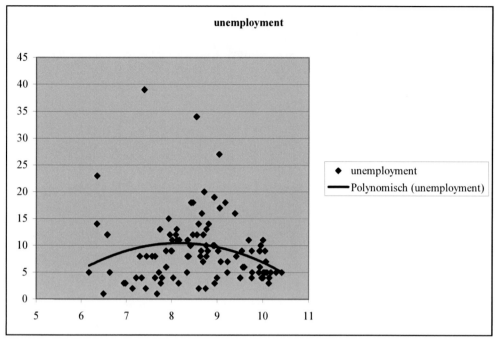

x-axis: n-log GDP PPP per capita.

Graph 8.1. Unemployment and development level.

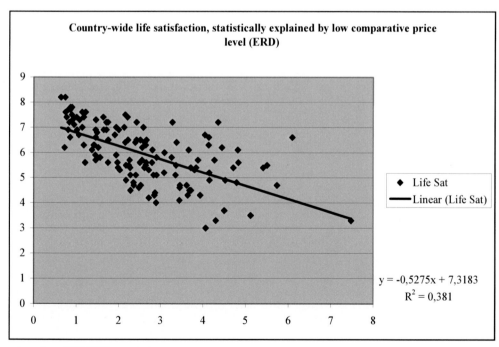

x-axis: n-log GDP PPP per capita.

Graph 8.2. Life satisfaction, unemployment and low comparative price levels.

Table 8.1. The determinants of unemployment

	unemployment	Dummy for being landlocked	Dummy for transition economy	Urbanization ratio, 1990	(1-S)/GNP	state interventionism (absence of ec. freedom)	MNC PEN 1995	low comparative international price level (ERD)	EU-membership (EU-15)	Muslims as % of total population	ln(GDP PPP pc)	ln (GDP PPP pc)^2	world bank pension reform	constant
		0,3935	-0,765	13,435	0,003	0,3297	0,1293	0,0862	0,4633	0,1835	-0,0021	0,0979	-1,9599	-52,649
		1,6563	0,553	9,025	0,0196	2,0204	0,8653	0,0347	1,64	0,0593	0,0459	1,9404	1,5906	36,002
		0,291	5,641											
		3,0746	90											
		1174	2863,8											
t-test; direction of influence	t-test and direction of influence	0,2376	-1,3835	1,4886	0,1553	0,1632	0,1494	**2,4866**	0,2825	**3,0931**	-0,0460	0,0505	-1,2322	-1,4624
	t-test and direction of influence^2	0,0564	1,9140	2,2161	0,0241	0,0266	0,0223	6,1830	0,0798	9,5674	0,0021	0,0025	1,5183	2,1385
	t-test and direction of influence^0,5	0,2376	1,3835	1,4886	0,1553	0,1632	0,1494	2,4866	0,2825	3,0931	0,0460	0,0505	1,2322	1,4624
	degrees of freedom	90,0000	90,0000	90,0000	90,0000	90,0000	90,0000	90,0000	90,0000	90,0000	90,0000	90,0000	90,0000	90,0000
error probability	error probability	0,8127	0,1699	0,1401	0,8770	0,8707	0,8815	**0,0147**	0,7782	**0,0026**	0,9634	0,9599	0,2211	0,1471
	F equation	3,0746	3,0746	3,0746	3,0746	3,0746	3,0746	3,0746	3,0746	3,0746	3,0746	3,0746	3,0746	3,0746
	error probability, entire equation	0,0011	0,0011	0,0011	0,0011	0,0011	0,0011	0,0011	0,0011	0,0011	0,0011	0,0011	0,0011	0,0011

Legend: As in all EXCEL 7.0 outprints, first row: un-standardized regression coefficients, second row: standard errors, second last row: t-Test and direction of the influence. The values immediately below the standard errors are R^2 (third row, left side entry), F, and degrees of freedom (fourth row). Below that: ss reg; ss resid, i.e. the sum of squares of the regression and the sum of squares of the residuals. The right-hand entry in the third row is the standard error of the estimate y. Below the EXCEL outprints; we present materials for the t-test and the F-test for our regression results.

Table 8.2. The determinants of life satisfaction

Life Sat	Dummy for being landlocked	Dummy for transition economy	Urbanization ratio, 1990	(I-S)/GNP	state interventionism (absence of ec. freedom)	MNC PEN 1995	low comparative international price level (ERD)	EU-membership (EU-15)	Muslims as % of total population	ln(GDP PPP pc)	ln (GDP PPP pc)^2	world bank pension reform	constant
	0,323	0,030	-0,083	0,002	0,107	-0,105	0,005	-0,253	-0,011	-0,005	-0,438	-0,324	5,843
	0,221	0,066	1,062	0,002	0,273	0,085	0,004	0,167	0,006	0,006	0,231	0,183	4,195
	0,585	0,766											
	14,237	**121,000**											
	100,357	71,077											
t-test and direction of influence	1,463	0,450	-0,078	0,743	0,392	-1,227	1,372	-1,518	**-1,823**	-0,841	**-1,898**	**-1,773**	1,393
t-test and direction of influence^2	2,141	0,203	0,006	0,553	0,154	1,505	1,881	2,304	3,324	0,708	3,604	3,144	1,940
t-test and direction of influence^0,5	1,463	0,450	0,078	0,743	0,392	1,227	1,372	1,518	1,823	0,841	1,898	1,773	1,393
degrees of freedom	121,000	121,000	121,000	121,000	121,000	121,000	121,000	121,000	121,000	121,000	121,000	121,000	121,000
error probability	0,146	0,653	0,938	0,459	0,695	0,222	0,173	0,132	**0,071**	0,402	**0,060**	**0,079**	0,166
F equation	14,237	14,237	14,237	14,237	14,237	14,237	14,237	14,237	14,237	14,237	14,237	14,237	14,237
error probability, entire equation	0,000	0,000	0,000	0,000	0,000	0,000	0,000	0,000	0,000	0,000	0,000	0,000	0,000

Legend: As in all EXCEL 7.0 outprints, first row: un-standardized regression coefficients, second row: standard errors, second last row: t-Test and direction of the influence. The values immediately below the standard errors are R^2 (third row, left side entry), F, and degrees of freedom (fourth row). Below that: ss reg; ss resid, i.e. the sum of squares of the regression and the sum of squares of the residuals. The right-hand entry in the third row is the standard error of the estimate y. Below the EXCEL outprints; we present materials for the t-test and the F-test for our regression results.

In graphical terms, our results can be presented as follows:

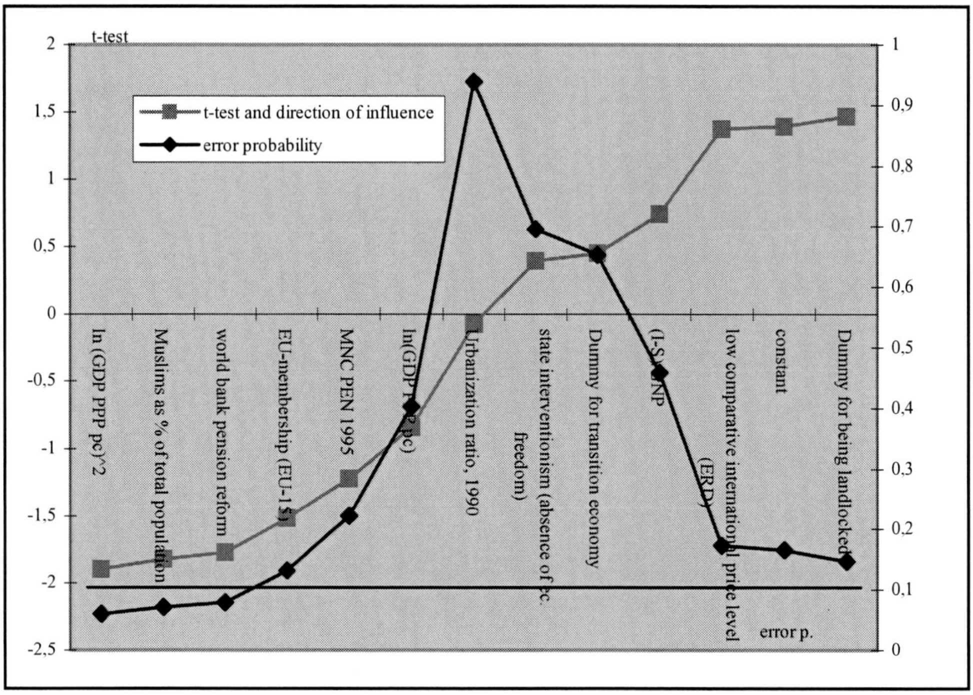

Graph 8.3. The determinants of life satisfaction.

As Tausch and associates have shown in Tausch (2007), however, results from a representative sample of all the Muslims in all of Europe (EEA + EFTA + EU-27), based on the European Commission's European Social Survey (ESS), render some support the Barro vision on religion in modern society, i.e. faith is good, but very regular religious service attendance is not so good for society. At least faith, and not social custom, should determine religious service attendance. Or to quote from the Surah 002.256 from the Holy Quran

> "Let there be no compulsion in religion: Truth stands out clear from Error: whoever rejects evil and believes in Allah hath grasped the most trustworthy hand-hold, that never breaks. And Allah heareth and knoweth all things." (University of Southern California Quran Search engine, YUSUFALI translation, available at: *http://www.usc.edu/dept/MSA/quran/ 002.qmt.html#002.256*)

The design of this multiple regression, working with the ESS survey data, was structured around the available cross-national aggregate results, and weighted "happiness" by such factors as poverty, religious service attendance, strength of religious feelings, feeling of safety, state of satisfaction with education in the country etc. **It turns out that the "materialist" explanations of self-declared "happiness", like absence of poverty, satisfaction with the education system, and safety, all contribute in a significant way to the feeling of happiness.**

But beyond that there is another dimension as well. Our findings about **human happiness** basically confirmed the approach chosen by Barro and his associates – human happiness of both the Muslims and the non-Muslims in Europe is **positively determined by a general, personal spirituality**, but it is also **positively, alas not significantly determined by the fact whether or not European Muslims have a low religious service attendance rate.** At any rate, our Muslim readership and above all Muslim Community leaders should take this result very seriously – it cannot be precluded *a priori* that there is a **mismatch between religious "demand"** (feelings of spirituality) **and "religious supply"** (the kinds of religious sermons and religious instruction being offered) in Europe.

The very low weekly religious attendance rates, documented in Tausch (2007) are an alarm signal; and Muslim Community leaders would be well advised to speak **not only about "empty Churches"** but also **"empty Mosques" in Europe**. Satisfaction with the **education system greatly increases, and poverty greatly reduces personal happiness.** A feeling of **personal unsafety** in the *banlieues* around you reduces to a considerable extent your personal feeling of happiness. But while non-Muslims generally tend to feel unhappier with the same level of poverty they are confronted with, religious discrimination is a factor for Muslims to feel unhappy, while the personal experience of religious discrimination does not play a significant role for happiness of the non-Muslim European inhabitants. Table 8.3 reports the multiple regression results for the representative sample of Muslims in Europe:

Table 8.3. Muslim Happiness in Europe
Muslims: HAPPY How happy are you, n = 799 ESS

model	R	R-Square	adjusted R	standard error of the estimate	Statistics of change		Durbin-Watson			
					Change in R^2	Change in F	df1	df2	Change in sign. of F	
4	,351(d)	0,123	0,119	2,007	0,007	6,175	1	788	0,013	1,852

Included variables

model		Non-standardized coefficients		Standardized coefficients			
		B	standard error	Beta	T	Significance	
4	(constant)	7,578	0,377		20,085	0	
	HINCFEL poverty	-0,632	0,081	**-0,262**	-7,77	0	
	STFEDU State of education in country nowadays	0,15	0,029	**0,173**	5,154	0	
	RLGDGR How religious are you	**0,086**	**0,028**	**0,103**	**3,076**	**0,002**	
	AESFDRK feeling unsafe	-0,217	0,087	**-0,083**	-2,485	0,013	

Excluded variables

model		Beta In	T	Significance	partial correlation	statistics of collinearity
4	**DSCRRLG** Discrimination of respondent's group: religion	-,030(d)	-0,902	0,367	-0,032	0,98
	RLGATND never attending religious services	,004(d)	0,119	0,905	0,004	0,865

In the following, we look into another very hotly contested phenomenon, i.e. the "relationship" between Muslim "culture" and "gender discrimination". It again will turn out that "Islam" is well compatible with a modern, liberal thought of the 21st Century.

Chapter 9

THE GENDER DIMENSION

Among the major social scientists of our time, Ronald T. **Inglehart** and his associate Pippa **Norris** were the most outspoken in proclaiming that in reality, **eros and gender issues** constitute the "true" dividing line between the West and Islam.

But we have come to the conclusion that, however valuable these insights may be, they underestimate the importance of the strong trade-off between gender issues and development levels. Without specifying this trade-off in a proper way, you will always get biased results from developing countries. Strong patterns of gender discrimination characterize not only much of the Muslim world, but also many other developing countries, including in Latin America. European periphery and semi-periphery nations are among the league of mediocre performers along the gender development and gender empowerment scales, developed by the researchers at the United Nations Development Programme.

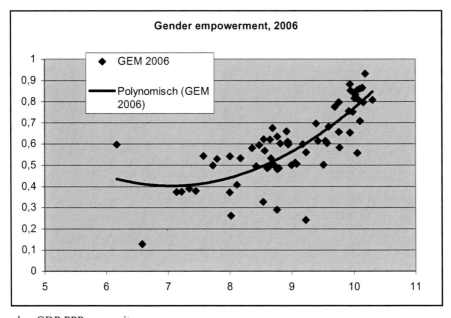

x-axis: n-log GDP PPP per capita.

Graph 9.1. Continued.

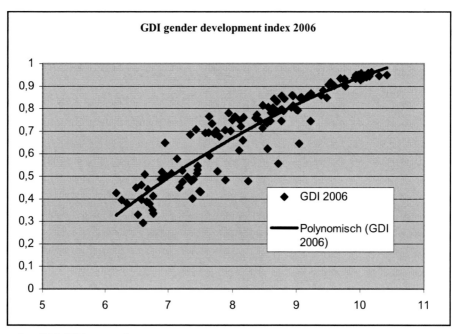

x-axis: n-log GDP PPP per capita.

Graph 9.1. Development levels and gender empowerment/gender development ratios.

As already presented in Chapters 6 and 8, we first present the important trade-off between development levels and gender empowerment or gender development (see also appendix). Without such a visualization of the very considerable trade-offs between gender empowerment/gender development on the one hand and development levels on the other hand, our whole debate about the issue remains abstract and does not include the all important **development level variable**. Comparing gender development/empowerment figures for Western countries and the Muslim world, as Inglehart and Norris do, without including the development level as a controlling variable, will always produce statistically very biased results.

Our calculations, based on the UNDP HRD data for gender empowerment and gender development, dramatically contradict all culturalist explanations of gender issues. The **gender development index** is **neatly, positively and significantly influenced by the share of Muslims per total population**, once we properly control for the development level. **Urbanization** significantly **improves** the chances for **gender development,** while two **globalization indicators**: low comparative international price levels and World Bank three pillar pension reforms, **significantly reduce the chances for an equitable gender development,** which *per se* would significantly **rise with rising levels of economic maturity** (ln GDP PPP per capita ^2). Our equation explains more than 9/10 of gender development, and the F-value is above 90. Our equation for **gender empowerment**, which explains 4/5 of this variable (with the F-value reaching more than 20), however, above all shows the limits of the **urbanization process**. It is **not Islam**, but the **urbanization process**, which reduces the chances for women for a more equitable share of the power in society, while the historical conquests of *"socialism"* in the **transition economies** and in countries, which practice **state interventionism,** significantly **improve** the gender empowerment index of a given country.

In addition, capitalist globalization – here in the form of **high foreign savings – significantly diminishes the power sharing by women**, while Muslim population shares even have a slightly positive effect on gender empowerment, once you properly control for the influence of the other variables.

Thus the interpretation, offered by Inglehart and Norris, has to be rejected. It is not "Islam", which is to be blamed for gender discrimnation, but gender development index is positively and significantly influenced by the share of Muslims per total population, once we properly control for the development level. Urbanization improves, while low comparative international price levels and World Bank three pillar pension reforms significantly reduce the chances for an equitable gender development, which per se would significantly rise with rising levels of economic maturity.

And it is not Islam, but the urbanization process, which reduces the chances for women for a more equitable share of the power in society, while the historical conquests of "socialism" in the transition economies and in countries, which practice state interventionism, significantly improve the gender empowerment index of a given country. In addition, high foreign savings significantly diminish the power sharing by women, while Muslim population shares even have a slightly positive effect on gender empowerment, once you properly control for the influence of the other variables.

Table 9.1. The gender dimension of development – results from multiple regressions

GEM 2006	Dummy for being landlocked	Dummy for transition economy	Urbanization ratio, 1990	(1-SJ)/GNP	state interventionism (absence of ec. freedom)	MNC PEN 1995	low comparative international price level (ERD)	EU-membership (EU-15)	Muslims as % of total population	ln(GDP PPP pc)	ln (GDP PPP pc)^2	world bank pension model	constant
	0,0228	0,04935	-0,7563	-0,0025	0,0539	0,00425	0,00103	0,00018	6,5E-05	6,1E-05	0,02513	-0,0325	3,35313
	0,02665	0,01101	0,18212	0,00044	0,03085	0,01975	0,00073	0,03241	0,00149	0,00078	0,03515	0,03317	0,73051
	0,8095	0,08236											
	20,1803	57											
	1,6427	0,38666											
t-test and direction of influence	0,85552	4,4801	-4,153	-5,64	1,7469	0,21519	1,40782	0,0057	0,04365	0,07859	0,71492	-0,9782	4,59015
t-test and direction of influence^2	0,73192	20,0709	17,2445	31,8073	3,05158	0,04631	1,98195	3,3E-05	0,00191	0,00618	0,51111	0,95694	21,0695
t-test and direction of influence^0,5	0,85552	4,48006	4,15265	5,63979	1,74688	0,21519	1,40782	0,0057	0,04365	0,07859	0,71492	0,97823	4,59015
degrees of freedom	57	57	57	57	57	57	57	57	57	57	57	57	57
error probability	0,39585	4E-05	0,00011	5,6E-07	0,08605	0,83039	0,16462	0,99547	0,96533	0,93764	0,47758	0,33209	2,5E-05
F equation	20,1803	20,1803	20,1803	20,1803	20,1803	20,1803	20,1803	20,1803	20,1803	20,1803	20,1803	20,1803	20,1803
error probability, entire equation	4,2E-17	4,2E-17	4,2E-17	4,2E-17	4,2E-17	4,2E-17	4,2E-17	4,2E-17	4,2E-17	4,2E-17	4,2E-17	4,2E-17	4,2E-17

GDI 2006	Dummy for being landlocked	Dummy for transition economy	Urbanization ratio, 1990	(I-S)/ GNP	state interventionism (absence of ec. freedom)	MNC PEN 1995	low comparative international price level (ERD)	EU-membership (EU-15)	Muslims as % of total population	ln(GDP PPP pc)	ln (GDP PPP pc)^2	world bank pension model	constant
	0,01178	-0,003	0,185	-0,0002	0,02099	0,00413	-0,0007	-0,0108	0,00113	0,00059	0,09446	-0,0471	-0,6302
	0,01777	0,00594	0,09606	0,00017	0,02173	0,00746	0,00034	0,01362	0,00054	0,00046	0,01914	0,01567	0,37843
	0,91102	0,0602											
	91,2891	107											
	3,97064	0,38783											
t-test and direction of influence	0,66288	-0,5079	1,9258	-1,141	0,966	0,55309	-1,951	-0,7936	2,0856	1,29898	4,93497	-3,005	-1,6653
t-test and direction of influence^2	0,43941	0,258	3,70889	1,30177	0,93316	0,30591	3,80738	0,62987	4,34992	1,68734	24,3539	9,02834	2,7731
t-test and direction of influence^0,5	0,66288	0,50793	1,92585	1,14095	0,966	0,55309	1,95125	0,79364	2,08565	1,29898	4,93497	3,00472	1,66526
degrees of freedom	107	107	107	107	107	107	107	107	107	107	107	107	
error probability	0,50883	0,61255	0,05678	0,25644	0,33622	0,58135	0,05364	0,42916	0,03939	0,19674	3E-06	0,00331	0,09879
F equation	91,2891	91,2891	91,2891	91,2891	91,2891	91,2891	91,2891	91,2891	91,2891	91,2891	91,2891	91,2891	91,2891
error probability, entire equation	9,4E-53	9,4E-53	9,4E-53	9,4E-53	9,4E-53	9,4E-53	9,4E-53	9,4E-53	9,4E-53	9,4E-53	9,4E-53	9,4E-53	9,4E-53

Legend: As in all EXCEL 7.0 outprints, first row: un-standardized regression coefficients, second row: standard errors, second last row: t-Test and direction of the influence. The values immediately below the standard errors are R^2 (third row, left side entry), F, and degrees of freedom (fourth row). Below that: ss $_{reg}$; ss $_{resid}$, i.e. the sum of squares of the regression and the sum of squares of the residuals. The right-hand entry in the third row is the standard error of the estimate y. Below the EXCEL outprints, we present materials for the t-test and the F-test for our regression results.

Chapter 10

THE DIMENSION OF HUMAN RIGHTS

The United States international think tank **"Freedom House"** made available data on political and civil rights fulfillment for the years 2003 – 2006, which might serve to correct and update our results, which were based up to now on Easterly, 2000 - 2002, referring to political and civil rights violations, 1998 (http://www.freedomhouse.org/template.cfm?page=276). Important optimistic or pessimistic arguments state that since 9/11, the compatibility (incompatibility) of Muslim "culture" with "democracy" has "increased" or "decreased". The complete world data set and its methodology is documented in the appendix of this work.

Above, we already explained that the available evidence, based on the Easterly data (2002), using the Freedom House materials for 1998, supports the view of the compatibility of Islam with democracy, once you properly control for the intervening variables. Does the picture change when you analyze the new data?

For the member countries of the Organization of the Islamic Conferences (OIC), we get the following Table in comparison with the "European orbit". This time, high numerical indicator values are a good indicator performance, while low numerical values are a bad indicator performance. Benin, Suriname, Mali, Senegal, Guyana, Albania and Turkey are the seven best civil rights performers in the Muslim world, while Turkmenistan, Uzbekistan, Sudan, Libya, Syria, Somalia and Saudi Arabia have – according to "Freedom House" - the worst performance in terms of civil rights. Benin and Suriname outperform Romania as the EU-27 country with the worst civil rights record. No way of doubting "Western" human rights – and Muslim nations as Benin and Suriname must be praised for their record:

Table 10.1a. The Freedom House data series for political rights and civil rights 2003 – 2006 for member states of the Organization of Islamic Conferences (OIC)

Country	PR 2006	CR 2006	Progress PR 2003-2006	Progress CR 2003-2006
Benin	30	48	3	0
Suriname	33	45	-3	-1
Mali	30	44	0	1
Senegal	33	43	2	6
Guyana	29	41	-1	-4
Albania	25	38	-1	-4

Table 10.1a. Continued

Country	PR 2006	CR 2006	Progress PR 2003-2006	Progress CR 2003-2006
Turkey	28	37	4	8
Sierra Leone	23	37	0	3
Burkina Faso	17	36	-3	2
Indonesia	30	35	4	3
Niger	27	35	4	6
Guinea-Bissau	25	34	4	9
Gambia	17	32	-3	-2
Mozambique	25	31	0	-3
Bangladesh	22	31	1	-2
Malaysia	19	31	2	6
Kyrgyzstan	16	31	5	9
Uganda	14	31	4	2
Comoros	18	30	5	3
Lebanon	16	30	10	6
Gabon	10	30	-6	-4
Nigeria	21	28	2	3
Jordan	15	27	5	2
Mauritania	11	27	-5	2
Morocco	17	26	0	2
Kuwait	18	25	0	1
Algeria	11	25	0	3
Pakistan	11	24	0	2
Djibouti	12	23	-6	-2
Azerbaijan	10	23	-1	-1
Guinea	9	23	-2	1
Brunei	6	23	0	-2
Bahrain	14	22	1	1
Kazakhstan	10	22	2	1
Maldives	9	22	0	0
Egypt	8	22	1	6
Tajikistan	9	21	-1	3
Afghanistan	16	19	8	4
Iraq	9	19	11	18
Yemen	13	18	3	1
Oman	10	18	0	1
Qatar	9	18	3	3
Chad	8	18	0	0
Togo	7	18	-2	-6
Tunisia	6	18	-2	-2
Cameroon	11	16	4	1
Iran	9	15	-1	-1
United Arab Emirates	7	15	0	-7
Cote d'Ivoire	6	15	-5	0
Saudi Arabia	4	8	1	2
Somalia	8	7	0	0
Syria	1	7	0	2
Libya	1	6	-1	0
Sudan	1	6	1	3
Uzbekistan	0	3	-3	-6
Turkmenistan	0	1	0	-3

Source: Compiled from Freedom House and Organization of Islamic Conferences websites.

Table 10.1b. The Freedom House data series for political rights and civil rights 2003 – 2006 for countries of the "European orbit"

Country	PR 2006 Political Rights	CR 2006 Civil Rights		world rank political rights	world rank civil rights	average rank freedom house scores
Finland	40	60	EU-27	1	1	1
Iceland	40	60	EEA+EFTA	2	2	2
Luxembourg	40	60	EU-27	3	3	3
Norway	40	60	EEA+EFTA	4	4	4
Sweden	40	60	EU-27	6	6	6
Liechtenstein	40	59	EEA+EFTA	8	8	8
Netherlands	40	59	EU-27	9	9	9
Switzerland	40	59	EEA+EFTA	10	10	10
Austria	40	58	EU-27	11	13	12
Denmark	40	58	EU-27	12	14	13
Ireland	40	58	EU-27	13	15	14
Malta	39	59	EU-27	16	12	14
Belgium	39	58	EU-27	17	16	16,5
Portugal	40	57	EU-27	14	20	17
Germany	39	58	EU-27	18	17	17,5
United Kingdom	39	57	EU-27	24	25	24,5
Estonia	39	56	EU-27	25	29	27
Cyprus	38	57	EU-27	28	26	27
Spain	38	57	EU-27	29	27	28
France	38	55	EU-27	30	34	32
Hungary	37	56	EU-27	41	30	35,5
Italy	39	53	EU-27	26	47	36,5
Poland	38	54	EU-27	35	43	39
Slovenia	38	54	EU-27	36	44	40
Czech Republic	37	55	EU-27	44	37	40,5
Slovakia	37	54	EU-27	47	45	46
Lithuania	36	54	EU-27	55	46	50,5
Greece	37	51	EU-27	49	56	52,5
Latvia	36	53	EU-27	56	52	54
South Africa	36	52	EU-27	58	55	56,5
Bulgaria	36	51	EU-27	59	58	58,5
Croatia	35	49	EU candidate	62	62	62
Romania	30	45	EU-27	84	80	82
Turkey	28	37	EU candidate	94	106	100
Macedonia	25	36	EU candidate	105	109	107

A **Western educated mind** would exclaim at this point that the "evidence" is "clear" – "Islam" does not "favor" democracy and human rights! Up to now, advanced research in international political sciene tended to confirm the rather pessimistic results, which emerge from a simple bi-variate analysis. A wide array of very serious available studies, authored by such well-known figures in comparative cross-national research, such as Barro and Mc Cleary, Donno and Russett, Fish, and Midlarsky, all looked into the relationship between democracy and Islam, and none of these studies, with all the politometric and econometric details duly considered, implied a straightforward falsification of the Islamo-pessimist hypotheses forwarded by Huntington.

But duly re-considering the quantitative, multivariate research on Islam and democracy, inherent in the works of Barro and Mc Cleary, Donno and Russett, Fish, and Midlarsky, we emphasize at this point however that **most social scientific processes of development** first of all are a **curve-linear function** of **development level**. This is also true for democracy. Results, which are based on linear trade-offs, will bias against the middle income countries, which are in the midst of the challenges of modernization, characterized by rapid economic growth, high income inequalities, and decreasing rates of employment, especially for women.

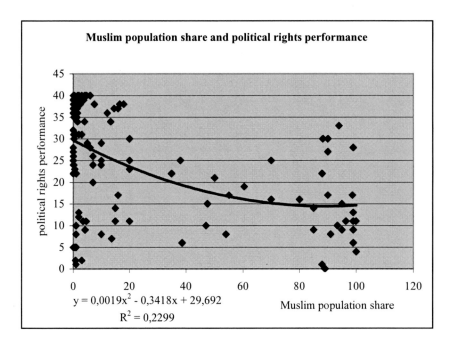

Graph 10.1. Muslim population share and the political rights performance.

Not introducing this important and very qualifying element, established in development economics by Nobel laureate **Simon Kuznets,** severely biases the research results in whatever direction. Supporters and opponents of neo-liberal capitalist globalization alike will in addition maintain that the whole arrays of variables of **"globalization"** and **"neo-liberal policies"** have to be entered in the multiple regressions on Muslim country democratic performance as additional, controlling variables. Supporters of neo-liberal globalization will claim that markets empower democracies, while dependency and world scholars will claim the opposite. In the theoretical chapters above, we introduced the entire canon of standard **world-system development research,** which of course also has to take into account other possible influencing variables, such as **geography, world political orientation (EU-integration)** and **recent development history** (Easterly, 2000 - 2002). This canon must also be tested for its relationships with democracy.

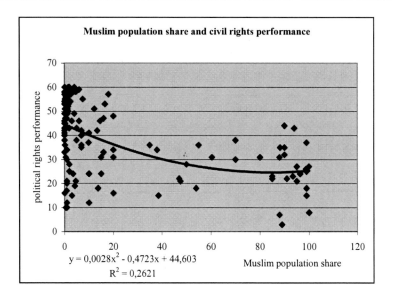

Graph 10.2. Muslim population share and the civil rights performance.

Since the essays on Islam and democracy, presented by Barro and Mc Cleary, Donno and Russett, Fish, and Midlarsky, in a way at least do not dispell clearly the negative trade-off between Islam and democracy, presented by Fish, we concentrate our analysis of existing findings on the essay, written by Fish. In this most famous quantitative essay supporting Huntington, which was published in *"World Politics"* in 2002, Fish suggested the following causal factors behind a good or bad human rights performance of a country:

Table 10.2. The causal factors of a good or bad democratic performance according to Fish (2002)

REGRESSIONS OF FREEDOM HOUSE SCORES ON HYPOTHESIZED DETERMINANTS[a]

Variable	Model 1	Model 2	Model 3	Model 4	Model 5
Constant	0.17	−0.15	0.27	−0.15	0.19
	(0.84)	(0.70)	(0.81)	(0.60)	(0.62)
Islamic religious tradition	−1.24***	−1.27***	−1.26***	−1.34***	−1.68***
	(0.27)	(0.27)	(0.27)	(0.27)	(0.27)
Economic development	1.40***	1.48***	1.40***	1.50***	1.39***
	(0.21)	(0.19)	(0.20)	(0.17)	(0.17)
Sociocultural division	−0.32		−0.30		
	(0.43)		(0.42)		
Economic performance	0.07	0.06	0.06		
	(0.05)	(0.04)	(0.04)		
British colonial heritage	0.25	0.18			
	(0.30)	(0.30)			
Communist heritage	0.20				
	(0.27)				
OPEC membership	−1.36**	−1.46**	−1.42**	−1.53**	
	(0.46)	(0.45)	(0.46)	(0.48)	
Adj. R^2	.55	.55	.55	.55	.51
N	149	149	149	149	149

* $p<0.05$; ** $p<0.01$; *** $p<0.001$.

[a] Entries in this table and all others are unstandardized regression coefficients with White-corrected robust standard errors in parentheses.

For the 149 analyzed countries, Fish suggests that with **rising incomes** (linear formulation), **political and civil rights suffer most in OPEC countries and/or in Muslim countries**. In the course of his quantitative analysis, Fish bases his theory then on a supposed negative trade off between gender equality performance and Islam. With rising incomes, you get rising gender equality and gender equality; and Islam is supposed to be – *ceteris paribus* – a major blockade against gender equality.

Fish then went on to test for the interaction between **development level, Islam, gender policy and democracy.** Does the "bad" Huntingtonian effect of "Islam" on "democracy" disappear, when you control properly for the gender dimension?

Table 10.3. The causal factors of a good or bad gender policy performance according to Fish (2002)

REGRESSIONS OF LITERACY GAP, SEX RATIO, WOMEN IN GOVERNMENT, AND THE GENDER EMPOWERMENT MEASURE ON HYPOTHESIZED DETERMINANTS[a]

	Dependent Variable: Literacy Gap		*Dependent Variable: Sex Ratio*		*Dependent Variable: Women in Government*		*Dependent Variable: Gender Empowerment Measure*	
	Model 1	*Model 2*	*Model 3*	*Model 4*	*Model 5*	*Model 6*	*Model 7*	*Model 8*
Constant	26.98***	42.69***	86.56***	95.82***	15.50***	5.07	0.12	−0.05
	(6.01)	(3.90)	(6.87)	(3.11)	(3.68)	(2.75)	(0.09)	(0.07)
Economic development	−6.46***	−10.21***	2.99	0.53	−0.95	1.83*	0.10***	0.15***
	(1.58)	(1.04)	(1.95)	(0.92)	(0.99)	(0.87)	(0.02)	(0.02)
Islamic religious tradition	11.10***	6.65***	6.68**	4.65**	−7.46***	−5.35***	−0.15***	−0.11***
	(2.09)	(1.77)	(2.21)	(1.56)	(1.23)	(0.95)	(0.03)	(0.03)
Sample	MC	all	MC	all	MC	all	MC	all
Adj. R^2	.51	.47	.17	.11	.29	.19	.73	.64
N	89	153	88	154	90	155	54	92

* $p<0.05$; ** $p<0.01$; *** $p<0.001$.
[a] MC-Muslim and Catholic countries; all - all available countries.

He reports the following results:

Table 10.4. The causal factors of a good or bad democratic performance, duly considering gender policy according to Fish (2002)

REGRESSIONS OF FREEDOM HOUSE SCORES ON HYPOTHESIZED DETERMINANTS

Variable	Model 1	Model 2	Model 3	Model 4	Model 5	Model 6	Model 7	Model 8
Constant	0.14 (0.63)	1.81* (0.91)	-0.21 (0.62)	5.90*** (1.62)	0.23 (0.62)	-0.19 (0.56)	0.51 (0.82)	0.67 (0.83)
Economic development	1.39*** (0.17)	0.99*** (0.23)	1.49*** (0.17)	1.52*** (0.16)	1.37*** (0.17)	1.21*** (0.16)	1.36*** (0.22)	0.88* (0.38)
Islamic religious tradition	-1.70*** (0.27)	-1.43*** (0.27)	-1.55*** (0.27)	-1.25*** (0.26)	-1.71*** (0.26)	-1.27*** (0.25)	-1.66*** (0.37)	-1.29*** (0.36)
Literacy gap		-0.04** (0.01)						
Sex ratio				-0.06*** (0.02)				
Women in government						0.08*** (0.02)		
Gender empowerment measure							3.32* (1.51)	
Adj. R²	.50	.53	.51	.54	.50	.57	.55	.58
N	153			154		155		92

* $p<0.05$; ** $p<0.01$; *** $p<0.001$.

The results seem to suggest that **"Islam" has a negative effect on "democratic performance"**, even when controlling for the **separate effects** of **gender inequality** on **democracy.** So far, so bad. If these results are true – and in essence they were at least not 100 % **contradicted** by Barro and Mc Cleary, Donno and Russett, and Midlarsky –they bode ill for efforts to "democratize" the "Muslim world".

However, we most fundamentally **disagree** with the results, presented by Fish in *"World Politics"*. As we already hinted at above, it is important to introduce **neo-liberal policies** (state sector influence versus economic freedom), **globalization, geography, development history** and the **non-linear trade off between development level and development performance** into the equations as additional control variables.

The **non-linear trade-off** between development level and democratic performance as well as the systematic inclusion of dependency and globalization variables seem to be the decisive factors, which explain **why** our results **differ** from those reported by Fish. One study, known in the literature, Hoeft, already demonstrated that **some** indicators of **globalization negatively** affect **democratic performance** (air departures and foreign direct investment inflow), while **Muslim population shares** are still **negatively related to the democratic outcome,** and **GDP per capita** (linear formulation) **does not affect at all democracy**.

But our main objection here is that **Muslim populations** in world society are **largely concentrated in the countries of the semi-periphery and the periphery.** Graph 10.3 analyzes this relationship, which is also vital for the trade-off between "Islam" and "democracy":

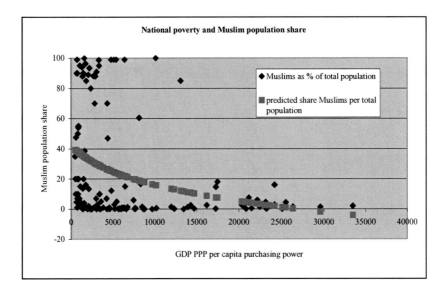

Graph 10.3. Muslim population shares in the countries of the world according to level of per capita purchasing power.

Democratic performance in the world system clearly is a **non-linear function of the attained development level:**

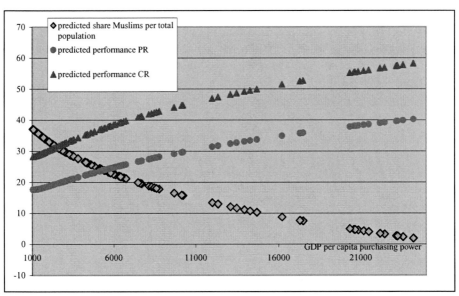

Sources: our own non-linear trend extrapolations, based on our data for 134 countries, based on Freedom House (democracy), Nationmaster (Muslim population share) and UNDP (real purchasing power per capita).
Political and civil rights performance – Freedom House point scale (y-axis).
Muslim population shares – precentages (y-axis).
GDP per capita purchasing power (x-axis).

Graph 10.4. political rights preformance, civil rights performance, Muslim population share and development level.

In addition to quantitatively questioning the results reported by Fish, we also look into the **changes** in **political and civil rights performance over time**. To this end, we first predicted 2006 performance on the 2003 data in a simple bi-variate OLS-regression. High positive residuals from this regression will be high positive changes to the better, while high negative changes will be high negative changes to the worse. Of course, we only interpret results, which are significant at least at the 10 % level.

political rights performance	PR t-test and direction of influence
EU-membership (EU-15)	-5,57626
Muslims as % of total population	3,73973
(I-S)/GNP	-3,60082
constant	3,40698
world bank pension model	-2,9441
Dummy for transition economy	2,30726
ln (GDP PPP pc)^2	2,27001
ln(GDP PPP pc)	-2,26003
Urbanization ratio, 1990	-2,11584
low comparative international price level (ERD)	-1,88497

Political rights are **positively** influenced, above all, by the **share of Muslims per total population**, by the status of a country as a **transition economy**, and by **economic maturity**. The **negative** effects are wielded by **EU-membership**, by **foreign savings**, by **World Bank pension models**, by the first part of the **"crisis of modernization"** (Kuznets) effect, by **urbanization**, and by **low comparative price levels**. In all, **61.5 %** of total variance are explained.

Civil rights are again **positively** influenced, above all, by the **share of Muslims per total population**, by **economic maturity**, and by the status of a country as a **transition economy**. The **negative** effects are again wielded by **EU-membership**, by **foreign savings**, by **World Bank pension models**, and again by the first part of the **"crisis of modernization"** (Kuznets) effect, and finally by **urbanization**. **72.9 %** of total variance are explained.

civil rights performance	CL t-test and direction of influence
EU-membership (EU-15)	-6,71466
(I-S)/GNP	-4,15706
Muslims as % of total population	3,95312
constant	3,61
ln (GDP PPP pc)^2	3,018
world bank pension model	-2,9031
ln(GDP PPP pc)	-2,84952
Dummy for transition economy	2,25373
Urbanization ratio, 1990	-1,98061

The **dynamics of political rights performance** over time, 2003 – 2006 took a **positive** turn in **landlocked countries**, in the **Muslim world**, and in the **transition economies**, while in **highly urbanized societies setbacks** in **political rights performances** were registered. **14.1 %** of total variance are explained.

DYN political rights performance	DYN PR t-test and direction of influence
constant	2,24446
Urbanization ratio, 1990	-1,88855
Dummy for being landlocked	1,74521
Muslims as % of total population	1,73017
Dummy for transition economy	1,70115

The **dynamics of civil rights performance** were **negatively** determined by **state interventionism**. **10.6 %** of total variance are explained.

DYN civil rights performance	DYN CR t-test and direction of influence
state interventionism (absence of ec. freedom)	-1,77541

Our full results are given in Table 10.5:.

Thus, we presented evidence, which raises serious questions about the Islamo-pessimistic interpretation, forwarded by Fish (2002).

Table 10.5. The multivariate results for the determination of the political and human rights performance

PR 2006 political rights performance, 2006	Dummy for being landlocked	Dummy for transition economy	Urbanization ratio, 1990	(1-S)/GNP	state interventionism (absence of ec. freedom)	MNC PEN 1995	low comparative international price level (ERD)	EU-membership (EU-15)	Muslims as % of total population	ln(GDP PPP pc)	ln (GDP PPP pc)^2	world bank pension model	constant
	3,30959	1,52015	-22,475	-0,07499	2,09159	-0,71241	-0,07198	-9,2912	0,23533	-0,12604	5,23764	-5,38337	142,884
	2,20698	0,65886	10,6223	0,02083	2,72461	0,85163	0,03818	1,6662	0,06293	0,05577	2,30733	1,82853	41,9387
	0,6512	7,66238											
	18,8275	121											
	13264,8	7104,16											
t-test and direction of influence	1,4996	2,3073	-2,116	-3,601	0,76767	-0,83652	-1,885	-5,576	3,7397	-2,26	2,27	-2,944	3,40698
t-test and direction of influence^2	2,2488	5,32346	4,47679	12,9659	0,58931	0,69977	3,55311	31,0947	13,9856	5,10775	5,15292	8,66771	11,6075
t-test and direction of influence^0,5	1,4996	2,30726	2,11584	3,60082	0,76767	0,83652	1,88497	5,57626	3,73973	2,26003	2,27001	2,9441	3,40698
degrees of freedom	121	121	121	121	121	121	121	121	121	121	121	121	121
error probability	0,13632	0,0227	0,0364	0,0005	0,44418	0,40451	0,0618	2E-07	0,0003	0,0256	0,025	0,0039	0,00089
F equation	18,8275	18,8275	18,8275	18,8275	18,8275	18,8275	18,8275	18,8275	18,8275	18,8275	18,8275	18,8275	18,8275
error probability, entire equation	2,2E-22	2,2E-22	2,2E-22	2,2E-22	2,2E-22	2,2E-22	2,2E-22	2,2E-22	2,2E-22	2,2E-22	2,2E-22	2,2E-22	2,2E-22

Table 10.5. Continued

PR 2006 political rights performance, 2006	Dummy for being landlocked	Dummy for transition economy	Urbanization ratio, 1990	(1-S)/GNP	state interventionism (absence of ec. freedom)	MNC PEN 1995	low comparative international price level (ERD)	EU-membership (EU-15)	Muslims as % of total population	ln(GDP PPP pc)	ln (GDP PPP pc)^2	world bank pension model	constant
	3,77379	1,60356	-22,7199	-0,09349	3,35248	-0,98819	-0,06153	-12,0822	0,26863	-0,17162	7,52005	-5,73265	163,498
	2,38337	0,71151	11,4712	0,02249	2,94237	0,9197	0,04124	1,79937	0,06796	0,06023	2,49173	1,97467	45,2905
	0,7287	8,27477											
	27,0859	121											
	22255,4	8285,09											
t-test and direction of influence	1,58339	2,25373	-1,98061	-4,15706	1,13938	-1,07447	-1,49211	-6,71466	3,95312	-2,84952	3,018	-2,9031	3,61
t-test and direction of influence^2	2,50711	5,07929	3,9228	17,2812	1,29819	1,15449	2,22638	45,0867	15,6272	8,11974	9,10833	8,42796	13,0321
t-test and direction of influence^0,5	1,58339	2,25373	1,98061	4,15706	1,13938	1,07447	1,49211	6,71466	3,95312	2,84952	3,018	2,9031	3,61
degrees of freedom	121	121	121	121	121	121	121	121	121	121	121	121	121
error probability	0,11594	0,02601	0,0499	6E-05	0,25679	0,28475	0,13827	6,5E-10	0,00013	0,00515	0,0031	0,00439	0,00045
F equation	27,0859	27,0859	27,0859	27,0859	27,0859	27,0859	27,0859	27,0859	27,0859	27,0859	27,0859	27,0859	27,0859
error probability, entire equation	9,6E-29	9,6E-29	9,6E-29	9,6E-29	9,6E-29	9,6E-29	9,6E-29	9,6E-29	9,6E-29	9,6E-29	9,6E-29	9,6E-29	9,6E-29

	Dummy for being landlocked	Dummy for transition economy	Urbanization ratio, 1990	(1-SJ)/GNP	state interventionism (absence of ec. freedom)	MNC PEN 1995	low comparative international price level (ERD)	EU-membership (EU-15)	Muslims as % of total population	ln(GDP PPP pc)	ln (GDP PPP pc)^2	world bank pension model	constant
PR Resid 2006 Dynamics of the political rights performance, 2003 - 2006													
	1,65156	0,4806	-8,60188	0,00658	-0,96076	-0,11678	-0,02622	-0,80635	0,04668	0,00843	-0,68947	-1,0656	40,3621
	0,94634	0,28251	4,55475	0,00893	1,16829	0,36518	0,01637	0,71446	0,02698	0,02391	0,98937	0,78406	17,983
	0,1405	3,28557											
	1,64826	121											
	213,516	1306,2											
t-test and direction of influence	1,7452	1,7011	-1,889	0,73703	-0,82236	-0,31979	-1,60143	-1,12861	1,7302	0,35241	-0,69688	-1,35908	2,24446
t-test and direction of influence^2	3,04575	2,8939	3,56663	0,54321	0,67628	0,10226	2,56456	1,27377	2,9935	0,1242	0,48565	1,8471	5,0376
t-test and direction of influence^0,5	1,74521	1,70115	1,88855	0,73703	0,82236	0,31979	1,60143	1,12861	1,73017	0,35241	0,69688	1,35908	2,24446
degrees of freedom	121	121	121	121	121	121	121	121	121	121	121	121	121
error probability	0,0835	0,0915	0,0613	0,46253	0,41249	0,74968	0,11189	0,26129	0,0861	0,72514	0,48721	0,17665	0,02662
F equation	1,64826	1,64826	1,64826	1,64826	1,64826	1,64826	1,64826	1,64826	1,64826	1,64826	1,64826	1,64826	1,64826
error probability, entire equation	0,08709	0,08709	0,08709	0,08709	0,08709	0,08709	0,08709	0,08709	0,08709	0,08709	0,08709	0,08709	0,08709
CL Resid 2006 Dynamics of the civil rights performance, 2003 - 2006	Dummy for being landlocked	Dummy for transition economy	Urbanization ratio, 1990	(1-SJ)/GNP	state interventionism (absence of ec. freedom)	MNC PEN 1995	low comparative international price level (ERD)	EU-membership (EU-15)	Muslims as % of total population	ln(GDP PPP pc)	ln (GDP PPP pc)^2	world bank pension model	constant
	0,90358	0,06783	-0,80181	0,01097	-1,75404	0,14199	0,00336	-0,77633	0,03716	0,01019	-0,17907	0,04454	2,95726
	0,80027	0,23891	3,85171	0,00755	0,98796	0,30881	0,01385	0,60418	0,02282	0,02022	0,83665	0,66304	15,2073
	0,1063	2,77843											
	1,19874	121											
	111,047	934,083											

Table 10.5. Continued

PR 2006 political rights performance, 2006	Dummy for being landlocked	Dummy for transition economy	Urbanization ratio, 1990	(1-S)/GNP	state interventionism (absence of ec. freedom)	MNC PEN 1995	low comparative international price level (ERD)	EU-membership (EU-15)	Muslims as % of total population	ln(GDP PPP pc)	ln (GDP PPP pc)^2	world bank pension model	constant
t-test and direction of influence	1,1291	0,28391	-0,20817	1,45326	-1,775	0,45979	0,24256	-1,28494	1,629	0,50376	-0,21403	0,06718	0,19446
t-test and direction of influence^2	1,27487	0,08061	0,04333	2,11197	3,15209	0,21141	0,05884	1,65108	2,65235	0,25377	0,04581	0,00451	0,03782
t-test and direction of influence^0,5	1,1291	0,28391	0,20817	1,45326	1,77541	0,45979	0,24256	1,28494	1,6286	0,50376	0,21403	0,06718	0,19446
degrees of freedom	121	121	121	121	121	121	121	121	121	121	121	121	121
error probability	0,26109	0,77696	0,83545	0,14874	0,0783	0,64649	0,80876	0,20127	0,106	0,61535	0,83088	0,94655	0,84614
F equation	1,19874	1,19874	1,19874	1,19874	1,19874	1,19874	1,19874	1,19874	1,19874	1,19874	1,19874	1,19874	1,19874
error probability, entire equation	0,29166	0,29166	0,29166	0,29166	0,29166	0,29166	0,29166	0,29166	0,29166	0,29166	0,29166	0,29166	0,29166

Legend: As in all EXCEL 7.0 outprints, first row: un-standardized regression coefficients, second row: standard errors, second last row: t-Test and direction of the influence. The values immediately below the standard errors are R^2 (third row, left side entry), F, and degrees of freedom (fourth row). Below that: ss reg; ss resid, i.e. the sum of squares of the regression and the sum of squares of the residuals. The right-hand entry in the third row is the standard error of the estimate y. Below the EXCEL outprints; we present materials for the t-test and the F-test for our regression results.

Chapter 11

CONCLUDING FINAL TESTS AND THEORETICAL SURVEYS

Winding up our journey across the field of comparative development studies, we now look at the patterns of effects, which can be established. First, we present the results of all the t-tests (t-tests and directions of the influence) from our 17 multiple regressions. Results, which are significant at least at the 10 % level, are printed in **bold** letters. Logically enough, we take the fact into account that the variables

Somewhat heroically combining the results, we arrive at the following graph:

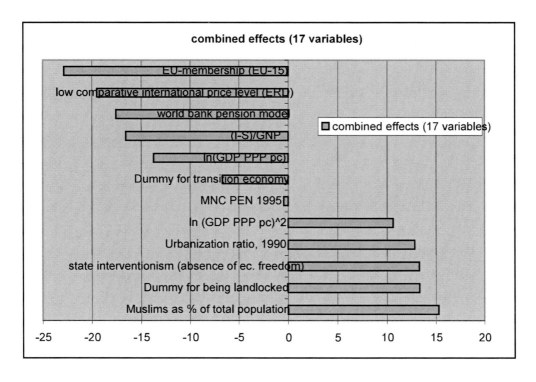

Graph 11.1. Overview of the combined effects – 17 variables.

Table 11.1. The combined effects

Dependent variable	Dummy for being landlocked	Dummy for transition economy	Urbanization ratio, 1990	(1-S)/GNP	state interventionism (absence of ec. freedom)	MNC PEN 1995	low comparative international price level (ERD)	EU-membership (EU-15)	Muslims as % of total population	ln(GDP PPP pc)	ln (GDP PPP pc)^2	world bank pension model	constant
freedom from early death before age 60	0,2307	-2,3417	3,26	2,81613	1,05261	1,24658	-1,0841	-1,43073	2,321	1,17921	1,988	-2,3515	-4,80479
freedom from civil liberty violations, 1998	0,28862	1,32502	-1,03106	-4,8469	0,99156	-0,75813	-2,007	-5,3844	2,786	-2,4466	0,97513	0,96691	0,9715
freedom from CO2 emissions per capita	1,943	-6,5757	5,989	-0,95851	2,498	-1,59787	-3,2264	-0,56049	2,019	-2,9465	-3,182	0,4715	-5,23804
economic growth, 1990-2003	0,93993	-0,81007	1,22829	0,51077	-0,20917	0,34387	0,4725	-2,4769	1,3579	-3,666	-0,91152	-2,719	-1,03284
eco-social market economy (GDP output per kg energy use)	2,5221	2,1151	-1,555	0,16926	2,1656	-2,241	-2,032	-0,21285	1,9432	-1,8539	-3,692	1,39024	1,50518
female economic activity rate as % of male economic activity rate	0,1731	5,9595	-6,119	-3,556	-0,38123	1,50135	-1,08617	-0,82755	-0,75783	-2,793	6,04619	-0,50433	7,47637
life expectancy, 1995-2000	0,01782	-2,29	3,3168	1,76825	0,95341	0,72024	-1,458	-1,39491	2,5228	1,3764	2,3814	-2,087	-2,28591
freedom from political rights violations,1998	-0,07015	0,84052	-0,52246	-5,4036	1,10522	-0,30651	-3,0612	-4,8015	4,075	-2,2938	1,56619	-2,6578	0,54826
social cohesion (small quintile ratio (share of income/consumption richest 20% to poorest 20%))	0,15522	2,583	-2,4001	2,167	1,758	1,6244	-0,9485	-0,49471	-0,31076	-1,04022	3,188	1,23961	1,93708
HDI 2005	0,40108	-1,918	3,6236	-1,096	1,12366	0,29352	-1,7936	-1,11434	2,0723	1,4968	4,699	-2,599	-3,28619

Table 11.1. The combined effects

Dependent variable	Dummy for being landlocked	Dummy for transition economy	Urbanization ratio, 1990	(1-S)/GNP	state interventionism (absence of ec. freedom)	MNC PEN 1995	low comparative international price level (ERD)	EU-membership (EU-15)	Muslims as % of total population	ln(GDP PPP pc)	ln(GDP PPP pc)^2	world bank pension model	constant
ESI-Index	1,35048	0,96938	-0,80424	**-2,5558**	-1,12	-0,80284	-0,24842	**-1,7871**	-0,42167	-0,40849	0,59455	0,30085	2,25328
HPI-Index Happy Planet Index	1,6	**-4,163**	**4,32**	1,211	0,314	0,166	-0,999	-1,276	-0,024	-0,395	**-2,218**	**-1,957**	-3,503
Life Satisfaction	1,463	0,45	-0,078	0,743	0,392	-1,227	1,372	-1,518	**-1,823**	-0,841	**-1,898**	**-1,773**	1,393
freedom from high ecological footprint	1,039	**-8,195**	**7,307**	-0,595	0,122	-0,016	-0,369	1,51	0,515	-0,516	**-4,525**	**1,866**	-7,032
Gender empowerment index	0,85552	**4,4801**	**-4,153**	**-5,64**	**1,7469**	0,21519	1,40782	0,0057	0,04365	0,07859	0,71492	-0,9782	4,59015
Gender development index	0,66288	-0,5079	**1,9258**	-1,141	0,966	0,55309	**-1,951**	-0,7936	**2,0856**	**1,29898**	**4,93497**	**-3,005**	-1,6653
freedom from unemployment	-0,2376	1,3835	-1,4886	-0,1553	-0,1632	-0,1494	**-2,4866**	-0,2825	**-3,0931**	0,046	-0,0505	1,2322	1,4624
Total	13,3347	-6,69525	12,81903	-16,5627	13,31536	-0,43451	-19,4986	-22,8398	15,31109	-13,7245	10,61133	-17,5776	-6,71085

- civil liberty violations, 1998
- CO2 emissions per capita
- early death before age 60
- political rights violations,1998
- quintile ratio (share of income/consumption richest 20% to poorest 20%))
- unemployment

are measuring **deficits** of development, and that the **signs** for their **t-values** have to be **reversed** to make their results comparable with the other, **positive indicators like life expectancy**, **economic growth etc.** Our outprint takes this already into account (Table 11.1).

EU-15 membership has the strongest combined negative effect (< -20.0). By comparison, the results for the effects of EU-15 membership are miserable indeed. Only one indicator, freedom from a high ecological footprint, is influenced in a positive way, while all the other indicators are influenced in a detrimental way by the dummy variable: EU-15 membership. Old Europe is in a mess indeed, while Muslim population shares have the strongest positive effect (> +15.0):

By contrast, the effects of Muslim population shares are much more positive in their effects than a large Islamophobic or at least Islamoskeptic public in Western Europe would believe. Only unemployment and life satisfaction are being determined statistically in a negative, significant fashion by this variable, while other effects, including the effects on key development indicators, are very positive, once we control properly for the other intervening variables.

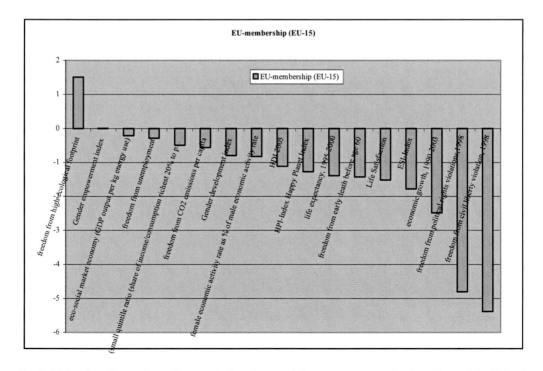

Graph 11.2a. the effects of Muslim population share and the EU – compared – the effects of the EU-15.

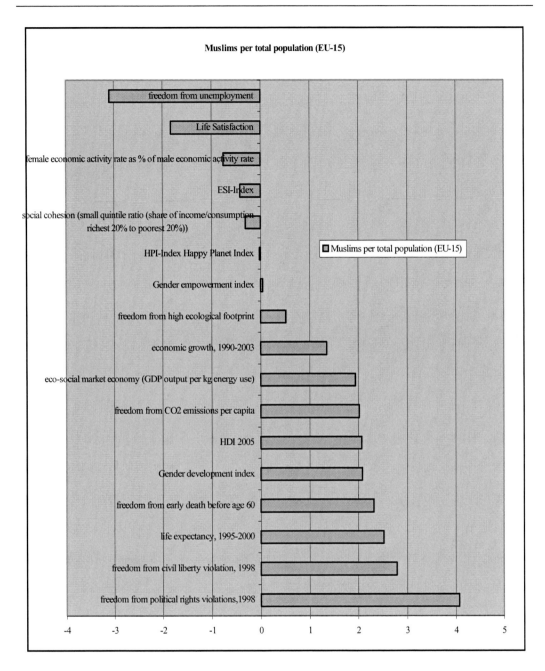

Graph 11.2b. the effects of Muslim population share and the EU – compared – the effects of the percentage share of Muslim piopulation per total population.

Graph 11.3 and Graph 11.4 now present the determinants of the two central aspects of the EU's Lisbon process, economic convergence (economic growth) and social cohesion:

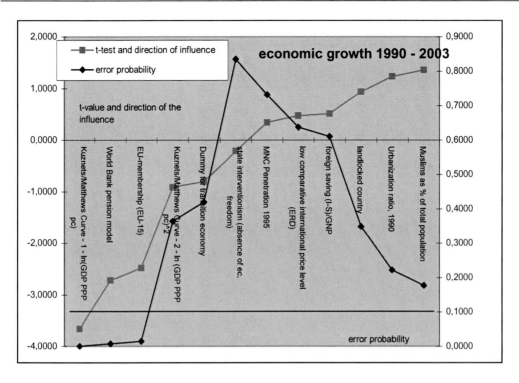

Graph 11.3. The determinants of economic growth.

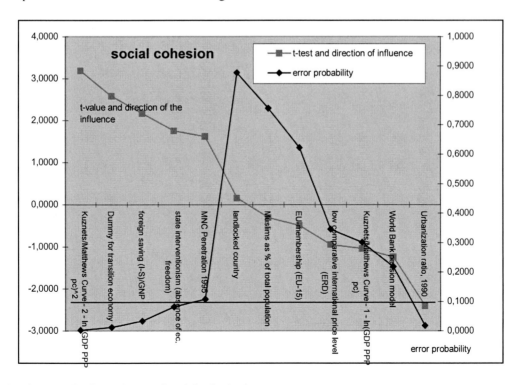

Graph 11.4. The determinants of social cohesion.

Economic growth is, by and large, determined by the *"Matthews effect"* (see Chapter 2 and Chapter 5 of this work), by the negative long-term effects of **EU-15 membership** and by the prohibitively high costs of establishing a **three-pillar pension model** of the World Bank type. All the other factors, which are so often mentioned in the public and in the scientific debate, do not wield **any** significant influence on the economic growth rates for the years 1990 – 2003.

Social cohesion, by contrast, is largely a function of the **"Kuznets curve"**; in addition, significant predictors working in the direction of social cohesion are the **legacies of Communism** and **state sector influence**, and the beneficial effects of **foreign saving** on income distribution, known since the early writings on **"dependencia"** by such authors as Paul Israel Singer from Brazil. A huge negative effect, **reducing social cohesion,** is wielded by the unequal process of **urbanization**. Again, all the other factors, including the classic dependency indicators transnational core capital penetration, unequal exchange (i.e. low comparative international price levels), and World Bank pension models, do not present significant results for the determination of social cohesion.

We also should state here that the original 14 EU Lisbon indicators (see Chapter 5) can be neatly projected onto the UNDP Human Development Index (UNDP HDI), for the UNDP HDI has more than 2/3 of variance in common with the Lisbon process. To this end, we projected the results from the 14 EU-Commission Lisbon indicators in the EU-27 onto a single new Lisbon Index, and compared this Lisbon Index with the UNDP HDI:

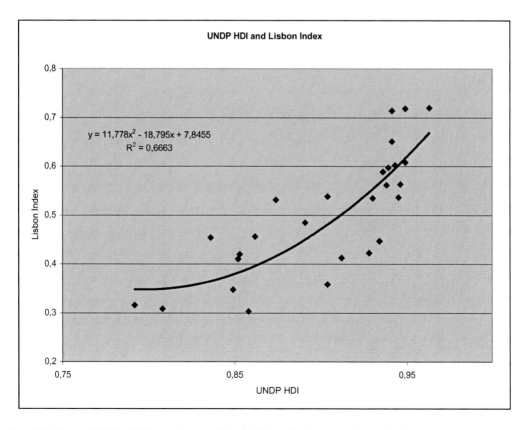

Graph 11.5a. the UNDP HDI, and the combined Lisbon development index in the EU-27.

Based on UNDP HDR 2005 and A. Tausch (2006) 'On heroes, villains and statisticians'. The Vienna Institute Monthly Report, No. 7, July 2006: 20 - 23. Vienna: The Vienna Institute for International Economic Studies (wiiw) and UNDP HDR 2005

What are now the determinants of the HDI as the best proxy for the EU-27 Lisbon process? Without question, **globalization** (**low comparative prices** and **World Bank pension reforms**) and the **transition process** from former Communism **quite negatively affect the results for the "global Lisbon race" as measured by the UNDP HDI or the original 14 EU Lisbon indicators**, while **Muslim population share, urbanization,** and income levels of a **mature economy** are positively related to the global "Lisbon results":

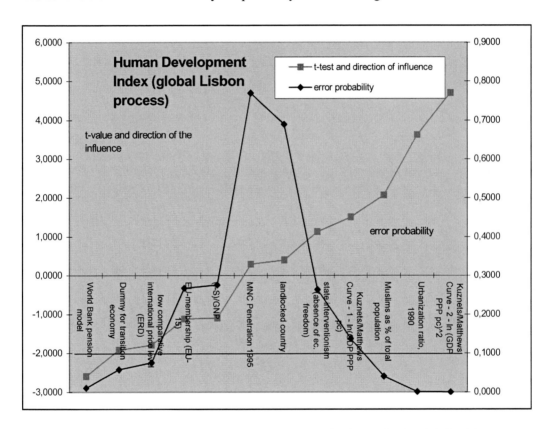

Graph 11.5b. The determinants of the Human Development Index (proxy for the global „Lisbon process").

In the following, we present materials, which further argue against a strategy of **low comparative prices,** which is so inherent in the 14 central Lisbon targets and in EU-27 policy making. The relationships of the exchange rate deviation index – low comparative international prices – with our main development indicators are clear-cut and mostly negative in terms of a coherent and reasonable development strategy:

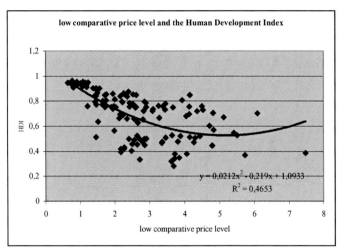
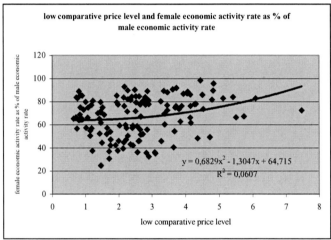
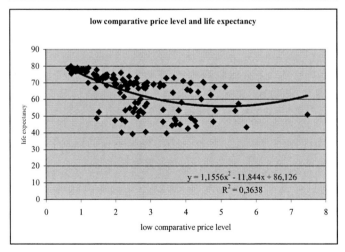

Graph 11.6. (Continued)

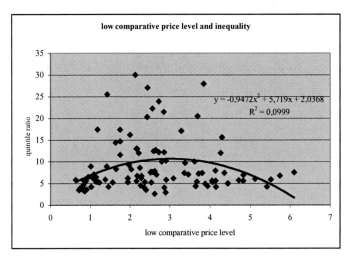

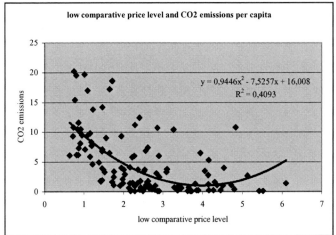

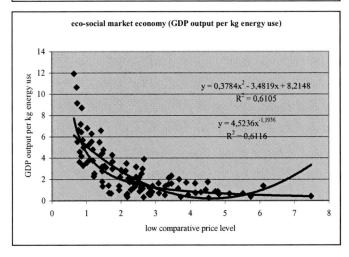

Concluding Final Tests and Theoretical Surveys 113

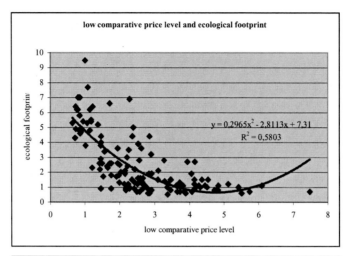

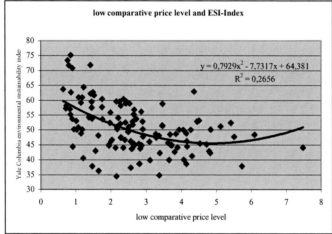

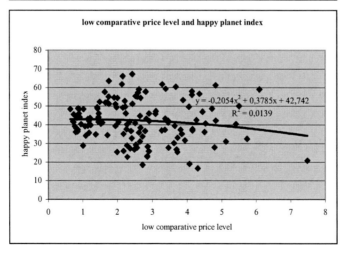

Graph 11.6. (Continued)

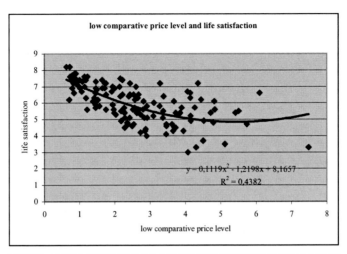

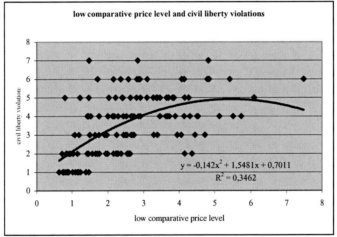

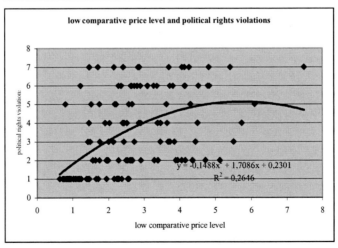

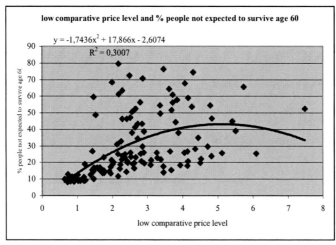
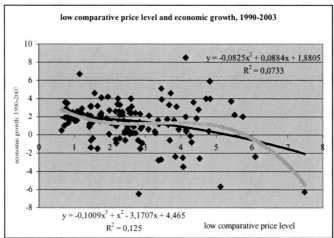
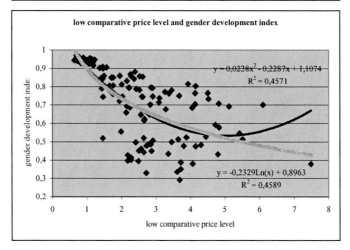

Graph 11.6. (Continued)

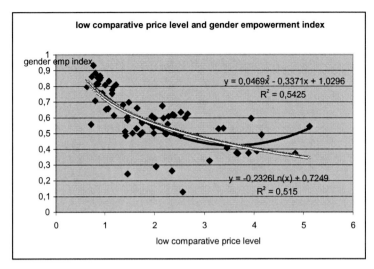

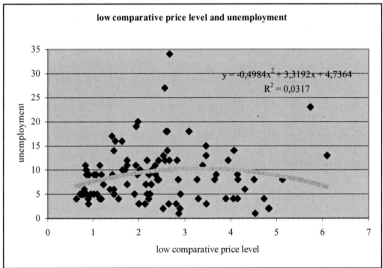

Graph 11.6. The direct effects of unequal exchange (low comparative price levels).

In 1998, and in comparison to the US, Canada and Australia, much of Europe was still a high-price region, while the Muslim countries were all low-price regions:

Table 11.3. Correlations with low comparative price level

	Pearson corr with ERD (low comparative price level)
state interventionism (absence of ec. freedom)	**0,7200901**
Civil liberty violations, 1998	**0,5486686**
% people not expected to survive age 60	**0,5001052**
Political rights violations,1998	**0,4863031**
(I-S)/GNP	0,3155311
Dummy for being landlocked	0,3022229
Muslims as % of total population	0,2345463

	Pearson corr with ERD (low comparative price level)
female economic activity rate as % of male economic activity rate	0,2265049
Dummy for transition economy	0,2142904
unemployment	**0,0989824**
quintile ratio (share of income/consumption richest 20% to poorest 20%)	**0,0409626**
MNC PEN 1995	-0,102825
HPI Happy Planet Index	**-0,108603**
economic growth, 1990-2003	**-0,255094**
world bank pension reform	-0,287537
EU-membership (EU-15)	**-0,440185**
ESI-Index environment sustainability index	**-0,456914**
Life Expectancy (1)	**-0,523999**
CO2 emissions per capita	-0,542198
life expectancy (2) 1995-2000	**-0,550141**
Life Satisfaction	**-0,617249**
HDI 2005 Human Development Index	**-0,624761**
eco-social market economy (GDP output per kg energy use)	**-0,656772**
EF ecological footprint	-0,666201
Urbanization ratio, 1990	**-0,669909**
ln(GDP PPP pc)	**-0,707477**
ln (GDP PPP pc)^2	**-0,721117**

Our following maps show the dramatic world shifts in price levels relative to the United States in recent years, and support our hypothesis that largely **unequal exchange** (or neo-liberal price reform strategies), **are to blame for many of the present ills of Europe and the Muslim world**. Contrary to what European policy makers expected with their Eurostat **politically binding price level indicator**, which is, after all, **one of their 14 main Lisbon targets,** the United States as the Lisbon competition country was a high price region throughout much of the late 1990s and the early 2000s. Also, our multivariate analysis in the preceeding Chapters showed the very negative effects of a low ERDI on the majority of our 17 indicators. The only exceptions were economic growth, life satisfaction and the gender empowerment index.

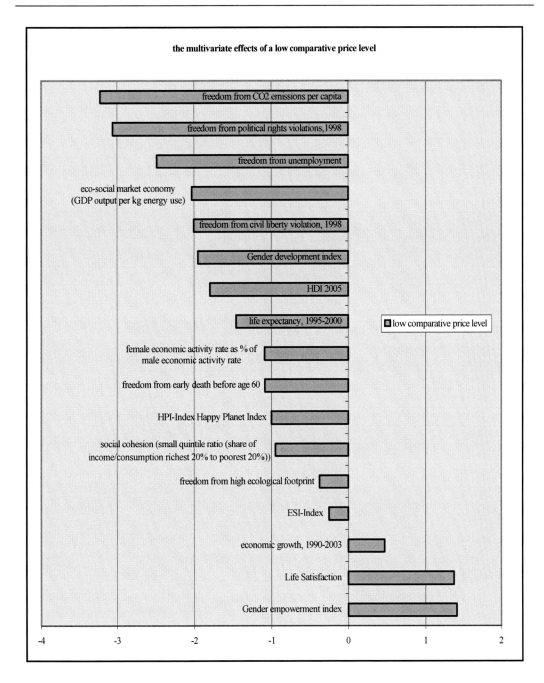

Graph 11.6. the effects of the "crown jewel" of neo-liberal EU policy: low comparative price levels in 134 nations of the world, duly considering the effects of other variables.

Our following maps show that the Lisbon process reference country, the US, always was a high-price country:

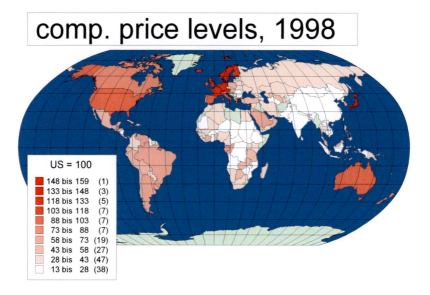

Legend: "bis" is the shorthand for "ranging from" "to". Countries marked in green color: missing values.

Map 11.1. Comparative price levels (US=100) in the world system, 1998.

In 2002 however, important European countries had a lower relative price level than the United States, while most Muslim countries pushed through a neo-liberal price reform policy path:

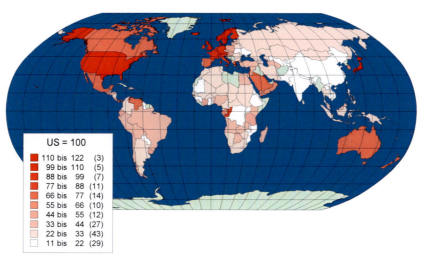

Legend: "bis" is the shorthand for "ranging from" "to". Countries marked in green color: missing values.

Map 11.2. Comparative price levels, 2002 (US=100). The United States became a global high-price country, while several European countries and the Muslim world lost their relative position.

It is important to grasp the **"tectonic shifts"** that underlie this process. Our following map shows the radical character of the neo-liberal transformation that many European nations, but also Egypt, Iran and Turkey had undergone in what Rao called *"the growing price convergence from growing globalization."* Europe pushed liberal, free trade policies, pushing down its price level in a much more radical fashion than the United States of America:

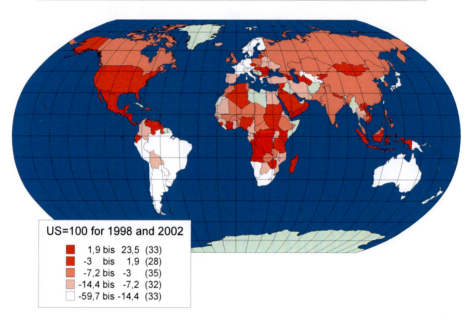

Legend: "bis" is the shorthand for "ranging from" "to". Countries marked in green color: missing values.
DYN price level = (100/ERD 2002*0,9927670) – (100/ERD 1998*1,01248497)
ERD US 2002 = 0,9927670; ERD US 1998 = 1,01248497

Map 11.3. comparisons of the shifts, 1998 – 2002 in the "Atlantic arena" and the world in genral.

By and large, it is shown that the member countries of the "old" EU-15, and especially the Euro zone countries, are on the losing side in that transnational equation. No "old" European country improved its position; on the contrary, "old Europe" becomes a region that is itself a victim of unequal transfer. It also emerges that *ceteris paribus* the Muslim world indeed became the main loser of these tectonic shifts.

It is entirely conceivable that these pressures – as Gernot Kohler has shown and as we already hinted at above – also explain a good part of the negative trends on the labor markets in the Muslim countries and in Europe (Tausch/Heshmati, 2007).

The cross-national, multi-variate effects of EU-15-membership are dismal indeed:

Table 11.4. the predicament of the EU-15 – t-values and directions of the influence for the variable "EU-15-membership" in our multiple regressions

	EU-membership (EU-15)
freedom from high ecological footprint	1,510
Gender empowerment index	0,006
eco-social market economy (GDP output per kg energy use)	-0,213
freedom from unemployment	-0,283
social cohesion (small quintile ratio (share of income/consumption richest 20% to poorest 20%))	-0,495
freedom from CO_2 emissions per capita	-0,560
Gender development index	-0,794
female economic activity rate as % of male economic activity rate	-0,828
HDI 2005	-1,114
HPI-Index Happy Planet Index	-1,276
life expectancy, 1995-2000	-1,395
freedom from early death before age 60	-1,431
Life Satisfaction	-1,518
ESI-Index	-1,787
economic growth, 1990-2003	-2,477
freedom from political rights violations, 1998	-4,802
freedom from civil liberty violations, 1998	-5,384

Two final tests for this Chapter should be presented, which further highlight the point that it is not "Islam", but the very nature of the way, the European economy is organized, is today's problem number 1 in Europe. Europe (EU-27) presents a strange combination of state interventions and neoliberalism, which are responsible for the negative effects of EU-membership.

The central question for the following test is: does Europe attract enough "human capital"? More and more, international inward migration flows become an asset of ascending countries in the center, as the present author argued at length elsewhere (Tausch, 2007). The UN Economic and Social Council 2004 data on international migration flows neatly render themselves for a calculation about the determinants of global inward migration flows. While the **transition economies,** mainly due to the large influxes in the former USSR and in former Yugoslavia, were quite significant net migration destination countries, and while there was a non-linear **"Kuznets effect"** of inward migration, surprisingly enough **urbanization** is **negatively** related to **inward migration flows**, and **positively related to outward migration flows**, reflecting the fact that outward migration from the semi-periphery and periphery countries mainly affects already highly, and often prematurely urbanized societies in Africa, Asia, Latin America and the Caribbean, the Pacific and on the outer rims of Europe. But in addition, it clearly emerges that **state interventions,** which are higher in Europe than in other Western democracies, **deter inward migration** and **induce outward migration flows**. Human beings are in search of economic opportunities, and in search of economic freedom. Not "Islam" drives people out of their countries, but state bureaucracies, which bloc the economic ascent of the economically most motivated individuals:

Table 11.5. Voting with your feet: net inward migration rates in the world economy, 1960 - 2000

total net migration rate 1950-2000 as % of total population, 2000	Dummy for being landlocked	Dummy for transition economy	Urbanization ratio, 1990	(1-S)/GNP	state interventionism (absence of ec. freedom)	MNC PEN 1995	low comparative international price level (ERD)	EU-membership (EU-15)	Muslims as % of total population	ln(GDP PPP pc)	ln(GDP PPP pc)^2	world bank pension model	constant
	-2,9888	2,69237	-41,546	0,03421	-8,1162	0,66027	0,02814	1,10176	0,01461	0,1601	-4,7355	-0,1805	143,223
	2,31568	0,71798	11,5551	0,02143	2,85254	0,96931	0,06003	1,8549	0,10748	0,06615	2,64325	1,96127	45,3872
	0,3977	6,78466											
	4,51143	82											
	2492,02	3774,59											
t-test and direction of influence	-1,2907	3,7500	-3,5954	1,5968	-2,8453	0,6812	0,4688	0,5940	0,1360	2,4203	-1,7915	-0,0920	3,1556
t-test and direction of influence^2	1,6658	14,0621	12,9272	2,5498	8,0955	0,4640	0,2198	0,3528	0,0185	5,8579	3,2096	0,0085	9,9577
t-test and direction of influence^0,5	1,2907	3,7500	3,5954	1,5968	2,8453	0,6812	0,4688	0,5940	0,1360	2,4203	1,7915	0,0920	3,1556
degrees of freedom	82,0000	82,0000	82,0000	82,0000	82,0000	82,0000	82,0000	82,0000	82,0000	82,0000	82,0000	82,0000	82,0000
error probability	0,2004	0,0003	0,0006	0,1142	0,0056	0,4977	0,6405	0,5542	0,8922	0,0177	0,0769	0,9269	0,0022
F equation	4,5114	4,5114	4,5114	4,5114	4,5114	4,5114	4,5114	4,5114	4,5114	4,5114	4,5114	4,5114	4,5114
error probability, entire equation	0,0000	0,0000	0,0000	0,0000	0,0000	0,0000	0,0000	0,0000	0,0000	0,0000	0,0000	0,0000	0,0000

Legend: As in all EXCEL 7.0 outprints, first row: un-standardized regression coefficients, second row: standard errors, second last row: t-Test and direction of the influence. The values immediately below the standard errors are R^2 (third row, left side entry), F, and degrees of freedom (fourth row). Below that: ss reg; ss resid, i.e. the sum of squares of the regression and the sum of squares of the residuals. The right-hand entry in the third row is the standard error of the estimate y. Below the EXCEL outprints; we present materials for the t-test and the F-test for our regression results.

Table 11.6a. "Islam's bloody borders"? Once again, Huntington is refuted – the linear formulation

UNDP Conflict Index	Dummy for being landlocked	Dummy for transition economy	Urbanization ratio, 1990	(I-S)/GNP	state interventionism (absence of ec. freedom)	MNC PEN 1995	low comparative international price level (ERD)	EU-membership (EU-15)	Muslims as % of total population	ln(GDP PPP pc)	ln (GDP PPP pc)^2	world bank pension reform	constant
	6,37665	-1,1812	19,8273	-0,081	-6,4876	3,54245	-0,1135	0,56687	0,10521	0,02394	-15,131	-4,0715	-78,685
	6,0255	1,79881	29,0009	0,05686	7,43872	2,32513	0,10425	4,54907	0,1718	0,15227	6,29946	4,99225	114,501
	0,1211	20,9198											
	1,38917	121											
	7295,44	52954,3											
t-test and direction of influence	1,0583	-0,6567	0,6837	-1,4251	-0,8721	1,5235	-1,0882	0,1246	0,6124	0,1572	-2,4020	-0,8156	-0,6872
t-test and direction of influence^2	1,1200	0,4312	0,4674	2,0309	0,7606	2,3212	1,1843	0,0155	0,3751	0,0247	5,7696	0,6651	0,4722
t-test and direction of influence^0,5	1,0583	0,6567	0,6837	1,4251	0,8721	1,5235	1,0882	0,1246	0,6124	0,1572	2,4020	0,8156	0,6872
degrees of freedom	121,0000	121,0000	121,0000	121,0000	121,0000	121,0000	121,0000	121,0000	121,0000	121,0000	121,0000	121,0000	121,0000
error probability	0,2920	0,5126	0,4955	**0,1567**	0,3849	0,1302	0,2787	0,9010	0,5414	0,8753	**0,0178**	0,4164	0,4933
F equation	1,3892	1,3892	1,3892	1,3892	1,3892	1,3892	1,3892	1,3892	1,3892	1,3892	1,3892	1,3892	1,3892
error probability, entire equation	0,1801	0,1801	0,1801	0,1801	0,1801	0,1801	0,1801	0,1801	0,1801	0,1801	0,1801	0,1801	0,1801

Legend: As in all EXCEL 7.0 outprints, first row: un-standardized regression coefficients, second row: standard errors, second last row: t-Test and direction of the influence. The values immediately below the standard errors are R^2 (third row, left side entry), F, and degrees of freedom (fourth row). Below that: ss reg; ss resid, i.e. the sum of squares of the regression and the sum of squares of the residuals. The right-hand entry in the third row is the standard error of the estimate y. Below the EXCEL outprints; we present materials for the t-test and the F-test for our regression results

Table 11.6b. "Islam's bloody borders"? Once again, Huntington is refuted – the non-linear formulation

UNDP Conflict Index	Dummy for being landlocked	Dummy for transition economy	Urbanization ratio, 1990	(I-S)/GNP	state interventionism (absence of ec. freedom)	MNC PEN 1995	low comparative international price level (ERD)	EU-membership (EU-15)	ln (Muslims+1)	(ln (Muslims+1))^2	ln(GDP PPP pc)	ln (GDP PPP pc)^2	world bank pension reform	constant
	6,58434	-1,9544	32,3791	-1,7222	7,02863	-7,7059	3,07732	-0,1327	0,06359	0,11635	0,03915	-15,389	-3,3786	-130,82
	6,01346	1,92249	31,0939	1,02655	4,97131	7,47306	2,35153	0,10508	4,54779	0,17189	0,15253	6,29297	5,03759	123,905
	0,1316													
	1,39874	120												
	7928,28	52321,4												
t-test and direction of influence	1,0949	-1,0166	1,0413	-1,6777	1,4138	-1,0312	1,3086	-1,2633	0,0140	0,6769	0,2567	**-2,4454**	-0,6707	-1,0558
t-test and direction of influence^2	1,1989	1,0335	1,0844	2,8146	1,9989	1,0633	1,7126	1,5960	0,0002	0,4581	0,0659	5,9800	0,4498	1,1148
t-test and direction of influence^0,5	1,0949	1,0166	1,0413	1,6777	1,4138	1,0312	1,3086	1,2633	0,0140	0,6769	0,2567	2,4454	0,6707	1,0558
degrees of freedom	120,0000	120,0000	120,0000	120,0000	120,0000	120,0000	120,0000	120,0000	120,0000	120,0000	120,0000	120,0000	120,0000	120,0000
error probability	0,2757	0,3114	0,2998	**0,0960**	0,1600	0,3045	0,1932	0,2089	0,9889	0,4998	0,7979	**0,0159**	0,5037	0,2932
F equation	1,3987	1,3987	1,3987	1,3987	1,3987	1,3987	1,3987	1,3987	1,3987	1,3987	1,3987	1,3987	1,3987	1,3987
error probability, entire equation	0,1696	0,1696	0,1696	0,1696	0,1696	0,1696	0,1696	0,1696	0,1696	0,1696	0,1696	0,1696	0,1696	0,1696

Legend: As in all EXCEL 7.0 outprints, first row: un-standardized regression coefficients, second row: standard errors, second last row: t-Test and direction of the influence. The values immediately below the standard errors are R^2 (third row, left side entry), F, and degrees of freedom (fourth row). Below that: ss reg; ss resid, i.e. the sum of squares of the regression and the sum of squares of the residuals. The right-hand entry in the third row is the standard error of the estimate y. Below the EXCEL outprints; we present materials for the t-test and the F-test for our regression results.

Huntington said all along that Muslim countries are not only characterized by an incompatibility to reconcile society with modernity, but also that Muslim countries are characterized by higher conflict intensity, especially on the "borders" of the Muslim cultural orbit. So this hypothesis will be tested in the following.

To properly test this hypothesis, we used again our predictor set, and the **data series** about the **percentage of a given population**, affected **by violent internal or external conflicts 1980 – 2000** (UNDP, 2004) as the dependent variable. To properly test the Huntington hypothesis, we introduced a linear formulation about the trade-off between "Islam" and "conflict", and a non-linear trade-off, which particularly takes into account that the conflict level could be highest at medium shares of the Muslim population per total population (i.e. the "bloody border" thesis; Huntington would quote here examples like Nigeria), while at very high and very low shares of Muslims per total population, conflict would be less extended. However, both formulations (a simple linear trade-off; or the equation conflict = natural log (Muslim population share +1) and [natural log (Muslim population share +1)]^2) do not wield **any** significant results. **Conflict** levels are a **diminishing function of very mature levels of per capita purchasing powers**. **Globalization (foreign savings)** has indeed a **conflict-diminishing effect**. But the R^2 of the entire equations is relatively low (< 1/6) and the error p is above 10 %.

We now proceed to present the theoretical summary of our results achieved so far. Our global comparisons, attained by multiple regressions, show 9 important conclusions:

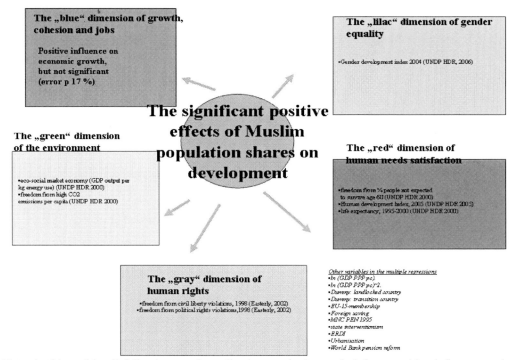

Note: in this and in all following graphs, a lined arrow is the symbol for a positive influence, and a dotted arrow is a symbol for a negative influence.

Graph 11.8. the significant positive effects of the share of Muslim population on development.

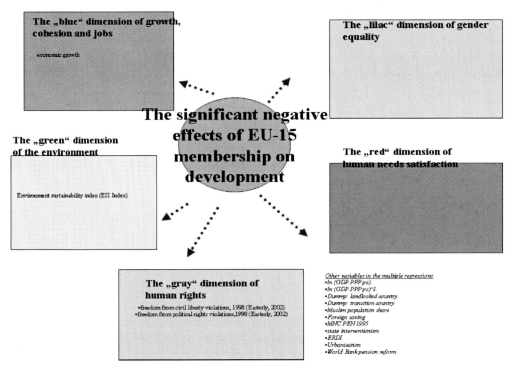

Graph 11.9. The significant negative effects of EU-15 membership.

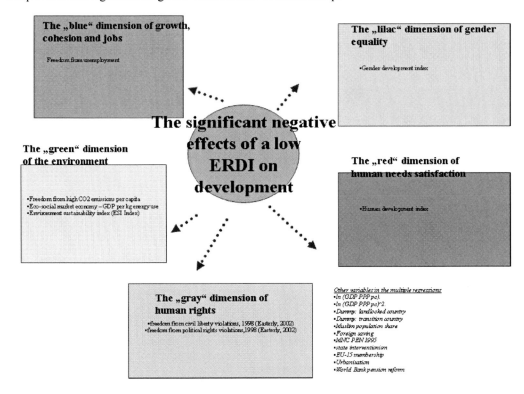

Graph 11.10. The significant negative effects of the EU strategy to lower the comparative international price level.

1) *first of all, Islam is hardly to blame for global and European development problems, let alone, Muslim migration is to blame for the failure of the European Lisbon process*
2) *it emerges that the European Union, the way it is constructed, is not the answer, but part of the very problem of stagnation and deficient development*
3) *in particular, the Lisbon target "low comparative price levels" contradicts the other Lisbon targets*
4) *Europe is characterized by an aging society and the pension crisis. But World Bank pension models will not propel economic growth and sustainable development*
5) *further opening up to global markets and unfettered globalization will not provide sustainable development to the European political economy*
6) *many of the ills of the Muslim world are in reality caused by the crisis of modernization ("things get worse, before the get better")*
7) *the "Limits to Growth" in the richest countries create serious social and ecological tensions*
8) *urbanization negatively affects development in many ways*
9) *the positive effects of globalization are very limited.*

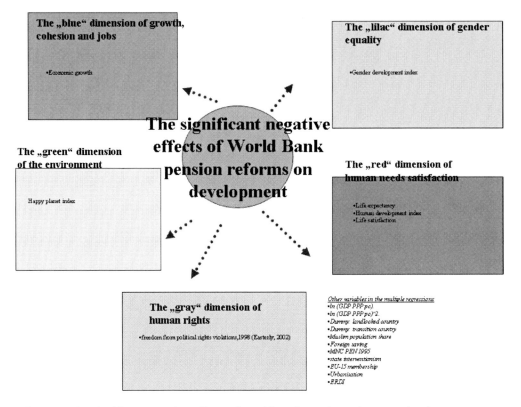

Graph 11.11. The significant negative effects of World Bank pension reforms on development.

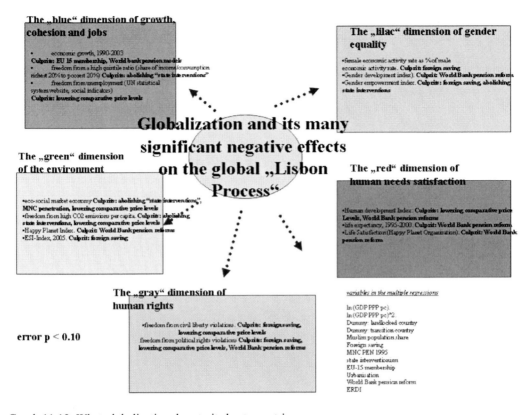

Graph 11.12. What globalization does to its host countries.

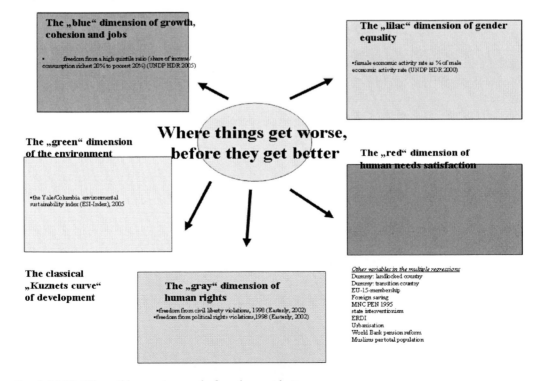

Graph 11.13. Where things get worse before they get better.

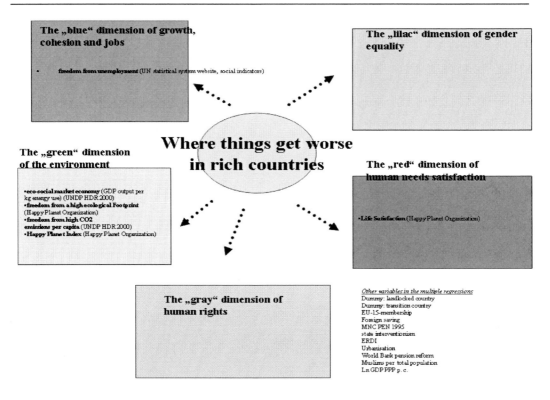

Graph 11.14. Where things get even worse in the highly developed countries.

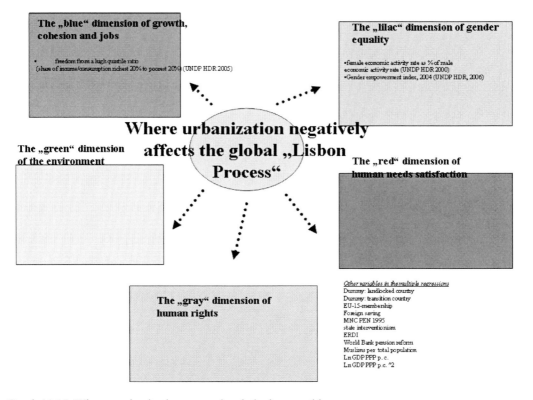

Graph 11.15. Where modernization proceeds relatively smoothly.

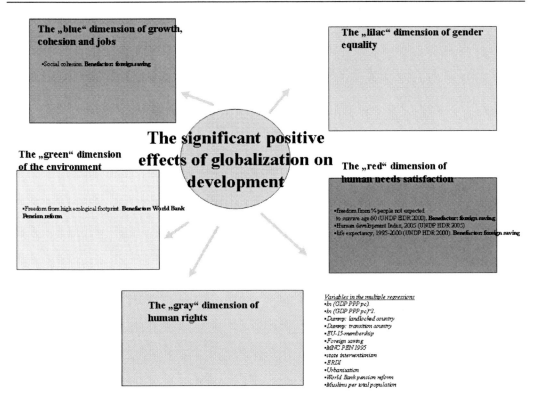

Graph 11.16. Where globalization has positive effects.

Chapter 12

GENERAL CONCLUSIONS FOR THE "GLOBAL LISBON INDEX" AND ITS COMPONENTS

Confronted with such a variety of dependent variables, our readers might be tempted to ask: and what are the "overall effects", and which concrete steps should be recommended to the policy-makers? In Chapter 5, we already presented a methodology by which we constructed two different global, overall "Lisbon Process Indicators (LPIs)". One is based on the simple aggregation of the 17 component dimension indicators, while we call the other indicator "Lisbon Process Indicator (LPI-2)". This indicator is based on the means of the five master component dimension indicators – for economic growth, the environment, human rights, basic human needs satisfaction, and gender equality. Both indicators correlate very closely with each other, i.e. their common variance is more than 96 %.

Our study by the way shows the close correlations of the new two "master indices" of "development" with the indices, developed by Nobel Laureate Amartya Sen and his team at the UNDP more than a decade and a half ago. Our Lisbon Indicator (LPI-1) correlates closest (+0.85) with the **UNDP GDI** *(gender development indicator),* while "the closest match" for the Lisbon Indicator (LPI-2), which reflects the 5 dimensions in an equal fashion, is again best correlated with the UNDP GDI (gender development indicator, +0.83). Also, the **close relationship with the UNDP Human Development Indicator is really outstanding – the correlation with the LPI-1 is +0.84, and with the LPI-2 +0.82.** As it is well known, the GDI – gender-related development index – is a composite indicator that, as the UNDP website has it *"measures the average achievement of a population in the same dimensions as the HDI [human development index, i.e. combining income, education, and longetivity], while adjusting for gender inequalities in the level of achievement in the three basic aspects of human development."* (see appendix). Among all the indicators, used here, the UNDP GDI turns out to be the single most important yardstick, which is capable of capturing so many dimensions of the development process at once, closely followed by the UNDP Human Development Index. Now, confronted with the concluding policy-making question as to what are the overall effects of our independent variables on the "development process", we would like to present analyses, which show the effects of our 12 predictors on our Lisbon Process Indicator (LPI-1) (linear combination of the 17 component processes) or LPI-2 (linear combination of the 5 dimensions growth, environment, human rights, basic human needs, gender equality, in turn combining the 17 component processes).

Readers should note that the regression model for the Global Lisbon Process Index (LPI-1) is based on 134 countries, while the regression model for the Global Lisbon Process Index (LPI-2) is based on 133 countries. Since the country Chad has now available data for any of the 3 components, on which the "growth" dimension is based, we dropped Chad from the sample.

What are the **significant predictors** (error p equal or <.10)? It again turns out that first of all **things get worse, before they get better** – the old wisdom of classical development economics **(Kuznets)** and political science modernization theory of the postwar period. In addition, it emerges that in both specifications, **foreign savings, "economic freedom", low comparative international price levels,** and **World Bank type pension reforms** are **not compatible with a solid and long-run development path,** based on our knowledge of 17 component variables, integrating the dimensions growth, environment, human rights, basic human needs satisfaction, and gender equality. In addition, **European Union membership** (EU-15, "old Europe") in both specifications has the numerically **highest negative effect** on the global Lisbon process; while **Muslim population shares** in no way bloc the development process, on the **contrary**. Both regression analyses have excellent statistical properties; the F values are each time above 25.00; and the R^2 exceeds in each case 7/10. Neo-liberal globalization strategies are condemned to failure; while European decision makers in particular would be strongly advised to re-think their Lisbon strategy, which pushes countries towards accepting strategies, which, *inter alia,* lower instead of increase the comparative international price level. In our sample, the countries with the lowest comparative price level were Congo, Dem. Rep. of the; Kyrgyzstan; Ethiopia; Nepal; Lao People's Dem. Rep.; Moldova, Rep. of; Cambodia; Viet Nam; Angola; India; Azerbaijan; while the classical high-price countries are: Switzerland; Japan; Denmark; Luxembourg; Norway; Singapore; Sweden; Germany; France; Finland; Austria; Netherlands; Iceland; Belgium; United Kingdom; United States; Italy; Israel; Australia; Ireland; Spain; New Zealand; Greece; Lebanon; Canada; and Portugal. **Is a price level of say, the Congo's dimension, really the aim of the Lisbon process?**

Balassa and Samuelson assumed that rising international price levels for the periphery country are a good thing. The ultraliberal underlying assumptions of the current Commission, member governments and Eurostat on the subject were already implied by Rao, who mentioned in a UNDP paper, back in 1998 **that neo-liberal economics sustain the expectation of a growing price convergence from growing globalization** *(Rao J. M., 1998: 14-15).* **Falling relative price levels in countries like Germany over the last years would suggest in the neo-classical argument that the price of the non-tradables in the German economy decreased dramatically over time.** Structuralist economists, like Stanford Professor emeritus Pan Yotopoulos, usually warn the weaker countries of the periphery that

> "Currency substitution represents an asymmetric demand from Mexicans to hold dollars as a store of value, a demand that is not reciprocated by Americans holding pesos as a hedge against the devaluation of the dollar!" (Yotopoulos and Sawada, 2005)

Their argument, which they established in a 1999 paper, refined in their 2005 analysis, was the so-called Y-Proposition, and this Y-position is very relevant today:

"in free currency markets hard currencies fluctuate, while soft currencies depriciate systematically (...) The alternative scenario deprives devaluation of any of its remedial properties that in the conventional view lead to a process of stable interactions and equilibrium...."

Yotopoulos and other critics think that the basic problem of international currency markets is **asymmetric reputation**. This process of asymmetric reputation of the periphery deepens the cycle of underdevelopment:

"Mexico cannot service its foreign debt from the proceeds of producing nontradables. These are traded in pesos. It has instead to shift resources away from the nontradable sector to produce tradable output in order to procure the dollars for servicing the debt (...) The process (...) can create a negative feedback loop that leads to resource misallocation in soft-currency countries (...) This shift of resources represents misallocation and produces inefficiency and output losses (...) Distortions inherent in free currency markets lead to a systematic devaluation of soft currencies – to „high" nominal exchange rates. Devaluation of the exchange rate means increasing prices of tradables and leads to increased exports. But not all exports are a bargain to produce compared to the alternative of producing nontradables (...) Countries graduate from being exporters of sugar and copra to exporting their teak forests, and on to systematically exporting nurses and doctors, while they remain underdeveloped all the same. If this happens, it may represent competitive devaluation trade as opposed to comparative advantage trade." (Yotopoulos and Sawada, 2005)

The authors further explain their ideas by an econometric analysis of economic growth rates in 62 countries from 1970 onwards that shows how this process of competitive devaluation trade leads to stagnation. They also present an economic model in the tradition of Paul Krugman that shows how currency substitution triggers financial crises. In their 2005 paper, the authors show the relevance of their theories with time series data from 153 countries. Thus, if they are correct, a high ratio between purchasing power and GDP at exchange rates, i.e. an **under-valued currency, will lead to development stagnation. The countries with the strongest currencies, like Denmark, the UK, Sweden, are typical centers of the capitalist world economy with a favorable ratio of tradables to non-tradables, while the countries with a Eurostat "good" low price level, like Turkey, are countries with an unfavorable relation between tradables and non-tradables,** suffering from what neo-Marxists like to call "unequal transfer" or "unequal exchange" (price reform/low international price level).

In addition to the above specified dependency theory and world systems theory arguments, **urbanization** positively affects Lisbon Process Index Indicator (LPI-1), but not Lisbon Process Index Indicator (LPI-2):

Table 12.1. The determinants of the global Lisbon process

Global Lisbon Index (1)	Dummy for being landlocked	Dummy for transition economy	Urbanization ratio, 1990	(I-S)/GNP	state interventionism (absence of ec. freedom)	MNC PEN 1995	low comparative international price level (ERD)	EU-membership (EU-15)	Muslims as % of total population	ln(GDP PPP pc)	ln(GDP PPP pc)^2	world bank pension reform	constant
	0,02879	-0,006	0,16834	-0,0004	0,04152	-0,0024	-0,001	-0,0614	0,0013	-0,0015	0,03843	-0,0443	-0,0919
	0,01974	0,00589	0,09501	0,00019	0,02437	0,00762	0,00034	0,0149	0,00056	0,0005	0,02064	0,01636	0,37513
	0,7197	0,06854											
	25,8951	121											
	1,45971	0,5684											
t-test and direction of influence	1,4583	-1,0226	**1,7718**	**-2,2870**	**1,7035**	-0,3185	**-3,0694**	**-4,1214**	**2,3058**	**-3,0642**	**1,8622**	**-2,7069**	-0,2451
t-test and direction of influence^2	2,1267	1,0458	3,1392	5,2303	2,9020	0,1014	9,4211	16,9863	5,3166	9,3896	3,4679	7,3275	0,0601
t-test and direction of influence^0,5	1,4583	1,0226	1,7718	2,2870	1,7035	0,3185	3,0694	4,1214	2,3058	3,0642	1,8622	2,7069	0,2451
degrees of freedom	121,0000	121,0000	121,0000	121,0000	121,0000	121,0000	121,0000	121,0000	121,0000	121,0000	121,0000	121,0000	121,0000
error probability	0,1473	0,3085	**0,0790**	**0,0239**	**0,0910**	0,7507	**0,0026**	**0,0001**	**0,0228**	**0,0027**	**0,0650**	**0,0078**	0,8068
F equation	25,8951	25,8951	25,8951	25,8951	25,8951	25,8951	25,8951	25,8951	25,8951	25,8951	25,8951	25,8951	25,8951
error probability, entire equation	0,0000	0,0000	0,0000	0,0000	0,0000	0,0000	0,0000	0,0000	0,0000	0,0000	0,0000	0,0000	0,0000

overall Global Lisbon Index (2)	Dummy for being landlocked	Dummy for transition economy	Urbanization ratio, 1990	(1-SJ)/GNP	state interventionism (absence of ec. freedom)	MNC PEN 1995	low comparative international price level (ERD)	EU-membership (EU-15)	Muslims as % of total population	ln(GDP PPP pc)	ln (GDP PPP pc)^2	world bank pension reform	constant
	0,02843	0,00445	0,00184	-0,0006	0,04579	0,00078	-0,0012	-0,0759	0,00167	-0,0018	0,06137	-0,05	0,61134
	0,01982	0,00592	0,09553	0,00019	0,02447	0,00765	0,00034	0,01497	0,00057	0,0005	0,02076	0,01656	0,37716
	0,764	0,06883											
	32,3797	120											
	1,84071	0,56848											
t-test and direction of influence	1,4341	0,7512	0,0192	-3,1704	1,8707	0,1013	-3,3884	-5,0711	2,9533	-3,5973	2,9564	-3,0170	1,6209
t-test and direction of influence^2	2,0566	0,5643	0,0004	10,0515	3,4997	0,0103	11,4811	25,7157	8,7220	12,9406	8,7400	9,1022	2,6273
t-test and direction of influence^0,5	1,4341	0,7512	0,0192	3,1704	1,8707	0,1013	3,3884	5,0711	2,9533	3,5973	2,9564	3,0170	1,6209
degrees of freedom	120,0000	120,0000	120,0000	120,0000	120,0000	120,0000	120,0000	120,0000	120,0000	120,0000	120,0000	120,0000	120,0000
error probability	0,1541	0,4540	0,9847	0,0019	0,0638	0,9194	0,0010	0,0000	0,0038	0,0005	0,0037	0,0031	0,1077
F equation	32,3797	32,3797	32,3797	32,3797	32,3797	32,3797	32,3797	32,3797	32,3797	32,3797	32,3797	32,3797	32,3797
error probability, entire equation	0,0000	0,0000	0,0000	0,0000	0,0000	0,0000	0,0000	0,0000	0,0000	0,0000	0,0000	0,0000	0,0000

Legend: As in all EXCEL 7.0 outprints, first row: un-standardized regression coefficients, second row: standard errors, second last row: t-Test and direction of the influence. The values immediately below the standard errors are R^2 (third row, left side entry), F, and degrees of freedom (fourth row). Below that: ss reg; SS resid, i.e. the sum of squares of the regression and the sum of squares of the residuals. The right-hand entry in the third row is the standard error of the estimate y. Below the EXCEL outprints; we present materials for the t-test and the F-test for our regression results

The causal links of the above Table can be further specified in the following graph. It portrays the determinants of the global Lisbon Process Indicator (LPI-1) only, since the determinants of LPI-2 are pretty similar, as we saw above:

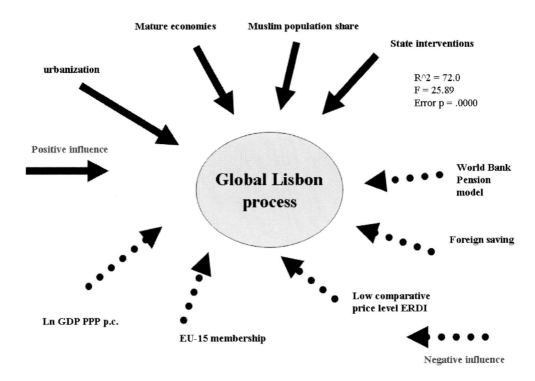

Graph 12.1. The final causal model.

The summarizing Table 12.2 finally shows the rankings of the highly developed countries in the global Lisbon process. European decision makers would be well advised to re-think their strategies, indeed. Not the United States (rank on the global Lisbon scale – 38) should be the target country, but the **north-west European welfare democracies Switzerland, Iceland, Austria, Sweden, Norway, Denmark, Finland, the Netherlands, and Ireland,** who all maximized

- their economic growth, 1990-2003 (UNDP HDR, 2005)
- their eco-social market economy (GDP output per kg energy use) (UNDP HDR 2000)
- their female economic activity rate as % of male economic activity rate (UNDP HDR 2000)
- their freedom from % people not expected to survive age 60 (UNDP HDR 2000)
- their freedom from a high ecological Footprint (Happy Planet Organization)
- their freedom from a high quintile ratio (share of income/consumption richest 20% to poorest 20%) (UNDP HDR 2005)
- their freedom from civil liberty violations, 1998 (Easterly, 2000 - 2002)
- their freedom from high CO_2 emissions per capita (UNDP HDR 2000)
- their freedom from political rights violations, 1998 (Easterly, 2000 - 2002)

- their freedom from unemployment (UN statistical system website, social indicators)
- their Gender development index 2004 (UNDP HDR, 2006)
- their Gender empowerment index, 2004 (UNDP HDR, 2006)
- their Happy Planet Index (Happy Planet Organization)
- their Human development Index, 2005 (UNDP HDR 2005)
- their life expectancy, 1995-2000 (UNDP HDR 2000)
- their Life Satisfaction (Happy Planet Organization)
- their the Yale/Columbia environmental sustainability index (ESI-Index), 2005

Pushing Europe downwards the path of falling comparative prices will only increase the growth impediments of the growingly multicultural Europe:

Table 12.2. The global Lisbon race

Country code	Global Lisbon Index	world rank	country group
Switzerland	0,82715	1	EEA/EFTA
Iceland	0,81502	2	EEA/EFTA
Austria	0,81147	3	EU-27
Sweden	0,807	4	EU-27
Norway	0,80098	5	EEA/EFTA
Denmark	0,79661	6	EU-27
Finland	0,77986	7	EU-27
Netherlands	0,7726	8	EU-27
Ireland	0,76347	9	EU-27
Japan	0,76012	10	other OECD democracies
Canada	0,75274	13	other OECD democracies
Cyprus	0,75226	14	EU-27
Germany	0,75064	15	EU-27
Luxembourg	0,74795	16	EU-27
Italy	0,74482	17	EU-27
New Zealand	0,74296	18	other OECD democracies
Slovenia	0,73988	19	EU-27
France	0,73665	21	EU-27
United Kingdom	0,73603	23	EU-27
Belgium	0,73226	24	EU-27
Spain	0,73157	25	EU-27
Portugal	0,72986	26	EU-27
Australia	0,72463	27	other OECD democracies
Israel	0,69906	32	other OECD democracies
Greece	0,68434	34	EU-27
Hungary	0,6801	36	EU-27
United States	**0,6761**	**38**	**other OECD democracies**
Poland	0,66212	42	EU-27
Slovakia	0,66206	43	EU-27
Latvia	0,66192	44	EU-27
Lithuania	0,6563	47	EU-27
Croatia	0,6423	49	EU-candidate

Table 12.2. The global Lisbon race

Country code	Global Lisbon Index	world rank	country group
Romania	0,6406	51	EU-27
Bulgaria	0,62485	60	EU-27
Estonia	0,62176	63	EU-27
Czech Republic	0,61236	69	EU-27
Turkey	0,5676	80	EU-candidate

On this sober note, we have reached the end of our journey.

APPENDIX

HAPPINESS IS POSSIBLE. TEACHINGS OF CLASSICAL MUSLIM PHILOSOPHY AS REFLECTED IN MUSLIMPHILOSPHY.COM

al-Kindi, Abu Yusuf Ya'qub ibn Ishaq (d. c.866–873)

> Human beings are what they truly are in the soul, not in the body. Whoever wishes for what is not in nature wishes for what does not exist. The reader is admonished that unhappiness follows such an attitude. Al-Kindi advocates maintaining an internal balance through the mechanism of the individual's interior autonomy. If worldly property becomes a concern and is then lost or damaged, this will upset an individual's mental equilibrium. The virtues are wisdom, courage and temperance. (http://www.muslimphilosophy.com/ip/kin.htm)

al-RAZI, Abu Bakr Muhammad b. Zakariyya', known to the Latins as Rhazes (ca.250/854-313/925 or 323/935), physician, philosopher and alchemist

> The attempt to maximise one's happiness by serving the appetites and passions is a self-defeating strategy, Wisdom, then, springs not from the thought of death, as many philosophers and pious teachers have supposed, but from overcoming that thought. As long as the fear of death persists, one will incline away from reason and toward passion (hawa').' The argument is Epicurean. The passions here, as in Epicurus, are thought of as neuroses, compulsions, pleasureless addictions, to use al-Razi's description (his word for an addict is mudmin). The glutton, the miser, even the sexual obsessive, are, by al-Razi's analysis, as much moved by the fear of death as by natural appetites. For natural needs, as Epicurus would explain, are always in measure. The unwholesome excess that makes vice a disease comes from the irrational and unselfconscious mental linking of natural pleasures and gratifications with security, that is, a sense of freedom from the fear of death. God has provided what we need to know, not in the arbitrary and divisive gift of special revelation, which only foments bloodshed and contention, but in reason, which belongs equally to all. Ordinary men are fully capable of thinking for themselves and need no guidance from another. A philosopher, he urges, does not slavishly follow the actions and ideas of some master. But he also affirms a belief in progress, at least for individuals, and denies that one is

trapped within the teachings of the great founders of traditions. (http://www. muslimphilosophy.com/ip/rep/H021.htm)

al-Farabi, Abu Nasr (c.870-950)

At the heart of al-Farabi's political philosophy is the concept of happiness (sa'ada). The virtuous society (al-ijtima' al-fadil) is defined as that in which people cooperate to gain happiness. The virtuous city (al-madina al-fadila) is one where there is cooperation in achieving happiness. The virtuous world (al-ma'mura al-fadila) will only occur when all its constituent nations collaborate to achieve happiness. If salvation in some form is reserved for the inhabitants of the virtuous city, and if the essence of that city is happiness, then it is no exaggeration to say that salvation is the reward of those who cooperate in the achievement of human happiness (sa'ada). http://www.muslimphilosophy.com/ip/rep/H021.htm

al-Sijistani, Abu Sulayman Muhammad (c.932-c.1000)

Knowledge implies two types: natural and supernatural. There are four degrees of knowledge: sensible knowledge possessed by non-reasoning animals; absolutely and exclusively intelligible knowledge possessed by the celestial bodies; the sensible-intelligible knowledge tied up with the imagination of those who have not reached perfect purity; and the intelligible-sensible knowledge which has been arrived at through rational and speculative investigation. This is the highest knowledge humans, including such persons as philosophers, augurs (kahins) and prophets, can acquire. Intuition, however, is the noblest kind of knowledge because it presents itself by itself in the soul and is not subject to generation and corruption. Through reason we overcome all obstacles to reach God through the intellect, which is the medium between human beings and the supernatural world. Reason has the power to contact the super-sensible beings until it reaches the First Being.

Having been greatly interested in the body-soul relationship, al-Sijistani distinguished between soul (nafs) and spirit (ruh), considering the soul to be a simple substance imperceptible to the senses and not subject to change or corruption. According to him, human beings are so by virtue of having a soul and not by the possession of a body, although the soul cannot make a human being by itself. The soul is the principle of knowledge, the body the principle of action. Because of the rival elements, nature versus reason, that constitute a human being and pull him in opposite directions, it is important to take reason as a guide. It alone can ensure our ultimate happiness, namely the knowledge of God and the good which he has reserved for the virtuous. One should aim high towards the celestial world in order to reach eternal life." (http://www.muslimphilosophy.com/ip/rep/H040)

Ibn Miskawayh, Ahmad ibn Muhammad (c.940-1030)

Ibn Miskawayh's discussion of virtue combines Aristotelian with Platonic ideas. Virtue is the perfection of the aspect of the soul (that is, human reason) that represents the essence of humanity and distinguishes it from lower forms of existence. Our virtue increases in so far as we develop and improve our ability to deliberate and apply reason to our lives. We should do this in accordance with the mean, the point most distant from two extremes, and justice results when we manage to achieve this. Ibn Miskawayh combines the Platonic division of virtues with an Aristotelian understanding of what virtue actually is, and adds to this the idea that the more these virtues can be treated as a unity, the better. This is because, he argues, that unity is equivalent to perfection, while multiplicity is equivalent to a meaningless plurality of physical objects. This idea is not just based upon a Pythagorean aesthetic. Ibn Miskawayh argues further that the notion of justice when it deals with eternal and immaterial principles is a simple idea, while human justice by contrast is variable and depends upon the changing nature of particular states and communities. The law of the state is based upon the contingent features of the time, while the divine law specifies what is to be done everywhere and at every time. The highest form of happiness exists when we can abandon the requirements of this world and are able to receive the emanations flowing from above that will perfect our intellects and enable us to be illuminated by divine light. The eventual aim seems to be the throwing off of the trappings of our physical existence and following entirely spiritual aims in mystical contemplation of the deity. This mystical level of happiness seems to rank higher than mere intellectual perfection, yet Ibn Miskawayh is particularly interesting in the practical advice he gives on how to develop our ordinary capacity for virtue. He regards the cultivation of our moral health in a very Aristotelian way as akin to the cultivation of physical health, requiring measures to preserve our moral equilibrium. We ought to keep our emotions under control and carry out practices that help both to restrain us on particular occasions and also to develop personality traits that will maintain that level of restraint throughout our lives. To eradicate faults, we must investigate their ultimate causes and seek to replace these with more helpful alternatives. Take the fear of death, for example: this is a baseless fear, since the soul is immortal and cannot die. Our bodies will perish, but they must do so since we are contingent; to acknowledge that contingency and also to wish that we were not thus contingent is some sort of contradiction. If we are worried by the pain involved in dying, then it is the pain we fear, not death itself. Ibn Miskawayh argues, along with al-Kindi and the Cynics and Stoics who no doubt influenced him on this issue, that to reconcile ourselves to reality we have to understand the real nature of our feelings. We have to use reason to work out what we should do and feel, since otherwise we are at the mercy of our feelings and the varying influences that come to us from outside ourselves. (http://www.muslimphilosophy.com/ip/rep/H042)

Ibn Bajja, Abu Bakr Muhammad ibn Yahya ibn as-Say'igh (d. 1138)

Ibn Bajja rejects the Sufi concept that the ultimate human end is the pleasure (al-ladhdha) which results from witnessing (mushahadat) the divine world internally, in a higher sensible form as presented by the common sense, imagination and memory. According to him, this amounts to saying that 'having pleasure internally is the ultimate objective of knowing the Truth through the internal senses'. However, this is not the case since this pleasure is not sought for its own sake. In support of his view, Ibn Bajja mentions among other things that if pleasure of the internal senses were the ultimate human end, then reason (which is a higher power than the internal senses) as well as its knowledge would be superfluous and futile.

Because knowledge of the internal senses is higher than that of the external senses, the objects of the former being more enduring than those of the latter, the pleasure of the internal senses is higher than that of the external senses. The assertion that the former objects are more enduring than the latter is demonstrated by the fact that one can imagine the existence of something that has ceased to exist externally. However, even knowledge of the internal senses still falls short of reaching the sublimity of the knowledge of reason since the objects of the former do not endure as much as those of the latter. Only the objects of the latter endure permanently, unaffected by the forgetfulness or even the removal of their subject. Knowledge of these permanent objects gives the knower a permanent status since the knower and the known in this case are one. It also gives the highest and most permanent pleasure. The state of happiness is one which cannot be described in language, owing to its nobility, pleasure, beauty and goodness. When human beings reach this ultimate end, they become simple intellects of which it is true to say that they are nothing but divine. The knower, or happy person, may exist in society in either a virtuous or a nonvirtuous city. A virtuous city is one whose members are all complete in knowledge, while in a nonvirtuous city the contrary is the case. If perfected people exist in a nonvirtuous city, they must live in isolation from the rest of society, for their complete knowledge makes them 'strangers' or 'weeds', that is, those whose true opinions are contrary to the opinions of society. While isolation from society is not natural or essential for a human being in the natural or virtuous city, it is accidental to one's nature and must be practised in order to preserve oneself from the corruption of the nonvirtuous cities." (http://www.muslimphilosophy.com/ip/rep/H023.htm) "

Ibn Rush Abu'l Walid Muhammad (1126 – 98)

Ibn Rushd argued that a distinction should be drawn between moral notions and divine commands. Here he follows an Aristotelian approach. Since everything has a nature, and this nature defines its end, we as things also have natures and ends at which our behaviour is directed. The purpose of a plant is to grow and the aim of a saw is to cut, but what is the purpose of a human being? One of our ultimate aims is to be happy and to avoid actions which lead to unhappiness. It is not difficult here to align Islamic and Aristotelian principles: moral virtue leads to happiness since, if we do what we should in accordance with our nature, we will be able to achieve happiness. This happiness may be interpreted in a number of ways, either as a mixture of social and religious activities or as an entirely intellectual ideal. However, the latter is possible only for a very few, and neither religion nor philosophy would approve of it as the ultimate aim for the majority of the community. There is an essential social dimension to human happiness which makes the identification of happiness with correct moral and religious behaviour much easier to establish. It is conceivable that someone would try to live completely apart from the community to concentrate upon entirely intellectual pursuits, but this way of living is inferior to a life in which there is a concentration upon intellectual thought combined with integration within the practices of a particular society. One might expect that Ibn Rushd, who was working within an Islamic context, would identify happiness and misery with some aspect of the afterlife, but he was unable to accept the traditional view of the afterlife as containing surviving individuals like ourselves. What the notion of the afterlife is supposed to achieve is an understanding that the scope of personal action is wider than might immediately appear to be the case. Without religious language and imagery, ordinary believers may find it difficult to grasp that our moral actions affect not only ourselves but the happiness of the whole community, not just at a particular time or in a particular place but as a species. When we behave badly we damage our own chances of human flourishing, and this affects our personal opportunities for achieving happiness and growing as people. It also affects our relationships with other people, resulting in a weakening of society. While it is possibly true that the misery consequent upon evil-doing may not follow us personally after our death, it may well follow the community. The importance of the notion of an afterlife is that it points to the wider terms of reference in which moral action has life. In his commentary on Plato's Republic, Ibn Rushd modifies Plato in terms of his own Aristotelian views and applies the text to the contemporary state. He uses Plato's idea of the transformation and deterioration of the ideal state into four imperfect states to illustrate aspects of past and contemporary political organization in the Islamic world. He takes mischievous pleasure in comparing the theologians of his own time, the mutakallimun, to Plato's sophists. He describes the theologians as a genuine danger to the state and to the purity of Islam, and suggests to the ruler that a ban on the publicizing of their activities is advisable. In this and many of his other works, Ibn Rushd stresses the importance of a careful understanding of the relationship between religion and philosophy in the state. However, it is worth emphasizing that the only advantage which religion has over reason is that the former involves a practical form of knowledge which is not necessarily possessed by the latter. (http://www.muslimphilosophy.com/ir/art/ibn%20rushd-rep.htm)

MULTIVARIATE RESULTS FOR THE CORE DEPENDENT VARIABLES OF OUR MODEL

Life Satisfaction	Dummy for being landlocked	Dummy for transition economy	Urbanization ratio, 1990	(1-S)/GNP	state interventionism (absence of ec. freedom)	MNC PEN 1995	low comparative international price level (ERD)	EU-membership (EU-15)	Muslims as % of total population	ln(GDP PPP pc)	ln (GDP PPP pc)^2	world bank pension reform	constant
	0,323	0,030	-0,083	0,002	0,107	-0,105	0,005	-0,253	-0,011	-0,005	-0,438	-0,324	5,843
	0,221	0,066	1,062	0,002	0,273	0,085	0,004	0,167	0,006	0,006	0,231	0,183	4,195
	0,585	0,766											
	14,237	121,000											
	100,357	71,077											
t-test and direction of influence	1,463	0,450	-0,078	0,743	0,392	-1,227	1,372	-1,518	**-1,823**	-0,841	**-1,898**	**-1,773**	1,393
t-test and direction of influence^2	2,141	0,203	0,006	0,553	0,154	1,505	1,881	2,304	3,324	0,708	3,604	3,144	1,940
t-test and direction of influence^0,5	1,463	0,450	0,078	0,743	0,392	1,227	1,372	1,518	1,823	0,841	1,898	1,773	1,393
degrees of freedom	121,000	121,000	121,000	121,000	121,000	121,000	121,000	121,000	121,000	121,000	121,000	121,000	121,000
error probability	0,146	0,653	0,938	0,459	0,695	0,222	0,173	0,132	**0,071**	0,402	**0,060**	**0,079**	0,166
F equation	14,237	14,237	14,237	14,237	14,237	14,237	14,237	14,237	14,237	14,237	14,237	14,237	14,237
error probability, entire equation	0,000	0,000	0,000	0,000	0,000	0,000	0,000	0,000	0,000	0,000	0,000	0,000	0,000
EF Ecological Footprint	Dummy for being landlocked	Dummy for transition economy	Urbanization ratio, 1990	(1-S)/GNP	state interventionism (absence of ec. freedom)	MNC PEN 1995	low comparative international price level (ERD)	EU-membership (EU-15)	Muslims as % of total population	ln(GDP PPP pc)	ln (GDP PPP pc)^2	world bank pension reform	constant
	-0,235	0,553	-7,947	0,001	-0,034	0,001	0,001	-0,258	-0,003	0,003	1,069	-0,349	30,191
	0,226	0,067	1,087	0,002	0,279	0,087	0,004	0,171	0,006	0,006	0,236	0,187	4,294
	0,852	0,784											
	58,237	121,000											
	430,034	74,458											

EF Ecological Footprint	Dummy for being landlocked	Dummy for transition economy	Urbanization ratio, 1990	(1-S)/GNP	state interventionism (absence of ec. freedom)	MNC PEN 1995	low comparative international price level (ERD)	EU-membership (EU-15)	Muslims as % of total population	ln(GDP PPP pc)	ln (GDP PPP pc)^2	world bank pension reform	constant
t-test and direction of influence	-1,039	**8,195**	**-7,307**	0,595	-0,122	0,016	0,369	-1,510	-0,515	0,516	**4,525**	**-1,866**	7,032
t-test and direction of influence^2	1,079	67,153	53,399	0,355	0,015	0,000	0,136	2,281	0,265	0,266	20,472	3,481	49,445
t-test and direction of influence^0,5	1,039	8,195	7,307	0,595	0,122	0,016	0,369	1,510	0,515	0,516	4,525	1,866	7,032
degrees of freedom	121,000	121,000	121,000	121,000	121,000	121,000	121,000	121,000	121,000	121,000	121,000	121,000	121,000
error probability	0,301	0,000	0,000	0,553	0,903	0,987	0,713	0,134	0,607	0,607	0,000	0,064	0,000
F equation	58,237	58,237	58,237	58,237	58,237	58,237	58,237	58,237	58,237	58,237	58,237	58,237	58,237
error probability, entire equation	0,000	0,000	0,000	0,000	0,000	0,000	0,000	0,000	0,000	0,000	0,000	0,000	0,000
HPI Happy Planet Index	Dummy for being landlocked	Dummy for transition economy	Urbanization ratio, 1990	(1-S)/GNP	state interventionism (absence of ec. freedom)	MNC PEN 1995	low comparative international price level (ERD)	EU-membership (EU-15)	Muslims as % of total population	ln(GDP PPP pc)	ln (GDP PPP pc)^2	world bank pension reform	constant
	4,487	-3,485	58,304	0,032	1,088	0,180	-0,048	-2,702	-0,002	-0,028	-6,503	-4,548	-186,645
	2,804	0,837	13,497	0,026	3,462	1,082	0,049	2,117	0,080	0,071	2,932	2,323	53,288
	0,276	9,736											
	3,847	121,000											
	4375,470	11469,325											
t-test and direction of influence	1,600	**-4,163**	**4,320**	1,211	0,314	0,166	-0,999	-1,276	-0,024	-0,395	**-2,218**	**-1,957**	-3,503
t-test and direction of influence^2	2,561	17,328	18,661	1,466	0,099	0,028	0,998	1,629	0,001	0,156	4,921	3,832	12,268
t-test and direction of influence^0,5	1,600	4,163	4,320	1,211	0,314	0,166	0,999	1,276	0,024	0,395	2,218	1,957	3,503
degrees of freedom	121,000	121,000	121,000	121,000	121,000	121,000	121,000	121,000	121,000	121,000	121,000	121,000	121,000
error probability	0,112	0,000	0,000	0,228	0,754	0,868	0,320	0,204	0,981	0,693	0,028	0,053	0,001
F equation	3,847	3,847	3,847	3,847	3,847	3,847	3,847	3,847	3,847	3,847	3,847	3,847	3,847
error probability, entire equation	0,000	0,000	0,000	0,000	0,000	0,000	0,000	0,000	0,000	0,000	0,000	0,000	0,000

Table. Continued

	Dummy for being landlocked	Dummy for transition economy	Urbanization ratio, 1990	(1-S)/GNP	state interventionism (absence of ec. freedom)	MNC PEN 1995	low comparative international price level (ERD)	EU-membership (EU-15)	Muslims as % of total population	ln(GDP PPP pc)	ln (GDP PPP pc)^2	world bank pension model	constant
Human Development Index HDI 2005	0,00672	-0,0096	0,29242	-0,00017	0,02326	0,0019	-0,00052	-0,01411	0,00099	0,00063	0,08237	-0,0361	-1,04701
	0,01677	0,00501	0,0807	0,00016	0,0207	0,00647	0,00029	0,01266	0,00048	0,00042	0,01753	0,01389	0,31861
	0,9123	0,05821											
	104,867	121											
	4,26422	0,41002											
t-test and direction of influence	0,40108	-1,918	3,6236	-1,096	1,12366	0,29352	-1,79356	-1,11434	2,0723	1,4968	4,699	-2,599	-3,28619
t-test and direction of influence^2	0,16087	3,67757	13,1308	1,20166	1,26261	0,08615	3,21686	1,24176	4,29457	2,24048	22,0806	6,75303	10,7991
t-test and direction of influence^0,5	0,40108	1,9177	3,62365	1,0962	1,12366	0,29352	1,79356	1,11434	2,07233	1,49682	4,699	2,59866	3,28619
degrees of freedom	121	121	121	121	121	121	121	121	121	121	121	121	121
error probability	0,68907	0,05751	0,00043	0,27517	0,26338	0,76963	0,07538	0,26734	0,0404	0,137	7E-06	0,0105	0,00133
F equation	104,867	104,867	104,867	104,867	104,867	104,867	104,867	104,867	104,867	104,867	104,867	104,867	104,867
error probability, entire equation	1,3E-60	1,3E-60	1,3E-60	1,3E-60	1,3E-60	1,3E-60	1,3E-60	1,3E-60	1,3E-60	1,3E-60	1,3E-60	1,3E-60	1,3E-60
Yale Columbia Environment Sustainability Index ESI-Index	2,66396	0,58816	-7,8798	-0,04764	-2,7725	-0,61607	-0,01074	-2,69734	-0,03358	-0,02186	1,20586	0,50561	87,1714
	1,9726	0,60673	9,79788	0,01864	2,47217	0,76736	0,04322	1,50938	0,07963	0,05352	2,02818	1,68061	38,6864
	0,3963	6,68845											
	6,12586	112											
	3288,52	5010,37											

Yale Columbia Environment Sustainability Index ESI-Index	Dummy for being landlocked	Dummy for transition economy	Urbanization ratio, 1990	(1-S)/GNP	state interventionism (absence of ec. freedom)	MNC PEN 1995	low comparative international price level (ERD)	EU-membership (EU-15)	Muslims as % of total population	ln(GDP PPP pc)	ln (GDP PPP pc)^2	world bank pension model	constant
t-test and direction of influence	1,35048	0,96938	-0,80424	-2,55581	-1,12	-0,80284	-0,24842	**-1,78705**	-0,42167	-0,40849	0,59455	0,30085	2,25328
t-test and direction of influence^2	1,8238	0,9397	0,6468	6,53218	1,25772	0,64455	0,06171	3,19353	0,17781	0,16686	0,35349	0,09051	5,07729
t-test and direction of influence^0,5	1,35048	0,96938	0,80424	2,55581	1,12148	0,80284	0,24842	1,78705	0,42167	0,40849	0,59455	0,30085	2,25328
degrees of freedom	112	112	112	112	112	112	112	112	112	112	112	112	112
error probability	0,17958	0,33444	0,42296	0,01193	0,264	0,42377	0,80426	0,07664	0,67407	0,68369	0,55334	0,76409	0,02619
F equation	6,12586	6,12586	6,12586	6,12586	6,12586	6,12586	6,12586	6,12586	6,12586	6,12586	6,12586	6,12586	6,12586
error probability, entire equation	7E-09	7E-09	7E-09	7E-09	7E-09	7E-09	7E-09	7E-09	7E-09	7E-09	7E-09	7E-09	7E-09

economic growth, 1990-2003	Dummy for being landlocked	Dummy for transition economy	Urbanization ratio, 1990	(1-S)/GNP	state interventionism (absence of ec. freedom)	MNC PEN 1995	low comparative international price level (ERD)	EU-membership (EU-15)	Muslims as % of total population	ln(GDP PPP pc)	ln (GDP PPP pc)^2	world bank pension model	constant
	0,5209	-0,13562	3,31979	0,00268	-0,14286	0,07358	0,0046	-1,0415	0,02149	-0,05132	-0,52988	-1,2622	-11,024
	0,55419	0,16742	2,70277	0,00524	0,68301	0,21399	0,00973	0,42049	0,01583	0,014	0,58132	0,46419	10,6734
	0,3195	1,92033											
	4,61627	118											
	204,278	435,143											
t-test and direction of influence	0,93993	-0,81007	1,22829	0,51077	-0,20917	0,34387	0,4725	**-2,47688**	1,3579	**-3,666**	-0,91152	**-2,719**	-1,03284
t-test and direction of influence^2	0,88346	0,65621	1,5087	0,26088	0,04375	0,11825	0,22329	6,13492	1,84401	13,4395	0,83087	7,39378	1,06677
t-test and direction of influence^0,5	0,93993	0,81007	1,22829	0,51077	0,20917	0,34387	0,47254	2,47688	1,35794	3,666	0,91152	2,71915	1,03284
degrees of freedom	118	118	118	118	118	118	118	118	118	118	118	118	118
error probability	0,34918	0,41953	0,22178	0,61047	0,83468	0,73155	0,6374	0,01467	0,1771	0,0004	0,36388	0,0075	0,30379
F equation	4,61627	4,61627	4,61627	4,61627	4,61627	4,61627	4,61627	4,61627	4,61627	4,61627	4,61627	4,61627	4,61627

Table. Continued

economic growth, 1990-2003	Dummy for being landlocked	Dummy for transition economy	Urbanization ratio, 1990	(1-S)/GNP	state interventionism (absence of ec. freedom)	MNC PEN 1995	low comparative international price level (ERD)	EU-membership (EU-15)	Muslims as % of total population	ln(GDP PPP pc)	ln(GDP PPP pc)^2	world bank pension model	constant
error probability, entire equation	1,3E-06	1,3E-06	1,3E-06	1,3E-06	1,3E-06	1,3E-06	1,3E-06	1,3E-06	1,3E-06	1,3E-06	1,3E-06	1,3E-06	1,3E-06
life expectancy, 1995-2000	Dummy for being landlocked	Dummy for transition economy	Urbanization ratio, 1990	(1-S)/GNP	state interventionism (absence of ec. freedom)	MNC PEN 1995	low comparative international price level (ERD)	EU-membership (EU-15)	Muslims as % of total population	ln(GDP PPP pc)	ln(GDP PPP pc)^2	world bank pension model	constant
	0,02837	-1,08837	25,4202	0,02657	1,87425	0,44256	-0,04016	-1,67693	0,11454	0,05539	3,96443	-2,75384	-69,1697
	1,59236	0,47537	7,66407	0,01503	1,96583	0,61446	0,02755	1,20218	0,0454	0,04024	1,66476	1,3193	30,2592
	0,7836	5,52849											
	36,5128	121											
	13391,8	3698,26											
t-test and direction of influence	0,01782	-2,29	3,3168	1,76825	0,95341	0,72024	-1,458	-1,39491	2,5228	1,3764	2,3814	-2,087	-2,28591
t-test and direction of influence^2	0,00032	5,24188	11,0011	3,12672	0,90899	0,51874	2,12452	1,94576	6,36428	1,89444	5,67099	4,35701	5,22537
t-test and direction of influence^0,5	0,01782	2,28952	3,31679	1,76825	0,95341	0,72024	1,45757	1,39491	2,52275	1,37638	2,38138	2,08735	2,28591
degrees of freedom	121	121	121	121	121	121	121	121	121	121	121	121	121
error probability	0,98581	0,0238	0,0012	0,07954	0,34228	0,47277	0,1475	0,1656	0,0129	0,1712	0,0188	0,039	0,024
F equation	36,5128	36,5128	36,5128	36,5128	36,5128	36,5128	36,5128	36,5128	36,5128	36,5128	36,5128	36,5128	36,5128
error probability, entire equation	9,8E-37	9,8E-37	9,8E-37	9,8E-37	9,8E-37	9,8E-37	9,8E-37	9,8E-37	9,8E-37	9,8E-37	9,8E-37	9,8E-37	9,8E-37

Political rights violations,1998	Dummy for being landlocked	Dummy for transition economy	Urbanization ratio, 1990	(1-S)/GNP	state interventionism (absence of ec. freedom)	MNC PEN 1995	low comparative international price level (ERD)	EU-membership (EU-15)	Muslims as % of total population	ln(GDP PPP pc)	ln (GDP PPP pc)^2	world bank pension model	constant
	0,02732	-0,09773	0,9794	0,01986	-0,53143	0,04607	0,02063	1,41188	-0,04526	0,02258	-0,63775	0,85766	-4,05782
	0,38949	0,11627	1,87461	0,00368	0,48084	0,1503	0,00674	0,29405	0,01111	0,00984	0,4072	0,3227	7,40131
	0,641	1,35225											
	18,0003	121											
	394,98	221,258											
t-test and direction of influence	0,07015	-0,84052	0,52246	5,4036	-1,10522	0,30651	3,0612	4,8015	-4,075	2,2938	-1,56619	2,6578	-0,54826
t-test and direction of influence^2	0,00492	0,70648	0,27296	29,199	1,2215	0,09395	9,37085	23,0543	16,6091	5,26143	2,45296	7,06375	0,30059
t-test and direction of influence^0,5	0,07015	0,84052	0,52246	5,40361	1,10522	0,30651	3,06118	4,80149	4,07542	2,29378	1,56619	2,65777	0,54826
degrees of freedom	121	121	121	121	121	121	121	121	121	121	121	121	121
error probability	0,94419	0,40227	0,60231	3E-07	0,27126	0,75974	0,0027	5E-06	8E-05	0,0235	0,11991	0,0089	0,58453
F equation	18,0003	18,0003	18,0003	18,0003	18,0003	18,0003	18,0003	18,0003	18,0003	18,0003	18,0003	18,0003	18,0003
error probability, entire equation	2,5E-23	2,5E-23	2,5E-23	2,5E-23	2,5E-23	2,5E-23	2,5E-23	2,5E-23	2,5E-23	2,5E-23	2,5E-23	2,5E-23	2,5E-23
Civil liberty violations, 1998	Dummy for being landlocked	Dummy for transition economy	Urbanization ratio, 1990	(1-S)/GNP	state interventionism (absence of ec. freedom)	MNC PEN 1995	low comparative international price level (ERD)	EU-membership (EU-15)	Muslims as % of total population	ln(GDP PPP pc)	ln (GDP PPP pc)^2	world bank pension model	constant
	-0,0824	-0,11294	1,41687	0,01306	-0,3495	0,08353	0,00991	1,16064	-0,02268	0,01765	-0,29107	0,22873	-5,27092
	0,28552	0,08524	1,37419	0,00269	0,35248	0,11018	0,00494	0,21556	0,00814	0,00722	0,2985	0,23656	5,42557
	0,6598	0,99128											
	19,5541	121											
	230,572	118,898											
t-test and direction of influence	-0,28862	-1,32502	1,03106	4,8469	-0,99156	0,75813	2,007	5,3844	-2,786	2,4466	-0,97513	0,96691	-0,9715
t-test and direction of influence^2	0,0833	1,75568	1,06308	23,4923	0,98319	0,57476	4,02793	28,9922	7,75959	5,98595	0,95089	0,93491	0,9438
t-test and direction of influence^0,5	0,28862	1,32502	1,03106	4,84688	0,99156	0,75813	2,00697	5,38444	2,7856	2,44662	0,97513	0,96691	0,9715

Table. Continued

Civil liberty violations, 1998	Dummy for being landlocked	Dummy for transition economy	Urbanization ratio, 1990	(1-S)/GNP	state interventionism (absence of ec. freedom)	MNC PEN 1995	low comparative international price level (ERD)	EU-membership (EU-15)	Muslims as % of total population	ln(GDP PPP pc)	ln (GDP PPP pc)^2	world bank pension model	constant
degrees of freedom	121	121	121	121	121	121	121	121	121	121	121	121	121
error probability	0,77337	0,18766	0,30457	4E-06	0,32339	0,44985	0,047	4E-07	0,0062	0,0159	0,33144	0,33552	0,33324
F equation	19,5541	19,5541	19,5541	19,5541	19,5541	19,5541	19,5541	19,5541	19,5541	19,5541	19,5541	19,5541	19,5541
error probability, entire equation	9,4E-25	9,4E-25	9,4E-25	9,4E-25	9,4E-25	9,4E-25	9,4E-25	9,4E-25	9,4E-25	9,4E-25	9,4E-25	9,4E-25	9,4E-25

% people not expected to survive age 60	Dummy for being landlocked	Dummy for transition economy	Urbanization ratio, 1990	(1-S)/GNP	state interventionism (absence of ec. freedom)	MNC PEN 1995	low comparative international price level (ERD)	EU-membership (EU-15)	Muslims as % of total population	ln(GDP PPP pc)	ln (GDP PPP pc)^2	world bank pension model	constant
	-0,67774	2,05375	-46,0983	-0,07807	-3,8176	-1,41317	0,0551	3,17324	-0,19445	-0,08754	-6,10642	5,72347	268,23
	2,93777	0,87702	14,1395	0,02772	3,62679	1,13363	0,05083	2,21792	0,08376	0,07424	3,07134	2,434	55,8255
	0,7322	10,1996											
	27,5717	121											
t-test and direction of influence	-0,2307	2,3417	-3,26	-2,81613	-1,05261	-1,24658	1,0841	1,43073	-2,321	-1,17921	-1,988	2,3515	4,80479
	34419,8	12587,8											
t-test and direction of influence^2	0,05322	5,48374	10,6292	7,9306	1,10799	1,55397	1,1752	2,04698	5,38902	1,39055	3,95292	5,52941	23,086
t-test and direction of influence^0,5	0,2307	2,34174	3,26024	2,81613	1,05261	1,24658	1,08407	1,43073	2,32143	1,17921	1,9882	2,35147	4,80479
degrees of freedom	121	121	121	121	121	121	121	121	121	121	121	121	121
error probability	0,81794	0,0208	0,0014	0,00568	0,29462	0,21496	0,2805	0,15509	0,0219	0,24063	0,049	0,0203	4,5E-06
F equation	27,5717	27,5717	27,5717	27,5717	27,5717	27,5717	27,5717	27,5717	27,5717	27,5717	27,5717	27,5717	27,5717
error probability, entire equation	4,3E-31	4,3E-31	4,3E-31	4,3E-31	4,3E-31	4,3E-31	4,3E-31	4,3E-31	4,3E-31	4,3E-31	4,3E-31	4,3E-31	4,3E-31

quintile ratio (share of income/consumption richest 20% to poorest 20%)	Dummy for being landlocked	Dummy for transition economy	Urbanization ratio, 1990	(1-S)/GNP	state interventionism (absence of ec. freedom)	MNC PEN 1995	low comparative international price level (ERD)	EU-membership (EU-15)	Muslims as % of total population	ln(GDP PPP pc)	ln (GDP PPP pc)^2	world bank pension model	constant
	-0,26802	-1,31851	19,8771	-0,03707	-3,54933	-1,23455	0,03248	0,70355	0,01855	0,04992	-6,19603	1,77188	-63,529
	1,72666	0,51036	8,28173	0,01711	2,01853	0,76	0,03424	1,42216	0,0597	0,04799	1,94377	1,42939	32,7963
	0,316	5,2702											
	3,46512	90											
	1154,93	2499,75											
t-test and direction of influence	-0,15522	-2,583	2,4001	-2,167	-1,758	-1,6244	0,9485	0,49471	0,31076	1,04022	-3,188	1,23961	-1,93708
t-test and direction of influence^2	0,02409	6,67431	5,76056	4,69564	3,09186	2,63868	0,89966	0,24473	0,09657	1,08206	10,161	1,53663	3,75227
t-test and direction of influence^0,5	0,15522	2,58347	2,40012	2,16694	1,75837	1,6244	0,9485	0,49471	0,31076	1,04022	3,18763	1,23961	1,93708
degrees of freedom	90	90	90	90	90	90	90	90	90	90	90	90	90
error probability	0,87699	0,0114	0,0184	0,0329	0,0821	0,10779	0,34541	0,62201	0,7567	0,30102	0,002	0,21834	0,05587
F equation	3,46512	3,46512	3,46512	3,46512	3,46512	3,46512	3,46512	3,46512	3,46512	3,46512	3,46512	3,46512	3,46512
error probability, entire equation	0,00016	0,00016	0,00016	0,00016	0,00016	0,00016	0,00016	0,00016	0,00016	0,00016	0,00016	0,00016	0,00016

CO2 emissions per capita	Dummy for being landlocked	Dummy for transition economy	Urbanization ratio, 1990	(1-S)/GNP	state interventionism (absence of ec. freedom)	MNC PEN 1995	low comparative international price level (ERD)	EU-membership (EU-15)	Muslims as % of total population	ln(GDP PPP pc)	ln (GDP PPP pc)^2	world bank pension model	constant
	-1,46819	1,59269	-23,5245	0,00702	-2,32819	0,54124	0,05468	0,34168	-0,05653	0,05971	2,57767	-0,31429	81,528
	0,75582	0,24221	3,92803	0,00732	0,932	0,33873	0,01695	0,60961	0,02799	0,02027	0,81008	0,66658	15,5646
	0,7472	2,61691											
	27,5822	112											
	2266,67	767,001											
t-test and direction of influence	-1,943	6,5757	-5,989	0,95851	-2,498	1,59787	3,2264	0,56049	-2,019	2,9465	3,182	-0,4715	5,23804
t-test and direction of influence^2	3,77339	43,2403	35,8668	0,91874	6,24029	2,55318	10,4094	0,31415	4,07764	8,68186	10,1251	0,22231	27,4371

Table. Continued

CO2 emissions per capita	Dummy for being landlocked	Dummy for transition economy	Urbanization ratio, 1990	(1-S)/GNP	state interventionism (absence of ec. freedom)	MNC PEN 1995	low comparative international price level (ERD)	EU-membership (EU-15)	Muslims as % of total population	ln(GDP PPP pc)	ln (GDP PPP pc)^2	world bank pension model	constant
t-test and direction of influence^{0,5}	1,94252	6,57574	5,98889	0,95851	2,49806	1,59787	3,22635	0,56049	2,01932	2,9465	3,18199	0,4715	5,23804
degrees of freedom	112	112	112	112	112	112	112	112	112	112	112	112	112
error probability	0,0546	2E-09	3E-08	0,33987	0,0139	0,11289	0,0016	0,57627	0,0458	0,0039	0,0019	0,6382	7,7E-07
F equation	27,5822	27,5822	27,5822	27,5822	27,5822	27,5822	27,5822	27,5822	27,5822	27,5822	27,5822	27,5822	27,5822
error probability, entire equation	7E-30	7E-30	7E-30	7E-30	7E-30	7E-30	7E-30	7E-30	7E-30	7E-30	7E-30	7E-30	7E-30

eco-social market economy (GDP output per kg energy use)	Dummy for being landlocked	Dummy for transition economy	Urbanization ratio, 1990	(1-S)/GNP	state interventionism (absence of ec. freedom)	MNC PEN 1995	low comparative international price level (ERD)	EU-membership (EU-15)	Muslims as % of total population	ln(GDP PPP pc)	ln (GDP PPP pc)^2	world bank pension model	constant
	0,96149	0,27053	-3,25367	0,00067	1,01667	-0,36437	-0,01949	-0,06846	0,02821	-0,0201	-1,5258	0,53151	12,701
	0,38122	0,1279	2,09287	0,00397	0,46947	0,16261	0,00959	0,32165	0,01452	0,01084	0,41331	0,38232	8,43817
	0,71441	1,3049											
	19,8035	95											
	404,65	161,763											
t-test and direction of influence	2,5221	2,1151	-1,555	0,16926	2,1656	-2,241	-2,032	-0,21285	1,9432	-1,85386	-3,692	1,39024	1,50518
t-test and direction of influence^2	6,36112	4,47369	2,41692	0,02865	4,6897	5,02107	4,12844	0,0453	3,7762	3,4368	13,6282	1,93277	2,26558
t-test and direction of influence^{0,5}	2,52213	2,11511	1,55464	0,16926	2,16557	2,24078	2,03186	0,21285	1,94324	1,85386	3,69163	1,39024	1,50518
degrees of freedom	95	95	95	95	95	95	95	95	95	95	95	95	95
error probability	0,0133	0,037	0,1234	0,86595	0,0328	0,0274	0,045	0,8319	0,0549	0,06686	0,0004	0,1677	0,13559
F equation	19,8035	19,8035	19,8035	19,8035	19,8035	19,8035	19,8035	19,8035	19,8035	19,8035	19,8035	19,8035	19,8035
error probability, entire equation	2,9E-22	2,9E-22	2,9E-22	2,9E-22	2,9E-22	2,9E-22	2,9E-22	2,9E-22	2,9E-22	2,9E-22	2,9E-22	2,9E-22	2,9E-22

female economic activity rate as % of male economic activity rate	Dummy for being landlocked	Dummy for transition economy	Urbanization ratio, 1990	(I-S)/GNP	state interventionism (absence of ec. freedom)	MNC PEN 1995	low comparative international price level (ERD)	EU-membership (EU-15)	Muslims as % of total population	ln(GDP PPP pc)	ln (GDP PPP pc)^2	world bank pension model	constant
	0,6381	6,5583	-108,566	-0,12369	-1,73496	2,13565	-0,06928	-2,30312	-0,07965	-0,26016	23,3015	-1,54033	523,72
	3,68632	1,10049	17,7423	0,03478	4,55091	1,42248	0,06378	2,78306	0,1051	0,09315	3,85392	3,05419	70,0501
	0,4922	12,7984											
	9,77458	121											
	19212,9	19819,8											
t-test and direction of influence	0,1731	5,95595	-6,119	-3,556	-0,38123	1,50135	-1,08617	-0,82755	-0,75783	-2,793	6,04619	-0,50433	7,47637
t-test and direction of influence^2	0,02996	35,5152	37,4427	12,6434	0,14534	2,25406	1,17977	0,68484	0,57431	7,79965	36,5564	0,25435	55,8961
t-test and direction of influence^0,5	0,1731	5,95946	6,11905	3,55575	0,38123	1,50135	1,08617	0,82755	0,75783	2,79279	6,04619	0,50433	7,47637
degrees of freedom	121	121	121	121	121	121	121	121	121	121	121	121	121
error probability	0,86286	3E-08	1E-08	0,0005	0,7037	0,13587	0,27956	0,40955	0,45003	0,0061	1,7E-08	0,61494	1,3E-11
F equation	9,77458	9,77458	9,77458	9,77458	9,77458	9,77458	9,77458	9,77458	9,77458	9,77458	9,77458	9,77458	9,77458
error probability, entire equation	3,1E-14	3,1E-14	3,1E-14	3,1E-14	3,1E-14	3,1E-14	3,1E-14	3,1E-14	3,1E-14	3,1E-14	3,1E-14	3,1E-14	3,1E-14

Legend: As in all EXCEL 7.0 outprints, first row: un-standardized regression coefficients, second row: standard errors, second last row: t-Test and direction of the influence. The values immediately below the standard errors are R^2 (third row, left side entry), F, and degrees of freedom (fourth row). Below that: ss reg; ss resid, i.e. the sum of squares of the regression and the sum of squares of the residuals. The right-hand entry in the third row is the standard error of the estimate y. Below the EXCEL outprints; we present materials for the t-test and the F-test for our regression results

DATA FOR THE ANALYSIS

The Independent Variables

Country code	Dummy for being landlocked	Dummy for transition economy	Urbanization ratio, 1990	(I-S)/GNP	state interventionism (absence of ec. freedom)	MNC PEN 1995	low comparative international price level (ERD)	EU-membership (EU-15)	Muslims as % of total population	ln(GDP PPP pc)	ln (GDP PPP pc)^2	world bank pension reform
Albania	0	1	35,7	22,678	3,7	8,7	3,4622	0	70	7,9389	63,027	0
Algeria	0	0	51,7	-0,0791	3,45	3,5	3,0917	0	99	8,4747	71,821	0
Angola	0	0	27,6	-10,187	4,5	58	4,793	0	1	7,5073	56,36	0
Argentina	0	0	86,5	2,5073	2,1	10,8	1,496	0	1,5	9,3938	88,243	1
Armenia	1	1	67,5	33,139	3,1	1,2	4,5051	0	2	7,6364	58,315	0
Australia	0	0	85,1	0,569	1,9	27,9	1,0878	0	1,5	10,019	100,38	1
Austria	1	0	64,5	0,5743	2,05	7,5	0,8634	1	4,7	10,05	101,01	0
Azerbaijan	1	1	54,4	34,373	4,2	6,1	4,5305	0	93,4	7,6846	59,054	0
Bahrain	0	0	87,6	-36,074	1,8	41,1	1,7161	0	85	9,4812	89,893	0
Bangladesh	0	0	15,7	5,0873	3,75	0,5	3,8894	0	88	7,2162	52,073	0
Belarus	1	1	66,8	5,9737	4,1	0,5	2,8987	0	0,5	8,7514	76,586	0
Belgium	0	0	96,5	-4,5312	2,1	40,8	0,915	1	3,5	10,053	101,06	0
Belize	0	0	47,5	4,9877	2,8	25,8	1,7164	0	1	8,4263	71,003	0
Benin	0	0	34,5	8,8146	2,9	18,9	2,2822	0	20	6,7653	45,77	0
Bolivia	1	0	55,6	9,1732	2,65	23,4	2,2468	0	0,01	7,7272	59,709	1
Botswana	1	0	41,5	-1,2089	2,95	23	1,988	0	1	8,7165	75,978	0
Brazil	0	0	74,7	2,664	3,5	6	1,4308	0	0,02	8,7986	77,415	0
Bulgaria	0	1	66,5	1,0566	3,4	3,4	3,9417	0	12,2	8,4782	71,88	0
Burkina Faso	1	0	13,6	16,238	3,4	3,4	3,6241	0	55	6,7683	45,809	0
Burundi	1	0	6,3	11,533	4	3,4	4,0689	0	10	6,345	40,259	0
Cambodia	0	0	17,5	9,509	3	12,1	4,8345	0	3,5	7,1365	50,929	0
Cameroon	0	0	40,3	-1,4917	3,4	13,3	2,4167	0	20	7,2959	53,23	0

Country code	Dummy for being landlocked	Dummy for transition economy	Urbanization ratio, 1990	(I-S)/GNP	state interventionism (absence of ec. freedom)	MNC PEN 1995	low comparative international price level (ERD)	EU-membership (EU-15)	Muslims as % of total population	ln(GDP PPP pc)	ln (GDP PPP pc)^2	world bank pension reform
Canada	0	0	76,6	-1,6389	2	21,1	1,2302	0	2	10,068	101,37	0
Chad	1	0	21,1	12,409	3,8	24,4	3,7235	0	54	6,7527	45,6	0
Chile	0	0	83,3	1,3332	2	23,8	1,7609	0	0,02	9,081	82,465	1
China	0	0	26,2	-4,347	3,4	19,6	4,1404	0	3	8,0409	64,656	0
Colombia	0	0	70	5,658	2,9	6,9	2,4314	0	0,2	8,7004	75,698	1
Congo	0	0	53,4	8,7923	3,9	26,7	1,4629	0	2	6,9025	47,645	0
Congo, Dem. Rep. of the	1	0	27,9	-0,8978	4,7	9,6	7,4759	0	10	6,7122	45,053	0
Costa Rica	0	0	47,1	1,8549	2,85	23,3	2,1612	0	0,1	8,6973	75,643	0
Côte d'Ivoire	0	0	40,4	-6,3471	3,45	16,2	2,2833	0	38,6	7,3767	54,415	0
Croatia	0	1	54	9,0022	3,5	2,5	1,4609	0	1,3	8,8172	77,742	1
Cyprus	0	0	51,4	6,494	2,55	17,8	1,4666	0	18	9,769	95,432	0
Czech Republic	1	1	64,9	1,4061	2,2	14,1	2,4004	0	0,2	9,4224	88,781	0
Denmark	0	0	84,8	-3,3496	2,25	13,2	0,733	1	3	10,095	101,91	1
Dominican Republic	0	0	58,3	8,9272	2,9	14,3	2,5975	0	0,02	8,4333	71,12	0
Ecuador	0	0	55,1	7,201	3,1	19,4	1,976	0	0	8,0075	64,12	0
Egypt	0	0	43,9	6,4592	3,5	23,4	2,357	0	91	8,0198	64,317	0
Estonia	0	1	71,8	9,6571	2,2	14,1	2,2864	0	0,75	8,9467	80,043	0
Ethiopia	0	0	13,4	11,851	3,5	2,9	5,7373	0	47,5	6,3522	40,35	0
Fiji	0	0	39,3	-1,2935	3,3	41,2	1,9146	0	7	8,3502	69,727	0
Finland	0	0	61,4	-8,8483	2,2	6,5	0,8586	1	0,2	9,945	98,903	0
France	0	0	74	-3,9388	2,5	12,3	0,8504	1	7,5	9,9606	99,213	0
Gabon	0	0	44,6	-10,935	3,1	15,2	1,5235	0	1	8,7567	76,679	0
Gambia	0	0	25,7	10,946	3,4	48,4	4,2721	0	90	7,2811	53,014	0
Georgia	0	1	56	13,97	3,65	1,7	3,4563	0	9,9	8,1175	65,894	0
Germany	0	0	85,3	-1,5138	2,2	7,8	0,8344	1	3,7	10,006	100,13	0

Table. Continued

Country code	Dummy for being landlocked	Dummy for transition economy	Urbanization ratio, 1990	(1-S)/GNP	state interventionism (absence of ec. freedom)	MNC PEN 1995	low comparative international price level (ERD)	EU-membership (EU-15)	Muslims as % of total population	ln(GDP PPP pc)	ln(GDP PPP pc)^2	world bank pension reform
Ghana	0	0	33,9	9,7045	3,1	12,7	4,4479	0	16	7,4586	55,63	0
Greece	0	0	58,8	8,2749	2,75	11,2	1,1877	1	1,3	9,5427	91,064	0
Guatemala	0	0	38	8,3262	2,7	15	2,1373	0	0,01	8,162	66,618	0
Guinea	0	0	25,7	1,7576	3,1	3,5	3,3628	0	85	7,4856	56,035	0
Guinea-Bissau	0	0	20	20,25	4,3	7,8	3,8482	0	38	6,4228	41,252	0
Guyana	0	0	33,2	11,651	3,2	57,4	4,3627	0	10	8,1324	66,136	0
Haiti	0	0	28,8	17,645	4	5,8	3,3738	0	0,04	7,2322	52,305	0
Honduras	0	0	40,7	6,205	3,35	16,5	3,2875	0	0,04	7,7968	60,79	0
Hungary	0	1	62	2,559	2,55	26,7	2,2688	0	0,6	9,2333	85,254	1
Iceland	0	0	90,6	-0,6157	2,15	1,8	0,9023	0	0,1	10,131	102,64	0
India	0	0	25,5	2,7251	3,8	1,6	4,7201	0	13,4	7,6386	58,348	0
Indonesia	0	0	30,6	-10,096	3,5	25	4,1428	0	88,22	7,8828	62,139	0
Iran, Islamic Rep. of	0	0	56,3	1,6114	4,55	2,6	3,1036	0	99	8,5411	72,95	0
Ireland	0	0	56,9	-17,78	1,85	14,4	1,1482	1	0,49	9,975	99,5	0
Israel	0	0	90,3	11,115	2,75	7,1	1,0693	0	14,6	9,7585	95,229	0
Italy	0	0	66,7	-4,3276	2,3	5,8	1,0246	1	1,7	9,9323	98,651	0
Jamaica	0	0	51,5	13,104	2,5	32,3	1,9476	0	0,2	8,1283	66,069	0
Japan	0	0	77,4	-1,1846	2,15	0,6	0,7189	0	0,2	10,054	101,09	0
Jordan	0	0	68	21,167	2,9	9,2	2,9107	0	95	8,1159	65,868	0
Kazakhstan	1	1	57,6	4,462	3,7	14,6	3,2675	0	47	8,3844	70,299	1
Kenya	0	0	24,1	7,7012	3,05	8,1	2,799	0	7	6,8872	47,433	0
Korea, Rep. of	0	0	73,8	-12,923	2,4	2	1,5672	0	0,04	9,5088	90,417	0

Country code	Dummy for being landlocked	Dummy for transition economy	Urbanization ratio, 1990	(I-S)/GNP	state interventionism (absence of ec. freedom)	MNC PEN 1995	low comparative international price level (ERD)	EU-membership (EU-15)	Muslims as % of total population	ln(GDP PPP pc)	ln (GDP PPP pc)^2	world bank pension reform
Kyrgyzstan	1	1	38,2	16,117	3,6	9,7	6,0966	0	80	7,7479	60,03	0
Lao People's Dem. Rep.	1	0	18,1	1,1531	4,6	11,6	5,4188	0	1	7,4582	55,625	0
Latvia	0	1	71,2	13,22	2,65	12,5	2,3671	0	0,02	8,6532	74,877	0
Lebanon	0	0	84,2	40,416	3,2	1	1,2153	0	70	8,3725	70,099	0
Lesotho	1	0	20,1	91,239	3,55	143,8	2,8532	0	2	7,3941	54,672	0
Lithuania	0	1	68,8	11,9	2,9	5,8	2,5338	0	0,6	8,7697	76,907	0
Luxembourg	1	0	86,3	-16,046	1,8	40,8	0,7429	1	2	10,419	108,57	0
Madagascar	0	0	23,5	7,9699	3,2	5,4	2,907	0	7	6,6278	43,928	0
Malawi	1	0	11,8	13,318	3,65	17,5	2,492	0	20	6,2602	39,19	0
Malaysia	0	0	49,7	-21,797	2,7	32,3	2,2173	0	60,4	9,0042	81,076	0
Mali	1	0	23,8	10,826	2,9	6,6	2,7251	0	90	6,524	42,562	0
Mauritania	0	0	43,5	13,016	3,8	8,6	3,8122	0	99,9	7,3544	54,087	0
Mauritius	0	0	40,5	0,1097	2,85	6,3	2,2284	0	16,6	9,0255	81,459	0
Mexico	0	0	72,5	1,9598	3	14,4	2,0062	0	0,3	8,9495	80,093	1
Moldova, Rep. of	1	1	47,8	28,759	3,2	6,5	5,1226	0	0,07	7,5738	57,363	0
Mongolia	1	1	58	5,8	3,15	4,2	4,0549	0	4	7,3401	53,877	0
Morocco	0	0	48,2	7,9628	2,75	10,1	2,6653	0	98,7	8,1032	65,661	0
Mozambique	0	0	26,6	18,769	3,8	8,7	3,7261	0	20	6,6625	44,389	0
Namibia	0	0	31	0,174	2,9	74	2,6682	0	3	8,5518	73,134	0
Nepal	1	0	8,9	11,226	3,6	0,9	5,5101	0	4,2	7,0537	49,755	0
Netherlands	0	0	88,7	-7,0114	2,05	28	0,8949	1	6	10,007	100,14	1
New Zealand	0	0	84,7	-0,6514	1,7	43,1	1,1841	0	0,17	9,7577	95,214	0
Niger	1	0	16,1	7,1021	3,8	19,2	3,6956	0	90	6,6055	43,632	0
Nigeria	0	0	35	8,2295	3,3	50	2,6494	0	50	6,6781	44,597	0
Norway	0	0	72,3	-7,0574	2,3	12,8	0,7678	0	1,6	10,179	103,61	0

Table. Continued

Country code	Dummy for being landlocked	Dummy for transition economy	Urbanization ratio, 1990	(1-S)/GNP	state interventionism (absence of ec. freedom)	MNC PEN 1995	low comparative international price level (ERD)	EU-membership (EU-15)	Muslims as % of total population	ln(GDP PPP pc)	ln (GDP PPP pc)^2	world bank pension reform
Pakistan	0	0	31,9	4,4215	3,4	9,1	3,6485	0	96,35	7,4471	55,459	0
Panama	0	0	53,7	9,2981	2,4	41	1,7556	0	0,3	8,5658	73,373	0
Papua New Guinea	0	0	15	2,0276	3,3	36,1	2,6508	0	0,04	7,7661	60,312	0
Paraguay	1	0	48,7	4,4276	2,8	7,1	2,4361	0	0,01	8,3635	69,948	0
Peru	0	0	68,9	4,7437	2,45	10,3	1,7547	0	0	8,3621	69,924	1
Philippines	0	0	48,8	4,263	2,85	8,2	3,386	0	5	8,1762	66,85	0
Poland	0	1	61,8	5,1738	2,8	6,2	1,9487	0	0,08	8,9384	79,896	1
Portugal	0	0	33,5	8,7018	2,3	17,1	1,3778	1	0,35	9,5957	92,077	0
Romania	0	1	53,6	8,4817	3,3	3,2	4,1528	0	0,3	8,639	74,633	0
Russian Federation	0	1	74	-4,9369	3,7	1,6	2,8584	0	15	8,7734	76,972	0
Rwanda	1	0	5,3	17,515	4	17	2,8696	0	4,6	6,4922	42,149	0
Saudi Arabia	0	0	78,5	-5,2206	2,95	17,5	1,47	0	100	9,226	85,119	0
Senegal	0	0	40,4	4,7102	3,05	8,3	2,5125	0	94	7,1751	51,482	0
Singapore	0	0	100	-17,786	1,45	71,5	0,8024	0	16	10,095	101,9	0
Slovakia	1	1	56,5	11,165	3	4,4	2,6212	0	0,05	9,1797	84,267	0
Slovenia	0	0	50,5	1,4488	3	9,4	1,4615	0	2,5	9,5675	91,538	0
South Africa	0	0	48,8	-1,237	2,9	9,9	2,5643	0	1,5	9,0464	81,837	0
Spain	0	0	75,3	-1,1989	2,4	18,7	1,1498	1	2,5	9,6935	93,964	0
Sri Lanka	0	0	21,3	6,4513	2,9	10	3,6777	0	7	7,9993	63,989	0
Swaziland	1	0	26,4	-6,9014	3	41,1	2,7255	0	1	8,2469	68,011	0
Sweden	0	0	83,1	-7,0114	2,35	12,9	0,8076	1	4	9,9359	98,723	1
Switzerland	1	0	59,7	-4,4401	1,9	18,6	0,6381	0	4,4	10,147	102,96	1

Country code	Dummy for being landlocked	Dummy for transition economy	Urbanization ratio, 1990	(I-S)/GNP	state interventionism (absence of ec. freedom)	MNC PEN 1995	low comparative international price level (ERD)	EU-membership (EU-15)	Muslims as % of total population	ln(GDP PPP pc)	ln (GDP PPP pc)^2	world bank pension reform
Syrian Arab Republic	0	0	50,2	11,166	4	8	2,8349	0	88	7,9696	63,514	0
Tajikistan	1	1	32,2	-0,586	4	7	2,8133	0	95	6,9479	48,273	0
Tanzania, U. Rep. of	0	0	20,8	6,6117	3,4	6,2	2,1824	0	35	6,1741	38,119	0
Thailand	0	0	18,7	-16,504	2,7	10,4	2,5257	0	5	8,6044	74,035	0
Togo	0	0	28,5	6,6696	3,8	23,4	4,1582	0	13,7	7,2242	52,189	0
Trinidad and Tobago	0	0	69,1	15,045	2,35	67,5	1,656	0	6	8,9206	79,578	0
Tunisia	0	0	57,9	3,2037	3	61	2,6233	0	99	8,5949	73,872	0
Turkey	0	0	61,2	3,47	2,75	3	2,0322	0	99	8,7675	76,868	0
Uganda	1	0	11,2	9,4138	3	4,7	3,4649	0	15	6,9792	48,71	0
United Kingdom	0	0	89,1	0,4734	1,9	17,6	0,9499	1	2,7	9,9202	98,41	1
United States	0	0	75,2	1,4049	1,8	7,3	1,0125	0	1,4	10,296	106	0
Uruguay	0	0	88,9	0,5263	2,55	8	1,4206	0	0,01	9,0622	82,123	1
Uzbekistan	1	1	40,6	0,24	4,4	1	2,1609	0	89	7,627	58,171	0
Venezuela	0	0	84	0,0558	3,3	9	1,6454	0	0,5	8,667	75,118	0
Viet Nam	0	0	19,7	7,4101	4,3	28,5	4,8247	0	0,85	7,4317	55,23	0
Yemen	0	0	28,9	19,146	3,85	44,8	2,5689	0	99	6,5783	43,274	0
Zambia	1	0	42	9,0085	2,9	43,7	2,1801	0	1,1	6,5785	43,276	0
Zimbabwe	1	0	28,4	1,8275	3,9	4,8	4,3053	0	1	7,8896	62,245	0

The Dependent Variables (1)

% people not expected to survive age 60	CO2 emissions per capita	female economic activity rate as % of male economic activity rate	eco-social market economy (GDP output per kg energy use)	life expectancy, 1995-2000	quintile ratio (share of income/consumption richest 20% to poorest 20%)	economic growth, 1990-2003	Country code	HDI 2005	ESI-Index
13,9	0,6	72,534	2,3451	72,75	..	5,1	Albania	0,78	58,8
18,5	3,3	36,272	1,634	68,89	6,1	0,6	Algeria	0,722	46
54,4	0,4	81,728	0,8792	46,49	..	0,4	Angola	0,445	42,9
16,5	3,7	44,398	4,7751	72,89	..	1,3	Argentina	0,863	62,7
19,8	1	85,865	1,7503	70,47	..	2,8	Armenia	0,759	53,2
8,9	17	74,898	3,841	78,25	7	2,6	Australia	0,955	61
10,9	7,3	64,303	8,6995	77,02	3,2	1,8	Austria	0,936	62,7
22,1	4	73,452	0,2588	69,86	..	-2,6	Azerbaijan	0,729	45,4
14,6	18,6	36,956	0,6869	72,86	..	1,5	Bahrain	0,846	..
37,9	0,2	76,166	1,7088	58,13	4,9	3,1	Bangladesh	0,52	44,1
26,1	6	81,283	0,8266	67,98	2,9	0,9	Belarus	0,786	52,8
10,1	10,5	64,495	4,9985	77,21	3,6	1,8	Belgium	0,945	44,4
13,7	1,6	30,731	..	74,69	..	2,2	Belize	0,753	..
46,2	0,1	89,828	1,0275	53,43	..	2,2	Benin	0,431	47,5
32,8	1,3	57,041	1,7207	61,39	8,6	1,3	Bolivia	0,687	59,5
68,3	1,4	77,632	..	47,39	..	2,7	Botswana	0,565	55,9
26,8	1,7	52,329	4,341	66,78	25,5	1,2	Brazil	0,792	62,2
18,3	6,5	86,741	0,5311	71,05	4,4	0,6	Bulgaria	0,808	50
64,3	0,1	90,588	..	44,39	10	1,7	Burkina Faso	0,317	45,7
67,8	(.)	88,661	..	42,44	5,3	-3,5	Burundi	0,378	40
46,6	(.)	95,657	..	53,36	6,9	4	Cambodia	0,571	50,1
46,2	0,3	57,343	1,5271	54,73	..	0,2	Cameroon	0,497	52,5
9,3	13,8	80,644	2,5293	78,98	5,2	2,3	Canada	0,949	64,4

% people not expected to survive age 60	CO2 emissions per capita	female economic activity rate as % of male economic activity rate	eco-social market economy (GDP output per kg energy use)	life expectancy, 1995-2000	quintile ratio (share of income/consumption richest 20% to poorest 20%)	economic growth, 1990-2003	Country code	HDI 2005	ESI-Index
56,1	(.)	76,186	...	47,19	...	...	Chad	0,341	45
13,8	3,4	47,061	2,98	74,94	17,4	4,1	Chile	0,854	53,6
18	2,8	86,158	0,7503	69,83	7,9	8,5	China	0,755	38,6
20,7	1,8	59,071	3,1826	70,43	20,3	0,4	Colombia	0,785	58,9
59,4	1,9	70,626	1,7768	48,55	...	-1,4	Congo	0,512	53,8
52,4	(.)	72,365	0,4074	50,79	...	-6,3	Congo, Dem. Rep. of the	0,385	44,1
11,6	1,4	44,58	3,4921	76,03	13	2,6	Costa Rica	0,838	59,6
63,4	0,9	50,298	2,0218	46,72	6,2	-0,4	Côte d'Ivoire	0,42	47,3
16,4	3,9	71,561	2,7811	72,64	...	2,1	Croatia	0,841	59,5
10	7,1	61,589	4,4477	77,76	...	3,2	Cyprus	0,891	
14,2	12,4	84,426	1,3357	73,88	3,5	1,5	Czech Republic	0,874	46,6
12,8	10,8	83,642	9,1381	75,65	3,6	1,9	Denmark	0,941	58,2
19	1,6	45,805	2,5391	70,61	12,5	4	Dominican Republic	0,749	43,7
21,5	2,1	37,722	2,2217	69,52	9,2	0,1	Ecuador	0,759	52,4
23	1,5	43,169	1,6837	66,27	4	2,5	Egypt	0,659	44
23,8	11,2	82,155	0,9907	68,68	6,7	3,3	Estonia	0,853	58,2
65,5	(.)	67,264	0,3962	43,32	6,7	2	Ethiopia	0,367	37,8
14,6	1	42,436	...	72,66	...	1,8	Fiji	0,752	
11,3	11,6	85,651	4,1795	76,83	3,6	2,5	Finland	0,941	75,1
11,3	6,2	75,21	6,4439	78,12	5,6	1,6	France	0,938	55,2
48,6	3,3	75,179	3,277	52,42	...	-0,4	Gabon	0,635	61,7
53,7	0,2	77,735	...	47	12	-0,1	Gambia	0,47	50
17,5	0,6	76,872	1,619	72,73	...	-2,7	Georgia	0,732	51,5
10,7	10,5	68,689	7,1605	77,21	4,7	1,3	Germany	0,93	57
34,9	0,2	98,351	1,0211	60	5	1,8	Ghana	0,52	52,8

The Dependent Variables (1) (Continued)

Country code	% people not expected to survive age 60	CO2 emissions per capita	female economic activity rate as % of male economic activity rate	eco-social market economy (GDP output per kg energy use)	life expectancy, 1995-2000	quintile ratio (share of income/consumption richest 20% to poorest 20%)	economic growth, 1990-2003	HDI 2005	ESI-Index
Greece	8,9	7,7	56,82	4,7961	78,11	5,4	2,1	0,912	50,1
Guatemala	31,1	0,6	39,564	2,7957	64,04	30	1,1	0,663	44
Guinea	54,4	0,2	89,403	...	46,5	7,4	1,6	0,466	48,1
Guinea-Bissau	57,7	0,2	62,651	...	44,95	28	-2,4	0,348	48,6
Guyana	28,2	1,1	48,359	...	64,41	7,4	3,6	0,72	62,9
Haiti	49,6	0,2	69,455	1,5427	53,75	...	-2,8	0,475	34,8
Honduras	22,8	0,7	45,722	1,3555	69,4	17,1	0,2	0,667	47,4
Hungary	21,6	6	71,513	1,8707	70,87	4,5	2,6	0,862	52
Iceland	8,4	8,1	85,372	3,3025	79,04	...	2,1	0,956	70,8
India	29,7	1,1	49,268	0,8889	62,59	5,7	4	0,602	45,2
Indonesia	26,7	1,2	66,2	1,6443	65,13	5,6	2	0,697	48,8
Iran, Islamic Rep. of	21,3	3,8	35,227	0,7171	69,22	...	2,1	0,736	39,8
Ireland	10	9,8	50,478	6,2928	76,35	6,4	6,7	0,946	59,2
Israel	9,3	9,3	66,023	5,2411	77,75	6,2	1,6	0,915	50,9
Italy	9	7,1	57,344	6,807	78,17	4,2	1,5	0,934	50,1
Jamaica	13,3	4	85,244	1,0122	74,82	6,2		0,738	44,7
Japan	8,2	9,3	66,409	10,631	79,96	3,4	1	0,943	57,3
Jordan	19,5	2,5	32,396	1,3886	70,15	5,8	0,9	0,753	47,8
Kazakhstan	25,8	10,4	80,196	0,5301	67,64	...	0,4	0,761	48,6
Kenya	56,3	0,3	84,018	0,6804	52,04	10	-0,6	0,474	45,3
Korea, Rep. of	16,7	9	68,587	3,11	72,42	5,2	4,6	0,901	43
Kyrgyzstan	25,4	1,4	82,733	1,4011	67,64	7,5	-2,4	0,702	48,4
Lao People's Dem. Rep.	44,9	0,1	83,996	...	53,23	4,2	3,7	0,545	52,4

% people not expected to survive age 60	CO2 emissions per capita	female economic activity rate as % of male economic activity rate	eco-social market economy (GDP output per kg energy use)	life expectancy, 1995-2000	quintile ratio (share of income/consumption richest 20% to poorest 20%)	economic growth, 1990-2003	Country code	HDI 2005	ESI-Index
25	3,7	81,437	1,2342	68,42	5,3	2,2	Latvia	0,836	60,4
19	4,6	37,472	2,2933	69,92		2,9	Lebanon	0,759	40,5
43,3	...	55,776		56,02	21,5	2,3	Lesotho	0,497	
23,3	3,7	79,331	0,879	69,89	5,2	0,5	Lithuania	0,852	58,9
10,6	20,2	56,564	5,5403	76,67	3,9	3,6	Luxembourg	0,949	
38,8	0,1	77,872		57,51	10,2	-0,9	Madagascar	0,499	50,2
72,5	0,1	90,276		39,27		0,9	Malawi	0,404	49,3
16,1	5,8	59,697	2,103	72	12	3,4	Malaysia	0,796	54
43,2	(.)	80,503		53,3	12,2	2,4	Mali	0,333	53,7
44,4	1,3	73,621		53,5	7,4	1,6	Mauritania	0,477	42,6
18,7	1,5	47,115		71,38		4	Mauritius	0,791	
18,9	3,7	46,063	2,8817	72,18	16,2	1,4	Mexico	0,814	46,2
25,7	2,7	82,828	0,6512	67,52	6	-5,7	Moldova, Rep. of	0,671	51,2
25,9	3,5	87,049		65,85	5,6	-2,5	Mongolia	0,679	50
23	1	51,491	3,9011	66,64	7	1	Morocco	0,631	44,8
60,9	0,1	91,844	0,3722	45,23	7,2	4,6	Mozambique	0,379	44,8
52,4		67,069		52,41		0,9	Namibia	0,627	56,8
39,1	0,1	66,36	0,6782	57,32	5,9	2,2	Nepal	0,526	47,7
9,3	10	65,198	5,6838	77,92	5,5	2,1	Netherlands	0,943	53,7
11,1	8,3	77,178	3,7636	76,9	17,4	2,1	New Zealand	0,933	61
51,6	0,1	74,964		48,5	20,5	-0,6	Niger	0,281	45
52,2	0,7	55,665	0,3426	50,08	12,7		Nigeria	0,453	45,4
9,1	15,4	83,1	6,6023	78,14	3,7	2,9	Norway	0,963	73,4
26,7	0,7	40,546	1,145	63,95	4,3	1,1	Pakistan	0,527	39,9
15,1	2,5	53,909	3,6479	73,6	14,7	2,4	Panama	0,804	57,7

The Dependent Variables (1) (Continued)

% people not expected to survive age 60	CO2 emissions per capita	female economic activity rate as % of male economic activity rate	eco-social market economy (GDP output per kg energy use)	life expectancy, 1995-2000	quintile ratio (share of income/consumption richest 20% to poorest 20%)	economic growth, 1990-2003	Country code	HDI 2005	ESI-Index
41,2	0,6	77,503	...	57,88	12,6	0,2	Papua New Guinea	0,523	55,2
19,7	0,7	42,261	2,2266	69,61	27,1	-0,6	Paraguay	0,755	59,7
23	1,1	42,209	4,2685	68,32	11,6	2,1	Peru	0,762	60,4
21,8	0,9	60,183	2,157	68,3	9,7	1,2	Philippines	0,758	42,3
17,3	9,3	79,337	1,3601	72,52	5,3	4,2	Poland	0,858	45
12,6	4,9	70,036	5,489	75,29	5,9	2,2	Portugal	0,904	54,2
20,7	5,3	76,138	0,7222	69,95	4,2	0,6	Romania	0,849	46,2
29,7	10,7	80,792	0,5564	66,56	12,2	-1,5	Russian Federation	0,795	56,1
70,7	0,1	89,033	...	40,5	4	0,7	Rwanda	0,45	44,8
16,8	14,2	24,853	1,3417	71,42	...	-0,6	Saudi Arabia	0,772	37,8
47	0,4	71,766	1,7918	52,32	7,5	1,3	Senegal	0,458	51,1
10,6	19,5	63,901	3,6113	77,1	...	3,5	Singapore	0,907	
16,4	7,4	84,539	1,1464	72,95	2,6	2,4	Slovakia	0,849	52,8
14,6	6,8	79,559	3,1805	74,45	4,2	3,1	Slovenia	0,904	57,5
50,5	6,9	58,702	1,5047	54,73	22,3	0,1	South Africa	0,658	46,2
10,1	5,9	54,889	5,5289	78	5,4	2,4	Spain	0,928	48,8
15,3	0,4	54,382	2,01	73,11	5,4	3,3	Sri Lanka	0,751	48,5
34,5	0,4	51,854	...	60,23	23,9	0,2	Swaziland	0,498	
8,7	6,2	88,808	4,5895	78,55	3,6	2	Sweden	0,949	71,7
9,8	6,1	65,201	11,924	78,65	5,8	0,5	Switzerland	0,947	63,7
20,7	3,1	35,547	1,2017	68,89	...	1,4	Syrian Arab Republic	0,721	43,8
25,3	1	77,335	0,5758	67,18	...	-6,5	Tajikistan	0,652	38,6
61,1	0,1	92,892	0,3774	47,92	6,7	1	Tanzania, U. Rep. of	0,418	50,3

% people not expected to survive age 60	CO2 emissions per capita	female economic activity rate as % of male economic activity rate	eco-social market economy (GDP output per kg energy use)	life expectancy, 1995-2000	quintile ratio (share of income/consumption richest 20% to poorest 20%)	economic growth, 1990-2003	Country code	HDI 2005	ESI-Index
25,8	3,5	84,606	2,1908	68,81	7,6	2,8	Thailand	0,778	49,8
58,9	0,2	61,65	..	48,84	..	0,4	Togo	0,512	44,5
15	17,2	57,039	0,6957	73,8	8,3	3,2	Trinidad and Tobago	0,801	36,3
19,6	1,8	45,919	2,9831	69,5	7,8	3,1	Tunisia	0,753	51,8
20,1	2,9	59,367	2,7432	69,02	8,2	1,3	Turkey	0,75	46,6
76,3	(.)	88,132	..	39,64	7	3,9	Uganda	0,508	51,3
9,8	9,5	73,183	5,1361	77,18	6,5	2,5	United Kingdom	0,939	50,2
12,6	19,7	79,936	3,5721	76,7	8,9	2,1	United States	0,944	53
15,5	1,8	65	6,5824	73,93	8,9	0,9	Uruguay	0,84	71,8
25,1	4,1	83,607	0,5453	67,52	5,5	-0,5	Uzbekistan	0,694	34,4
17	6,5	51,922	1,423	72,41	14,4	-1,5	Venezuela	0,772	48,1
23,9	10,8	89,539	0,6089	67,39	5,6	5,9	Viet Nam	0,704	42,3
38	1,1	36,224	1,211	57,99	7,6	2,4	Yemen	0,489	37,3
79,5	0,3	76,158	0,6384	40,09	13	-0,9	Zambia	0,394	51,1
74,5	1,6	78,011	0,8084	44,13	15,6	-0,8	Zimbabwe	0,505	41,2

The Dependent Variables (2)

Country	unemployment	Civil liberty violations, 1998	Political rights violations, 1998
Albania	15,00	5	4
Algeria	18,00	5	6
Angola		6	6
Argentina	16,00	3	3
Armenia	8,00	4	4
Australia	5,00	1	1
Austria	5,00	1	1
Azerbaijan	1,00	4	6
Bahrain		6	7
Bangladesh	4,00	4	2
Belarus	2,00	6	6
Belgium	9,00	2	1
Belize	10,00	2	1
Benin		2	2
Bolivia	5,00	3	1
Botswana	20,00	2	2
Brazil	9,00	4	3
Bulgaria	12,00	3	2
Burkina Faso		4	5
Burundi	14,00	6	7
Cambodia	2,00	6	6
Cameroon	8,00	5	7
Canada	7,00	1	1
Chad		4	6
Chile	7,00	2	3
China	4,00	6	7
Colombia	12,00	4	3
Congo		5	7
Congo, Dem, Rep, of the		6	7
Costa Rica	7,00	2	1
Cote d'Ivoire		4	6
Croatia	14,00	4	4
Cyprus	5,00	1	1
Czech Republic	8,00	5	4
Denmark	5,00	1	1
Dominican Republic	18,00	2	2
Ecuador	9,00	3	2
Egypt	11,00	6	6
Estonia	10,00	2	1
Ethiopia	23,00	4	4
Fiji	5,00	3	4
Finland	9,00	1	1
France	10,00	2	1
Gabon		4	5
Gambia		5	7
Georgia	13,00	4	3

Country	unemployment	Civil liberty violations, 1998	Political rights violations,1998
Germany	11,00	2	1
Ghana		3	3
Greece	9,00	3	1
Guatemala	3,00	4	3
Guinea		5	6
Guinea-Bissau		5	3
Guyana		2	2
Haiti		5	4
Honduras	4,00	3	2
Hungary	7,00	2	1
Iceland	3,00	1	1
India	4,00	3	2
Indonesia	9,00	4	6
Iran		6	6
Ireland	4,00	1	1
Israel	9,00	3	1
Italy	9,00	2	1
Jamaica	11,00	2	2
Japan	5,00	2	1
Jordan		5	4
Kazakhstan	8,00	5	6
Kenya		5	6
Korea	4,00	2	2
Kyrgyzstan	13,00	5	5
Laos		6	7
Latvia	9,00	2	1
Lebanon		5	6
Lesotho	39,00	4	4
Lithuania	13,00	2	1
Luxembourg	5,00	1	1
Madagascar	5,00	4	2
Malawi		3	2
Malaysia	4,00	5	5
Mali		3	3
Mauritania		5	6
Mauritius	9,00	2	1
Mexico	3,00	4	3
Moldova	8,00	4	2
Mongolia	4,00	3	2
Morocco	12,00	4	5
Mozambique		4	3
Namibia	34,00	3	2
Nepal		4	3
Netherlands	4,00	1	1
New Zealand	4,00	1	1
Niger		5	7
Nigeria		4	6
Norway	5,00	1	1

The Dependent Variables (2) (Continued

Country	unemployment	Civil liberty violations, 1998	Political rights violations,1998
Pakistan	8,00	5	4
Panama	12,00	3	2
Papua New Guinea	3,00	3	2
Paraguay	8,00	3	4
Peru	11,00	4	5
Philippines	11,00	3	2
Poland	19,00	2	1
Portugal	6,00	1	1
Romania	8,00	2	2
Russia	8,00	4	4
Rwanda	1,00	6	7
Saudi Arabia	5,00	7	7
Senegal		4	4
Singapore	5,00	5	5
Slovakia	18,00	2	2
Slovenia	6,00	2	1
South Africa	27,00	2	1
Spain	11,00	2	1
Sri Lanka	9,00	4	3
Swaziland		4	6
Sweden	6,00	1	1
Switzerland	4,00	1	1
Syria	12,00	7	7
Tajikistan	3,00	6	6
Tanzania	5,00	4	5
Thailand	2,00	3	2
Togo		5	6
Trinidad and Tobago	10,00	2	1
Tunisia	14,00	5	6
Turkey	10,00	5	4
Uganda	3,00	4	4
United Kingdom	5,00	2	1
United States of America	5,00	1	1
Uruguay	17,00	2	1
Uzbekistan		6	7
Venezuela	16,00	3	2
Vietnam	2,00	7	7
Yemen	12,00	6	5
Zambia	12,00	4	5
Zimbabwe	6,00	4	5

The Life Satisfaction Dimension

Country	Life Satisfaction	Life Expectancy	EF ecological footprint	HPI Happy Planet Index
Albania	4,6	73,8	1,5	42,1
Algeria	5,2	71,1	1,5	45,9
Angola	4,8	40,8	0,8	27,9
Argentina	6,8	74,5	2,6	52,2
Armenia	3,7	71,5	1	36,1
Australia	7,3	80,3	7,7	34,1
Austria	7,8	79	4,6	48,8
Azerbaijan	4,9	66,9	1,5	40,7
Bahrain	7,2	74,3	6,6	34,4
Bangladesh	5,7	62,8	0,6	53,2
Belarus	4	68,1	3,2	25,8
Belgium	7,3	78,9	4,9	44
Belize	6,9	71,9	2,6	52
Benin	5,4	54	1	40,1
Bolivia	5,5	64,1	1,2	46,2
Botswana	5,4	36,3	1,3	25,4
Brazil	6,3	70,5	2,2	48,6
Bulgaria	4,3	72,2	2,7	31,6
Burkina Faso	4,7	47,5	1,1	30,1
Burundi	3	43,6	0,7	19
Cambodia	5,6	56,2	1,1	42,2
Cameroon	5,1	45,8	0,9	32,8
Canada	7,6	80	6,4	39,8
Chad	4,5	43,6	1,3	25,4
Chile	6,5	77,9	2,6	51,3
China	6,3	71,6	1,5	56
Colombia	7,2	72,4	1,3	67,2
Congo	5,7	52	0,9	41,6
Congo, Dem, Rep, of the	3,3	43,1	0,7	20,7
Costa Rica	7,5	78,2	2,1	66
Cote d'Ivoire	4,5	45,9	0,9	28,8
Croatia	5,9	75	2,9	43,7
Cyprus	6,9	78,6	4	46
Czech Republic	6,4	75,6	5	36,6
Denmark	8,2	77,2	6,4	41,4
Dominican Republic	7	67,2	1,6	57,1
Ecuador	5,6	74,3	1,8	49,3
Egypt	4,8	69,8	1,5	41,6
Estonia	5,1	71,3	6,9	22,7
Ethiopia	4,7	47,6	0,7	32,5
Fiji	6,7	67,8	1,7	54,5
Finland	7,7	78,5	7	37,4
France	6,6	79,5	5,8	36,4
Gabon	6,2	54,5	1,7	40,5
Gambia	5,7	55,7	1,1	42,5
Georgia	4,1	70,5	0,8	41,2

The Life Satisfaction Dimension (Continued)

Country	Life Satisfaction	Life Expectancy	EF ecological footprint	HPI Happy Planet Index
Germany	7,2	78,7	4,8	43,8
Ghana	6,2	56,8	1,1	47
Greece	6,3	78,3	5,4	35,7
Guatemala	7	67,3	1,2	61,7
Guinea	5,1	53,7	1	37,4
Guinea-Bissau	5,4	44,7	0,7	35,1
Guyana	7,2	63,1	1,5	56,6
Haiti	5,5	51,6	0,5	43,3
Honduras	7,2	67,8	1,4	61,8
Hungary	5,7	72,7	3,5	37,6
Iceland	7,8	80,7	4,9	48,4
India	5,4	63,3	0,8	48,7
Indonesia	6,6	66,8	1,2	57,9
Iran	6	70,4	2,1	47,2
Ireland	7,6	77,7	6,2	39,4
Israel	6,7	79,7	5,3	39,1
Italy	6,9	80,1	3,8	48,3
Jamaica	7	70,8	2,6	51
Japan	6,2	82	4,3	41,7
Jordan	5,1	71,3	1,9	42
Kazakhstan	5,8	63,2	2,8	36,9
Kenya	5,6	47,2	0,9	36,7
Korea	5,8	77	3,4	41,1
Kyrgyzstan	6,6	66,8	1,1	59
Laos	5,4	54,7	1	40,3
Latvia	4,7	71,6	4,4	27,3
Lebanon	5,6	72	2,3	43,6
Lesotho	4,3	36,3	0,6	23,1
Lithuania	4,7	72,3	3,9	29,3
Luxembourg	7,6	78,5	4,9	45,6
Madagascar	5,8	55,4	0,8	46
Malawi	4,6	39,7	0,7	26,7
Malaysia	7,4	73,2	3	52,7
Mali	5,3	47,9	1,1	33,7
Mauritania	5,3	52,7	1,1	37,3
Mauritius	6,5	72,2	2,4	49,6
Mexico	6,9	75,1	2,5	54,4
Moldova	3,5	67,7	1,2	31,1
Mongolia	6,7	64	1,9	49,6
Morocco	5,6	69,7	0,9	54,4
Mozambique	5,4	41,9	0,7	33
Namibia	6,5	48,3	1,6	38,4
Nepal	5,5	61,6	0,6	50
Netherlands	7,5	78,4	4,7	46
New Zealand	7,4	79,1	5,5	41,9

Country	Life Satisfaction	Life Expectancy	EF ecological footprint	HPI Happy Planet Index
Niger	4,5	44,4	1,1	26,8
Nigeria	5,5	43,4	1,2	31,1
Norway	7,4	79,4	6,2	39,2
Pakistan	4,3	63	0,7	39,4
Panama	7,2	74,8	1,8	63,5
Papua New Guinea	6,3	55,3	1,3	44,8
Paraguay	6,5	71	2,2	51,1
Peru	5,6	70	0,9	55,1
Philippines	6,4	70,4	1,2	59,2
Poland	5,9	74,3	3,6	39,3
Portugal	6,1	77,2	5,2	34,8
Romania	5,2	71,3	2,7	37,7
Russia	4,3	65,3	4,4	22,8
Rwanda	4,4	43,9	0,7	28,3
Saudi Arabia	7,3	71,8	4,4	42,7
Senegal	5,6	55,7	1,2	40,8
Singapore	6,9	78,7	6,2	36,1
Slovakia	5,4	74	3,6	35,8
Slovenia	6,6	76,4	3,8	44
South Africa	5,7	48,4	2,8	27,8
Spain	7	79,5	4,8	43
Sri Lanka	6,1	74	1,1	60,3
Swaziland	4,2	32,5	1,1	18,4
Sweden	7,7	80,2	7	38,2
Switzerland	8,2	80,5	5,3	48,3
Syria	5,1	73,3	1,9	43,2
Tajikistan	6,1	63,6	0,6	57,7
Tanzania	5,5	46	0,9	35,1
Thailand	6,5	70	1,6	55,4
Togo	4,9	54,3	0,9	36,9
Trinidad and Tobago	6,9	69,9	2,3	51,9
Tunisia	6,4	73,3	1,4	58,9
Turkey	5,3	68,7	2	41,4
Uganda	4,7	47,3	1,5	27,7
United Kingdom	7,1	78,4	5,4	40,3
United States of America	7,4	77,4	9,5	28,8
Uruguay	6,3	75,4	2,6	49,3
Uzbekistan	6,4	66,5	1,9	49,2
Venezuela	7,4	72,9	2,4	57,5
Vietnam	6,1	70,5	0,8	61,2
Yemen	6,2	60,6	0,7	55
Zambia	4,9	37,5	0,8	25,9
Zimbabwe	3,3	36,9	1	16,6

The Gender Dimension

Country code	GDI 2006 gender development index	GEM 2006 gender empowerment index
Albania	0,78	
Algeria	0,713	
Angola	0,431	
Argentina	0,859	0,697
Armenia	0,765	
Australia	0,956	0,833
Austria	0,937	0,815
Azerbaijan	0,733	
Bahrain	0,849	
Bangladesh	0,524	0,374
Belarus	0,793	
Belgium	0,943	0,855
Belize		0,495
Benin	0,412	
Bolivia	0,687	0,499
Botswana	0,555	0,501
Brazil	0,789	0,486
Bulgaria	0,814	0,595
Burkina Faso	0,335	
Burundi	0,38	
Cambodia	0,578	0,373
Cameroon	0,497	
Canada	0,947	0,81
Chad	0,35	
Chile	0,85	0,506
China	0,765	
Colombia	0,787	0,506
Congo	0,519	
Congo, Dem. Rep. of the	0,378	
Costa Rica	0,831	0,675
Côte d'Ivoire	0,401	
Croatia	0,844	0,602
Cyprus	0,9	0,584
Czech Republic	0,881	0,615
Denmark	0,94	0,861
Dominican Republic	0,745	
Ecuador		0,542
Egypt		0,262
Estonia	0,856	0,608
Ethiopia		
Fiji		
Finland	0,943	0,853
France	0,94	
Gabon		
Gambia		
Georgia		0,407

Country code	GDI 2006 gender development index	GEM 2006 gender empowerment index
Germany	0,928	0,816
Ghana	0,528	
Greece	0,917	0,614
Guatemala	0,659	
Guinea	0,434	
Guinea-Bissau		
Guyana		
Haiti		
Honduras	0,676	0,53
Hungary	0,867	0,56
Iceland	0,958	0,866
India	0,591	
Indonesia	0,704	
Iran, Islamic Rep. of	0,736	0,326
Ireland	0,951	0,753
Israel	0,925	0,656
Italy	0,934	0,653
Jamaica	0,721	
Japan	0,942	0,557
Jordan	0,747	
Kazakhstan	0,772	
Kenya	0,487	
Korea, Rep. of	0,905	0,502
Kyrgyzstan	0,701	
Lao People's Dem. Rep.	0,545	
Latvia	0,843	0,621
Lebanon		
Lesotho	0,486	
Lithuania	0,856	0,635
Luxembourg	0,949	
Madagascar	0,507	
Malawi	0,394	
Malaysia	0,795	0,5
Mali	0,329	
Mauritania	0,478	
Mauritius	0,792	
Mexico	0,812	0,597
Moldova, Rep. of	0,692	0,544
Mongolia	0,685	0,388
Morocco	0,615	
Mozambique	0,387	
Namibia	0,622	0,623
Nepal	0,513	
Netherlands	0,945	0,844
New Zealand	0,932	0,797
Niger	0,292	
Nigeria	0,443	
Norway	0,962	0,932

The Gender Dimension (Continued)

Country code	GDI 2006 gender development index	GEM 2006 gender empowerment index
Pakistan	0,513	0,377
Panama	0,806	0,568
Papua New Guinea	0,521	
Paraguay		
Peru	0,759	0,58
Philippines	0,761	0,533
Poland	0,859	0,61
Portugal	0,902	0,681
Romania	0,804	0,492
Russian Federation	0,795	0,482
Rwanda	0,449	
Saudi Arabia	0,744	0,242
Senegal	0,451	
Singapore		0,707
Slovakia	0,853	0,599
Slovenia	0,908	0,603
South Africa	0,646	
Spain	0,933	0,776
Sri Lanka	0,749	0,372
Swaziland	0,479	
Sweden	0,949	0,883
Switzerland	0,944	0,797
Syrian Arab Republic	0,702	
Tajikistan	0,648	
Tanzania, U. Rep. of	0,426	0,597
Thailand	0,781	0,486
Togo	0,476	
Trinidad and Tobago	0,805	0,66
Tunisia	0,744	
Turkey	0,745	0,289
Uganda	0,498	
United Kingdom	0,938	0,755
United States	0,946	0,808
Uruguay	0,847	0,513
Uzbekistan	0,694	
Venezuela	0,78	0,532
Viet Nam	0,708	
Yemen	0,462	0,128
Zambia	0,396	
Zimbabwe	0,483	

The Human Rights Dimension: Replicating our Findings with Freedom House Data, 2003 - 2006

Data download: http://www.freedomhouse.org/template.cfm?page=276

Country	Political Rights 2006	2003	Civil Rights 2003	2004	2005	2006	PR PRED 2006	PR Resid 2006	CL PRED 2006	CL Resid 2006
Albania	25	26	42	42	40	38	26,2946	-1,29464	42,5944	-4,59441
Algeria	11	11	22	22	25	25	11,5878	-0,58781	22,8152	2,18477
Angola	8	8	22	22	22	21	8,64645	-0,64645	22,8152	-1,81523
Argentina	34	24	41	46	48	50	24,3337	9,66627	46,5502	3,44975
Armenia	13	20	34	32	28	28	20,4119	-7,41191	32,7048	-4,70482
Australia	39	39	57	57	57	57	39,0406	-0,04056	57,4288	-0,4288
Austria	40	40	58	59	59	58	40,021	-0,02101	59,4067	-1,40672
Azerbaijan	10	11	24	24	22	23	11,5878	-1,58781	24,7932	-1,79315
Bahrain	14	13	21	21	21	22	13,5487	0,45128	21,8263	0,17373
Bangladesh	22	21	33	33	32	31	21,3924	0,60763	33,6938	-2,69378
Belarus	5	9	15	14	14	10	9,6269	-4,6269	14,9036	-4,90356
Belgium	39	39	56	59	59	58	39,0406	-0,04056	59,4067	-1,40672
Belize	36	37	52	51	52	52	37,0796	-1,07965	51,495	0,50496
Benin	30	27	48	49	49	48	27,2751	2,7249	49,5171	-1,51713
Bolivia	28	31	43	42	43	43	31,1969	-3,19692	42,5944	0,40559
Botswana	31	34	48	48	48	47	34,1383	-3,13828	48,5282	-1,52817
Brazil	32	32	41	42	43	45	32,1774	-0,17737	42,5944	2,40559
Bulgaria	36	36	50	50	51	51	36,0992	-0,09919	50,5061	0,49391
Burkina Faso	17	20	34	33	34	36	20,4119	-3,41191	33,6938	2,30622
Burundi	25	9	18	17	17	24	9,6269	15,3731	17,8704	6,12956
Cambodia	11	11	20	23	23	24	11,5878	-0,58781	23,8042	0,19581
Cameroon	11	7	15	14	16	16	7,66599	3,33401	14,9036	1,09644
Canada	39	39	57	59	59	59	39,0406	-0,04056	59,4067	-0,40672
Chad	8	8	18	18	18	18	8,64645	-0,64645	18,8594	-0,8594
Chile	39	34	53	56	56	57	34,1383	4,86172	56,4398	0,56016
China	2	3	12	10	15	15	3,74417	-1,74417	10,9477	4,05227
Colombia	24	23	32	34	34	36	23,3533	0,64672	34,6827	1,31726
Congo (Brazzaville)	12	11	28	30	30	25	11,5878	0,41219	30,7269	-5,72691
Congo (Kinshasa)	8	6	12	13	13	12	6,68554	1,31446	13,9146	-1,9146
Costa Rica	38	38	52	52	54	54	38,0601	-0,0601	52,484	1,516
Cote d'Ivoire	6	11	15	20	15	15	11,5878	-5,58781	20,8373	-5,83732
Croatia	35	31	49	48	48	49	31,1969	3,80308	48,5282	0,47183
Cyprus	38	39	57	57	57	57	39,0406	-1,04056	57,4288	-0,4288
Czech Republic	37	37	47	52	56	55	37,0796	-0,07965	52,484	2,516
Denmark	40	40	59	59	59	58	40,021	-0,02101	59,4067	-1,40672
Dominican Republic	32	30	48	46	46	46	30,2165	1,78354	46,5502	-0,55025

The Human Rights Dimension: Replicating our Findings with Freedom House Data, 2003 – 2006 (Continued)

Country	Political Rights 2006	2003	Civil Rights 2003	2004	2005	2006	PR PRED 2006	PR Resid 2006	CL PRED 2006	CL Resid 2006
Ecuador	27	24	40	40	41	41	24,3337	2,66627	40,6165	0,3835
Egypt	8	7	16	16	18	22	7,66599	0,33401	16,8815	5,11852
Estonia	39	37	50	52	55	56	37,0796	1,92035	52,484	3,516
Ethiopia	15	12	20	20	21	21	12,5683	2,43173	20,8373	0,16268
Fiji	20	22	41	41	41	42	22,3728	-2,37282	41,6055	0,39455
Finland	40	40	59	60	60	60	40,021	-0,02101	60,3957	-0,39568
France	38	39	56	57	57	55	39,0406	-1,04056	57,4288	-2,4288
Gabon	10	16	34	32	31	30	16,4901	-6,49009	32,7048	-2,70482
Gambia	17	20	34	33	34	32	20,4119	-3,41191	33,6938	-1,69378
Georgia	24	19	32	32	34	37	19,4315	4,56855	32,7048	4,29518
Germany	39	38	56	58	59	58	38,0601	0,9399	58,4178	-0,41776
Ghana	37	31	41	44	47	47	31,1969	5,80308	44,5723	2,42767
Greece	37	36	45	50	52	51	36,0992	0,90081	50,5061	0,49391
Guatemala	22	22	33	30	30	33	22,3728	-0,37282	30,7269	2,27309
Guinea	9	11	22	25	22	23	11,5878	-2,58781	25,7821	-2,78211
Guinea-Bissau	25	21	25	28	30	34	21,3924	3,60763	28,749	5,25101
Guyana	29	30	45	45	44	41	30,2165	-1,21646	45,5613	-4,56129
Haiti	5	9	16	12	14	16	9,6269	-4,6269	12,9256	3,07436
Honduras	26	27	41	40	40	40	27,2751	-1,2751	40,6165	-0,6165
Hungary	37	37	52	52	55	56	37,0796	-0,07965	52,484	3,516
Iceland	40	40	58	60	60	60	40,021	-0,02101	60,3957	-0,39568
India	34	31	40	41	42	42	31,1969	2,80308	41,6055	0,39455
Indonesia	30	26	32	34	34	35	26,2946	3,70536	34,6827	0,31726
Iran	9	10	16	15	15	15	10,6074	-1,60736	15,8925	-0,89252
Ireland	40	38	55	58	58	58	38,0601	1,9399	58,4178	-0,41776
Israel	37	40	43	43	43	46	40,021	-3,02101	43,5834	2,41663
Italy	39	38	54	54	53	53	38,0601	0,9399	54,4619	-1,46192
Jamaica	31	30	43	43	42	43	30,2165	0,78354	43,5834	-0,58337
Japan	37	36	52	52	52	51	36,0992	0,90081	52,484	-1,484
Jordan	15	10	25	25	27	27	10,6074	4,39264	25,7821	1,21789
Kazakhstan	10	8	21	20	22	22	8,64645	1,35355	20,8373	1,16268
Kenya	26	18	30	39	40	40	18,451	7,549	39,6275	0,37246
Korea, Rpublic of	36	32	51	49	49	49	32,1774	3,82263	49,5171	-0,51713
Kyrgyzstan	16	11	22	24	25	31	11,5878	4,41219	24,7932	6,20685
Laos	1	3	9	11	12	12	3,74417	-2,74417	11,9367	0,06332
Latvia	36	36	50	50	51	53	36,0992	-0,09919	50,5061	2,49391
Lebanon	16	6	24	24	25	30	6,68554	9,31446	24,7932	5,20685
Lesotho	31	30	41	41	41	43	30,2165	0,78354	41,6055	1,39455
Lithuania	36	38	51	52	52	54	38,0601	-2,0601	52,484	1,516
Luxembourg	40	44	57	60	60	60	43,9428	-3,94283	60,3957	-0,39568
Madagascar	24	24	34	37	37	36	24,3337	-0,33373	37,6496	-1,64962
Malawi	23	23	32	32	34	34	23,3533	-0,35328	32,7048	1,29518

Country	Political Rights 2006	2003	Civil Rights 2003	2004	2005	2006	PR PRED 2006	PR Resid 2006	CL PRED 2006	CL Resid 2006
Malaysia	19	17	25	28	30	31	17,4705	1,52946	28,749	2,25101
Mali	30	30	43	45	44	44	30,2165	-0,21646	45,5613	-1,56129
Mauritania	11	16	25	24	23	27	16,4901	-5,49009	24,7932	2,20685
Mauritius	38	36	52	52	53	53	36,0992	1,90081	52,484	0,516
Mexico	35	33	44	44	44	45	33,1578	1,84217	44,5723	0,42767
Moldova	24	28	32	32	33	33	28,2556	-4,25555	32,7048	0,29518
Mongolia	34	34	48	49	49	49	34,1383	-0,13828	49,5171	-0,51713
Morocco	17	17	24	24	27	26	17,4705	-0,47054	24,7932	1,20685
Mozambique	25	25	34	34	34	31	25,3142	-0,31419	34,6827	-3,68274
Namibia	31	33	43	43	42	46	33,1578	-2,15783	43,5834	2,41663
Nepal	9	21	29	28	25	19	21,3924	-12,3924	28,749	-9,74899
Netherlands	40	40	58	60	59	59	40,021	-0,02101	60,3957	-1,39568
New Zealand	39	39	58	57	57	57	39,0406	-0,04056	57,4288	-0,4288
Niger	27	23	29	33	35	35	23,3533	3,64672	33,6938	1,30622
Nigeria	21	19	25	26	26	28	19,4315	1,56855	26,7711	1,22893
Norway	40	40	60	60	60	60	40,021	-0,02101	60,3957	-0,39568
Pakistan	11	11	22	24	23	24	11,5878	-0,58781	24,7932	-0,79315
Panama	36	36	46	44	44	47	36,0992	-0,09919	44,5723	2,42767
Papua New Guinea	26	31	43	43	38	38	31,1969	-5,19692	43,5834	-5,58337
Paraguay	25	20	39	38	38	38	20,4119	4,58809	38,6386	-0,63858
Peru	32	32	43	42	41	42	32,1774	-0,17737	42,5944	-0,59441
Philippines	29	31	42	42	42	43	31,1969	-2,19692	42,5944	0,40559
Poland	38	37	51	52	54	54	37,0796	0,92035	52,484	1,516
Portugal	40	40	58	58	57	57	40,021	-0,02101	58,4178	-1,41776
Romania	30	32	46	47	44	45	32,1774	-2,17737	47,5392	-2,53921
Russia	11	17	25	25	25	24	17,4705	-6,47054	25,7821	-1,78211
Rwanda	11	4	18	20	20	21	4,72463	6,27537	20,8373	0,16268
Saudi Arabia	4	3	6	6	5	8	3,74417	0,25583	6,99189	1,00811
Senegal	33	31	37	41	42	43	31,1969	1,80308	41,6055	1,39455
Singapore	17	17	26	29	34	33	17,4705	-0,47054	29,7379	3,26205
Slovakia	37	36	47	51	53	54	36,0992	0,90081	51,495	2,50496
Slovenia	38	38	54	54	53	54	38,0601	-0,0601	54,4619	-0,46192
South Africa	36	36	52	52	52	52	36,0992	-0,09919	52,484	-0,484
Spain	38	39	53	53	53	57	39,0406	-1,04056	53,473	3,52704
Sri Lanka	24	26	33	37	36	35	26,2946	-2,29464	37,6496	-2,64962
Swaziland	1	8	25	19	19	20	8,64645	-7,64645	19,8484	0,15164
Sweden	40	40	59	60	60	60	40,021	-0,02101	60,3957	-0,39568
Switzerland	40	40	60	52	60	59	40,021	-0,02101	52,484	6,516
Syria	1	1	5	6	7	7	1,78326	-0,78326	6,99189	0,00811
Tajikistan	9	10	18	19	21	21	10,6074	-1,60736	19,8484	1,15164
Tanzania	22	22	36	36	36	36	22,3728	-0,37282	36,6607	-0,66066
Thailand	29	30	42	44	39	38	30,2165	-1,21646	44,5723	-6,57233
Togo	7	9	24	24	25	18	9,6269	-2,6269	24,7932	-6,79315
Trinidad & Tobago	28	29	43	43	43	46	29,236	-1,23601	43,5834	2,41663

The Human Rights Dimension: Replicating our Findings with Freedom House Data, 2003 – 2006 (Continued)

Country	Political Rights 2006	2003	Civil Rights 2003	2004	2005	2006	PR PRED 2006	PR Resid 2006	CL PRED 2006	CL Resid 2006
Tunisia	6	8	20	14	18	18	8,64645	-2,64645	14,9036	3,09644
Turkey	28	24	29	33	38	37	24,3337	3,66627	33,6938	3,30622
Uganda	14	10	29	30	30	31	10,6074	3,39264	30,7269	0,27309
United Kingdom	39	40	57	58	58	57	40,021	-1,02101	58,4178	-1,41776
United States of America	37	37	55	56	55	56	37,0796	-0,07965	56,4398	-0,43984
Uruguay	39	36	54	54	55	58	36,0992	2,90081	54,4619	3,53808
Uzbekistan	0	3	9	9	9	3	3,74417	-3,74417	9,95877	-6,95877
Venezuela	23	26	32	32	34	31	26,2946	-3,29464	32,7048	-1,70482
Vietnam	2	2	11	12	15	17	2,76372	-0,76372	12,9256	4,07436
Yemen	13	10	17	23	22	18	10,6074	2,39264	23,8042	-5,80419
Zambia	22	20	33	33	34	34	20,4119	1,58809	33,6938	0,30622
Zimbabwe	5	6	15	14	14	10	6,68554	-1,68554	14,9036	-4,90356

Migration and Conflict

Data sources:
    UNDP (2004) (Disaster Risk, average percentage of people affected by conflicts, 1980 – 2000, per total population.
    UN United Nations Department of Economic and Social Affairs (2004) (World Economic and Social Report; net migration rates per total population, 1950 – 2000).

Country code	total net migration rate 1950-2000 as % of total population, 2000
Algeria	-7,000
Angola	-2,500
Argentina	3,243
Australia	23,158
Austria	6,250
Azerbaijan	8,750
Bangladesh	-0,652
Belarus	-8,000
Belgium	5,000
Benin	-10,000
Bolivia	-7,500
Brazil	0,058
Bulgaria	-11,250
Burkina Faso	-12,500
Burundi	-20,000
Cambodia	-3,077

Country code	total net migration rate 1950-2000 as % of total population, 2000
Cameroon	0,000
Canada	18,710
Chad	-1,250
Chile	-3,333
China	-0,431
Colombia	-5,714
Congo, Dem. Rep. of the	0,000
Côte d'Ivoire	13,750
Czech Republic	2,000
Denmark	4,000
Dominican Republic	-7,500
Ecuador	-1,667
Egypt	-5,147
Ethiopia	0,152
Finland	-4,000
France	7,966
Georgia	-8,000
Germany	11,585
Ghana	-4,000
Greece	5,455
Guatemala	-10,909
Guinea	-2,500
Haiti	-10,000
Honduras	-3,333
Hungary	-4,000
India	-0,433
Indonesia	-1,038
Iran, Islamic Rep. of	-0,303
Israel	28,333
Italy	-1,379
Japan	0,394
Jordan	26,000
Kazakhstan	-8,750
Kenya	0,323
Korea, Rep. of	-0,851
Lao People's Dem. Rep.	-6,000
Madagascar	-0,625
Malawi	-3,636
Malaysia	2,609
Mali	-11,667
Mexico	-8,788
Morocco	-6,207
Mozambique	-5,000
Nepal	-2,500
Netherlands	5,000
Niger	-0,909
Nigeria	-0,174
Pakistan	-0,210
Papua New Guinea	0,000

Continued

Country code	total net migration rate 1950-2000 as % of total population, 2000
Paraguay	-6,000
Peru	-4,231
Philippines	-5,526
Poland	-3,590
Portugal	-18,000
Romania	-5,455
Russian Federation	1,986
Rwanda	-1,250
Saudi Arabia	18,636
Senegal	2,222
Slovakia	-2,000
South Africa	2,273
Spain	0,244
Sri Lanka	-6,842
Sweden	7,778
Switzerland	15,714
Syrian Arab Republic	-2,353
Tanzania, U. Rep. of	2,000
Thailand	-1,639
Tunisia	-9,000
Turkey	-2,647
Uganda	0,000
United Kingdom	0,509
United States	11,263
Uzbekistan	-1,600
Venezuela	5,000
Viet Nam	-2,308
Yemen	-2,222
Zambia	2,000
Zimbabwe	-0,769

Country code	UNDP Conflict Index
Albania	0
Algeria	37
Angola	79
Argentina	0
Armenia	0
Australia	0
Austria	0
Azerbaijan	0,8
Bahrain	0
Bangladesh	4
Belarus	0
Belgium	0
Belize	0
Benin	0
Bolivia	0

Country code	UNDP Conflict Index
Botswana	0
Brazil	0
Bulgaria	0
Burkina Faso	0
Burundi	16
Cambodia	75
Cameroon	0
Canada	0
Chad	43
Chile	0
China	0
Colombia	100
Congo	6
Congo, Dem. Rep. of the	18
Costa Rica	0
Côte d'Ivoire	0
Croatia	4
Cyprus	0
Czech Republic	0
Denmark	0
Dominican Republic	0
Ecuador	0
Egypt	0
Estonia	0
Ethiopia	24
Fiji	0
Finland	0
France	0
Gabon	0
Gambia	0
Georgia	0
Germany	0
Ghana	0
Greece	0
Guatemala	76
Guinea	3
Guinea-Bissau	0
Guyana	0
Haiti	0
Honduras	0
Hungary	0
Iceland	0
India	3
Indonesia	1
Iran, Islamic Rep. of	22
Ireland	0
Israel	99
Italy	0
Jamaica	0
Japan	0
Jordan	0
Kazakhstan	0
Kenya	0

Continued

Country code	UNDP Conflict Index
Korea, Rep. of	0
Kyrgyzstan	0
Lao People's Dem. Rep.	6
Latvia	0
Lebanon	25
Lesotho	0
Lithuania	0
Luxembourg	0
Madagascar	0
Malawi	0
Malaysia	0
Mali	0
Mauritania	0
Mauritius	0
Mexico	0
Moldova, Rep. of	0
Mongolia	0
Morocco	0
Mozambique	46
Namibia	40
Nepal	0
Netherlands	0
New Zealand	0
Niger	0
Nigeria	0
Norway	0
Pakistan	0
Panama	0
Papua New Guinea	0
Paraguay	0
Peru	70
Philippines	100
Poland	0
Portugal	0
Romania	0
Russian Federation	0
Rwanda	23
Saudi Arabia	0
Senegal	6
Singapore	0
Slovakia	0
Slovenia	3,7
South Africa	22
Spain	0
Sri Lanka	65
Swaziland	0
Sweden	0
Switzerland	0
Syrian Arab Republic	4
Tajikistan	15
Tanzania, U. Rep. of	0

Country code	UNDP Conflict Index
Thailand	11
Togo	0
Trinidad and Tobago	0
Tunisia	0
Turkey	3
Uganda	45
United Kingdom	2
United States	0
Uruguay	0
Uzbekistan	0
Venezuela	0
Viet Nam	10
Yemen	4
Zambia	0
Zimbabwe	0

MULTIPLE REGRESSIONS FOR THE MUSLIM POPULATION EUROPE ON TRUST IN THE POLICE, SATISFACTION WITH DEMOCRACY, PERSONAL HAPPINESS, AVOIDING VAT, DOCUMENT FRAUD, INSURANCE FRAUD, SOCIAL BENEFITS FRAUD AS EXPLAINED BY RELIGIOUS DISCRIMINATION, SATISFACTION WITH EDUCATION, STRENGTH OF RELIGIOUS FEELINGS, SECULARISM (NON-ATTENDANCE OF WEEKLY PRAYER MEETINGS), FEELING OF UNSAFETY AND POVERTY

From:

Arno Tausch, with Christian Bischof and Karl Mueller (2007), ""MUSLIM CALVINISM", INTERNAL SECURITY AND THE LISBON PROCESS IN EUROPE". Amsterdam: Rozenberg Publishers

Muslims: TRSTPLC Trust in the Police, n = 806

model	R	R-Square	adjusted R	standard error of the estimate	Statistics of change					Durbin Watson
					Change in R^2	Change in F	df1	df2	Change in sign. of F	
2	,345(b)	0,119	0,117	2,56	0,006	5,401	1	782	0,02	1,929

Included Variables

model		Non-standardized coefficients	Standardized coefficients			
		B	standard error	Beta	T	Significance
2	(constant)	4,17	0,26		16,048	0
	STFEDU State of education in country nowadays	0,363	0,037	0,328	9,717	0
	DSCRRLG Discrimination of respondent's group: religion	-0,538	0,231	-0,078	-2,324	0,02

Excluded Variables

model		Beta In	T	Significance	partial correlation	statistics of collinearity
2	RLGDGR How religious are you	,062(b)	1,847	0,065	0,066	0,996
	RLGATND never attending religious services	-,054(b)	-1,62	0,106	-0,058	0,996
	AESFDRK feeling unsafe	-,021(b)	-0,629	0,53	-0,022	0,996
	HINCFEL poverty	,013(b)	0,399	0,69	0,014	0,986

Muslims: STFDEM How Satisfied with the Way Democracy Works in Country, n = 776

model	R	R-Square	adjusted R	standard error of the estimate	Statistics of change					Durbin Watson
2	,386(b)	0,149	0,147	2,232	0,005	3,998	1	755	0,046	1,838

Included Variables

model		Non-standardized coefficients	Standardized coefficients			
		B	standard error	Beta	T	Significance
2	(constant)	4,197	0,23		18,251	0
	STFEDU State of education in country nowadays	0,366	0,033	0,373	11,052	0
	DSCRRLG Discrimination of respondent's group: religion	-0,408	0,204	-0,067	-1,999	0,046

Excluded Variables

model		Beta In	T	Significance	partial correlation	statistics of collinearity
2	**RLGDGR How religious are you**	**,008(b)**	**0,25**	**0,803**	**0,009**	**0,996**
	RLGATND never attending religious services	**,018(b)**	**0,532**	**0,595**	**0,019**	**0,995**
	AESFDRK feeling unsafe	-,048(b)	-1,426	0,154	-0,052	0,996
	HINCFEL poverty	-,010(b)	-0,288	0,773	-0,011	0,981

Muslims: HAPPY How Happy Are you, n = 799

model	R	R-Square	adjusted R	standard error of the estimate	Statistics of change				Durbin-Watson
					Change in R^2	Change in F	df1	df2	Change in sign. of F
4	,351(d)	0,123	0,119	2,007	0,007	6,175	1	788	0,013	1,852

Included Variables

model		Non-standardized coefficients		Standardized coefficients		
		B	standard error	Beta	T	Significance
4	(constant)	7,578	0,377		20,085	0
	HINCFEL poverty	-0,632	0,081	-0,262	-7,77	0
	STFEDU State of education in country nowadays	0,15	0,029	0,173	5,154	0
	RLGDGR How religious are you	**0,086**	**0,028**	**0,103**	**3,076**	**0,002**
	AESFDRK feeling unsafe	-0,217	0,087	-0,083	-2,485	0,013

Excluded Variables

model		Beta In	T	Significance	partial correlation	statistics of collinearity
4	DSCRRLG Discrimination of respondent's group: religion	-,030(d)	-0,902	0,367	-0,032	0,98
	RLGATND never attending religious services	**,004(d)**	**0,119**	**0,905**	**0,004**	**0,865**

THE AGGREGATED DIMENSIONS AND THE CORRELATIONS WITH THE GLOBAL LISBON PROCESS

Date for the dependent variables: see Table 5.1a and Graph 5.3a; Appendix and Graph 5.3b

The global Lisbon Process Indicator (LPI) (1) and (2), combining 17 variables, correlate in the following fashion with the different components of the indicator:

	correlations with "global Lisbon process Index" (1)	correlations with "global Lisbon processs Index" (2)	(difference (1) - (2))*100
UNDP type component index: HPI Happy Planet Index	0,4854	0,34572	13,9679
UNDP type component index: CO_2 emissions per capita	-0,4146	-0,4758	6,12215
UNDP type component index: % people not expected to survive age 60	0,79143	0,73245	5,89748
UNDP type component index: EF ecological footprint	-0,6181	-0,6764	5,82926
UNDP type component index: life expectancy, 1995-2000	0,81817	0,76884	4,93249
UNDP type component index: Life Satisfaction	0,73138	0,68642	4,49635
UNDP type component index: unemployment	0,30145	0,26573	3,57138
UNDP type component index: eco-social market economy (GDP output per kg energy use)	0,70113	0,66981	3,1321
UNDP type component index: HDI 2005	0,84144	0,81778	2,36561
UNDP type component index: GDI 2006	0,8535	0,83435	1,91492
UNDP type component index: ESI-Index	0,61326	0,6044	0,88693
UNDP type component index: economic growth, 1990-2003	0,42824	0,43142	-0,3186
UNDP type component index: quintile ratio (share of income/consumption richest 20% to poorest 20%)	0,32893	0,3688	-3,9862

UNDP type component index: GEM 2006	0,78439	0,82995	-4,556
UNDP type component index: Political rights violations,1998	0,7713	0,83269	-6,14
UNDP type component index: Civil liberty violation, 1998	0,75304	0,82719	-7,4154
UNDP type component index: female economic activity rate as % of male economic activity rate	-0,0196	0,09405	-11,367

The Different Disaggregated Components of the Global Lisbon Process Indicators (LPIs)

	growth, social cohesion, jobs	environment	gender equality	human needs satisfaction	human rights
Albania	0,702	0,629	0,689	0,696	0,417
Algeria	0,633	0,542	0,392	0,663	0,250
Angola	0,460	0,487	0,491	0,279	0,167
Argentina	0,563	0,675	0,607	0,823	0,667
Armenia	0,718	0,575	0,768	0,610	0,500
Australia	0,780	0,333	0,850	0,941	1,000
Austria	0,809	0,648	0,785	0,943	1,000
Azerbaijan	0,630	0,488	0,660	0,645	0,333
Bahrain	0,533	0,198	0,498	0,843	0,083
Bangladesh	0,826	0,614	0,450	0,479	0,667
Belarus	0,819	0,418	0,758	0,597	0,167
Belgium	0,769	0,437	0,805	0,927	0,917
Belize	0,672	0,797	0,268	0,809	0,917
Benin	0,580	0,559	0,532	0,374	0,833
Bolivia	0,732	0,638	0,496	0,569	0,833
Botswana	0,557	0,637	0,525	0,309	0,833
Brazil	0,489	0,679	0,520	0,700	0,583
Bulgaria	0,706	0,428	0,734	0,666	0,750
Burkina Faso	0,638	0,619	0,479	0,180	0,417
Burundi	0,586	0,388	0,500	0,096	0,083
Cambodia	0,839	0,608	0,565	0,433	0,167
Cameroon	0,631	0,564	0,374	0,392	0,167
Canada	0,778	0,411	0,862	0,956	1,000
Chile	0,670	0,599	0,535	0,828	0,750
China	0,909	0,536	0,770	0,736	0,083
Colombia	0,508	0,736	0,558	0,784	0,583
Congo	0,340	0,593	0,481	0,342	0,167

Continued

	growth, social cohesion, jobs	environment	gender equality	human needs satisfaction	human rights
Congo, Dem. Rep. of the	0,013	0,327	0,387	0,218	0,083
Costa Rica	0,690	0,726	0,584	0,884	0,917
Côte d'Ivoire	0,638	0,525	0,254	0,225	0,333
Croatia	0,616	0,583	0,683	0,771	0,500
Cyprus	0,771	0,551	0,658	0,891	1,000
Czech Republic	0,772	0,335	0,765	0,822	0,417
Denmark	0,806	0,530	0,893	0,949	1,000
Dominican Republic	0,630	0,606	0,481	0,769	0,833
Ecuador	0,663	0,603	0,345	0,689	0,750
Egypt	0,762	0,534	0,208	0,589	0,167
Estonia	0,756	0,301	0,739	0,687	0,917
Ethiopia	0,613	0,347	0,577	0,187	0,500
Fiji	0,724	0,857	0,239	0,783	0,583
Finland	0,784	0,491	0,900	0,938	1,000
France	0,731	0,508	0,826	0,892	0,917
Gabon	0,407	0,622	0,685	0,473	0,417
Gambia	0,542	0,706	0,720	0,337	0,167
Georgia	0,469	0,593	0,527	0,641	0,583
Germany	0,727	0,538	0,800	0,914	0,917
Ghana	0,733	0,609	0,676	0,525	0,667
Greece	0,754	0,446	0,657	0,876	0,833
Guatemala	0,485	0,648	0,374	0,654	0,583
Guinea	0,682	0,672	0,545	0,301	0,250
Guinea-Bissau	0,173	0,672	0,514	0,251	0,500
Guyana	0,749	0,832	0,320	0,697	0,833
Haiti	0,247	0,529	0,607	0,385	0,417
Honduras	0,613	0,635	0,452	0,727	0,750
Hungary	0,793	0,472	0,677	0,740	0,917
Iceland	0,760	0,579	0,912	0,972	1,000
India	0,836	0,574	0,389	0,551	0,750
Indonesia	0,749	0,631	0,589	0,670	0,333
Iran, Islamic Rep. of	0,573	0,483	0,350	0,699	0,167
Ireland	0,887	0,492	0,703	0,936	1,000
Israel	0,733	0,457	0,721	0,893	0,833
Italy	0,755	0,572	0,684	0,913	0,917

	growth, social cohesion, jobs	environment	gender equality	human needs satisfaction	human rights
Jamaica	0,803	0,514	0,731	0,810	0,833
Japan	0,789	0,614	0,690	0,897	0,917
Jordan	0,688	0,531	0,391	0,674	0,417
Kazakhstan	0,638	0,401	0,735	0,673	0,250
Kenya	0,562	0,529	0,548	0,356	0,250
Korea, Rep. of	0,855	0,435	0,658	0,786	0,833
Kyrgyzstan	0,593	0,630	0,699	0,691	0,333
Lao People's Dem. Rep.	0,811	0,714	0,591	0,419	0,083
Latvia	0,757	0,464	0,735	0,655	0,917
Lebanon	0,627	0,487	0,172	0,701	0,250
Lesotho	0,299	0,559	0,355	0,372	0,500
Lithuania	0,685	0,470	0,738	0,676	0,917
Luxembourg	0,840	0,384	0,706	0,937	1,000
Madagascar	0,664	0,734	0,521	0,469	0,667
Malawi	0,493	0,636	0,521	0,147	0,750
Malaysia	0,746	0,558	0,563	0,824	0,333
Mali	0,621	0,582	0,406	0,343	0,667
Mauritania	0,682	0,621	0,471	0,393	0,250
Mauritius	0,745	0,790	0,525	0,766	0,917
Mexico	0,659	0,572	0,549	0,798	0,583
Moldova, Rep. of	0,582	0,505	0,634	0,529	0,667
Mongolia	0,693	0,678	0,585	0,675	0,750
Morocco	0,683	0,645	0,422	0,620	0,417
Mozambique	0,786	0,513	0,527	0,253	0,583
Namibia	0,312	0,620	0,561	0,471	0,750
Nepal	0,730	0,602	0,447	0,463	0,583
Netherlands	0,796	0,512	0,805	0,943	1,000
New Zealand	0,651	0,498	0,833	0,922	1,000
Niger	0,370	0,599	0,341	0,227	0,167
Nigeria	0,631	0,491	0,322	0,345	0,333
Norway	0,827	0,511	0,931	0,947	1,000
Pakistan	0,753	0,522	0,284	0,489	0,417
Panama	0,621	0,705	0,570	0,830	0,750
Papua New Guinea	0,676	0,739	0,529	0,496	0,750
Paraguay	0,438	0,651	0,237	0,738	0,583
Peru	0,661	0,730	0,498	0,678	0,417
Philippines	0,664	0,616	0,561	0,719	0,750

Continued

	growth, social cohesion, jobs	environment	gender equality	human needs satisfaction	human rights
Poland	0,714	0,400	0,729	0,773	0,917
Portugal	0,776	0,507	0,738	0,833	1,000
Romania	0,744	0,449	0,638	0,709	0,833
Russian Federation	0,600	0,344	0,651	0,593	0,500
Rwanda	0,810	0,616	0,554	0,168	0,083
Saudi Arabia	0,644	0,311	0,272	0,804	0,000
Senegal	0,671	0,585	0,438	0,384	0,500
Singapore	0,781	0,269	0,626	0,891	0,333
Slovakia	0,715	0,440	0,745	0,752	0,833
Slovenia	0,817	0,532	0,752	0,845	0,917
South Africa	0,346	0,405	0,494	0,465	0,917
Spain	0,743	0,512	0,724	0,911	0,917
Sri Lanka	0,780	0,656	0,462	0,754	0,583
Swaziland	0,335	0,651	0,323	0,424	0,333
Sweden	0,800	0,538	0,930	0,960	1,000
Switzerland	0,757	0,703	0,785	0,980	1,000
Syrian Arab Republic	0,619	0,507	0,379	0,650	0,000
Tajikistan	0,474	0,577	0,623	0,647	0,167
Tanzania, U. Rep. of	0,748	0,544	0,570	0,288	0,417
Thailand	0,804	0,604	0,663	0,720	0,750
Togo	0,460	0,650	0,388	0,307	0,250
Trinidad and Tobago	0,734	0,346	0,622	0,816	0,917
Tunisia	0,703	0,662	0,481	0,732	0,250
Turkey	0,693	0,539	0,449	0,674	0,417
Uganda	0,827	0,508	0,584	0,178	0,500
United Kingdom	0,784	0,453	0,801	0,916	0,917
United States	0,746	0,201	0,857	0,919	1,000
Uruguay	0,614	0,758	0,618	0,801	0,917
Uzbekistan	0,647	0,463	0,700	0,679	0,083
Venezuela	0,503	0,543	0,533	0,814	0,750
Viet Nam	0,897	0,508	0,751	0,672	0,000
Yemen	0,707	0,568	0,136	0,491	0,250
Zambia	0,568	0,517	0,427	0,138	0,417
Zimbabwe	0,591	0,417	0,504	0,144	0,417

The Global Lisbon Indicator, Calculated by the Method, Presented in Graph 5.3b of this Work, Combined with the Results, Achieved by the Method, Presented in Graph 5.3a of this Work

	growth, social cohesion, jobs	environment	gender equality	human needs satisfaction	human rights	overall Global Lisbon Index (2) - 17 components, broken down into 5 categories, which enter the final index on an equal basis	overall global Lisbon Index (2) ranking	Country code	Global Lisbon Index (17 sub-components)	overall global Lisbon Index (2) ranking	positive or negative bias of "17" measure [rank differences Index 17 and Index 17/5/1]
Albania	0,702	0,629	0,689	0,696	0,417	0,626	61	Albania	0,636	53	8
Algeria	0,633	0,542	0,392	0,663	0,250	0,496	103	Algeria	0,534	91	12
Angola	0,460	0,487	0,491	0,279	0,167	0,377	130	Angola	0,381	130	0
Argentina	0,563	0,675	0,607	0,823	0,667	0,667	46	Argentina	0,684	35	11
Armenia	0,718	0,575	0,768	0,610	0,500	0,634	56	Armenia	0,619	66	-10
Australia	0,780	0,333	0,850	0,941	1,000	0,781	13	Australia	0,725	27	-14
Austria	0,809	0,648	0,785	0,943	1,000	0,837	5	Austria	0,811	3	2
Azerbaijan	0,630	0,488	0,660	0,645	0,333	0,551	84	Azerbaijan	0,551	84	0
Bahrain	0,533	0,198	0,498	0,843	0,083	0,431	116	Bahrain	0,451	116	0
Bangladesh	0,826	0,614	0,450	0,479	0,667	0,607	66	Bangladesh	0,597	73	-7
Belarus	0,819	0,418	0,758	0,597	0,167	0,552	83	Belarus	0,549	85	-2
Belgium	0,769	0,437	0,805	0,927	0,917	0,771	20	Belgium	0,732	24	-4
Belize	0,672	0,797	0,268	0,809	0,917	0,693	39	Belize	0,718	28	11
Benin	0,580	0,559	0,532	0,374	0,833	0,576	75	Benin	0,543	86	-11
Bolivia	0,732	0,638	0,496	0,569	0,833	0,654	50	Bolivia	0,636	54	-4
Botswana	0,557	0,637	0,525	0,309	0,833	0,572	76	Botswana	0,543	87	-11
Brazil	0,489	0,679	0,520	0,700	0,583	0,594	70	Brazil	0,611	71	-1
Bulgaria	0,706	0,428	0,734	0,666	0,750	0,657	49	Bulgaria	0,625	60	-11
Burkina Faso	0,638	0,619	0,479	0,180	0,417	0,467	108	Burkina Faso	0,447	118	-10
Burundi	0,586	0,388	0,500	0,096	0,083	0,331	132	Burundi	0,319	132	0

Continued

	growth, social cohesion, jobs	environment	gender equality	human needs satisfaction	human rights	overall Global Lisbon Index (2) - 17 components, broken down into 5 categories, which enter the final index on an equal basis	overall global Lisbon Index (2) ranking	Country code	Global Lisbon Index (17 sub-components)	overall global Lisbon Index (2) ranking	positive or negative bias of "17" measure [rank differences Index 17 and Index 17/5/1]
Cambodia	0,839	0,608	0,565	0,433	0,167	0,522	95	Cambodia	0,540	88	7
Cameroon	0,631	0,564	0,374	0,392	0,167	0,426	119	Cameroon	0,449	117	2
Canada	0,778	0,411	0,862	0,956	1,000	0,801	10	Canada	0,753	13	-3
Chile	0,670	0,599	0,535	0,828	0,750	0,676	43	Chile	0,672	39	4
China	0,909	0,536	0,770	0,736	0,083	0,607	67	China	0,629	57	10
Colombia	0,508	0,736	0,558	0,784	0,583	0,634	57	Colombia	0,658	46	11
Congo	0,340	0,593	0,481	0,342	0,167	0,385	129	Congo	0,426	123	6
Congo, Dem. Rep. of the	0,013	0,327	0,387	0,218	0,083	0,206	133	Congo, Dem. Rep. of the	0,241	133	0
Costa Rica	0,690	0,726	0,584	0,884	0,917	0,760	24	Costa Rica	0,754	11	13
Côte d'Ivoire	0,638	0,525	0,254	0,225	0,333	0,395	128	Côte d'Ivoire	0,398	127	1
Croatia	0,616	0,583	0,683	0,771	0,500	0,630	59	Croatia	0,642	49	10
Cyprus	0,771	0,551	0,658	0,891	1,000	0,774	16	Cyprus	0,752	14	2
Czech Republic	0,772	0,335	0,765	0,822	0,417	0,622	62	Czech Republic	0,612	69	-7
Denmark	0,806	0,530	0,893	0,949	1,000	0,836	6	Denmark	0,797	6	0
Dominican Republic	0,630	0,606	0,481	0,769	0,833	0,664	47	Dominican Republic	0,664	41	6
Ecuador	0,663	0,603	0,345	0,689	0,750	0,610	65	Ecuador	0,622	62	3
Egypt	0,762	0,534	0,208	0,589	0,167	0,452	110	Egypt	0,504	99	11
Estonia	0,756	0,301	0,739	0,687	0,917	0,680	42	Estonia	0,622	63	-21
Ethiopia	0,613	0,347	0,577	0,187	0,500	0,445	114	Ethiopia	0,397	128	-14
Fiji	0,724	0,857	0,239	0,783	0,583	0,637	54	Fiji	0,713	29	25
Finland	0,784	0,491	0,900	0,938	1,000	0,823	7	Finland	0,780	7	0
France	0,731	0,508	0,826	0,892	0,917	0,775	15	France	0,737	21	-6
Gabon	0,407	0,622	0,685	0,473	0,417	0,521	96	Gabon	0,533	93	3

	growth, social cohesion, jobs	environment	gender equality	human needs satisfaction	human rights	overall Global Lisbon Index (2) - 17 components, broken down into 5 categories, which enter the final index on an equal basis	overall global Lisbon Index (2) ranking	Country code	Global Lisbon Index (17 sub-components)	overall global Lisbon Index (2) ranking	positive or negative bias of "17" measure [rank differences Index 17 and Index 17/5/1]
Gambia	0,542	0,706	0,720	0,337	0,167	0,494	104	Gambia	0,485	107	-3
Georgia	0,469	0,593	0,527	0,641	0,583	0,563	80	Georgia	0,579	78	2
Germany	0,727	0,538	0,800	0,914	0,917	0,779	14	Germany	0,751	15	-1
Ghana	0,733	0,609	0,676	0,525	0,667	0,642	52	Ghana	0,620	65	-13
Greece	0,754	0,446	0,657	0,876	0,833	0,713	32	Greece	0,684	34	-2
Guatemala	0,485	0,648	0,374	0,654	0,583	0,549	85	Guatemala	0,577	79	6
Guinea	0,682	0,672	0,545	0,301	0,250	0,490	106	Guinea	0,489	106	0
Guinea-Bissau	0,173	0,672	0,514	0,251	0,500	0,422	121	Guinea-Bissau	0,427	122	-1
Guyana	0,749	0,832	0,320	0,697	0,833	0,686	41	Guyana	0,739	20	21
Haiti	0,247	0,529	0,607	0,385	0,417	0,437	115	Haiti	0,452	115	0
Honduras	0,613	0,635	0,452	0,727	0,750	0,636	55	Honduras	0,634	56	-1
Hungary	0,793	0,472	0,677	0,740	0,917	0,720	30	Hungary	0,680	36	-6
Iceland	0,760	0,579	0,912	0,972	1,000	0,845	3	Iceland	0,815	2	1
India	0,836	0,574	0,389	0,551	0,750	0,620	63	India	0,616	67	-4
Indonesia	0,749	0,631	0,589	0,670	0,333	0,594	71	Indonesia	0,620	64	7
Iran, Islamic Rep. of	0,573	0,483	0,350	0,699	0,167	0,454	109	Iran, Islamic Rep. of	0,478	109	0
Ireland	0,887	0,492	0,703	0,936	1,000	0,804	9	Ireland	0,763	9	0
Israel	0,733	0,457	0,721	0,893	0,833	0,727	29	Israel	0,699	32	-3
Italy	0,755	0,572	0,684	0,913	0,917	0,768	22	Italy	0,745	17	5
Jamaica	0,803	0,514	0,731	0,810	0,833	0,738	28	Jamaica	0,703	30	-2
Japan	0,789	0,614	0,690	0,897	0,917	0,781	11	Japan	0,760	10	1
Jordan	0,688	0,531	0,391	0,674	0,417	0,540	87	Jordan	0,556	83	4
Kazakhstan	0,638	0,401	0,735	0,673	0,250	0,539	88	Kazakhstan	0,530	94	-6
Kenya	0,562	0,529	0,548	0,356	0,250	0,449	111	Kenya	0,453	114	-3
Korea, Rep. of	0,855	0,435	0,658	0,786	0,833	0,714	31	Korea, Rep. of	0,678	37	-6
Kyrgyzstan	0,593	0,630	0,699	0,691	0,333	0,589	72	Kyrgyzstan	0,610	72	0

Continued

	growth, social cohesion, jobs	environment	gender equality	human needs satisfaction	human rights	overall Global Lisbon Index (2) - 17 components, broken down into 5 categories, which enter the final index on an equal basis	overall global Lisbon Index (2) ranking	Country code	Global Lisbon Index (17 sub-components)	overall global Lisbon Index (2) ranking	positive or negative bias of "17" measure [rank differences Index 17 and Index 17/5/1]
Lao People's Dem. Rep.	0,811	0,714	0,591	0,419	0,083	0,524	94	Lao People's Dem. Rep.	0,536	90	4
Latvia	0,757	0,464	0,735	0,655	0,917	0,706	35	Latvia	0,662	44	-9
Lebanon	0,627	0,487	0,172	0,701	0,250	0,447	112	Lebanon	0,503	100	12
Lesotho	0,299	0,559	0,355	0,372	0,500	0,417	122	Lesotho	0,401	126	-4
Lithuania	0,685	0,470	0,738	0,676	0,917	0,697	36	Lithuania	0,656	47	-11
Luxembourg	0,840	0,384	0,706	0,937	1,000	0,774	18	Luxembourg	0,748	16	2
Madagascar	0,664	0,734	0,521	0,469	0,667	0,611	64	Madagascar	0,612	70	-6
Malawi	0,493	0,636	0,521	0,147	0,750	0,509	101	Malawi	0,474	111	-10
Malaysia	0,746	0,558	0,563	0,824	0,333	0,605	68	Malaysia	0,628	58	10
Mali	0,621	0,582	0,406	0,343	0,667	0,524	93	Mali	0,501	102	-9
Mauritania	0,682	0,621	0,471	0,393	0,250	0,483	107	Mauritania	0,490	105	2
Mauritius	0,745	0,790	0,525	0,766	0,917	0,748	25	Mauritius	0,754	12	13
Mexico	0,659	0,572	0,549	0,798	0,583	0,632	58	Mexico	0,638	52	6
Moldova, Rep. of	0,582	0,505	0,634	0,529	0,667	0,583	73	Moldova, Rep. of	0,566	81	-8
Mongolia	0,693	0,678	0,585	0,675	0,750	0,676	44	Mongolia	0,672	40	4
Morocco	0,683	0,645	0,422	0,620	0,417	0,557	81	Morocco	0,589	75	6
Mozambique	0,786	0,513	0,527	0,253	0,583	0,533	90	Mozambique	0,491	104	-14
Namibia	0,312	0,620	0,561	0,471	0,750	0,543	86	Namibia	0,539	89	-3
Nepal	0,730	0,602	0,447	0,463	0,583	0,565	79	Nepal	0,559	82	-3
Netherlands	0,796	0,512	0,805	0,943	1,000	0,811	8	Netherlands	0,773	8	0
New Zealand	0,651	0,498	0,833	0,922	1,000	0,781	12	New Zealand	0,743	18	-6
Niger	0,370	0,599	0,341	0,227	0,167	0,341	131	Niger	0,361	131	0
Nigeria	0,631	0,491	0,322	0,345	0,333	0,425	120	Nigeria	0,413	124	-4
Norway	0,827	0,511	0,931	0,947	1,000	0,843	4	Norway	0,801	5	-1

	growth, social cohesion, jobs	environment	gender equality	human needs satisfaction	human rights	overall Global Lisbon Index (2) - 17 components, broken down into 5 categories, which enter the final index on an equal basis	overall global Lisbon Index (2) ranking	Country code	Global Lisbon Index (17 sub-components)	overall global Lisbon Index (2) ranking	positive or negative bias of "17" measure [rank differences Index 17 and Index 17/5/1]
Pakistan	0,753	0,522	0,284	0,489	0,417	0,493	105	Pakistan	0,501	101	4
Panama	0,621	0,705	0,570	0,830	0,750	0,695	38	Panama	0,701	31	7
Papua New Guinea	0,676	0,739	0,529	0,496	0,750	0,638	53	Papua New Guinea	0,635	55	-2
Paraguay	0,438	0,651	0,237	0,738	0,583	0,529	91	Paraguay	0,595	74	17
Peru	0,661	0,730	0,498	0,678	0,417	0,597	69	Peru	0,628	59	10
Philippines	0,664	0,616	0,561	0,719	0,750	0,662	48	Philippines	0,655	48	0
Poland	0,714	0,400	0,729	0,773	0,917	0,707	34	Poland	0,662	42	-8
Portugal	0,776	0,507	0,738	0,833	1,000	0,771	21	Portugal	0,730	26	-5
Romania	0,744	0,449	0,638	0,709	0,833	0,674	45	Romania	0,641	51	-6
Russian Federation	0,600	0,344	0,651	0,593	0,500	0,538	89	Russian Federation	0,520	96	-7
Rwanda	0,810	0,616	0,554	0,168	0,083	0,446	113	Rwanda	0,456	113	0
Saudi Arabia	0,644	0,311	0,272	0,804	0,000	0,406	127	Saudi Arabia	0,430	120	7
Senegal	0,671	0,585	0,438	0,384	0,500	0,516	98	Senegal	0,512	97	1
Singapore	0,781	0,269	0,626	0,891	0,333	0,580	74	Singapore	0,580	77	-3
Slovakia	0,715	0,440	0,745	0,752	0,833	0,697	37	Slovakia	0,662	43	-6
Slovenia	0,817	0,532	0,752	0,845	0,917	0,772	19	Slovenia	0,740	19	0
South Africa	0,346	0,405	0,494	0,465	0,917	0,525	92	South Africa	0,484	108	-16
Spain	0,743	0,512	0,724	0,911	0,917	0,761	23	Spain	0,732	25	-2
Sri Lanka	0,780	0,656	0,462	0,754	0,583	0,647	51	Sri Lanka	0,658	45	6
Swaziland	0,335	0,651	0,323	0,424	0,333	0,413	124	Swaziland	0,433	119	5
Sweden	0,800	0,538	0,930	0,960	1,000	0,846	1	Sweden	0,807	4	-3
Switzerland	0,757	0,703	0,785	0,980	1,000	0,845	2	Switzerland	0,827	1	1
Syrian Arab Republic	0,619	0,507	0,379	0,650	0,000	0,431	117	Syrian Arab Republic	0,475	110	7
Tajikistan	0,474	0,577	0,623	0,647	0,167	0,497	102	Tajikistan	0,533	92	10
Tanzania, U. Rep. of	0,748	0,544	0,570	0,288	0,417	0,513	100	Tanzania, U. Rep. of	0,510	98	2

Continued

	growth, social cohesion, jobs	environment	gender equality	human needs satisfaction	human rights	overall Global Lisbon Index (2) - 17 components, broken down into 5 categories, which enter the final index on an equal basis	overall global Lisbon Index (2) ranking	Country code	Global Lisbon Index (17 sub-components)	overall global Lisbon Index (2) ranking	positive or negative bias of "17" measure [rank differences Index 17 and Index 17/5/1]
Thailand	0,804	0,604	0,663	0,720	0,750	0,708	33	Thailand	0,694	33	0
Togo	0,460	0,650	0,388	0,307	0,250	0,411	126	Togo	0,428	121	5
Trinidad and Tobago	0,734	0,346	0,622	0,816	0,917	0,687	40	Trinidad and Tobago	0,641	50	-10
Tunisia	0,703	0,662	0,481	0,732	0,250	0,566	77	Tunisia	0,613	68	9
Turkey	0,693	0,539	0,449	0,674	0,417	0,554	82	Turkey	0,568	80	2
Uganda	0,827	0,508	0,584	0,178	0,500	0,519	97	Uganda	0,492	103	-6
United Kingdom	0,784	0,453	0,801	0,916	0,917	0,774	17	United Kingdom	0,736	23	-6
United States	0,746	0,201	0,857	0,919	1,000	0,745	26	United States	0,676	38	-12
Uruguay	0,614	0,758	0,618	0,801	0,917	0,741	27	Uruguay	0,737	22	5
Uzbekistan	0,647	0,463	0,700	0,679	0,083	0,514	99	Uzbekistan	0,526	95	4
Venezuela	0,503	0,543	0,533	0,814	0,750	0,629	60	Venezuela	0,622	61	-1
Viet Nam	0,897	0,508	0,751	0,672	0,000	0,565	78	Viet Nam	0,589	76	2
Yemen	0,707	0,568	0,136	0,491	0,250	0,430	118	Yemen	0,461	112	6
Zambia	0,568	0,517	0,427	0,138	0,417	0,413	125	Zambia	0,408	125	0
Zimbabwe	0,591	0,417	0,504	0,144	0,417	0,415	123	Zimbabwe	0,392	129	-6

THE MULTIVARIATE RESULTS FOR THE DETERMINANTS OF THE COMPONENTS OF THE "GLOBAL LISBON INDEX" (2)

growth, social cohesion, jobs	Dummy for being landlocked	Dummy for transition economy	Urbanization ratio, 1990	(1-S)/GNP	state interventionism (absence of ec. freedom)	MNC PEN 1995	low comparative international price level (ERD)	EU-membership (EU-15)	Muslims as % of total population	ln(GDP PPP pc)	ln (GDP PPP pc)^2	world bank pension reform	constant
	0,0073	0,00578	-0,0438	0,00053	0,0482	0,0081	-0,0015	-0,0928	0,00026	-0,0026	0,06772	-0,0463	1,01406
	0,03814	0,0114	0,18378	0,00036	0,04708	0,01472	0,00066	0,02881	0,00109	0,00096	0,03993	0,03186	0,72558
	0,2953	0,13241											
	4,19057	120											
	0,88165	2,1039											
t-test and direction of influence	0,19136	0,50706	-0,2385	1,46935	1,02383	0,5505	-2,272	-3,221	0,23854	-2,6529	1,69588	-1,4544	1,39759
t-test and direction of influence^2	0,03662	0,25711	0,05689	2,15898	1,04822	0,30305	5,16266	10,3772	0,0569	7,03793	2,87602	2,11518	1,95326
t-test and direction of influence^0,5	0,19136	0,50706	0,23851	1,46935	1,02383	0,5505	2,27215	3,22136	0,23854	2,65291	1,69588	1,45437	1,39759
degrees of freedom	120	120	120	120	120	120	120	120	120	120	120	120	120
error probability	0,84857	0,61304	0,81189	0,14436	0,30798	0,583	**0,0249**	**0,0016**	0,81187	**0,0091**	**0,0925**	0,14846	0,16481
F equation	4,19057	4,19057	4,19057	4,19057	4,19057	4,19057	4,19057	4,19057	4,19057	4,19057	4,19057	4,19057	4,19057
error probability, entire equation	1,7E-05	1,7E-05	1,7E-05	1,7E-05	1,7E-05	1,7E-05	1,7E-05	1,7E-05	1,7E-05	1,7E-05	1,7E-05	1,7E-05	1,7E-05
environment	Dummy for being landlocked	Dummy for transition economy	Urbanization ratio, 1990	(1-S)/GNP	state interventionism (absence of ec. freedom)	MNC PEN 1995	low comparative international price level (ERD)	EU-membership (EU-15)	Muslims as % of total population	ln(GDP PPP pc)	ln (GDP PPP pc)^2	world bank pension reform	constant
	0,0646	-0,0429	0,69061	-0,0003	0,03198	-0,0262	-0,0008	-0,015	0,00109	-0,0022	-0,0983	0,00973	-1,926
	0,0292	0,00872	0,14069	0,00028	0,03604	0,01127	0,00051	0,02205	0,00083	0,00074	0,03057	0,02439	0,55545
	0,3651	0,10136											

Continued

environment	Dummy for being landlocked	Dummy for transition economy	Urbanization ratio, 1990	(I-S)/GNP	state interventionism (absence of ec. freedom)	MNC PEN 1995	low comparative international price level (ERD)	EU-membership (EU-15)	Muslims as % of total population	ln(GDP PPP pc)	ln (GDP PPP pc)^2	world bank pension reform	constant
	5,75096	120											
	0,70907	1,23296											
t-test and direction of influence	2,2125	-4,919	4,9089	-1,0015	0,88723	-2,329	-1,5764	-0,6821	1,31434	-3,048	-3,216	0,39887	-3,4675
t-test and direction of influence^2	4,89498	24,1952	24,0969	1,00301	0,78717	5,42613	2,48509	0,46529	1,72749	9,28908	10,3396	0,15909	12,0237
t-test and direction of influence^0,5	2,21246	4,91886	4,90886	1,00151	0,88723	2,32941	1,57642	0,68212	1,31434	3,0478	3,21552	0,39887	3,46752
degrees of freedom	120	120	120	120	120	120	120	120	120	120	120	120	120
error probability	0,0288	3E-06	3E-06	0,3186	0,37673	0,0215	0,11756	0,49648	0,19124	0,0028	0,0017	0,6907	0,00073
F equation	5,75096	5,75096	5,75096	5,75096	5,75096	5,75096	5,75096	5,75096	5,75096	5,75096	5,75096	5,75096	5,75096
error probability, entire equation	9E-08	9E-08	9E-08	9E-08	9E-08	9E-08	9E-08	9E-08	9E-08	9E-08	9E-08	9E-08	9E-08

gender equality	Dummy for being landlocked	Dummy for transition economy	Urbanization ratio, 1990	(I-S)/GNP	state interventionism (absence of ec. freedom)	MNC PEN 1995	low comparative international price level (ERD)	EU-membership (EU-15)	Muslims as % of total population	ln(GDP PPP pc)	ln (GDP PPP pc)^2	world bank pension reform	constant
	0,04518	0,05796	-0,8616	-0,0009	0,03672	0,02944	-0,0006	-0,0184	0,00013	-0,0015	0,20445	-0,0556	3,71333
	0,03105	0,00928	0,14964	0,00029	0,03834	0,01198	0,00054	0,02346	0,00089	0,00078	0,03252	0,02594	0,5908
	0,6528	0,10782											
	18,8011	120											
	2,62255	1,39489											
t-test and direction of influence	1,45502	6,2462	-5,758	-3,141	0,95773	2,4568	-1,0928	-0,7854	0,15012	-1,917	6,2876	-2,145	6,28524

gender equality	Dummy for being landlocked	Dummy for transition economy	Urbanization ratio, 1990	(1-S)/GNP	state interventionism (absence of ec. freedom)	MNC PEN 1995	low comparative international price level (ERD)	EU-membership (EU-15)	Muslims as % of total population	ln(GDP PPP pc)	ln (GDP PPP pc)^2	world bank pension reform	constant
t-test and direction of influence^2	2,1171	39,0149	33,1543	9,86548	0,91724	6,03594	1,19429	0,61693	0,02254	3,67472	39,5333	4,59997	39,5042
t-test and direction of influence^0,5	1,45502	6,24619	5,75797	3,14094	0,95773	2,45682	1,09284	0,78545	0,15012	1,91696	6,28755	2,14475	6,28524
degrees of freedom	120	120	120	120	120	120	120	120	120	120	120	120	120
error probability	0,14827	7E-09	7E-08	0,0021	0,34013	0,0154	0,27665	0,43374	0,88092	0,0576	5E-09	0,034	5,5E-09
F equation	18,8011	18,8011	18,8011	18,8011	18,8011	18,8011	18,8011	18,8011	18,8011	18,8011	18,8011	18,8011	18,8011
error probability, entire equation	2,8E-22	2,8E-22	2,8E-22	2,8E-22	2,8E-22	2,8E-22	2,8E-22	2,8E-22	2,8E-22	2,8E-22	2,8E-22	2,8E-22	2,8E-22
human needs satisfaction	Dummy for being landlocked	Dummy for transition economy	Urbanization ratio, 1990	(1-S)/GNP	state interventionism (absence of ec. freedom)	MNC PEN 1995	low comparative international price level (ERD)	EU-membership (EU-15)	Muslims as % of total population	ln(GDP PPP pc)	ln (GDP PPP pc)^2	world bank pension reform	constant
	0,02063	-0,0158	0,41727	0,00046	0,03851	0,0033	-0,0004	-0,0384	0,00119	0,00066	0,05396	-0,0641	-1,6633
	0,03137	0,00937	0,15116	0,0003	0,03873	0,0121	0,00054	0,02369	0,00089	0,00079	0,03285	0,0262	0,59679
	0,8085	0,10891											
	42,2133	120											
	6,00825	1,42331											
t-test and direction of influence	0,65781	-1,682	2,7605	1,53614	0,9943	0,27267	-0,6842	-1,6192	1,33506	0,83008	1,6429	-2,446	-2,7871
t-test and direction of influence^2	0,43272	2,82907	7,62059	2,35972	0,98863	0,07435	0,46808	2,62173	1,7824	0,68903	2,69913	5,98365	7,76805
t-test and direction of influence^0,5	0,65781	1,68198	2,76054	1,53614	0,9943	0,27267	0,68416	1,61918	1,33506	0,83008	1,6429	2,44615	2,78712
degrees of freedom	120	120	120	120	120	120	120	120	120	120	120	120	120
error probability	0,51192	0,0952	0,0067	0,12714	0,32208	0,78557	0,49519	0,10803	0,18438	0,40814	0,10302	0,0159	0,00618

Continued

human needs satisfaction	Dummy for being landlocked	**Dummy for transition economy**	Urbanization ratio, 1990	(1-S)/GNP	state interventionism (absence of ec. freedom)	MNC PEN 1995	low comparative international price level (ERD)	EU-membership (EU-15)	Muslims as % of total population	ln(GDP PPP pc)	ln (GDP PPP pc)^2	**world bank pension reform**	constant
F equation	42,2133	42,2133	42,2133	42,2133	42,2133	42,2133	42,2133	42,2133	42,2133	42,2133	42,2133	42,2133	42,2133
error probability, entire equation	2,5E-37	2,5E-37	2,5E-37	2,5E-37	2,5E-37	2,5E-37	2,5E-37	2,5E-37	2,5E-37	2,5E-37	2,5E-37	2,5E-37	2,5E-37
human rights	Dummy for being landlocked	Dummy for transition economy	Urbanization ratio, 1990	**(1-S)/GNP**	state interventionism (absence of ec. freedom)	MNC PEN 1995	low comparative international price level (ERD)	EU-membership (EU-15)	Muslims as % of total population	ln(GDP PPP pc)	ln (GDP PPP pc)^2	world bank pension reform	constant
	0,00444	0,01719	-0,1932	-0,0028	0,07352	-0,0107	-0,0026	-0,2151	0,00567	-0,0034	0,07901	-0,0935	1,91865
	0,05264	0,01573	0,25365	0,0005	0,06499	0,02031	0,00091	0,03976	0,0015	0,00133	0,05512	0,04397	1,00146
	0,6766	0,18276											
	20,9198	120											
	8,38458	4,00797											
t-test and direction of influence	0,08432	1,09282	-0,7618	-5,542	1,13133	-0,5279	-2,808	-5,409	3,7753	-2,525	1,43344	-2,126	1,91586
t-test and direction of influence^2	0,00711	1,19425	0,5804	30,7093	1,2799	0,27867	7,88221	29,2527	14,2526	6,37659	2,05474	4,51849	3,6705
t-test and direction of influence^0,5	0,08432	1,09282	0,76184	5,5416	1,13133	0,52789	2,80753	5,40858	3,77526	2,52519	1,43344	2,12567	1,91586
degrees of freedom	120	120	120	120	120	120	120	120	120	120	120	120	120
error probability	0,93294	0,27666	0,44765	**2E-07**	0,26017	0,59855	**0,0058**	**3E-07**	**0,0002**	**0,0129**	0,15433	**0,0356**	0,05776
F equation	20,9198	20,9198	20,9198	20,9198	20,9198	20,9198	20,9198	20,9198	20,9198	20,9198	20,9198	20,9198	20,9198
error probability, entire equation	4,7E-24	4,7E-24	4,7E-24	4,7E-24	4,7E-24	4,7E-24	4,7E-24	4,7E-24	4,7E-24	4,7E-24	4,7E-24	4,7E-24	4,7E-24

Legend: As in all EXCEL 7.0 outprints, first row: un-standardized regression coefficients, second row: standard errors, second last row: t-Test and direction of the influence. The values immediately below the standard errors are R^2 (third row, left side entry), F, and degrees of freedom (fourth row). Below that: ss $_{reg}$, ss $_{resid}$, i.e. the sum of squares of the regression and the sum of squares of the residuals. The right-hand entry in the third row is the standard error of the estimate y. Below the EXCEL outprints; we present materials for the t-test and the F-test for our regression results.

Documentation: The United Nations on Definitions of the UNDP Indicators

From: http://hdr.undp.org/statistics/faq/#31

What Is the Human Development Index (HDI)?

The HDI – human development index – is a summary composite index that measures a country's average achievements in three basic aspects of human development: longevity, knowledge, and a decent standard of living. Longevity is measured by life expectancy at birth; knowledge is measured by a combination of the adult literacy rate and the combined primary, secondary, and tertiary gross enrolment ratio; and standard of living by GDP per capita (PPP US$). For details on how to calculate the HDI, see pages 258-259 of Technical Note 1 and also the interactive HDI calculator and the Excel tool - interactive tools that help understand the calculation of the HDI.

How is the HDI Used?

- To capture the attention of policy makers, media and NGOs and to draw their attention away from the more usual economic statistics to focus instead on human outcomes. The HDI was created to re-emphasize that people and their capabilities should be the ultimate criteria for assessing the development of a country, not economic growth.
- To question national policy choices - asking how two countries with the same level of income per person can end up with such different human development outcomes (HDI levels). For example, Viet Nam and Pakistan have similar levels of income per person, but life expectancy and literacy differ greatly between the two countries, with Viet Nam having a much higher HDI value than Pakistan. These striking contrasts immediately stimulate debate on government policies on health and education, asking why what is achieved in one country is far from the reach of another.
- • To highlight wide differences within countries, between provinces or states, across gender, ethnicity, and other socioeconomic groupings. Highlighting internal disparities along these lines has raised national debate in many countries.

Is the HDI Enough to Measure a Country's Level of Development?

Not at all. The concept of human development is much broader than what can be captured in the HDI, or any other of the composite indices in this Report (see gender-related development index, gender empowerment measure, and human poverty index). The HDI, for example, does not reflect political participation or gender inequalities. The HDI and the other composite indices can only offer a broad proxy on some of the key the issues of human development, gender disparity, and human poverty. A fuller picture of a country's level of human development requires analysis of other human development indicators and information (see human development indicators).

Can GDP per Capita be Used to Measure Human Development instead of the HDI?

No. GDP per capita only reflects average national income. It tells nothing of how that income is distributed or how that income is spent - whether on universal health, education or military expenditure. Comparing rankings on GDP per capita and the HDI can reveal much about the results of national policy choices. For example, a country with a very high GDP per capita such as Kuwait, who has a relatively low level of educational attainment, can have a lower HDI rank than, say, Uruguay, who has roughly half the GDP per capita of Kuwait.

Why is GDP per Capita (PPP US$) Used over GDP per Capita (US$) in the HDI?

The human development index (HDI) attempts to make an assessment of 177 very diverse countries and areas, with very different price levels. To compare economic statistics across countries, the data must first be converted into a common currency. Unlike conventional exchange rates, PPP (Purchasing Power Parity) rates of exchange allow this conversion to take account of price differences between countries. GDP per capita (PPP US$) accounts for price differences between countries and therefore better reflects people's living standards. In theory, at the PPP rate, 1 PPP dollar has the same purchasing power in the domestic economy of a country as 1 US dollar has in the US economy. For further discussion on the use of PPP, see Box 2, p.135, in the Note on statistics in the Human Development Report 2001 (The why's and wherefore's of purchasing power parities).

Why doesn't the HDI Include Dimensions of Participation, Gender, and Equality?

As a simple summary index, the HDI is designed to reflect average achievements in three basic aspects of human development – leading a long and healthy life, being knowledgeable, and enjoying a decent standard of living. Participation, gender disparity and human deprivation are measured in other indices (see gender-related development index, gender empowerment measure, and the human poverty index) or other indicators of the Report. Measurement issues related to these indices demonstrate the conceptual and methodological challenges that remain to be tackled.

Where do Data for HDI Come from? What Are the Criteria for a Country to be Included in the HDI?

Currently, for various reasons, there still exist many data gaps in even some very basic areas of human development indicators. While actively advocating for the improvement of human development data, as a principle and for practical reasons, HDRO does not collect data directly from countries or make estimates to fill these data gaps in the Report.

The one exception is the human development index (HDI). The Human Development Report Office strives to include as many UN member countries as possible in the HDI. For a country to be included, data ideally should be available from the relevant international data agencies for all four components of the index (the primary sources of data are the United Nations Population Division for life expectancy at birth, the UNESCO Institute for Statistics for the adult literacy rate and combined gross enrolment ratio for primary, secondary and tertiary schools and the World Bank for GDP per capita [PPP US$]). But for a significant number of countries data are missing for one or more of these components.

Striving to include as many UN member countries as possible and in response to the desire of countries to be included in the HDI, the Human Development Report Office makes every effort in these cases to identify other reasonable estimates, working with international data agencies, the UN Regional Commissions, national statistical offices and UNDP country offices. In a few cases the Human Development Report Office has attempted to make an estimate in consultation with regional and national statistical offices or other experts. Read more...

Why Isn't the HDI Compiled for all UN Member Countries?

While the data in the Report demonstrate the wealth of human development statistics available, they also reveal many data gaps in basic areas of human development. Not all UN member countries have sufficient data available to calculate the HDI or other indices. However, for the 16 UN member countries not included in the HDI in HDR 2004, basic human development indicators (where available) are shown in Table 33 of the Report, p. 250.

Is the HDI Comparable over Time?

The HDI is comparable over time when it is calculated based on the same methodology and comparable trend data. HDR 2004 presents a time series in HDI for 1975, 1980, 1985, 1990, 1995, 2000 and 2002. This time series uses the latest HDI methodology and the most up-to-date trend data for each component of the index (please see indicator Table 2, Human development index trends, pp. 143-146). Please note that the HDI is designed to capture long-term progress in human development, rather than short-term changes. Read more...

Is the HDI Comparable across Editions of the HDR?

Due to revisions to the data series for some or all of the components of the HDI, changes in the HDI methodology, or variations in the country coverage, the HDI values and ranks presented in the 1990 through 2004 editions of the Report are not directly comparable. The year-to-year changes in the index often reflect data improvement, instead of real increase or decrease in the level of human development (see Statistical feature 2 Note to table 1: About this year's human development index, pp. 137-138).

The Human Development Report Offices strongly advises against constructing HDI trend analysis based on the HDI published in different editions of the Report. For the most up-to-date HDI trend data based on consistent country coverage, methodology and data, please refer to Table 2 (Human Development Index Trends, pp. 143-146) in HDR 2004.

Is the HDI Available before 1975?

Comparable data are not available for many countries for all components of the HDI before 1975, so 1975 is the first year for which the HDI was calculated in HDR 2004. Estimates for some indicators are available before this time, such as life expectancy, which are available since 1950.

Why was the HDI Methodology Changed in the 1999 HDR?

The methodology of the HDI has evolved and improved over time. In 1999, the formula used to treat the income component of the HDI was significantly refined, setting the methodology on a more solid analytical foundation (for details, see page 159 HDR 1999 Technical Note: Computing the indices).

Questions about Other Indices Used in the Human Development Report

What is the Gender-related Development Index (GDI)?
The GDI – gender-related development index – is a composite indicator that measures the average achievement of a population in the same dimensions as the HDI while adjusting for gender inequalities in the level of achievement in the three basic aspects of human development. It uses the same variables as the HDI, disaggregated by gender. For details on how to calculate the GDI see pages 258, 261-262 and 264 of Technical Note 1.

What Is the Gender Empowerment Measure (GEM)?
The GEM – gender empowerment measure – is a composite indicator that captures gender inequality in three key areas:

- Political participation and decision-making, as measured by women's and men's percentage shares of parliamentary seats;

- Economic participation and decision-making power, as measured by two indicators – women's and men's percentage shares of positions as legislators, senior officials and managers and women's and men's percentage shares of professional and technical positions;
- Power over economic resources, as measured by women's and men's estimated earned income (PPP US$).

For details on how to calculate the GEM see pages 258, and 263-264 of Technical Note 1.

How are the GDI and the GEM Used?

To draw attention to gender issues. The GDI adjusts the HDI for inequalities in the achievement of men and women. A comparison of a country's ranking on the HDI and its ranking on the GDI can indicate the existence of gender disparity . To illustrate that gender empowerment does not depend on income, it is useful to compare relative rankings on the GEM and the relative level of national income. For example,

- Poland ranks 27th in the GEM, ahead of Japan, in 38th place, yet income per person in Poland is about one third that of Japan's (10, 560 PPP US$ vs. 26, 190 PPP US$ for 2002).
- The UK and Finland have very similar income per person (26, 150 PPP US$ and 26, 190 PPP US$ for 2002) yet in the GEM Finland ranks 4th, the UK 18th.

Both indicators can be disaggregated to highlight gender inequality within countries, which can vary widely across regions.

What Is the Human Poverty Index (HPI-1 and HPI-2)?

Poverty has traditionally been measured as a lack of income - but this is far too narrow a definition. Human poverty is a concept that captures the many dimensions of poverty that exist in both poor and rich countries—it is the denial of choices and opportunities for living a life one has reason to value. The HPI-1–human poverty index for developing countries – measures human deprivations in the same three aspects of human development as the HDI (longevity, knowledge and a decent standard of living). HPI-2–human poverty index for selected high-income OECD countries–includes, in addition to the three dimensions in HPI-1, social exclusion.

For HPI-1 (developing countries): deprivations in longevity are measured by the probability at birth of not surviving to age 40; deprivations in knowledge are measured by the percentage of adults who are illiterate; deprivations in a decent standard of living are measured by two variables: the percentage of people not having sustainable access to an improved water source and the percentage of children below the age of five who are underweight.

For HPI-2 (selected high-income OECD countries): deprivations in longevity are measured by the probability at birth of not surviving to age 60; deprivations in knowledge are measured by the percentage of adults lacking functional literacy skills; deprivations in a decent standard of living are measured by the percentage of people living below the income poverty line, set at 50% of the adjusted median household disposable income; and social exclusion is measured by the rate of long-term (12 months or more) unemployment of the labour force. For details on how to calculate the HPI-1 and HPI-2 see pages 258 and 260 of Technical Note 1.

How is the HPI Used?

- To focus attention on the most deprived people and deprivations in basic human capabilities in a country, not on average national achievement. The human poverty indices focus directly on the number of people living in deprivation – presenting a very different picture from average national achievement. It also moves the focus of poverty debates away from concern about income poverty alone.
- To highlight the presence of human poverty in both the rich and poor countries. High income per person is no guarantee of a poverty-free country. Even among the richest countries, there is human poverty. The HPI-2 for selected high-income OECD countries (HPI-2) shows that out of 17 countries, the US has the second highest level of income per person, but also the highest rate of human poverty.
- To guide national planning for poverty alleviation. Many National Human Development Reports now break down the HPI by region or other socioeconomic groups to identify the areas or social groups within the country most deprived in terms of human poverty. The results can be dramatic, creating national debate and helping to reshape policies.

Why Aren't All the Countries Included in the GDI, GEM, and HPI?

Lack of data is a particular constraint in monitoring gender disparity and poverty. Coverage of the GDI in HDR 2004 is limited to 144 countries, GEM to 78 countries, and the HPI-1 to 95 developing countries and HPI-2 to 17 high-income OECD countries (see also "Why isn't HDI compiled for all UN member countries? ").

DOCUMENTATION: THE YALE/COLUMBIA ENVIRONMENTAL SUSTAINABILITY INDEX

The team, which developed the Index

Yale Center for Environmental Law and Policy 250 Prospect Street New Haven, CT 06511 USA (1-203) 432-3123 Fax (1-203) 432-3817 E-mail: ycelp@yale.edu Web: www.yale.edu/envirocenter *In Collaboration with:*	Center for International Earth Science Information Network (CIESIN) Columbia University PO Box 1000 61 Route 9W Palisades, NY 10964 USA (1-845) 365-8988 Fax (1-845) 365-8922 E-mail: ciesin.info@ciesin.columbia.edu Web: www.ciesin.columbia.edu
World Economic Forum 91-93 route de la Capite 1223 Cologny/Geneva Switzerland (41-22) 869-1212 Fax (41-22) 786-2744 E-mail: contact@weforum.org Web: www.weforum.org	**Joint Research Centre** European Commission Enrico Fermi 1 TP 361, 21020 Ispra Italy (39-03320)-785287 Fax: (39-0332)-785733 Web: www.jrc.cec.eu.int/uasa

A summary of the methodology is contained in:
http://sedac.ciesin.columbia.edu/es/esi/a_methodology.pdf

Data and data descitptions are downloadable from:
http://sedac.ciesin.columbia.edu/es/esi/downloads.html#data

The creators of the measure say on their website:
http://sedac.ciesin.columbia.edu/es/esi/ESI2005_policysummary.pdf

The 2005 Environmental Sustainability Index (ESI) benchmarks the ability of nations to protect the environment over the next several decades. It does so by integrating 76 data sets – tracking natural resource endowments, past and present pollution levels, environmental management efforts, and a society's capacity to improve its environmental performance – into 21 indicators of environmental sustainability.

These indicators permit comparison across the following five fundamental components of sustainability: Environmental Systems; Environmental Stresses; Human Vulnerability to Environmental Stresses; Societal Capacity to Respond to Environmental Challenges; and Global Stewardship.

The issues reflected in the indicators and the underlying variables were chosen through an extensive review of the environmental literature, assessment of available data, rigorous analysis, and broad-based consultation with policymakers, scientists, and indicator experts.

The Index is calculated by weighting the following components:

Variable Code	Variable Description	Indicator Description	Indicator Code	Component	Short Source
NO2	Urban population weighted NO2 concentration	Air Quality	SYS_AIR	SYSTEM	Organisation for Economic Co-operation and Development (OECD), United Nations Human Settlement Programme (UNHABITAT), World Health Organization, European Environment Agency, and World Resources Institute, plus country data.
SO2	Urban population weighted SO2 concentration	Air Quality	SYS_AIR	SYSTEM	Organisation for Economic Co-operation and Development (OECD), United Nations Human Settlement Programme (UNHABITAT), World Health Organization, European Environment Agency, and World Resources Institute, plus country data.

Continued

Variable Code	Variable Description	Indicator Description	Indicator Code	Component	Short Source
TSP	Urban population weighted TSP concentration	Air Quality	SYS_AIR	SYSTEM	Organisation for Economic Co-operation and Development (OECD), United Nations Human Settlement Programme (UNHABITAT), World Health Organization, European Environment Agency, and World Resources Institute, plus country data.
INDOOR	Indoor air pollution from solid fuel use	Air Quality	SYS_AIR	SYSTEM	World Health Organization.
ECORISK	Percentage of country's territory in threatened ecoregions	Biodiversity	SYS_BIO	SYSTEM	The Nature Conservancy and World Wildlife Fund.
PRTBRD	Threatened bird species as percentage of known breeding bird species in each country	Biodiversity	SYS_BIO	SYSTEM	IUCN-The World Conservation Union Species Survival Commission.
PRTMAM	Threatened mammal species as percentage of known mammal species in each country	Biodiversity	SYS_BIO	SYSTEM	IUCN-The World Conservation Union Species Survival Commission.
PRTAMPH	Threatened amphibian species as percentage of known amphibian species in each country	Biodiversity	SYS_BIO	SYSTEM	IUCN-The World Conservation Union Species Survival Commission, Conservation International-Center for Applied Biodiversity Science, and NatureServe.
NBI	National Biodiversity Index	Biodiversity	SYS_BIO	SYSTEM	Convention on Biological Diversity.
ANTH10	Percentage of total land area (including inland waters) having very low anthropogenic impact	Land	SYS_LAN	SYSTEM	Center for International Earth Science Information Network (CIESIN), Columbia University.

Variable Code	Variable Description	Indicator Description	Indicator Code	Component	Short Source
ANTH40	Percentage of total land area (including inland waters) having very high anthropogenic impact	Land	SYS_LAN	SYSTEM	Center for International Earth Science Information Network (CIESIN), Columbia University.
WQ_DO	Dissolved oxygen concentration	Water Quality	SYS_WQL	SYSTEM	United Nations Environment Programme (UNEP), Organisation for Economic Co-operation and Development (OECD), European Environment Agency (EEA), plus country data.
WQ_EC	Electrical conductivity	Water Quality	SYS_WQL	SYSTEM	United Nations Environment Programme (UNEP) and European Environment Agency (EEA), plus country data.
WQ_PH	Phosphorus concentration	Water Quality	SYS_WQL	SYSTEM	United Nations Environment Programme (UNEP), Organisation for Economic Co-operation and Development (OECD), European Environment Agency (EEA), plus country data.
WQ_SS	Suspended solids	Water Quality	SYS_WQL	SYSTEM	United Nations Environment Programme (UNEP) plus country data.
WATAVL	Freshwater availability per capita	Water Quantity	SYS_WQN	SYSTEM	Center for Environmental System Research, Kassel University.
GRDAVL	Internal groundwater availability per capita	Water Quantity	SYS_WQN	SYSTEM	United Nations Food and Agricultural Organization (FAO).
NOXKM	Anthropogenic NOx emissions per populated land area	Reducing Air Pollution	STR_AIR	STRESS	United Nations Framework Convention on Climate Change (UNFCCC), Organization for Economic Cooperation and Development (OECD), and Intergovernmental Panel on Climate Change (IPCC), plus country data.
SO2KM	Anthropogenic SO2 emissions per populated land area	Reducing Air Pollution	STR_AIR	STRESS	United Nations Framework Convention on Climate Change (UNFCCC), Organization for Economic Cooperation and Development (OECD), and Intergovernmental Panel on Climate Change (IPCC), plus country data.
VOCKM	Anthropogenic VOC emissions per populated land area	Reducing Air Pollution	STR_AIR	STRESS	United Nations Framework Convention on Climate Change (UNFCCC), Organization for Economic Cooperation and Development (OECD), and Intergovernmental Panel on Climate Change (IPCC), plus country data.

Continued

Variable Code	Variable Description	Indicator Description	Indicator Code	Component	Short Source
COALKM	Coal consumption per populated land area	Reducing Air Pollution	STR_AIR	STRESS	United States Energy Information Agency, plus country data.
CARSKM	Vehicles in use per populated land area	Reducing Air Pollution	STR_AIR	STRESS	United Nations Statistics Division (UNSD) plus country data.
FOREST	Annual average forest cover change rate from 1990 to 2000	Reducing Ecosystem Stress	STR_ECO	STRESS	United Nations Food and Agriculture Organization (FAO).
ACEXC	Acidification exceedance from anthropogenic sulfur deposition	Reducing Ecosystem Stress	STR_ECO	STRESS	Stockholm Environment Institute at York.
GR2050	Percentage change in projected population 2004-2050	Reducing Population Pressure	STR_POP	STRESS	Population Reference Bureau (PRB).
TFR	Total Fertility Rate	Reducing Population Pressure	STR_POP	STRESS	Population Reference Bureau (PRB).
EFPC	Ecological Footprint per capita	Reducing Waste & Consumption Pressures	STR_WAS	STRESS	Redefining Progress, plus country data.
RECYCLE	Waste recycling rates	Reducing Waste & Consumption Pressures	STR_WAS	STRESS	Organisation for Economic Co-operation and Development (OECD) and United Nations Human Settlement Programme (UNHABITAT), plus country data.
HAZWST	Generation of hazardous waste	Reducing Waste & Consumption Pressures	STR_WAS	STRESS	United Nations Environment Program, plus country data.
BODWAT	Industrial organic water pollutant (BOD) emissions per available freshwater	Reducing Water Stress	STR_WAT	STRESS	World Bank, plus country data.

Variable Code	Variable Description	Indicator Description	Indicator Code	Component	Short Source
FERTHA	Fertilizer consumption per hectare of arable land	Reducing Water Stress	STR_WAT	STRESS	World Bank, plus country data.
PESTHA	Pesticide consumption per hectare of arable land	Reducing Water Stress	STR_WAT	STRESS	United Nations Food and Agricultural Organization (FAO), plus country data.
WATSTR	Percentage of country under severe water stress	Reducing Water Stress	STR_WAT	STRESS	Center for Environmental Systems Research, University of Kassel.
OVRFSH	Productivity overfishing	Natural Resource Management	STR_NRM	STRESS	South Pacific Applied Geoscience Commission (SOPAC).
IRRSAL	Salinized area due to irrigation as percentage of total arable land	Natural Resource Management	STR_NRM	STRESS	United Nations Food and Agricultural Organization (FAO).
FORCERT	Percentage of total forest area that is certified for sustainable management	Natural Resource Management	STR_NRM	STRESS	The Forest Stewardship Council, and Pan-European Forest Certification Council.
WEFSUB	World Economic Forum Survey on subsidies	Natural Resource Management	STR_NRM	STRESS	World Economic Forum (WEF).
AGSUB	Agricultural subsidies	Natural Resource Management	STR_NRM	STRESS	Organisation for Economic Co-operation and Development (OECD), World Trade Organization, and European Commission's Directorate General Agriculture.
DISINT	Death rate from intestinal infectious diseases	Environmental Health	VUL_HEA	VULNER	World Health Organization (WHO).
DISRES	Child death rate from respiratory diseases	Environmental Health	VUL_HEA	VULNER	World Health Organization (WHO).
U5MORT	Children under five mortality rate per 1,000 live births	Environmental Health	VUL_HEA	VULNER	United Nations Statistics Division (UNSD).

Continued

Variable Code	Variable Description	Indicator Description	Indicator Code	Component	Short Source
UND_NO	Percentage of undernourished in total population	Basic Human Sustenance	VUL_SUS	VULNER	United Nations Food and Agriculture Organization (FAO).
WATSUP	Percentage of population with access to improved drinking water source	Basic Human Sustenance	VUL_SUS	VULNER	World Health Organization (WHO) and United Nations Children's Fund (UNICEF), plus country data.
DISCAS	Average number of deaths per million inhabitants from floods, tropical cyclones, and droughts	Exposure to Natural Disasters	VUL_DIS	VULNER	United Nations Development Programme (UNDP) Bureau for Crisis Prevention and Recovery.
DISEXP	Environmental Hazard Exposure Index	Exposure to Natural Disasters	VUL_DIS	VULNER	The World Bank.
PRAREA	Percentage of total land area under protected status	Environmental Governance	CAP_GOV	CAP	United Nations Environment Program - World Conservation Monitoring Centre (UNEP-WCMC), plus country data.
GASPR	Ratio of gasoline price to world average	Environmental Governance	CAP_GOV	CAP	World Bank.
CSDMIS	Percentage of variables missing from the CGSDI "Rio to Joburg Dashboard"	Environmental Governance	CAP_GOV	CAP	Consultative Group on Sustainable Development Indicators (CGSDI).
KNWLDG	Knowledge creation in environmental science, technology, and policy	Environmental Governance	CAP_GOV	CAP	Yale Center for Environmental Law and Policy (YCELP) Knowledge Divide Project, plus country data.
IUCN	IUCN member organizations per million population	Environmental Governance	CAP_GOV	CAP	IUCN-The World Conservation Union.

Variable Code	Variable Description	Indicator Description	Indicator Code	Component	Short Source
AGENDA21	Local Agenda 21 initiatives per million people	Environmental Governance	CAP_GOV	CAP	International Council for Local Environmental Initiatives (ICLEI).
GRAFT	Corruption measure	Environmental Governance	CAP_GOV	CAP	World Bank.
LAW	Rule of law	Environmental Governance	CAP_GOV	CAP	World Bank.
CIVLIB	Civil and Political Liberties	Environmental Governance	CAP_GOV	CAP	Freedom House.
WEFGOV	World Economic Forum Survey on environmental governance	Environmental Governance	CAP_GOV	CAP	World Economic Forum (WEF).
GOVEFF	Government effectiveness	Environmental Governance	CAP_GOV	CAP	World Bank.
POLITY	Democracy measure	Environmental Governance	CAP_GOV	CAP	Polity IV Project, University of Maryland.
ENEFF	Energy efficiency	Eco-efficiency	CAP_EFF	CAP	US Energy Information Agency (EIA).
RENPC	Hydropower and renewable energy production as a percentage of total energy consumption	Eco-efficiency	CAP_EFF	CAP	US Energy Information Agency.
DJSGI	Dow Jones Sustainability Group Index (DJSGI)	Private Sector Responsiveness	CAP_PRI	CAP	Dow Jones SAM Sustainability Group.
ECOVAL	Average Innovest EcoValue rating of firms headquartered in a country	Private Sector Responsiveness	CAP_PRI	CAP	Innovest Strategic Value Advisors.

Continued

Variable Code	Variable Description	Indicator Description	Indicator Code	Component	Short Source
ISO14	Number of ISO 14001 certified companies per billion dollars GDP (PPP)	Private Sector Responsiveness	CAP_PRI	CAP	Reinhard Peglau, Federal Environmental Agency, Germany.
WEFPRI	World Economic Forum Survey on private sector environmental innovation	Private Sector Responsiveness	CAP_PRI	CAP	World Economic Forum (WEF).
RESCARE	Participation in the Responsible Care Program of the Chemical Manufacturer's Association	Private Sector Responsiveness	CAP_PRI	CAP	International Council of Chemical Associations (ICCA).
INNOV	Innovation Index	Science and Technology	CAP_ST	CAP	World Economic Forum (WEF).
DAI	Digital Access Index	Science and Technology	CAP_ST	CAP	International Telecommunication Union (ITU).
PECR	Female primary education completion rate	Science and Technology	CAP_ST	CAP	United Nations Educational, Scientific and Cultural Organization (UNESCO), plus country data.
ENROL	Gross tertiary enrollment rate	Science and Technology	CAP_ST	CAP	United Nations Educational, Scientific and Cultural Organization (UNESCO), plus country data.
RESEARCH	Number of researchers per million inhabitants	Science and Technology	CAP_ST	CAP	United Nations Educational, Scientific and Cultural Organization (UNESCO), plus country data.
EIONUM	Number of memberships in environmental intergovernmental organizations	Participation in International Collaborative Efforts	GLO_COL	GLOBAL	Union of International Associations.

Variable Code	Variable Description	Indicator Description	Indicator Code	Component	Short Source
FUNDING	Contribution to international and bilateral funding of environmental projects and development aid	Participation in International Collaborative Efforts	GLO_COL	GLOBAL	Global Environmental Facility (GEF) and Organisation for Economic Co-operation and Development (OECD).
PARTICIP	Participation in international environmental agreements	Participation in International Collaborative Efforts	GLO_COL	GLOBAL	United Nations Framework Convention on Climate Change (UNFCCC), Vienna Convention on the Protection of the Ozone Layer, Convention on the Trade in Endangered Species (CITES), Basel Convention on the Transboundary Movement of Hazardous Waste, United Nation
CO2GDP	Carbon emissions per million US dollars GDP	Greenhouse Gas Emissions	GLO_GHG	GLOBAL	Carbon Dioxide Information Analysis Center (CDIAC), plus country data.
CO2PC	Carbon emissions per capita	Greenhouse Gas Emissions	GLO_GHG	GLOBAL	United Nations Statistics Division, Millennium Indicator Database.
SO2EXP	SO2 Exports	Reducing Transboundary Environmental Pressures	GLO_TBP	GLOBAL	Europe Meteorological Synthesizing Centre West and International Institute for Applied Systems Analysis.
POLEXP	Import of polluting goods and raw materials as percentage of total imports of goods and services	Reducing Transboundary Environmental Pressures	GLO_TBP	GLOBAL	United Nations Commodity Trade Statistics database (COMTRADE).

DOCUMENTATION: THE HAPPY PLANET INDEX, ECOLOGICAL FOOTPRINT AND LIFE SATISFACTION

The **Happy Planet Index** (HPI) is designed as a measure for the relative success or failure of countries in supporting good life for their citizens, whilst repecting the environmental resource limits, upon which our lives depend. We shortly present here the arguments of the "happy planet" organization regarding the logic of their new measures.

"The **HPI** incorporates three separate indicators: ecological footprint, life-satisfaction and life expectancy.

$$\text{Equation (1) Happy Planet Index} = \frac{\text{Life satisfaction} \times \text{Life expectancy}}{\text{Ecological Footprint}}$$

It represents the efficiency, with which countries convert the earth's finite resources into well-being experienced by their citizens.

Ecological footprint measures how much land area is required to sustain a given population at present levels of consumption, technological development and resource efficiency, and is expressed in global-average hectares (gha). The largest component elements of Footprint are the land used to grow food, trees and biofuels, areas of ocean used for fishing, and - most importantly - the land required to support the plant life needed to absorb and sequester CO_2 emissions from fossil fuels.

Footprint takes account of the fact that in a global economy people consume resources and ecological services from all over the world. Therefore, a Chiquita plantation in Costa Rica will not count towards Costa Rica's Footprint, but rather towards the Footprint of those countries where the bananas are consumed. For this reason, a country's Footprint can be significantly larger than its actual biocapacity. The Footprint of a country is thus best understood as a measure of its consumption, and its worldwide environmental impact.

The same methodology can be used to calculate, in the same units, the Earth's biocapacity - its biologically productive area. Currently, the biocapacity of the Earth is around 11.2 billion hectares or 1.8 global hectares per person in 2001 (assuming that no capacity is set aside for non-human species). In 2001, humanity's demand on the biosphere - its global ecological footprint - was 13.7 billion global hectares, or 2.2 global hectares per person. At present, therefore, our Footprint exceeds our biocapacity by 0.4 global hectares per person, or 23 per cent. This means that the planet's living stocks are being depleted faster than nature can regenerate them.". (http://www.happyplanetindex.org/list.htm.)

Their third measure is **life satisfaction**, taken from the "world value surveys" of Michigan University. International surveys tend to consider life satisfaction by asking respondents a question such as: *'If you consider your life overall, how satisfied would you say you are nowadays?'* Responses are given on a 0-10 scale, from not at all satisfied to extremely satisfied. Clearly this is not a perfect measure.

DOCUMENTATION: THE FREEDOM HOUSE INDEX OF POLITICAL RIGHTS AND CIVIL RIGHTS

http://www.freedomhouse.org/template.cfm?page=276

This year for the first time, Freedom House released the subcategory scores from the Freedom in the World 2006 survey and the aggregate scores from the 2003, 2004, 2005, and 2006 editions of Freedom in the World.

Freedom in the World is an annual comparative assessment of political rights and civil liberties that this year covers 192 countries and 14 related and disputed territories.

For the last 30 years of the survey, each country and territory has been assigned two numerical ratings--one for political rights and one for civil liberties--based on a 1 to 7 scale. Underlying those ratings are more detailed assessments of country situations based on a 40-point scale for political rights and a 60-point scale for civil liberties. Freedom House is releasing the aggregate scores for political rights and civil liberties for each country in order to provide more nuanced information about country trends beyond the 7-point rating scales used previously.

In addition, in order to generate debate and discussions within countries as to areas that are most in need of reform, Freedom House is releasing the ratings for the seven subcategories that compose assessments of what constitute political rights and civil liberties for the latest survey edition, Freedom in the World 2006. These subcategories, drawn from the Universal Declaration of Human Rights, represent the fundamental components of freedom, which include an individual's ability to:

- Participate freely in the political process;
- Vote freely in legitimate elections;
- Have representatives that are accountable to them;
- Exercise freedoms of expression and belief;
- Be able to freely assemble and associate;
- Have access to an established and equitable system of rule of law;
- Have social and economic freedoms, including equal access to economic opportunities and the right to hold private property.

We trust that this information will provide more transparency and a better understanding of how Freedom House measures political rights and civil liberties.

REFERENCES

INTERNET SOURCES

http://www.lalisio.com/members/m_TAUSCH/publications/114986208075/114986228444/?use_session=True&browser_type=Explorer&-C=&language=en

http://www.cgdev.org/content/expert/detail/2699/

Sources provided by the ILO, the UTIP project at the University of Texas, and the World Bank were used in this essay. These analyses of the dynamics in the world system calculated the time series correlations of globalization, economic growth (Global Development Network Growth Database, William Easterly and Mirvat Sewadeh, World Bank), unemployment (Laborsta ILO), and inequality (UTIP, University of Texas Inequality Project, Theil indices of inequality, based on wages in 21 economic sectors) since 1980.

http://www.worldbank.org/research/growth/GDNdata.htm

http://laborsta.ilo.org/

http://utip.gov.utexas.edu/

Aalberg T. (2005). "Stimulert eller demobilisert? En kvantitativ undersøkelse av mediebruk og politisk engasjement (Mobilized or demobilized? A quantitative study of media use and political engagement)." *Norsk Medietidsskrift* 12(2): 136-154. http://www.universitetsforlaget.no/tidsskrifter/samfunnsfag/article.jhtml?articleID=19641

Abbott J. P. and Worth O. (2002), *'Critical Perspectives on International Political Economy'* London and Basingstoke: Palgrave Macmillan.

Abdullah M. S. and Khoury A. Th. (1984), *'Mohammed für Christen. Eine Herausforderung'* Freiburg, Basel, Wien: Herder.

Achen Ch. H. (1982), *'Interpreting and Using Regression'* Beverly Hills: Sage University Papers.

Adams K. R. (2005), *'New Great Powers: Who Will They Be, and How Will They Rise?'*. Department of Political Science, University of Montana, Paper, prepared for presentation at the 2005 Annual Meeting of the International Studies Association, Honolulu, Hawaii, March 2-5, 2005, available at: http://www.umt.edu/polsci/faculty/adams/greatpower.rtf.

Addo H. (1986), *'Imperialism: the permanent stage of capitalism'* Tokyo: United Nations University.

Adler E. and Crawford B. (2002), *'Constructing a Mediterranean Region: A Cultural Approach'* The Hebrew University of Jerusalem, Department of International Relations, available at: http://ies.berkeley.edu/research/MeditAdlerCrawford.pdf.

Afheldt H. (1994), *'Wohlstand fuer niemand? Die Marktwirtschaft entlaesst ihre Kinder'* Munich: Kunstmann.

Aghion Ph. and Williamson J. G. (1998), *'Growth, Inequality and Globalization. Theory, History and Policy'* Cambridge: at the University Press.

Agnew J. (2001), 'The New Global Economy: Time-Space Compression, Geopolitics, and Global Uneven Development' *Journal of World-Systems Research, available at: http://jwsr.ucr.edu/index.php*VII, 2, Fall: 133-154.

Ahluwalia M. S. (1974), 'Income Inequality: Some Dimensions of the Problem' in *'Redistribution with Growth'* (Chenery H.B. et al. (Eds.)), pp. 3 - 37, New York and Oxford: Oxford University Press.

Ahulwalia M. S. (1976), 'Inequality, Poverty and Development'. *Journal of Development Economics 3,* pps. 307-342.

Aiginger K. and Guger A. (2005a), *'The European Socio-economic Model. Differences to the USA and Changes Over Time'*, London School of Economics – European Social Model Programme – Tandem Project to the British EU Presidency, 42 pages, available at: http://publikationen.wifo.ac.at/pls/wifosite/wifosite.wifo_search.frameset?p_filename=M ONOGRAPHIEN/PRIVATE26369/S_2005_EUROPEAN_MODEL_25777$.PDF.

Aiginger K. and Guger A. (2005b), *„Das europäische Gesellschaftsmodell'* Austrian Institute for Economic Research (WIFO) (Studie im Auftrag des Bundesministeriums für Wirtschaft und Arbeit, restricted).

Akerman J. (1936), *'Economic Progress and Economic Crises'* London and Basingstoke: Macmillan.

Albritton R. (2001), *'Phases of Capitalist Development: Booms, Crises, and Globalizations'* Basingstoke and London: Palgrave.

Alderson A. and Nielsen F. (1999), *„Income Inequality, Development and Dependence: A Reconsideration'* American Sociological Review, 64, 4, August: 606 – 631.

Alderson A. S., Beckfield J. and Nielsen F. (2005), 'Income Inequality Trends in Core Societies' in *'The Future of World Society'* (Herkenrath M. et al. (Eds.)) pp. 253 – 271; Sociological Institute, University of Zurich: Intelligent Book Production.

Alexander M. A. (2002), *'The Kondratiev Cycle: A Generational Interpretation'* Lincoln, NE: iUniverse.

Alexandratos N., Bruinsma J. and Yotopoulos P. A. (1983), *'Agriculture from the perspective of population growth: some results from 'Agriculture: toward 2000''* Rome: Food and Agriculture Organization of the United Nations, (FAO economic and social development paper; 30).

Almond G. (1991), 'Capitalism and Democracy' *PS. Political Science and Politics,* 24, 3, September: 467 - 474.

Almond G. A. (1938/1998) *'Plutocracy and politics in New York City'* Ph.D. thesis, Chicago University, re-published at Boulder, Colo.: Westview Press

Amato G. and Batt J. (1999), *'Final Report of the Reflection Group on The Longterm Implications of EU Enlargement: The Nature of the New Border'* The Robert Schuman Centre for Advanced Studies, European University Institute and The Forward Studies Unit, European Commission (mimeo).

Amin S. (1973), *'Le developpement inegal. Essai sur les formations sociales du capitalisme peripherique'* Paris: Editions de Minuit.

Amin S. (1976), *'Unequal Development: An Essay on the Social Formations of Peripheral Capitalism'* New York: Monthly Review Press.

Amin S. (1980), 'The Class Structure of the Contemporary Imperialist System', *Monthly Review* (USA), 31 (1980), 8: 9-26.

Amin S. (1984), 'Was kommt nach der Neuen Internationalen Wirtschaftsordnung? Die Zukunft der Weltwirtschaft' in *'Rote Markierungen International'* (Fischer H. and Jankowitsch P. (Eds.)), pp. 89 - 110, Vienna: Europaverlag.

Amin S. (1989), *'Eurocentrism'* Translated by Russell Moore. New York: Monthly Review Press.

Amin S. (1992), *'Empire of Chaos'* New York: Monthly Review Press.

Amin S. (1994a), 'The Future of Global Polarization', *Review* (Fernand Braudel Center, USA), XVII, 3 (Summer), p. 337-347.

Amin S. (1994b), 'Die neue kapitalistische Globalisierung - die Herrschaft des Chaos' *Starnberger Forschungsberichte,* 3, 4, May: 7 - 26.

Amin S. (1994c), *'Re-reading the postwar period: an intellectual itinerary'* Translated by Michael Wolfers. New York: Monthly Review Press.

Amin S. (1997a), *'Capitalism in the Age of Globalization'*. London, England: Zed Books.

Amin S. (1997b), *'Die Zukunft des Weltsystems. Herausforderungen der Globalisierung. Herausgegeben und aus dem Franzoesischen uebersetzt von Joachim Wilke'* Hamburg: VSA.

Amnesty International (current issues), *'Jahresbericht'* Frankfurt a.M.: Fischer TB.

Amsden A. H. *et al.* (1994), 'From Pseudo - Socialism to Pseudo - Capitalism: Eastern Europe's First Five Years' *Internationale Politik und Gesellschaft. International Politics and Society (Friedrich Ebert Foundation),* 2: 107 - 116.

Andall J. (Ed.)(2003), *'Gender and ethnicity in contemporary Europe'*. Oxford; New York: Berg

Angresano J. (1994), 'Evolving Socio - economic Conditions in Central and Eastern Europe: A Myrdalian View' *Development Policy Review,* 12: 251 - 275.

Apter D. (1987), *'Rethinking Development: Modernization, Dependency and Post - Modern Politics'* Newbury Park, CA.: Sage.

Armstrong K. (1992), *'Muhammad: a biography of the prophet'* San Francisco, Calif.: Harper SanFrancisco.

Armstrong K. (2006), *'Muhammad: a prophet for our time'* New York: Atlas Books/HarperCollins

Arrighi G. (1989), *'The Developmentalist Illusion: A Reconceptualization of the Semiperiphery'* paper, presented at the Thirteenth Annual Political Economy of the World System Conference, University of Illinois at Urbana - Champaign, April 28 - 30.

Arrighi G. (1991), *'World Income Inequalities and the Future of Socialism'* Fernand Braudel Centre, State University of New York at Binghamton.

Arrighi G. (1995), *'The Long 20th Century. Money, Power, and the Origins of Our Times'* London, New York: Verso.

Arrighi G. and Silver B. J. (1984), 'Labor Movements and Capital Migration: The United States and Western Europe in World - Historical Perspective' in *'Labor in the Capitalist World - Economy'* (Bergquist Ch. (Ed.)), pp. 183 - 216, Beverly Hills: Sage.

Arrighi G. and Silver B. J. (1999), *'Chaos and Governance in the Modern World System'* Minneapolis: University of Minnesota Press.

Arrighi G. et al. (1991), *'The Rise of East Asia. One Miracle or Many?'* State University of New York at Binghamton: Fernand Braudel Centre.

Arrighi G. et al. (1996a), *'Beyond Western Hegemonies'* I Meeting of the Social Science History Association, New Orleans, available at: http://www.marion.ohio-state.edu/fac/vsteffel/web597/arrighi_hegemony.pdf.

Arrighi G. et al. (1996b), *'Modelling Zones of the World-Economy: A Polynomial Regression Analysis (1964-1994)'* State University of New York at Binghamton: Fernand Braudel Center.

Arrighi G. et al. (1996c), *'The Rise of East Asia in World Historical Perspective'* State University of New York at Binghamton: Fernand Braudel Center.

Arrighi G., Hamashita T. and Selden M. (Eds.)(2003), *'Resurgence of East Asia: 500, 150 and 50 year perspectives'* London; New York: Routledge, 2003..

Attinà F. (2002), *'Politica di sicurezza e difesa dell'Unione europea: il cammino europeo dopo il trattato di Amsterdam'* Gaeta (Latina): Artistic & publishing company.

Attinà F. (2003a), 'Organisation, Competition and Change of the International System.' *International interactions,* vol. 16, no. 4, pp. 317.

Attinà F. (2003b), 'The Euro-Mediterranean Partnership Assessed: The Realist and Liberal Views' *European Foreign Affairs Review,* vol. 8, no. 2, pp. 181-199.

Attinà F. (2004), 'The Barcelona Process, the Role of the European Union and the Lesson of the Western Mediterranean' *Journal of North African Studies,* vol. 9, no. 2, pp. 140-152.

Attinà F. (2005), 'State aggregation in defense pacts: systematic explanations.', Jean Monnet Working Papers in Comparative and International Politics, Jean Monnet Centre EuroMed, Department of Political Studies, University of Catania, available at: http://www.fscpo.unict.it/EuroMed/jmwp56.pdf.

Australian Treasury (2001), *'Global poverty and inequality in the 20th Century: turning the corner?* Australian Treasury, available at: http://www.treasury.gov.au/publications/EconomicPublications/EconomicRoundUp/2001CentenaryEdition/dowload/Round2.pdf.

Avery W. P., Rapkin D. P. (1989), *'Markets, Politics, and Change in the Global Political Economy.'* Boulder, CO: Lynne Rienner Publications.

Axtmann R (2004), 'The State of the State: The Model of the Modern State and its Contemporary Transformation' *International Political Science Review,* vol. 25, no. 3, pp. 259-280.

Axtmann R. (1995), 'Kulturelle Globalisierung, kollektive Identitaet und demokratischer Nationalstaat' *Leviathan,* 1: 87 - 101.

Aydin H. et al. (2003), *'"Euro-Islam". Das neue Islamverständnis der Muslime in der Migration".* Stiftung Zentrum für Türkeistudien, Institut an der Universität Duisburg-Essen. Available at: http://www.renner-institut.at/download/texte/euroisla.pdf

Aydin H. et al. (2003), '"Euro-Islam". Das neue Islamverständnis der Muslime in der Migration". Stiftung Zentrum für Türkeistudien, Institut an der Universität Duisburg-Essen. Available at: http://www.renner-institut.at/download/texte/euroisla.pdf

Babones S. J. (2002), 'Population and Sample Selection Effects in Measuring International Income Inequality' *Journal of World-Systems Research,* available at: http://jwsr.ucr.edu/index.php*VIII, 1, Winter: 8 – 28.

Babones S. J. (2005), 'The Country-Level Income Structure of the World Economy' *Journal of World-Systems Research, available at: http://jwsr.ucr.edu/index.php*XI, 1, July: 29 – 55.

Bailey P.; Parisotto A. and Renshaw G. (1993*), 'Multinationals and Employment. The Global Economy of the 1990s'* Geneva: International Labor Office.

Balassa, B. (1964),"The Purchasing Power Parity Doctrine: A Reappraisal", *Journal of Political Economy,* vol. 72, December, pp. 584-596.

Baldassarri M., Mundell R. A. and McCallum, J. (1993), *'Debt, deficit and economic performance'* New York, N.Y.: St. Martin's Press.

Baldwin R. E. et al. (1997), *'The Costs and Benefits of Eastern Enlargement: The Impact on the EU and Central Europe'* Economic Policy, April (quoted from the typescript).

Balibar E. (1991), 'Es gibt keinen Staat in Europa: Racism and Politics in Europe Today' *New Left Review,* March/April, 186: 5 - 19.

Balic S. (2001), *'Islam für Europa. Neue Perspektiven einer alten Religion'.* Köln, Weimar, Wien: Böhlau

Bandt J. de et al. (Eds.)(1980), *'European Studies in Development. New Trends in European Development Studies'* Basingstoke and London: Macmillan.

Baran P. A. (1957), *'The Political Economy of Growth'* New York: Monthly Review Press.

Bardakoglu A. (2006), 'Religion and Society. New Perspectives from Turkey.' Ankara: P.P.R.A.

Barnes S. H. et al. (1979), *'Political Action. Mass Participation in Five Western Democracies'* Beverly Hills: Sage.

Barnett V. (2002), 'Which Was the 'Real' Kondratiev: 1925 or 1928?' *Journal of the History of Economic Thought,* Volume 24, Number 4, 1 December, pp. 475-478.

Barr K. (1979), 'Long Waves: A Selected Annotated Bibliography', *Review,* Vol 2, No 4, Spring: pp. 675-718. (This is a special issue of the *Review* on long waves.).

Barr N. (2001), 'The Truth About Pension Reform' *Finance and Development,* September 2001, 38, 3, available at: http://www.imf.org/external/pubs/ft/fandd/2001/09/barr.htm.

Barro R. J. (1991), 'Economic Growth in a Cross Section of Countries.', *Quarterly journal of economics,* 106[2]: 407-43.

Barro R. J. (1994), 'Sources of economic growth.' *Carnegie-Rochester conference series on public policy,* 1994, vol. 40, pp. 1.

Barro R. J. (1996a), 'Democracy and Growth.' *Journal of Economic Growth,* 1996, vol. 1, no. 1, pp. 1.

Barro R. J. (1996b), *'Getting It Right. Markets and Choices in a Free Society'* Cambridge, Mass.: MIT Press.

Barro R. J. (1999), 'Determinants of Democracy.' *Journal of political economy,* vol. 107, no. 6p2, pp. S158.

Barro R. J. (1999), 'Determinants of Democracy' The Journal of Political Economy, 107, 6:

Barro R. J. (2000), 'Inequality and Growth in a Panel of Countries.' *Journal of Economic Growth,* 2000, vol. 5, no. 1, pp. 5.

Barro R. J. (2001), 'Human Capital and Growth', *American Economic Review,* 2001, vol. 91, no. 2, pp. 12-17.

Barro R. J. (2003), 'Economic Growth in a Cross Section of Countries' *International Library of Critical Writings in Economics,* 2003, vol. 159, no. 1, pp. 350-386.

Barro R. J. (2004), 'Spirit of Capitalism Religion and Economic Development'. *Harvard International Review,* vol. 25, no. 4, pp. 64-67.

Barro R. J. (2004a), 'Determinants of economic growth in a panel of countries' *Annals of economics and finance,* Beijing: Peking University Press Bd. 4 (2003), 2, pp. 231-275.

Barro R. J. (2004b), 'Spirit of Capitalism, Religion and Economic Development' *Harvard International Review,* vol. 25, no. 4, pp. 64-67.

Barro R. J. and Grilli V. (1994), *'European Macroeconomics'* Basingstoke and London: Macmillan.

Barro R. J. and McCleary R. M. (2003), 'Religion and Economic Growth across Countries' *American Sociological Review,* Volume 68, Number 5, 1 October, pp. 760-781.

Barro R. J. and McCleary R. M. (2003a), 'Religion and Economic Growth across Countries Source' *American Sociological Review,* Volume 68, Number 5, 1 October 2003, pp. 760-781.

Barro R. J. and McCleary R. M. (2003b), 'Religion and Economic Growth' *NBER Working Paper Series,* 2003, no. 9682, (entire).

Barro R. J. and McCleary R. M. (2004), 'Religion and economic growth' *The Milken Institute review (Milken, Santa Monica, Cal.),* 6 (2004), 2, S. 36-45.

Barro R. J. and Sala-i-Martin X. (1991), 'Convergence across States and Regions' *Brookings Papers on Economic Activity,* 1: 107 - 179.

Barro R. J. and Sala-i-Martin X. (1995/98), *'Wirtschaftswachstum (Economic Growth)'* München: Oldenbourg (McGraw Hill, New York).

Barro, R. J. and Sala-i-Martin X. (1992), 'Convergence", *Journal of Political Economy,* vol. 100 (2), pp. 223-251.

Barta V. and Richter S. (1996), *'Eastern Enlargement of the European Union from a Western and an Eastern Persepctive'* Research Reports, 227, Vienna Institute for Comparative Economic Studies.

Bauer P. (1998), 'Die Union vor der Osterweiterung. Die Transformationsstaaten - Von der Startlinie ins Abseits?' *Oesterreichische Zeitschrift fuer Politikwissenschaft,* 27, 4: 363 - 376.

Bauer Th. and Zimmermann, K. F.(1999), *'Assessment of Possible Migration Pressure and Its Labour Market impact Following EU Enlargement to Central and Eastern Europe.'* A Study for the Department for Education and Employment, London, 1999.

Beaud M. (1990), *'Histoire du capitalisme de 1500 à nos jours'* 4e édition revue et corrigée en 1990, Paris: Éditions du Seuil.

Beck N. (1991), 'The Illusion of Cycles in International Relations' *International Studies Quarterly,* 35: 455 – 476.

Becker G. (1993), 'Europe Wastes Its Human Capital' *The Wall Street Journal Europe,* 18 - 19 June: 10.

Beckerman W. (1992), *'Economic Development and the Environment. Conflict or Complementarity?'* World Bank Policy Research Papers, WPS 961, Washington D.C.: The World Bank.

Beer L. (1999), 'Income Inequality and Transnational Corporate Penetration' *Journal of World Systems Research,* 5, 1: 1 – 25.

Beer L. and Boswell T. (2002), 'The Resilience of Dependency Effects in Explaining Income Inequality in the Global Economy: A Cross-National Analysis, 1975 – 1995'. *Journal of*

*World-Systems Research, available at: http://jwsr.ucr.edu/index.php*VIII, 1, Winter 2002: 30 – 59.

Beeson M. (2005), *'Global Governance'*. Article for the forthcoming *'International Encyclopedia of Public Policy"* (O'Hara Ph. (Ed.)), London and New York: Routledge.

Belkacem L. (2001), *'Poverty Dynamics in Algeria'* Kuwait: Arab Planning Institute at: http://www.erf.org.eg/html/Laabbas.pdf.

Bello W. (1989), 'Confronting the Brave New World Economic Order: Toward a Southern Agenda for the 1990s' *Alternatives,* XIV, 2: 135 - 168.

Bello W.; with Shea Cunningham and Bill Rau (1999), *'Dark Victory. The United States and Global Poverty'* London: Pluto Press.

Berger P. L. (1998), *'The Limits of Social Cohesion: Conflict and Mediation in Pluralist Societies: a Report of the Bertelsmann Foundation to the Club of Rome'* Boulder, CO: Westview Press.

Bergesen A. (1983), '1914 Again? Another Cycle of Interstate Competition and War' in *'Foreign Policy and the Modern World - System'* (Mc Gowan P. and Kegley Ch.W. Jr. (Eds.)), pp. 255 - 273, Beverly Hills: Sage.

Bergesen A. (1983), 'Modeling Long Waves of Crisis in the World - System' in *'Crisis in the World System'* (Bergesen A. (Ed.)), pp. 73 - 92, Beverly Hills: Sage.

Bergesen A. and Fernandez R. (1999), 'Who Has the Most Fortune 500 Firms? A Network Analysis of Global Economic Competition, 1956 - 89' in *'The Future of Global Conflict'* (Bornschier V. and Chase-Dunn Ch. K. (Eds.)), pp. 151 - 173, London, Thousand Oaks and New Delhi: Sage Publications.

Bergesen A. J. and Bata M. (2002), 'Global and National Inequality: Are They Connected?' *Journal of World-Systems Research, available at: http://jwsr.ucr.edu/index.php*VIII, 1, Winter: 130 – 144.

Berry A. *et al.* (1981), 'The Level of World Inequality: How Much Canada One Say?' Document 38, Laboratoire d'Economie Politique, CNRS, 45, rue d'Ulm, F - 75230 Paris Cedex 05.

Berry W. D. and Feldman S. (1985), *'Multiple Regression in Practice'* Beverly Hills: Sage University Papers.

Betcherman G. (2002), *'An Overview of Labor Markets World-Wide: key Trends and Major Policy Issues'* World Bank, available at: http://wbln0018.worldbank.org/HDNet/ HDdocs.nsf/2d5135ecbf351de6852566a90069b8b6/e27ab3ded55970b585256b9e004e02 cb/$FILE/0205.pdf.

Bhaduri A. and Laski K. (1996), *'Lessons to be drawn from main mistakes in the transition strategy'* Paper, presented at the 'Colloquium on Economic Transformation and Development of Central and Eastern Europe', OECD, Paris, 29/30 May 1996.

Bhagwati J.N. (1989), 'Nation States in an International Framework: An Economist's Perspective' *Alternatives,* XIV, 2: 231 - 244.

Bielinski J. (2006). "Konsens i jednorodnosc spoleczna w procesie budowania kapitalizmu w krajach postkomunistycznych (Role of Consensus and Social Homogeneity in the Process of Building Capitalism in Postcommunist Countries)." *Studia Socjologiczne* 180(1): 89-118.

Birdsall N. (2006), 'Latin America and Globalization: Prebisch had a point' in *'Raúl Prebisch. Power, Principle and the Ethics of Development. Essays in Honour of David H. Pollock marking the centennial celebrations of the birth of Raul Prebisch'* (Dosman E. (Ed.)), pp. 31 – 36, Washington and Buenos Aires: Inter-American Development Bank.

Birdsall N., de la Torre, A. (2001, with Menezes R.), *'Washington Contentious: Economic Policies for Social Equity in Latin America'* Washington D.C.: Center for Global Development; available at: http://www.cgdev.org/content/publications/detail/2923

Black J. (2005), *'Why Wars Happen'* London and Lexington, KY: Reaktion Books.

BM.I .SIAK (2006), *'Perspektiven und Herausforderungen in der Integration muslimischer MitbürgerInnen in Österreich'* Federal Ministry of the Interior, Republic of Austria, available at: http://www.bmi.gv.at/downloadarea/asyl_fremdenwesen/Perspektiven_Herausforderungen.pdf

BM.I.SIAK (2006), 'Perspektiven und Herausforderungen in der Integration muslimischer MitbürgerInnen in Österreich' Federal Ministry of the Interior, Republic of Austria, available at: http://www.bmi.gv.at/downloadarea/asyl_fremdenwesen/Perspektiven_Herausforderungen.pdf

Bobróvnikov A. V. (1989), 'La periodización y las peculiaridades de las crisis de la deuda externa en América Latina' en Davydov V., Lunin V. (eds.), *'La crisis de la deuda externa en la periferia latinoamericana del capitalismo mundial'*. Moscú: Instituto de América Latina, pp. 37-52 (in Russian).

Bobróvnikov A. V. (1994), 'Ondas largas en la economía y los procesos sociales', *América Latina,* No 4, pp. 4-12; No 7-8, pp. 65-75 (in Russian).

Bobróvnikov A. V. (1996), 'Los niveles de equilibrio en la economía', *Almanaque América Latina,* N 2, pp. 98-106.

Bobróvnikov A. V. (1999), 'Los epicentros regionales del desarrollo', *Iberoamérica,* N 4, pp. 49-67.

Bobróvnikov A. V. (2002), *'La dinamica ondularia en la economía periférica'* Ponencia en el Tercer Congreso Europeo de Latinoamericanistas 'Cruzando Fronteras en América Latina" Amsterdam, 3-6 julio de 2002, available from the author at: Instituto de Latinoamérica de la Academia de Ciencias de Rusia, Federación Rusa.

Bobróvnikov A. V. and Teperman, V. A. (2000), 'Latinoamerikanskie modeli social'no-·ekonomiceskogo razvitija' *Obscestvo i ekonomika (Moskva),* 9/10, pp. 256-281 [Obscestvo i ekonomika: mezdunarodnyj naucnyj i obscestvenno-politiceskij zurnal. - Moskva: Izdat. Nauka ISSN: 0207-3676].

Bodemann Y. M. and Yurdakul G. (Eds.) (2006), *'Migration, citizenship, ethnos'*. New York: Palgrave Macmillan, 2006.

Boehring W.R. and Schloeter - Paredes M.L. (1994*), 'Aid in place of migration?. A World Employment Programme Study'* Geneva: International Labor Office.

Boersch-Suppan A., Ludwig A., and Winter J. (2003), 'Aging, pension reforms and capital flows: a multi-country simulation model' MEA, University of Mannheim, available at: http://www.mea.uni-mannheim.de/mea_neu/pages/files/nopage_pubs/vksrytv2m35ucj2v_dp28.pdf.

Boff L. (1985), *'Church, charism and power: liberation theology and the institutional church'*. London: SCM Press.

Boff L. (2005), *'Global civilization: challenges to society and to Christianity.'* London; Oakville : Equinox Publishing.

Bollen K. A. (1980), 'Issues in the Comparative Measurement of Political Democracy' *American Sociological Review,* 45: 370 - 390.

Bollen K. A. and Jackman R. W. (1985), 'Political Democracy and the Size Distribution of Income.' *American Sociological Review,* 46, pps. 651-659.

Bornschier V. (1976), *'Wachstum, Konzentration und Multinationalisierung von Industrieunternehmen'* Frauenfeld and Stuttgart: Huber.

Bornschier V. (1988), *'Westliche Gesellschaft im Wandel'* Frankfurt a.M./ New York: Campus.

Bornschier V. (1992), *'The Rise of the European Community. Grasping Towards Hegemony or Therapy against National Decline in the World Political Economy?'.* Vienna: paper, presented at the First European Conference of Sociology, August 26 - 29.

Bornschier V. (1996), *'Western society in transition'* New Brunswick, N.J.: Transaction Publishers.

Bornschier V. (1999), 'Hegemonic Transition, West European Unification and the Future Structure of the Core' in in *'The Future of Global Conflict'* (Bornschier V. and Chase-Dunn Ch. K. (Eds.)), pp. 77 - 98, London, Thousand Oaks and New Delhi: Sage Publications.

Bornschier V. (2002), 'Changing Income Inequality in the Second Half of the 20th Century: Preliminary Findings and Propositions For Explanations" *Journal of World-Systems Research, available at: http://jwsr.ucr.edu/index.php*VIII, 1, Winter: 100 – 127.

Bornschier V. (Ed.)(1994*), 'Conflicts and new departures in world society'* New Brunswick, N.J.: Transaction Publishers.

Bornschier V. and Ballmer-Cao, T. H. (1979), 'Income Inequality: A Cross-National Study of the Relationships Between MNC-Penetration, Dimensions of the Power Structure and Income Distribution.' *American Sociological Review,* 44, pps. 438-506.

Bornschier V. and Chase-Dunn Ch. K (1985), *'Transnational Corporations and Underdevelopment'* N.Y., N.Y.: Praeger.

Bornschier V. and Chase-Dunn Ch. K. (1999), 'Technological Change, Globalization and Hegemonic Rivalry' in *'The Future of Global Conflict'* (Bornschier V. and Chase-Dunn Ch. K. (Eds.)), pp. 285 - 302, London, Thousand Oaks and New Delhi: Sage Publications.

Bornschier V. and Heintz P., reworked and enlarged by Th. H. Ballmer - Cao and J. Scheidegger (1979), *'Compendium of Data for World Systems Analysis'* Machine readable data file, Zurich: Department of Sociology, Zurich University.

Bornschier V. and Nollert M. (1994), 'Political Conflict and Labor Disputes at the Core: An Encompassing Review for the Post - War Era' in *'Conflicts and New Departures in World Society'* (Bornschier V. and Lengyel P. (Eds.)), pp. 377 - 403, New Brunswick (U.S.A.) and London: Transaction Publishers, World Society Studies, Volume 3.

Bornschier V. and Suter Chr. (1992), 'Long Waves in the World System' in *'Waves, Formations and Values in the World System'* (Bornschier V. and Lengyel P. (Eds.)), pp. 15 - 50, New Brunswick and London: Transaction Publishers.

Bornschier V. *et al.* (1980), *'Multinationale Konzerne, Wirtschaftspolitik und nationale Entwicklung im Weltsystem'* Frankfurt a.M.: Campus.

Bornschier V., Chase-Dunn Ch. and Rubinson R. (1977), 'Cross-National Evidence of the Effects of Foreign Investment and Aid on Economic Growth and Inequality: A Survey of Findings and a Reanalysis.' *American Journal of Sociology,* 84, pps. 487-506.

Borocz J. (1996), 'Leisure migration: a sociological study on tourism'. Oxford, OX, U.K. ; Tarrytown , N.Y., U.S.A.: Pergamon.

Borocz J. (1999), 'Intellectuals and politics in Central Europe' New York: Central European University Press

Borocz J. (2005), 'Redistributing Global Inequality: A Thought Experiment.' *Economic and Political Weekly,* February 26.

Borocz J. and Kovacz M. (Eds.) (2001), *'Empire's New Clothes: Unveiling EU Enlargement'* e-book, Central Europe's Review, Rutgers University, available at: http://www.rci.rutgers.edu/~eu/Empire.pdf

Borocz J. and Sarkar M. (2005), 'What Is the EU?' *International Sociology,* 20,2(June):153-73.

Borocz J. and Smith D. A. (1995), 'A new world order?: global transformations in the late twentieth century' Westport, Conn.: London: Greenwood Press.

Bosserelle E. (2001), 'Le cycle Kondratiev: mythe ou realite?' *Futuribles,* 2001, no. 267, pp. 63-78.

Boswell T. (1989), *'Revolutions in the World System'* Greenwich CT: Greenwood.

Boswell T. (1997), 'Review on George Modelski and William R. Thompson (1996)' *Journal of World Systems Research,* 3, 2, Spring 1977, electronic journal, available on the Internet at http://csf.colorado.edu/wsystems/jwsr.html.

Boswell T. (1999), 'Hegemony and Bifurcation Points in World History' in *'The Future of Global Conflict'* (Bornschier V. and Chase-Dunn Ch. K. (Eds.)), pp. 263 - 284, London, Thousand Oaks and New Delhi: Sage Publications.

Boswell T. and Bergesen A. (1987), *'America's Changing Role in the World-System'* New York: Frederic Praeger Publishers.

Boswell T. and Chase-Dunn Ch. K. (2000), *'The Spiral of Capitalism and Socialism. Toward Global Democracy'* Boulder, Colorado: Lynne Rienner.

Boswell T. and Dixon W. J. (1993), 'Marx's Theory of Rebellion: A Cross-National Analysis of Class Exploitation, Economic Development, and Violent Revolt.' *American sociological review,* 1993, vol. 58, no. 5, pp. 681.

Boswell T. and Dixon W.J. (1990), 'Dependency and Rebellion: A Cross - National Analysis' *American Sociological Review,* 55, August: 540 - 559.

Boswell T. and Sweat M. (1991), 'Hegemony, Long Waves, and Major Wars: A Time Series Analysis of Systemic Dynamics, 1496 - 1967' *International Studies Quarterly,* 35, 2: 123 - 149.

Botsford D. (1997), *'Britain and the European Union: How we got in and why we should get out'* Foreign Policy Perspectives, 28; also available on the Internet at: http://www.capital.demon.co.uk/LA/foreign/briteuro.txt.

Boxberger G. and Klimenta H. (1998), *'Die 10 Globalisierungslügen. Alternativen zur Allmacht des Marktes'* Munich: dtv.

Bozonnet J. (2004). "De-institutionalising environmentalism. The shift from civil institutions to a fake state institutionalisation. Local Institution Building for the Environment: Perspectives from East and West", Instituto de Sociologia Internationale di Gorizia, University of Trieste, Gorizia (Italy). http://www.interuniv.isig.it/envtrieste/Paper-Bozonnet.doc

Bradshaw Y. (1987), 'Urbanization and Underdevelopment: A Global Study of Modernization, Urban Bias, and Economic Dependency' *American Sociological Review*, 52: 224 - 239.

Bradshaw Y. and Huang J. (1991), 'Intensifying Global Dependency. Foreign Debt, Structural Adjustment, and Third - World Underdevelopment' *Sociological Quarterly*, 32, 3: 321 - 342.

Bradshaw Y. W. and Schafer M. J. (2000), 'Urbanization and Development: The Emergence of International Nongovernmental Organizations Amid Declining States'. *Sociological Perspectives*, vol. 43, no. 1, pp. 97.

Bradshaw Y. W., Noonan R; and Gash L. (1993), 'Borrowing against the Future: Children and Third World Indebtedness.' *Social forces*, vol. 71, no. 3, pp. 629.

Brecke P. (1999), *'Violent Conflicts 1400 A.D. to the Present in Different Regions of the World"*. The Sam Nunn School of International Affairs, Georgia Institute of Technology, Atlanta, GA 30332-0610, available at http://www.inta.gatech.edu/peter/PSS99_paper.html.

Breedlove W. L. and Armer J. M. (1996), 'Economic Disarticulation and Social Development in Less-Developed Nations: A Cross-National Study of Intervening Structures.' *Sociological focus*, vol. 29, no. 4, pp. 359 ff.

Breedlove W. L. and Armer J. M. (1997), 'Dependency, Techno-Economic Heritage, Disarticulation, and Social Development in Less Developed Nations. ' *Sociological perspectives*, vol. 40, no. 4, pp. 661 ff.

Breedlove W. L. and Patrick N. D. (1988), 'International Stratification and Inequality 1960-1980'. *International journal of contemporary sociology*, 1988, vol. 25, no. 3/4, pp. 105.

Bremer S. and Cusack T. (1996), *'The Process of War'* London and New York: Taylor and Francis.

Brenner R. (1998), 'Uneven Development and the Long Downturn: The Advanced Capitalist Economies from Boom to Stagnation, 1950-1998'. *New Left Review*, No. 229 (May-June), pp. 1-228.

Brolin J. (2007), *'The Bias of the World. Theories of Unequal Exchange in History'*. Lund: Lund University, Lund Studies in Human Ecology, 9 (entire).

Brooks S. and James E. J. (1999), 'The Political Economy of Pension Reform' Paper, presented at the World Bank Conference New Ideas about Old-Age Security, September 14-15, Washington D.C., available at: http://www.worldbank.org/knowledge/chiefecon/conferen/papers/polecon.htm.

Broswimmer F. J. (2003), *'Ecocide: A Short History of the Mass Extinction of Species'*. London: Pluto Press.

Bryceson D. and Vuorela U. (Eds.)(2002), *'The transnational family: new European frontiers and global networks'* Oxford; New York: Berg.

Bull B; Boas M; and McNeill D (2004), 'Private Sector Influence in the Multilateral System: A Changing Structure of World Governance?' *Global Governance*, vol. 10, no. 4, pp. 481-498.

Bullock B. and Firebaugh G. (1990), 'Guns and Butter? The Effect of Military, Economic and Social Development in the Third World'. *Journal of Political and Military Sociology*, 18:231-266.

Bundesministerium fuer Soziale Sicherheit und Generationen (2001), „Bericht ueber die soziale Lage 1999". Vienna: Federal Ministry for Social Security and Generations (Two volumes).

Bundesministerium fuer Soziale Sicherheit, Generationen und Konsumentenschutz (2005), „Bericht ueber die soziale Lage 2003 - 2004". Vienna: Federal Ministry for Social Security and Generations (Two volumes).

Burns T. J. et al. (1994), 'Demography, Development, and Deforestation in a World-System Perspective'. *International Journal of Comparative Sociology*, 35(3-4):221-239.

Burns T. J., Kentor J. D. and Jorgenson, A. (2002), 'Trade Dependence, Pollution and Infant Mortality in Less Developed Countries: A Study of World-System Influences on National Outcomes' Department of Sociology, University of Utah, available at: http://www.irows.ucr.edu/andrew/papers/tradedep.doc.

Burns T. J., Kick E. L. and Davis B. L. (2003), 'Theorizing and Rethinking Linkages Between the Natural Environment and the Modern World-System: Deforestation in the Late 20th Century' *Journal of World-Systems Research*, available at: http://jwsr.ucr.edu/index.phpVol. 9, Num. 2 (Summer 2003): 357 – 390.

Cadette W. (1999), 'Social Security Privatization: A Bad Idea' *Policy Notes*, Jerome Levy Economics Institute, 10; available at: http://www.levy.org/docs/pn/99-10.html.

Caminada K. and Goudswaard K. (2000*), 'International trends in income inequality and social policy'* ISSA Conference, Helsinki 'Social Security in the global village' available at: http://www.issa.int/pdf/helsinki2000/topic4/2goudswaard.PDF.

Caporaso J. A. (1978), 'Dependence, Dependency, and Power in the Global System: A Structural and Behavioral Analysis' *International Organization*, 32: 13 - 43.

Cardoso F. H. (1969), *'Mudancas sociais na América Latina'* Sao Paulo: DIFEL.

Cardoso F. H. (1972), *'O Modelo Politico Brasileiro, e outros ensaios'* Sao Paulo: DIFEL.

Cardoso F. H. (1973), 'Associated - Dependent Development. Theoretical and Practical Implications' in *'Authoritarian Brazil. Origins, Policies and Future'* (Stepan A. (Ed.)), New Haven and London: Yale University Press.

Cardoso F. H. (1977), 'El Consumo de la Teoria de la Dependencia en los Estados Unidos' *El Trimestre Economico*, 173, 44, 1, Enero: 33 - 52.

Cardoso F. H. (1979), *'Development under Fire'* Mexico D.F.: Instituto Latinoamericano de Estudios Transnacionales', DEE/D/24 i, Mayo (Mexico 20 D.F., Apartado 85 - 025).

Cardoso F. H. and Faletto E. (1971), *'Dependencia y desarrollo en América Latina'* Mexico D.F.: editorial siglo I.

Carroll E. (2000*), 'Globalization and social policy: social insurance quality, institutions, trade exposure and deregulation in 18 OECD nations, 1965-1995'* ISSA Conference, Helsinki 'Social Security in the global village' available at: http://www.issa.int/engl/reunion/2000/helsinki/2prog.htm.

Chan St. (1989), 'Income Inequality Among LDCs: A Comparative Analysis of Alternative Perspectives.' *International Studies Quarterly*, 33, pps. 45-65.

Chan St. and Clark C. (1992), *'Flexibility, Foresight, and Fortuna in Taiwan's Development: Navigating between Scylla and Charybdis'*. London and New York: Routledge.

Chan St. and Mintz A. (1992), *'Defense, Welfare, and Growth'* London and New York: Routledge.

Chase-Dunn Ch. (1999), 'Globalization: A World-Systems Perspective' *Journal of World-Systems Research, available at: http://jwsr.ucr.edu/index.php*V, 2: 165 – 185.

Chase-Dunn Ch. K. (1975), 'The Effects of International Economic Dependence on Development and Inequality: a Cross - national Study' *American Sociological Review*, 40: 720 - 738.

Chase-Dunn Ch. K. (1983), 'The Kernel of the Capitalist World Economy: Three Approaches' in *'Contending Approaches to World System Analysis'* (Thompson W.R. (Ed.)), pp. 55 - 78, Beverly Hills: Sage.

Chase-Dunn Ch. K. (1984), 'The World - System Since 1950: What Has Really Changed?' in *'Labor in the Capitalist World - Economy'* (Bergquist Ch. (Ed.)), pp. 75 - 104, Beverly Hills: Sage.

Chase-Dunn Ch. K. (1991), *'Global Formation: Structures of the World Economy'* London, Oxford and New York: Basil Blackwell.

Chase-Dunn Ch. K. (1992a), 'The Changing Role of Cities in World Systems' in *'Waves, Formations and Values in the World System'* (Bornschier V. and Lengyel P. (Eds.)), pp. 51 - 87, New Brunswick and London: Transaction Publishers.

Chase-Dunn Ch. K. (1992b), 'The National State as an Agent of Modernity' *Problems of Communism,* January - April: 29 - 37.

Chase-Dunn Ch. K. (1996), *'Conflict among Core States: World System Cycles and Trends'* Department of Sociology, Johns Hopkins University, available from the Internet at http://csf.colorado.edu/wsystems/archive/papers/c-d&hall/warprop.htm.

Chase-Dunn Ch. K. (2000), *'World State Formation: Historical Processes and Emergent Necessity'* Department of Sociology, Johns Hopkins University, available from the Internet at http://www.jhu.edu/.

Chase-Dunn Ch. K. (2005a), 'Social Evolution and the Future of World Society' in *'The Future of World Society'* (Herkenrath M. et al. (Eds.)) pp. 13 – 37; Sociological Institute, University of Zurich: Intelligent Book Production.

Chase-Dunn Ch. K. (Ed.), (1982), *'Socialist States in the World System'* Beverly Hills and London: Sage.

Chase-Dunn Ch. K. and Boswell T. (2005), 'Global Democracy: a world systems perspective'. Forthcoming at Protosociology, available at: http://www.irows.ucr.edu/cd/courses/181/globdemo.htm

Chase-Dunn Ch. K. and Grimes P. (1995), 'World - Systems Analysis' *Annual Review of Sociology,* 21: 387 - 417.

Chase-Dunn Ch. K. and Hall Th. D. (1997), *'Rise and Demise. Comparing World - Systems'* Boulder, Colorado: Westview Press.

Chase-Dunn Ch. K. and Podobnik B. (1995), 'The Next World War: World - System Cycles and Trends' *Journal of World Systems Research* 1, 6 (unpaginated electronic journal at world - wide - web site of the World System Network: *http://csf.colorado.edu/wsystems/jwsr.html).*

Chase-Dunn Ch., Kawano Y., and Brewer B. (2000), 'Trade Globalization since 1795: waves of integration in the world-system' *American Sociological Review,* 65: 77 – 95 (February).

Chenery H. and Syrquin M. (1975), 'Patterns of Development 1950-1970'. Oxford, London and New York: Oxford U. Press.

Chiti V. (1998), *'Euroland/Civiland. Europe in Wonderland'* Rennes: editions l'Aube.

Chojnacki S. (2004), *'Anything New or More of the Same? Types of War in the Contemporary International System"* Paper, prepared for the 5th Pan-European International Relations Conference 'Constructing World Orders", The Hague, September 9-11, 2004, available at: http://www.polwiss.fu-berlin.de/frieden/pdf/Chojnacki-Anything-New.pdf.

Chow P. C. Y. (2002), *'Taiwan's Modernization in Global Perspective'*. New York: Frederic Praeger.

Ciprut J. V. (2000), *'Of Fears and Foes: Security and Insecurity in an Evolving Global Political Economy'* New York: Frederic Praeger Publishers.

Clark A. E &. Lelkes O. (2005). *"Deliver Us From Evil: Religion As Insurance"*. Paris, PSE. http://www.pse.ens.fr/document/wp200543.pdf

Clark G. L. (2001a), *'European pensions and global finance: continuity or convergence?'* School of Geography and Environment, and the Said Business School, University of Oxford, available at: http://www.geog.ox.ac.uk/~jburke/wpapers/wpg01-02.html or http://www.pensions-research.org/papers/default.htm.

Clark G. L. (2001b), *'Requiem for a national ideal? Social solidarity, the crisis of French social security, and the role of global financial markets'* School of Geography and Environment, and the Said Business School, University of Oxford, available at: http://www.pensions-research.org/papers/default.htm.

Clark R. (1992), 'Economic Dependency and Gender Differences in Labor - Force Sectoral Change in Non - Core Nations' *Sociological Quarterly,* 33, 1: 83 - 98.

Clark R. *et al.* (1991), 'Culture, Gender, and Labor - Force Participation. A Cross - National Study' *Gender and Society,* 5, 1: 47 - 66.

Clauss G. and Ebner H. (1978), *'Grundlagen der Statistik. Fuer Psychologen, Paedagogen und Soziologen'* Berlin: Volk and Wissen.

Coenders M.,. Lubbers M., et al. (2005). *"Majorities' attitudes towards minorities, findings from the Eurobarometer and the European Social Survey."* Vienna, European Monitoring Centre on Racism and Xenophobia. http://www.eumc.eu.int/eumc/index.php?fuseaction=content.dsp_cat_content&catid=3fb38ad3e22bb&contentid=42369ad95426f

Cohen R. (1991), 'East - West and European migration in a global context' *New Community,* 18, 1: 9 - 26.

Cohn - Bendit D. (1993), 'Europe and its borders: the case for a common immigration policy' in *'Towards a European Immigration Policy'* (Ogata S. *et al.*), pp. 22 - 31, London: Philip Morris Institute for Public Policy Research.

Coleman J. S. (1965), *'Education and Political Development'* Princeton: Princeton University Press.

Commonwealth of Australia, Office of the Status of Women (2000), 'Women and Poverty' available at: http://osw.dpmc.gov.au/content/publications/beijing/a_poverty.html.

Coppel J. et al. (2001*), 'Trends in Immigration and Economic Consequences'* OECD Economics Department Working Papers, 284, available at: http://ideas.uqam.ca/ideas/data/Papers/oedoecdec284.html.

Corbetta R. and Dixon W. J. (2004), 'Multilateralism, Major Powers, and Militarized Disputes ' *Political Research Quarterly,* vol. 57, no. 1, pp. 5-14.

Corden W.M. (1987), 'How Valid is International Keynesianism?' International Monetary Fund, Research Department: *IMF Working Paper* WP/87/56.

Cordova A. (1973), *'Strukturelle Heterogenitaet und wirtschaftliches Wachstum'* Frankfurt a.M.: edition suhrkamp.

Cordova A. and Silva - Michelena H. (1972), *'Die wirtschaftliche Struktur Lateinamerikas. Drei Studien zur politischen Oekonomie der Unterentwicklung'* Frankfurt a.M.: edition suhrkamp.

Cornia G. A. (Ed.)(1993), *'Economies in Transition Studies, Regional Monitoring Report, 1'* Firenze: UNICEF.

Cornia G. A. (Ed.)(1994), *'Economies in Transition Studies, Regional Monitoring Report, 2'* Firenze: UNICEF.

Cornia G. A. (Ed.)(2004), *'Inequality, growth, and poverty in an era of liberalization and globalization'* Oxford; New York: Oxford University Press.

Cornia G. A. and Kiiski S. (2002), *'Trends in Income Distribution in the Post WWII Period: Evidence and Interpretation'* UNI WIDER available at http://www.wider.unu.edu/conference/conference-2001-1/cornia%20and%20kiiski.pdf.

Cornia G. A. and Paniccia R. (Eds.)(2000), *'Mortality crisis in transitional economies'* Oxford; New York: Oxford University Press.

Cornia G. A., Addison T. and Kiiski S. (2003), *'Income Distribution Changes and their Impact in the Post-World War II Period'* United Nations University, WIDER Institute Helsinki, Discussion Paper Wdp, 2003, no. 28, (entire).

Cornwall J. and Cornwall W. (2001), *'Capitalist Development in the Twentieth Century: An Evolutionary-Keynesian Analysis'* Cambridge: Cambridge University Press, 2001.

Cox R.W. (1994), 'Global Restructuring: Making Sense of the Changing International Political Economy, ' in: G. Stubbs and Underhill (eds.), *Political Economy and the Changing Global Order*.

Crafts N. (2000), *'Globalization and Growth in The Twentieth Century*, IMF Working Paper, WP/00/44, International Monetary Fund,. Available at: http://www.imf.org/external/pubs/ft/wp/2000/wp0044.pdf.

Crenshaw E. M. (1991), 'Foreign Investment as a Dependent Variable: Determinants of Foreign and Capital Penetration in Developing Nations, 1967 - 1978' *Social Forces,* 69, 4: 1169 - 1182.

Crenshaw E. M. (1992), 'Cross - National Determinants of Income Inequality: A Replication and Extension Using Ecological - Evolutionary Theory' *Social Forces,* 71: 339 - 363.

Crenshaw E. M. (1993), 'Polity, Economy and Technology: Alternative Explanations for Income Inequality.' *Social forces,* vol. 71, no. 3, pp. 807.

Crenshaw E. M. (1995), 'Democracy and Demographic Inheritance: The Influence of Modernity and Proto-Modernity on Political and Civil Rights, 1965 to 1980.' *American sociological review,* vol. 60, no. 5, pp. 702 ff.

Crenshaw E. M. and Ansari A. (1994), 'The Distribution of Income Across National Populations: Testing Multiple Paradigms.' *Social Science Research,* 23, 1, March, pps. 1-22.

Crenshaw E. M. and Jenkins J. C. (1996), 'Social Structure and Global Climate Change: Sociological Propositions Concerning the Greenhouse Effect.' *Sociological focus,* 1996, vol. 29, no. 4, pp. 341.

Crenshaw E. M. and Oakey, D. R. (1998), "Jump-Starting' Development: Hyperurbanization as a Long-Term Economic Investment.' *Sociological focus,* vol. 31, no. 4, pp. 321.

Crenshaw E. M.; Ameen A. Z.; and Christenson. M. (1997), 'Population Dynamics and Economic Development: Age-Specific Population Growth Rates and Economic Growth in Developing Countries, 1965 to 1990.' *American sociological review,* vol. 62, no. 6, pp. 974.

Crenshaw E. M.; Christenson M.; Oakey D. R. (2000), 'Demographic Transition in Ecological Focus.' *American Sociological Review,* vol. 65, no. 3, pp. 371.

Dadush U. and Brahmbhatt M. (1995), 'Anticipating Capital Flow Reversals' *Finance and Development,* December: 3 - 5.

Dahlmanns G. (2000), *'Mastering Germany's Pension Crisis'* Frankfurter Institut Stiftung Marktwirtschaft & Politik, available at: http:// www.aicgs.org/econ/dahlmanns.html.

Dasgupta P. (1995), *'An Inquiry into Well-Being and Destitution.'* New York and Oxford: Oxford University Press.

Datta A. (1993), 'Warum fluechten Menschen aus ihrer Heimat?' in *'Die Neuen Mauern. Krisen der Nord - Sued - Beziehungen'* (Datta A. (Ed.)), pp. 31 - 46, Wuppertal: P. Hammer.

David A. and Wheelwright T. (1989), *'The Third Wave. Australia and Asian Capitalism'* Sutherland, New South Wales: Left Book Club Cooperative Ltd.

Davis B. L., Kick E. L. and Burns T. J. (2004), 'Change Scores, Composites and Reliability Issues in Cross-National Development Research' *International Journal of Comparative Sociology,* vol. 45, no. 5, pp. 299-314.

Davydov V. M., Bobróvnikov A. V. and Teperman V. A. (2000), *'Fenomen finansovoj globalizacii: universal'nye processy i reakcija latinoamerikanskich stran'* Moskva: Inst. Latinskoj Ameriki RAN, 2000, ISBN: 5-201-05387-4.

Deacon B. (1992a), 'East European Welfare: Past, Present and Future in Comparative Context' in *'The New Eastern Europe. Social Policy Past, Present and Future'* (Deacon B. (Ed.)), pp. 1 - 31, London and Newbury Park: Sage.

Deacon B. (1992b), 'The Future of Social Policy in Eastern Europe' in *'The New Eastern Europe. Social Policy Past, Present and Future'* (Deacon B. (Ed.)), pp. 167 - 191, London and Newbury Park: Sage.

Deininger K. and Squire L. (1996), 'A New Data Set Measuring Inequality", *World Bank Economnic Review,* vol. 10, pp. 565-591.

del Sarto R. (2002), *'Israel's Contested Identity and the Mediterranean'* The Hebrew University of Jerusalem, Department of International Relations; available at: http://ies.berkeley.edu/research/DelSartoIsraelMed.pdf.

Delacroix J. and Ragin Ch. (1981), 'Structural Blockage: A Cross - National Study of Economic Dependency, State Efficacy, and Underdevelopment' *American Journal of Sociology,* 86, 6: 1311 - 1347.

Denemark R. A., Modelski G., Gills B. K. and Friedman J. (2000), *'World Systems History: The Social Science of Long-term Change'* London and New York: Routledge.

Dennis I. and Guio A. C. (2004), 'Armut und soziale Ausgrenzung in der EU' Statistik kurz gefasst, Eurostat, 16, available at: http://www.eds-destatis.de/de/downloads/sif/nk_04_16.pdfsearch=%22Armut%20und%20soziale%20Au sgrenzung%20in%20der%20EU%20Dennis%20Guio%22

Dennis I. and Guio A. C. (2004), 'Armut und soziale Ausgrenzung in der EU' Statistik kurz gefasst, Eurostat, 16, available at: http://www.eds-destatis.de/de/downloads/sif/nk_04_16.pdf#search=%22Armut%20und%20soziale%20Ausgrenzung%20in%20der%20EU%20Dennis%20Guio%22

Dennis I. and Guio A. C. (2004), 'Monetary poverty in the new Member States and Candidate Countries' Statistik kurz gefasst, Eurostat, 12, available at: www.eustatistics.gov.uk/Download.asp?KS-NK-04-012-EN_tcm90-17101.pdf

Dennis I. and Guio A. C. (2004), 'Monetary poverty in the new Member States and Candidate Countries' Statistik kurz gefasst, Eurostat, 12, available at: www.eustatistics.gov.uk/Download.asp?KS-NK-04-012-EN_tcm90-17101.pdf

Derlugian G. M. and Greer S. L. (2000), *'Questioning Geopolitics: Political Projects in a Changing World-System'* New York: Frederic Praeger.

Desai M. and Redfern, P. (1995), *'Global Governance, Ethics and Economics of the World Order'* London: Pinter.

Deshingkar G. (1989), 'Arms, Technology, Violence and the Global Military Order' in *'The Quest for Peace'* (Vaerynen R. et al. (Eds.)), pp. 260 - 274, London, Beverly Hills: Sage.

Deutsch K. W. (1960), 'Ansaetze zu einer Bestandsaufnahme von Tendenzen in der vergleichenden und internationalen Politik' in *'Political Science. Amerikanische Beitraege zur Politikwissenschaft'* (Krippendorff E. (Ed.)), Tuebingen: J.C.B. Mohr.

Deutsch K. W. (1966), *'Nationalism and Social Communication. An inquiry into the foundations of nationality'* Cambrigde, Massachusetts and London: M.I.T. Press.

Deutsch K. W. (1978), *'The Analysis of International Relations'* Englewood Cliffs, N.J.: Prentice Hall.

Deutsch K. W. (1979), *'Tides Among Nations'* New York: Free Press.

Deutsch K. W. (1982), 'Major Changes in Political Science' in *'International Handbook of Political Science'* (Andrews W.G. (Ed.)), pp. 9 - 33, Westport, Con.: Greenwood Press.

Devezas T. C. (Ed.) (2006), *'Kondratieff Waves, Warfare and World Security'* Volume 5 NATO Security through Sciences Series: Human and Societal Dynamics. Amsterdam: Iospress

Devezas T. C. and Corredine J. T. (2001), 'The biological determinants of long-wave behavior in socio-economic growth and development' *Technological Forecasting & Social Change,* 68: 1 – 57.

Devezas T. C. and Modelski G. (2003), 'Power law behavior and world system evolution: A millennial learning process' *Technological Forecasting and Social Change,* Volume 70, Issue 9, November: 819-859.

Devezas T. C., Linestone H. A. and Santos H. J. S. (2005), 'The growth dynamics of the Internet and the long wave theory' *Technological Forecasting and Social Change,* Volume 72, Issue 8, October: 913-935.

Die Presse (2005), *''Österreichs Sozialmodell ineffizient'* VON FRANZISKA ANNERL (Die Presse)' 28.10.2005, available at: http://www.diepresse.com/Artikel.aspx?channel=p&ressort=eu&id=515384&archiv=false.

Dittrich M. (2006), *'Muslims in Europe: addressing the challenges of radicalisation'.* European Policy Centre in strategic partnership with the King Baudouin Foundation and the Comagnia di San Paolo, Brussels, available at http://www.theepc.be/TEWN/pdf/602431467_EPC%20Working%20Paper%2023%20Muslims%20in%20Europe.pdf

Dittrich M. (2006), 'Muslims in Europe: addressing the challenges of radicalisation'. European Policy Centre in strategic partnership with the King Baudouin Foundation and the Comagnia di San Paolo, Brussels, available at http://www.theepc.be/TEWN/pdf/602431467_EPC%20Working%20Paper%2023%20Muslims%20in%20Europe.pdf

Dixon C. J., Drakakis-Smith D. and Watts H. D. (1986), *'Multinational Corporations and the Third World'* Boulder, CO: Westview Press.

Dixon W. J. (1984), 'Trade Concentration, Economic Growth and the Provision of Basic Human Needs' *Social Science Quarterly,* 65: 761 - 774.

Dixon W. J. (1994), 'Democracy and the Peaceful Settlement of International Conflict.' *The American Political Science Review,* 1994, vol. 88, no. 1, pp. 14.

Dixon W. J. and Boswell T. (1996a), 'Dependency, Disarticulation, and Denominator Effects: Another Look at Foreign Capital Penetration'. *The american journal of sociology,* 1996, vol. 102, no. 2, pp. 543.

Dixon W. J. and Boswell T. (1996b), 'Differential Productivity, Negative Externalities, and Foreign Capital Dependency: Reply to Firebaugh.' *The american journal of sociology,* vol. 102, no. 2, pp. 576.

Dollar D. (2005), 'Globalization, Poverty, and Inequality since 1980.' *World Bank Research Observer,* vol. 20, no. 2, pp. 145-175.

Dollar D. and Kraay A. (2000), *'Growth Is Good for the Poor'.* Development Research Group, The World Bank, available at: http://www.worldbank.org/research/growth/pdfiles/growthgoodforpoor.pdf; third (final) draft available at: http://www.worldbank.org/research/growth/pdfiles/GIGFTP3.pdf.

Dollar D. and Kraay A. (2001a), 'Trade, Growth and Poverty' *Finance and Development,* 38, 3, available at: http://www.imf.org/external/pubs/ft/fandd/2001/09/dollar.htm.

Donno D. (2004), "Islam, Authoritarianism, and Female and Empowerment: What Are the Linkages?" *World Politics* Volume 56, Number 4, July 2004, pp. 582-607

Donno D. and Russett B. (2004), 'Islam, Authoritarianism, and Female Empowerment: What Are the Linkages?' *World Politics,* vol. 56, no. 4, pp. 582-607.

Dowrick, S. and Akmal M. (2001b), 'Contradictory Trends in Global Income Inequality: A Tale of Two Biases", available from http://ecocomm.anu.edu.au/economics/staff/dowrick/dowrick.html.

Drekonja-Kornat G. and Tokatlian J. G. (Eds.)(1983), *'Teoría y práctica de la política exterior latinoamericana'* [Bogotá]: Centro de Estudios de la Realidad Colombiana, Fondo Editorial. Centro de Estudios Internacionales, Universidad de los Andes.

Dubiel I. (1983), *'Der klassische Kern der lateinamerikanischen Entwicklungstheorie. Ein metatheoretischer Versuch'* Munich: Eberhard.

Dubiel I. (1993), 'Andere Zeiten - Andere Wirtschaftstheorien. Elemente einer oekonomischen Theorie von morgen' in *'Kultur - Identitaet - Kommunikation. 2. Versuch'* (Ammon G. and Eberhard Th. (Eds.)), pp. 81 - 124, Munich: Eberhard - Verlag.

Dunaway W. A. and Wallerstein I. (Eds.)(2003), *'Emerging Issues in the 21st Century World System'* New York: Frederic Praeger/Greenwood.

Dunning J. H. (2001), 'Global Capitalism at Bay?' London and New York: Palgrave Macmillan.

Easterly W. G. (2000), *'The Middle Class Consensus and Economic Development'.* (May 2000). World Bank Policy Research Working Paper No. 2346. Available at SSRN: http://ssrn.com/abstract=630718

Easterly W. (2001), 'The Lost Decades. Developing Countries' Stagnation In Spite of Policy Reform, 1980-98", *Journal of Economic Growth,* vol. 6, No.2, pp. 135-157.

Easterly W. (2002), *'Inequality does Cause Underdevelopment: New evidence'.* Center for Global Development, Working Paper 1, January 2002, available at: http://www.cgdev.org/wp/cgd_wp001_rev.pdf.

Ehrhardt-Martinez K.; Crenshaw E. M.; and Jenkins J. C. (2002), 'Deforestation and the Environmental Kuznets Curve: A Cross-National Investigation of Intervening Mechanisms'. *Social Science Quarterly,* Volume 83, Number 1, March, pp. 226-243.

Elsenhans H. (1983), 'Rising mass incomes as a condition of capitalist growth: implications for the world economy' *International Organization,* 37, 1: 1 - 39.

Elsenhans H. (1992), *'Equality and development'* Dhaka, Bangladesh: Centre for Social Studies: Distributor, Dana Publishers.

Elsenhans H. (1993), *'Europe-India: new perspectives in changing power structures in the international system.'* [New Delhi]: Friedrich Ebert Stiftung.

Elsenhans H. (1996), ' *State, class, and development'.* New Delhi: Radiant Publishers.

Elsenhans H. (1999), *'A balanced European architecture: enlargement of the European Union to Central Europe and the Mediterranean = Une architecture européenne équilibré: l'ouverture de l'Union européenne vers l'Europe centrale et la Méditerranée'* Paris: Publisud.

Elsenhans H. (Ed.)(1978), *'Migration und Wirtschaftsentwicklung'* Frankfurt a.M.: Campus.

Elsenhans H. (Ed.)(1979), *'Agrarreform in der Dritten Welt'* Frankfurt/Main; New York: Campus-Verlag.

Emmanuel, A. (1972), *'Unequal Exchange: A Study of the Imperialism of Trade.'* New York, USA: Monthly Review Press [translated from the 1969 French original].

Erdenir B. (2006), 'The Future of Europe: Islamophobia?' Secretariat General for EU Affairs (EUSG) of Turkey, available at: http://www.turkishpolicy.com/default.asp?show=fall_2005_erdenir (Turkish Policy Quarterly, 2006).

Erdenir B. (2006), 'The Future of Europe: Islamophobia?' Secretariat General for EU Affairs (EUSG) of Turkey, available at: http://www.turkishpolicy.com/default.asp?show =fall_2005_erdenir (Turkish Policy Quarterly, 2006).

Esfahani H. S. (2000), *‚Political Economy of Growth in MENA Countries: A Framework for Country Case Studies'.* University of Illinois at Urbana-Champaign, available at: http://www.gdnet.org/pdf/325_H-Esfahani.pdf.

Esping - Andersen G. (1985), *'Politics against markets. The social democratic road to power'* Princeton: Princeton University Press.

European Commission (2000a), 'Modernising and Improving Social Protection in the European Union' available at: http://www.itcilo.it/english/actrav/telearn/global/ ilo/seura/eumode.htm.

European Commission (2000b), 'Progress report on the impact of ageing populations on public pension systems' Economic Policy Committee, available at: http://europa. eu.int/comm/economy_finance/document/epc/epc_ecfin_581_00_en.pdf.

European Commission (2001), 'White Paper on Governance. Working Group No. 5: An EU contribution to Better Governance beyond Our Borders'. Report of the Working Group: 'Strengthening Europe's Contribution to World Governance". Brussels, May 2001, available on the Internet at: http://europa.eu.int/comm/governance/areas/ group11/report_en.pdf.

European Commission (2003), *'Governance and Development. Communication from the Commission to the Council, the European Parliament and the European Economic and Social Committee.'* Brussels, 20. 10. 2003, COM (2003) 615 final. Available on the Internet at: http://europa.eu.int/eur-lex/en/com/cnc/2003/com2003_0615en01.pdf.

European Commission (2005), *'Communication from the Commission to the European Parliament, the Council, the European Economic and Social Committee and the Committee of the Regions'* Brussels, Commission of the European Communities, 20.10.2005, COM (2005) 525 final.

European Commission (current issues), *'Euro-Mediterranean statistics'*. Brussels: Eurostat.

European Commission (current issues), *'External Relations. Website of the GD External Relations* at: http://europa.eu.int/comm/external_relations/index.htm.

European Foundation for the Improvement of Living and Working Conditions (2005), *'Quality of life in Europe survey'* available at: http://www.eurofound.eu.int/publications/htmlfiles/ef04105.htm

European Roundtable of Industrialists, ERT (2001), *'European Pensions. An Appeal for Reform'*. Pension Schemes that Europe Can Really Afford' Brussels: ERT.

European Social Survey (2006), Data materials, freely available from: http://www.europeansocialsurvey.org/

European Social Survey (2006), Data materials, freely available from: http://www.europeansocialsurvey.org/

European Stability Initiative (2006), *'Islamic Calvinists. Change and Conservatism in Central Anatolia'*. European Stability Initiative, Berlin, Brussels, Istanbul, available at: http://www.esiweb.org/

Evans P. B. and Timberlake M. (1980), 'Dependence, Inequality, and the Growth of the Tertiary: A Comparative Analysis of Less Developed Countries.' *American Sociological Review,* 45, August, pps. 531-552.

Fahey T. Et al. (2005), 'First European Quality of Life Survey: Income inequalities and deprivation' European Foundation for the Improvement of Living and Wokring Conditions, available at: http://www.eurofound.eu.int/pubdocs/2005/93/en/1/ef0593en.pdf

Fahey T. Et al. (2005), 'First European Quality of Life Survey: Income inequalities and deprivation' European Foundation for the Improvement of Living and Wokring Conditions, available at: http://www.eurofound.eu.int/pubdocs/2005/93/en/1/ef0593en.pdf

Fain H. D. et al. (1997), 'World-System Position, Tropical Climate, National Development, and Infant Mortality: A Cross-National Analysis of 86 Countries'. *Human Ecology Review,* 3:197-203.

Falk R. (1995), *'On human governance: towards a new global politics'* Cambridge: Polity Press.

Falk. R. A. and Szentes T. (1997), 'A New Europe in the changing global system.' Tokyo ; New York: United Nations University

Feder E. (1972), *'Violencia y despojo del campesino: el latifundismo en América Latina'* Mexico D.F.: siglo I.

Ferrera M. (2005), ‚*The Caring Dimension of Europe: How to make it more visible and more vigorous'* University of Milan and URGE Turin (Discussion paper prepared for the UK Presidency, available at http://www.eu2005.gov.uk/servlet/Front?pagename=Open Market/Xcelerate/ShowPage&c=Page&cid=1107293391098&a=KArticle&aid=1119527 321606.

Fiala R. (1992), 'The International System, Labor Force Structure, and the Growth and Distribution of National Income, 1950 - 1980' *Sociological Perspectives,* 35, 2: 249 - 282.

Fink M. and Schuh U. (2005), ‚*Das Europäische Sozialmodell. Grundlagen, Ausgestaltung und Perspektiven'* Vienna: Institute for Advanced Studies (Studie im Auftrag des Bundesministeriums für Wirtschaft und Arbeit; restricted).

Firebaugh G. (1992), 'Growth Effects of Foreign and Domestic Investment' *American Journal of Sociology,* 98: 105 - 130.

Firebaugh G. (1996), 'Does Foreign Capital Harm Poor Nations? New Estimates Based on Dixon and Boswells Measures of Capital Penetration' *American Journal of Sociology,* 2, 102: 563 - 575.

Firebaugh G. (1999), 'Empirics of World Income Inequality", *American Journal of Sociology,* vol.104, pp. 1597-1630.

Firebaugh G. (2000), 'The Trend in Between-Nation Income Inequality' *Annual Review of Sociology,* vol. 26, pp. 323-496.

Firebaugh G. (2002), *'The Myth of Growing Global Income Inequality'* Paper, presented at Oxford University, available at http://www.nuff.ox.ac.uk/rc28/Papers/Firebaugh.PDF.

Firebaugh G. (2003), 'New geography of global income inequality' Cambridge, Mass.: Harvard University Press.

Firebaugh G. and Beck F. D. (1994), 'Does Economic Growth Benefit the Masses?' *American Sociological Review,* 59:631-653.

Firebaugh G. and Goesling B. (2004), 'Accounting for the Recent Decline in Global Income Inequality' *American Journal of Sociology,* vol. 110, no. 2, pp. 283-312.

Fischer - Welt - Almanach (current issues), *'Der Fischer Welt - Almanach. Zahlen, Daten, Fakten'* Frankfurt a.M.: Fischer Taschenbuch Verlag.

Fischer D. H. (1999), *'The Great Wave: Price Revolutions and the Rhythm of History'*. New York and Oxford: Oxford University Press.

Fish M. S. (2002), "Islam and Authoritarianism" *World Politics,* 55, Number 1, October 2002, pp. 4-37

Flechsig St. (1987), 'Raul Prebisch - ein bedeutender Oekonom Lateinamerikas und der Entwicklungslaender' *Wirtschaftswissenschaft,* 35, 5: 721 - 741.

Flechsig St. (1994), 'Raúl Prebisch (1901 - 1986) - ein bedeutendes theoretisches Vermaechtnis oder kein alter Hut' *Utopie kreativ,* 45/46, Juli/August: 136 - 155.

Flechsig St. (2000), 'The Heritage of Raúl Prebisch for a Humane World' *in 'Globalization, Liberation Theology and the Social Sciences. An Analysis of the Contradictions of Modernity at the Turn of the Millennium'* (Andreas Müller OFM et al.) Commack, New York: Nova Science.

Floro S. L. and Yotopoulos P. A. (1991), *'Informal credit markets and the new institutional economics: the case of Philippine agriculture'* Boulder, CO: Westview Press.

Fox L. and Palmer E. (2000), *'New approaches to multi-pillar pension systems: What in the world is going on?'* ISSA Conference, Helsinki 'Social Security in the global village' available at: http://www.issa.int/engl/reunion/2000/helsinki/2prog.htm.

Frank A. G. (1978a), *'Dependent accumulation and underdevelopment'* London: Macmillan.

Frank A. G. (1978b), *'World accumulation, 1492 - 1789'* London: Macmillan.

Frank A. G. (1980), *'Crisis in the world economy'* New York: Holmes & Meier Publishers.

Frank A. G. (1981), *'Crisis in the Third World'* New York: Holmes & Meier Publishers.

Frank A. G. (1983), 'World System in Crisis' in *'Contending Approaches to World System Analysis'* (Thompson W.R. (Ed.)), pp. 27 - 42, Beverly Hills: Sage.

Frank A. G. (1990), 'Revolution in Eastern Europe: lessons for democratic social movements (and socialists?), ' *Third World Quarterly,* 12, 2, April: 36 - 52.

Frank A. G. (1992), 'Economic ironies in Europe: a world economic interpretation of East - West European politics' *International Social Science Journal,* 131, February: 41 - 56.

Frank A. G. (1994), *'World System History".* University of Amsterdam, 23 April 1994, Prepared for presentation at the annual meeting of The New England Historical Association, Bentley College, Waltham, Mass., April 23, 1994, available at: http://www.hartford-hwp.com/archives/10/034.html.

Frank A. G. (1998), *'ReOrient: Global Economy in the Asian Age'.* Ewing, USA: University of California Press.

Frank A. G. and Frank - Fuentes M. (1990), *'Widerstand im Weltsystem'* Vienna: Promedia.

Frank A. G. and Gills B. (Eds.)(1993), *'The World System: Five Hundred or Five Thousand Years?'* London and New York: Routledge, Kegan&Paul.

Franzmeyer F./Brücker H. (1997), 'Europäische Union - Osterweiterung u. Arbeitskräftemigration' - DIW Berlin, 1997 (DIW-Wochenbericht 5).

Freeman Ch. and Louçã F. (2001), *'As time goes by: from the industrial revolutions to the information revolution.'* Oxford; New York: Oxford University Press.

Frey R. S. and Field C. (2000), 'The determinants of Infant Mortality in the Less Developed Countries: A Cross-National Test of Five Theories' *Social Indicators Research,* 52, no. 3 (2000): 215-234.

Friedman M. (1997), 'Monetary Unity, Political Disunity' *Transitions,* December: 32 - 33.

Froebel F. *et al.* (1977a), *'Die neue internationale Arbeitsteilung. Strukturelle Arbeitslosigkeit in den Industrielaendern und die Industrialisierung der Entwicklungslaender'* Reinbek: rororo aktuell (English translation: Cambridge University Press).

Froebel F. *et al.* (1977b), 'Internationalisierung von Kapital und Arbeitskraft' in *'Armut in Oesterreich'* (Junge Generation der SPOe Steiermark und Erklaerung von Graz fuer Solidarische Entwicklung (Eds.)), pp. 12 - 46, Graz: Leykam.

Froebel F. *et al.* (1984), 'The Current Development of the World Economy: Reproduction of Labor and Accumulation of Capital on a World Scale' in *'Transforming the World Economy? Nine Critical Essays on the New International Economic Order'* (Addo H. (Ed.)), pp. 51 - 118, London and Sydney: Hodder & Stoughton.

Froebel F. *et al.* (1986), *'Umbruch in der Weltwirtschaft'* Reinbek: rororo aktuell (English translation: Cambridge University Press).

Fuest C. (1996), 'Die finanzielle Last der EU - Ausgaben. Bleibt Europa noch finanzierbar?' *Die Neue Gesellschaft. Frankfurter Hefte,* 43, 7: 594 - 598.

Fukuyama F. (1991), 'Liberal Democracy as a Global Phenomenon' *PS: Political Science and Politics (Washington D.C.),* 24, 4: 659 - 664.

Fuller G. E. and Lesser I. O. (1995), *'A sense of siege: the geopolitics of Islam and the West'*. Boulder CO.: Westview Press, 1995.

Furtado C. (1970), 'Economic Development of Latin America: Historical Background and Contemporary Problems'. Cambridge: Cambridge U. Press.

Gaerber A. (1999), *'MENA-Region: Der Nahe Osten und Nordafrika. Zwischen Bilateralismus, Regionalismus und Globalisierung'* FES Analysen, Friedrich Ebert Stiftung, September.

Galbraith J. K. (2002), 'A perfect crime: global inequality' *Daedalus,* 2002, vol. 131, no. 1, pp. 11-25.

Galbraith J. K. and Berner M. (2001), *'Inequality and industrial change: a global view'* Cambridge; New York: Cambridge University Press.

Galbraith J. K. and Kum H. (2005), 'Estimating the Inequality of Household Incomes: A Statistical Approach to the Creation of a Dense and Consistent Global Data Set.' *The Review of Income and Wealth,* Volume 51, Number 1, March, pp. 115-143.

Galbraith J. K. and Pitts J. W. (2002), 'Is Inequality Decreasing?' *Foreign Affairs,* 2002, vol. 81, no. 4, pp. 178-183.

Galbraith, J.K. (1995), 'Global Keynesianism in the Wings, ' *World Policy Journal* (USA).

Galganek A. (1992), *'Zmiana w globalnym systemie miedzynarodowym. Supercycle i wojna hegemoniczna'* Poznan: Uniwersytet im. Adama Mickiewicza w Poznanie, Seria Nauki Polityczne, 13 (entire).

Galtung J. (1969), 'Violence, Peace and Peace Research. *Journal of Peace Research,* 6 (3), 167-191.

Galtung J. (1971), 'A Structural Theory of Imperialism' *Journal of Peace Research,* 8, 2: 81 - 118.

Galtung J. (1994), *'Human Rights in Another Key'*. Cambridge, United Kingdom: Polity Press.

Galtung J., Chase-Dunn, Ch. K. et al. (1985), *'Export Dependence and Economic Growth: a Reformulation and Respecification'* Social Forces, Vol. 64, pp. 857 - 894.

Garcia de Cortázar F. and Gonzáles Vesga J. M. (1995), *'Breve historia de Espana'* Madrid: Alianza Editorial, El Libro de Bolsillo.

Garson J. P. et al. (1997), 'Regional Integration and Outlook for Temporary and Permanent Migration in Central and Eastern Europe' in *'Migration, Free Trade and Regional Integration in Central and Eastern Europe'* pp. 299-333, Wien: Schriftenreihe des Bundeskanzleramts.

Gartner R. (1990), 'The Victims of Homicide: A Temporal and Cross - National Comparison' *American Sociological Review,* 55, February: 92 - 106.

Gavin B. (2001), *'European Union and Globalisation: Towards Global Democratic Governance'* Edward Elgar Publishing.

Geller D. S. and Singer J. D. (1998), *'Nations at War: A Scientific Study of International Conflict'* Cambridge: Cambridge University Press.

George S. and Gould E. (2000), 'Liberalisierung kommt auf leisen Sohlen' *Le Monde Diplomatique,* Deutschsprachige Ausgabe, Juli.

Gereffi G. and Miguel Korzeniewicz M. (1994), *'Commodity Chains and Global Capitalism'* New York: Frederic Praeger.

Ghazouani S. and Goaied M. (2001), *'The Determinants of Urban and Rural Poverty in Tunisia'* Laboratoire d' Economie Appliquée (LEA), Tunis, available via the Global Development Network at: http://www.gdnet.org/tm-frame.html?http://www.erf.org.eg/database/2030.pdf.

Ghobarah H. et al. (2001), *'The Political Economy of Comparative Human Misery and Well-being'* American Political Science Association Annual Meeting, San Francisco, available at: http://www.yale.edu/unsy/brussett/PoliticalEconomy(Dale_APSA)12.03.01.pdf.

Gholami R., Lee S. Y. T and Heshmati A. (2003), *'The Causal Relationship between Information and Communication Technology and Foreign Direct Investment'* Helsinki: Wider Discussion Paper Wdp, 2003, no. 30, (entire)

Ghose A. K. (2005), *'Foreign Capital and Investment in Developing Countries'*. Presentation at the Vienna Institute for International Economic Comparisons, available at: http://www.wiiw.ac.at/pdf/sie_ghose_presentation.ppt

Giering C. (1998), 'Die Europaeische Union vor der Erweiterung - Reformbedarf der Institutionen und Verfahren nach Amsterdam' *Oesterreichische Zeitschrift fuer Politikwissenschaft,* 27, 4: 391 - 405.

Gierus J. (1998), *'Russia's Road to Modernity'* Warsaw: Instytut Studiow Politycznych, Polskiej Akademii Nauk.

Gissinger R. and Gleditsch N. P. (1999), 'Globalization and Conflict: Welfare, Distribution, and Political unrest' *Journal of World-Systems Research, available at: http://jwsr.ucr.edu/index.php*5, 2: 327 – 365.

Goedings S. (1997), *'The Expected Effect of the Enlargement of the European Union with Central and Eastern European Countries in the Area of the Free Movement of Workers'* Study for the European Commission, DG V, Amsterdam: International Institute of Social History.

Goedings S. (1999), *'EU Enlargement to the East and Labour Migration to the West'* International Institute of Social History Amsterdam, Research Paper 36.

Goesling B. (2001), 'Changing Income Inequalities within and between Nations: New Evidence' *American Sociological Review,* 66, 5, October: 745 – 761.

Goesling B. and Firebaugh G. (2004), 'The Trend in International Health Inequality' *Population and Development Review,* Volume 30, Number 1, March 2004, pp. 131-146.

Goldfrank W. L. (1978), 'Fascism and the World Economy' in *'Social Change in the Capitalist World Economy'* (Kaplan B.H. (Ed.)), pp. 75 - 117, Beverly Hills: Sage.

Goldfrank W. L. (1982), 'The Soviet Trajectory' in *'Socialist States in the World - System'* (Chase-Dunn Ch. K. (Ed.)), pp. 147 - 156, Beverly Hills: Sage.

Goldfrank W. L. (1990), 'Fascism and the Great Transformation' in *'The Life and Work of Karl Polanyi'* (Polanyi - Levitt K. (Ed.)), Montreal: Black Rose (quoted from the author's typescript).

Goldfrank W. L. (1999), 'Beyond Cycles of Hegemony: Economic, Social and Military Factors' in *'The Future of Global Conflict'* (Bornschier V. and Chase-Dunn Ch. K. (Eds.)), pp. 66 - 76, London, Thousand Oaks and New Delhi: Sage Publications.

Goldfrank W. L. (1999), *'Ecology and the World-System'* Westport, CT: Greenwood Press.

Goldstein J. S. (1985a), 'Basic Human Needs: The Plateau Curve' *World Development,* 13, 5: 595 - 609.

Goldstein J. S. (1985b), 'Kondratiev Waves as War Cycles' *International Studies Quarterly,* 29, 4: 411 - 444.

Goldstein J. S. (1988), *'Long Cycles. Prosperity and War in the Modern Age'* New Haven and London: Yale University Press.
Goldstein J. S. (1994), *'Introduction to the Japanese Edition of Long Cycles'* Tokyo: Tsuge Shobo (quoted from the author's manuscript).
Goldstein J. S. (1996), *'International Relations'* New York, N.Y.: Harper Collins, College Publishers, 2nd edition.
Goldstein J. S. (2001), *'War and Gender: How Gender Shapes the War System and Vice Versa'* Cambridge: at the University Press, http://www.american.edu/academic.depts/sis/goldtext/wargendr.htm.
Goldstein J. S. (2005), *'The Predictive Power of Long Wave Theory, 1989-2004"*. Prepared for NATO conference on Kondratiev Waves and Warfare, Covilha, Portugal, Feb. 2005, available at: http://www.joshuagoldstein.com/jgkond.htm.
Gonzales Casanova P. (1973), *'Sociología de la explotación'* Mexico D.F.: Siglo I.
Gore A. (1994), *'Wege zum Gleichgewicht. Ein Marshallplan fuer die Erde'* Frankfurt a.M.: Fischer *('Earth in the Balance. Ecology and Human Spirit'* Boston, New York: Houghton Mifflin Company).
Gosh P. K. (1984), *'Multi-National Corporations and Third World Development'* Westport, CT: Greenwood Press.
Gower J. (1996), 'EU Enlargement to Central and Eastern Europe: Issues for the 1996 IGC' *Die Union. Oesterreichische Zeitschrift fuer Integrationsfragen,* 4: 85 - 93.
Gradstein M and Milanovic B. (2004), 'Does Liberte = Egalite? A Survey of the Empirical Links between Democracy and Inequality with Some Evidence on the Transition Economies' *Journal of Economic Surveys,* Volume 18, Number 4, September 2004, pp. 515-537.
Gray C. and Weig D. (1999), 'Pension System Issues and Their Relation to Economic Growth' CAER II Discussion paper No. 41, Harvard Institute for International Development, available at: http://www.hiid.harvard.edu/projects/caer/papers/paper41/paper41.html.
Gray C. S. (2005), 'How Has War Changed Since the End of the Cold War?" *Parameters. U.S. Army War College Quarterly,* Spring 2005: 14-26, available at: http://carlisle-www.army.mil/usawc/Parameters/05spring/gray.htm.
Griffin K. (1987), *'World Hunger and the World Economy. And Other Essays in Development Economics'* London, Basingstoke and New York: Macmillan/Saint Martin's Press.
Griffin K. (1996), *'Studies in Globalization and Economic Transitons'* Basingstoke and New York: Macmillan/Saint Martin's Press.
Griffin K. and Gurley J. (1985), 'Radical Analyses of Imperialism, the Third World, and the Transition to Socialism: A Survey Article' *Journal of Economic Literature,* 23, September: 1089 - 1143.
Griffin K. and Knight J. (Eds.)(1990), *'Human Development and the International Development Strategy for the 1990s'* London and Basingstoke: Macmillan.
Grimes P. and Kentor J. (2003), 'Exporting the Greenhouse: Foreign Capital Penetration and CO_2 Emissions 1980 – 1996' *Journal of World-Systems Research, available at: http://jwsr.ucr.edu/index.php*IX, 2, Summer: 261 – 275.
Grönlund K. and Setälä M. (2005). *"Legitimacy, Trust and Turnout"*. 2005 Annual Meeting of the American Political Science Association, Washington DC.

Gurr T. R. (1991), 'America as a Model for the World? A Skeptical View' *PS: Political Science and Politics (Washington D.C.)*, 24, 4: 664 - 667.

Gurr T. R. (1994), '*Ethnic conflict in world politics*' Boulder: Westview Press.

Gurr T. R. (1994), 'Peoples Against States: Ethnopolitical Conflict and the Changing World System' *International Studies Quarterly*, 38: 347 - 377.

Gwartney J. et al. (1998), '*The Size and Functions of Government And Economic Growth*' Joint Economic Committee Study, United States Congress, http://www.house.gov/jec/growth/function/function.htm.

Haddad M. (2002), '*Export Competitiveness: Where does the Middle East and North Africa* http://www.gdnet.org/tm-frame.html?http://www.popcouncil.org/pdfs/wp/132.pdf *Region Stand?*' United Nations Economic Commission for West Asia, Working Paper 2030. Access via Global Development Network at: http://www.gdnet.org/tm-frame.html? http://www.erf.org.eg/database/2030.pdf.

Hadden K. and London B. (1996), 'Educating Girls in the Third World: The Demographic, Basic Needs, and Economic Benefits'. *International journal of comparative sociology*, 1996, vol. 37, no. 1/2, pp. 31.

Hagell P. and Vasilová K. (2005). "*Functionality of rating scales in survey research*". 1st Congress of the European Association for Survey Research, Barcelona, Spain. http://www.easr.upf.edu

Hagfors R. (2000*), 'EMU convergence and the structure of social protection financing'* ISSA Conference, Helsinki 'Social Security in the global village' available at: http://www.issa.int/engl/reunion/2000/helsinki/2prog.htm.

Hainmueller J. and Hiscox M. J. (2004 (paper published in 2005)). "*Educated Preferences: Explaining Attitudes Toward Immigration in Europe*". Annual Meeting of the American Political Science Association, Chicago. http://www.people.fas.harvard.edu/~hiscox/EducatedPreferences.pdf

Haller M. (2003), 'Soziologische Theorie im systematisch-kritischen Vergleich' Wiesbaden: VS Verlag für Sozialwissenschaften (2. Auflage)

Haller M. (Ed.)(1990), '*Class Structure in Europe. New Findings from East-West Comparisons of Social Structure and Mobility*' Armonk, N.Y./ London: Sharpe

Haller M. (Ed.)(2001), '*The Making of the European Union. Contributions of the Social Sciences*' Berlin/Heidelberg/New York: Springer Verlag

Haller M. and Richter R. (Ed.)(1994), '*Toward a European Nation? Political Trends in Europe. East and West, Center and Periphery*' Armonk, N.Y./London: M. E. Sharpe

Haller M. and Schachner-Blazizek P. (Ed.)(1999), '*Beschäftigung in Europa. Ergebnisse eines interdisziplinären Symposiums des Europaforums Steiermark*' Graz: Leykam

Haller M. and Schachner-Blazizek P. (Eds.)(1994), '*Europa wohin? Wirtschaftliche Integration, soziale Gerechtigkeit und Demokratie*' Graz: Leykam Verlag

Halliday F. (2000), 'Global governance: prospects and problems' *Citizenship Studies*, vol.4, n°1, February pp19-33..

Haouas I; Yagoubi, M; and Heshmati A (2002a), '*The Impacts of Trade Liberalization on Employment and Wages in Tunisian Industries*' Helsinki: Wider Discussion Paper Wdp, 2002, no. 102, (entire)

Haouas I; Yagoubi, M; and Heshmati, A. (2002b), '*Labour-Use Efficiency in Tunisian Manufacturing Industries A Flexible Adjustment Model.*' Helsinki: Wider Discussion Paper Wdp, 2002, no. 103, (entire)

Harss C. and Maier K. (1998), 'HR Managers as the pathfinders of globalization". *Personalwirtschaft,* 2, 26-30.

Hausner J. (1999), *'Poland: Security Through Diversity'* Deutsche Stiftung für Internationale Entwicklung, available at http://www.dse.de/ef/kop5/hausner.htm.

Havlik P. (1996), 'Exchange Rates, Competitiveness and Labour Costs in Central and Eastern Europe, ' *WIIW Research Report* No. 231 (October). Abstract available online: http://www.wiiw.at/summ231.html.

Heidenreich M (1997), ‚Wirtschaftsregionen im weltweiten Innovationswettbewerb'. In: *Kölner Zeitschrift für Soziologie und Sozialpsychologie,* Jg. 49, Nr. 3, S. 500-527..

Heidenreich M (1998a), 'The changing system of European cities and regions'. *'European Planning Studies'.* Jg. 6, Nr. 3, S. 315-332..

Heidenreich M (1998b), ‚Die duale Berufsausbildung zwischen industrieller Prägung und wissensgesellschaftlichen Herausforderungen'. *Zeitschrift für Soziologie,* Jg. 27, Nr. 5, S. 321-340..

Heidenreich M. (1999), ‚Gibt es einen europäischen Weg in die Wissensgesellschaft?' In: G. Schmidt und R. Trinczek (Eds.) ‚Globalisierung. Ökonomische und soziale Herausforderungen am Ende des zwanzigsten Jahrhunderts'. Sonderband 13 der *'Sozialen Welt'.* Baden-Baden: Nomos, S. 293-323..

Heidenreich M. (2001a), ‚Die Zukunftsfähigkeit der industriellen Beziehungen. Das Beispiel des VW-Tarifmodells'. *Gegenwartskunde* Nr. 3/2001, S. 353-362.

Heidenreich M. (2001b), ‚Europäische Identität' in: *Soziologische Revue* 24, 2001: 301-308.

Heidenreich M. (2003a), 'Regional Inequalities in the enlarged Europe'. *Journal of European Social Policy,* Vol. 13, No 4, pp. 313-333.

Heidenreich M. (2003b), ‚Territoriale Ungleichheiten im erweiterten Europa.' *Kölner Zeitschrift für Soziolo-gie und Sozialpsychologie,* Jg. 55, Heft 1, 2003, S. 1ff..

Heidenreich M. (2004a), 'Knowledge-Based Work: An International Comparison'. *International Mana-gement, Thematic Issue Cultures, nations and Management.* Volume 8 No. 3, pp. 65-80.

Heidenreich M. (2004b), ‚Beschäftigungsordnungen im internationalen Vergleich'. *'Zeitschrift für Soziologie',* Jg. 33, Nr. 3, 206-227.

Heidenreich M. (2004c), ‚Mittel- und Osteuropa nach der EU-Erweiterung. Eine Gratwanderung zwischen wirtschaftlicher Modernisierung und sozialer Integration' (Vortrag, Bamberg 2004), available at: http://www.uni-bamberg.de/sowi/europastudien/ dokumente/modernisierung_mitteleuropa.pdf.

Heidenreich M. and Töpsch K. (1998), ‚Die Organisation von Arbeit in der Wissensgesellschaft.' *Industrielle Beziehungen,* Jg. 5, Nr. 1, S. 13-44.

Henke H. (Ed.)(2005); *'Crossing over: comparing recent migration in the United States and Europe'* Lanham: Lexington Books

Herrmann P. and Tausch A. (Eds.)(2005a), *'Dar al Islam--the Mediterranean, the world system and the wider Europe: the chain of peripheries and the new wider Europe'* New York: Nova Science Publishers.

Herrmann P. and Tausch A. (Eds.)(2005b), *'Dar al Islam--the Mediterranean, the world system, and the wider Europe: the 'cultural enlargement' of the EU and Europe's identity'* New York: Nova Science.

Hertz E. et al. (1994), 'Social and Environmental Factors and Life Expectancy, Infant Mortality, and Maternal Mortality Rates: Results of a Cross-National Comparison.' *Social Science and Medicine,* 39:105-114.

Heshmati A. (2003a), *'Measurement of a Multidimentional Index of Globalization and its Impact on Income Inequality'* Helsinki: WIDER Discussion Paper 2003:69, 36 pages.

Heshmati A. (2003b), 'Productivity Growth, Efficiency and Outsourcing in Manufacturing and Service Industries' *Journal of Economic Surveys,* Volume 17, Number 1, February 2003, pp. 79-112

Heshmati A. and Addison T. (2003), *'The New Global Determinants of FDI Flows to Developing Countries The Importance of ICT and Democratization'* Helsinki: Wider Discussion Paper Wdp, 2003, no. 45, (entire)

Hettne B. (1983), 'The Development of Development Theory' *Acta Sociologica,* 26, 3 - 4: 247 - 266.

Hettne B. (1989), 'Three Worlds of Crisis for the Nation State' in *'Crisis in Development'* (Bablewski Z. and Hettne B. (Eds.)), pp. 45 - 77, Goeteborg: United Nations University: European Perspectives Project 1986 - 87, Peace and Development Research Institute, Gothenburg University, P.A.D.R.I.G.U Papers.

Hettne B. (1994), 'The Political Economy of Post - Communist Development' *The European Journal of Development Research,* 6, 1, June: 39 - 60.

Hettne B. (1995a), *'Development theory and the three worlds: towards an international political economy of development'* 2nd ed. Essex, England: Longman Scientific & Technical; New York, NY. Copublished in the United States by John Wiley.

Hettne B. (1995b), *'International political economy: understanding global disorder.'* Halifax, N.S.: Fernwood Pub.; Cape Town: SAPES SA; Dhaka: University Press Ltd.; London; Atlantic Highlands, N.J.: Zed Books.

Hettne B. (2004), 'In Search of World Order" in *'Global Governance in the 21st Century: Alternative Perspectives on World Order'* (Hettne B. and Oden B. (Eds.)), pp. 6 – 25. Stockholm: Almkvist & Wiksell. Availabla also at: http://www.egdi.gov.se/pdf/study/study2002_2.pdf.

Hickmann Th. (1994), 'Wenn Ost und West zusammenwachsen sollen...' *Osteuropa - Wirtschaft,* 39, 2, Juni: 115 - 127.

Hilferding R. (1915), 'Europaer, nicht Mitteleuropaer' *Der Kampf (Vienna),* 8, 11 - 12: 357 - 365.

Hoeft M. K. (2003), *‚Prosperity, Islam and Democracy'* Center for the Study of Islam & Democracy, American University, Washington, available at: http://www.islam-democracy.org/4th_Annual_Conference-Hoeft_paper.asp

Hofbauer H and Komlosy A. (1994), 'Eastern Europe: From 'Second World' to First or Third World.' *Contention,* 1994, vol. 3, no. 2, pp. 129.

Hofbauer H and Komlosy A. (2000), 'Capital Accumulation and Catching-Up Development in Eastern Europe' *Review,* vol. 23, no. 4, pp. 459-502.

Holmes L. (1999), *'Corruption, Weak States and Economic Rationalism in Central and Eastern Europe'* International Anti-Corruption Conference (IAACC), 9th International Anti-Corruption Conference, published on the Internet: http://www.transparency.de/iacc/9th_papers/day1/ws2/d1ws2_lholmes.html.

Holtbruecke D. (1996), 'Oekonomische Voraussetzungen und Folgen einer Osterweiterung der Europaeischen Union' *Osteuropa,* 46, 6: 537 - 547.

Holzmann R. (1999), *'Mixed blessing of financial inflows: transition countries in comparative perspective'* (edited by János Gács, Robert Holzmann, Michael L. Wyzan). Northampton, Ma.; Cheltenham, UK: Edward Elgar Publishing.

Holzmann R. (2000a), *'Financing the Transition: The Importance of Growth Effects'* Pension Workshop, Harvard University, 19-30 June.

Holzmann R. (2000b), *'The Challenge of Coverage'* Pension Workshop, Harvard University, 19-30 June.

Holzmann R. (2004), *‚Toward a Reformed and Coordinated Pension System in Europe: Rationale and Potential Structure'* Social Protection Discussion Paper Series, The World Bank, No. 407. Download at http://wbln0018.worldbank.org/HDNet/HD.nsf/0/92c4513c14aceb8185256e280073869d?OpenDocument.

Holzmann R. (2005), 'Old-age income support in the 21st century: an international perspective on pension systems and reform' Washington, D.C.: World Bank.

Holzmann R. (Ed.)(1996), *'Maastricht: monetary constitution without a fiscal constitution? / Empirica-Economic Policy Forum and European Institute workshop'*, Saarbrucken, October 2-3, 1995; Robert Holzmann (ed.). Baden-Baden: Nomos Verlagsgesellschaft.

Holzmann R. (Ed.)(2001), *'New ideas about old age security: towards sustainable pension systems in the 21st Century'* Washington, DC: World Bank, 2001..

Holzmann R. (Ed.)(2002), *'Pension reform in Europe: process and progress / edited by Robert Holzmann, Mitchell Orenstein, and Michal Rutkowski'*. Washington, DC: The World Bank.

Holzmann R. et al. (1999*)*, *'Extending Coverage in multi-Pillar Pension Systems: Constraints and Hypotheses, Preliminary Evidence and Future Research Agenda'*. Paper, prepared for the World Bank Conference New Ideas about Old-Age Security, September 14-15, Washington D.C., available at: http://wbln0018.worldbank.org/HDNet/HDdocs.nsf/View+to+Link+WebPages/C84F825C6A3B40D485256840007A31ED?OpenDocument.

Hooghe L. (2001), *'The European Commission and the Integration of Europe: Images of Governance'* Cambridge: Cambridge University Press.

Hopkins T. K. (1982), 'The Study of the Capitalist World - Economy. Some Introductory Considerations' in *'World Systems Analysis. Theory and Methodology'* (Hopkins T.K. and Wallerstein I. *et al.*), pp. 3 - 38, Beverly Hills: Sage.

Hopkins T. K. and Wallerstein I. *et al.* (1982), 'Patterns of Development of the Modern World System' in *'World Systems Analysis. Theory and Methodology'* (Hopkins T. K. and Wallerstein I. *et al.*), pp. 41 - 82, Beverly Hills: Sage.

Huang J. (1995), 'Structural Disarticulation and Third World Human Development' *International Journal of Comparative Sociology,* 36, 3 - 4: 164 - 183.

Huber P. (1999), *'Labour Market Adjustment in Central and Eastern Europe: How Different?'* Austrian Institute for Economic Research (WIFO).

Huber P. (1999), *'Wirtschaftliche und soziale Folgen der Erweiterung der EU'* in *'Zukunft ohne Grenzen'* Wien: Institut für den Donauraum und Mitteleuropa.

Huebner K. (1994), 'Wege nach Nirgendwo: Oekonomische Theorie und osteuropaeische Transformation' *Berliner Journal fuer Soziologie,* 3: 345 - 364.

Huntington S. P. (1991), *'The Third Wave: Democratization in the Late Twentieth Century'* Norman, Oklahoma: University of Oklahoma Press.

Huntington S. P. (1993), 'The Clash of Civilizations?' *Foreign Affairs,* Summer: 22 - 49.

Huntington S. P. (1996), *'The clash of civilizations and the remaking of world order'* New York: Simon & Schuster.

ICMPD (1998), *'Auswirkungen der EU-Osterweiterung auf die Zuwanderung in die Europäische Union unter besonderer Berücksichtigung Österreichs'* Studie im Auftrag des Bundeskanzleramtes, Sektion IV, Wien (3 Bände): ICMPD.

IFO-Institut (1999), 'Auswirkungen der Arbeitnehmer-Frezügigkeit auf innereuropäische Migrationsbewegungen' Vorstudie im Auftrag des Bundesministeriums für Arbeit und Sozialordnung, München.

IFRI (Institut Francais des relations internationales) (1998), *'Ramses 98. Rapport Annuel Mondial sur le Système Economique et les Stratégies'* Paris: Dunod.

Inglehart R. and Carballo M. (1997), 'Does Latin America Exist? (And is there a Confucian Culture?): A Global Analysis of Cross - Cultural Differences' *PS: Political Science & Politics,* 30, 1, March: 47 - 52.

Inglehart R. and Norris P. (2003), 'The True Clash of Civilizations' *Foreign Policy,* March/April 2003, available at: http://www.globalpolicy.org/globaliz/cultural/2003/0304clash.htm

Inglehart R. and Norris P. (2003), 'The True Clash of Civilizations' Foreign Policy, March/April 2003, available at: http://www.globalpolicy.org/globaliz/cultural/2003/0304clash.htm

Inglehart R. and Norris P. (2004), *'Sacred and Secular: Religion and Politics Worldwide (Cambridge Studies in Social Theory, Religion and Politics) (Paperback)'*. Cambridge and New York: Cambridge University Press.

Inotai A. (2001a), 'Hungary's economic development at the crossroads: after transformation and before EU accession'. *South-East Europe review for labour and social affairs: SEER.* Düsseldorf: Hans-Böckler-Stiftung. Special issue, no. 1 (2001).

Inotai A. (2001b), *'Some reflections on possible scenarios for EU enlargement. Some key issues in understanding the negotiations on accession to the European Union'* Budapest: Institute for World Economics, Hungarian Academy of Sciences.

Inotai A. and Hettne B. (1999), *'Globalism and the new regionalism'* New York: St. Martin's Press.

Inotai A. and Hettne B. (2000), *'The new regionalism and the future of security and development'.* New York. St. Martin's Press

Inotai A. and Hettne B. (2001), *'Comparing regionalisms: implications for global development'* New York: Palgrave

Inotai A. and Sander H. (2002), *'World trade after the Uruguay Round. Prospects and Policy Options for the 21st Century'* London and New York: Routledge

International Labor Office and United Nations Centre on Transnational Corporations (1988), *'Economic and social effects of multinational enterprises in export processing zones'* Geneva: ILO.

International Labour Office (2000), *'World Labor Report 2000'* Geneva: ILO (available at Amazon.com and Barnes & Noble).

IOM (International Organization for Migration) (1999), *'Migration Potential in Central and Eastern Europe'* Geneva: IOM.

Israelewicz E. (2000), 'Demain, quel gouvernement pour le monde ?" *Revue des deux mondes,* février, pp 42-49.

J. Timmons Roberts J. T., Grimes P. E. and Jodie L. Manale J. L. (2003), 'Social Roots of Global Environmental Change: A World-Systems Analysis of Carbon Dioxide Emissions.' *Journal of World-Systems Research, available at: http://jwsr. ucr.edu/index.php*Vol. 9, Num. 2 (Summer 2003): 277 – 315.

Jabber P. (2001), *'Impact of the War on Terror on Certain Aspects of US Policy in the Middle East. A Medium-Term Assessment'* Prepared for the United States National Intelligence Council. Available at: http://www.fas.org/irp/nic/jabber_paper.htm.

Jackman R.W. (1975), *'Politics and Social Equality: A Comparative Analysis'* New York: Wiley.

Jaeger M. (2006). "Welfare regimes and attitudes towards redistribution: The regime hypothesis revisited." *European Sociological Review* 22(2): 157-170.

Jenkins J. C. and Scanlan S. J. (2001), 'Food Security in Less Developed Countries, 1970 to 1990' *American Sociological Review,* 66, 5, October: 718 – 744.

Jenkins R. (1987), *'Transnational Corporations and Uneven Development: The Internationalization of Capital and the Third World'* London and New York: Methuen.

Johnson R. B. (1986), 'Income Inequality in the Third World: A Comparison of Three Theories.' *International Review of Modern Sociology,* 16, pps. 69-81.

Jorgenson A. K. and Rice J. (2005), 'Structural Dynamics of International Trade and Material Consumption: A Cross-National Study of the Ecological Foodprints of Less-Developed Countries' *Journal of World-Systems Research, available at: http://jwsr.ucr.edu/index. php*XI, 1, July: 57-77.

Jourdon Ph. (2005), *'Wars on the Borders of Europe, and Socio-Economical Long Cycles'* Université de Montpellier, I, UFR de Sciences Economiques, available at http://www.sceco.univ-montp1.fr/webenseignants/poudou/JourdonPhiPort.pdf.

Juchler J. (1986), *'Sozialistische Gesellschaftsformation: allgemeine Theorie und Fallstudie (Polen 1945-1984)'* Frankfurt [am Main]; New York: Campus.

Juchler J. (1992a), *'Ende des Sozialismus - Triumph des Kapitalismus?: eine vergleichende Studie moderner Gesellschaftssysteme.'* Zurich: Seismo.

Juchler J. (1992b), 'The Socialist Societies: Rise and Fall of a Societal Formation' in *'Waves, Formations and Values in the World System'* (Bornschier V. and Lengyel P. (Eds.)), pp. 145 - 174, New Brun-swick (USA),: Transaction Publishers.

Juchler J. (1992c), 'The Socialist Societies: Rise and Fall of a Societal Formation' in *'Waves, Formations and Values in the World System'* (Bornschier V. and Lengyel P. (Eds.)), pp. 145 - 174, New Brunswick (USA),: Transaction Publishers.

Juchler J. (1992d), 'Zur Entwicklungsdynamik in den sozialistischen bzw. postsozialistischen Laendern' *Schweizerische Zeitschrift fuer Soziologie,* 17, 2: 273 - 307.

Juchler J. (1994), *'Osteuropa im Umbruch: politische, wirtschaftliche und gesellschaftliche Entwicklungen 1989-1993: Gesamtueberblick und Fallstudien'* Zuerich: Seismo Verlag.

Juchler J. (1995), 'Kontinuitaet oder Wende? Polen seit dem Wahlsieg der 'Postkommunisten'' Osteuropa, 45, 1: 65 - 76.

Juchler J. (2001), 'Zur Osterweiterung der EU - Gesellschaftliche Asymmetrien und ihre Risiken' *Europaische Rundschau,* vol. 29, no. 1, pp. 121-134.

Juchler J. (2003), 'Polens Transformationsentwicklung und der EU-Beitritt.' *Wirtschaft und Gesellschaft,* vol. 29, no. 1, pp. 103-130.

Juchler J. (2004), 'EU? Na gut Zur Akzeptanz der EU-Mitgliedschaft in Ostmitteleuropa'. *Osteuropa,* vol. 54, no. 7, pp. 52-64.

Kalecki M. (1972), *'The Last Phase in the Transformation of Capitalism'* New York: Monthly Review Press.

Kalecki M. (1979), *'Essays on Developing Economies. With an Introduction by Professor Joan Robinson'* Hassocks, Sussex: The Harvester Press.

Kanbur R. (2001), *'Income Distribution and Development'* World Development Report background paper at: http://www.worldbank.org/poverty/wdrpoverty/kanbur.htm.

Kanbur R. (2005), 'Growth, Inequality and Poverty: Some Hard Questions' *Journal of International Affairs- Columbia University,* vol. 58, no. 2, pp. 223-232.

Kanbur R. and Squire L. (2001), *'The Evolution of Thinking about Poverty: Exploring the Interactions'* World Development Report background paper at: http://www.worldbank.org/poverty/wdrpoverty/evolut.pdf.

Karatnycky A. (1994), 'Freedom in Retreat' *Freedom Review,* 25, 1: 4 - 9.

Karns M. P. P. and Mingst K. A. (2004), *'International Organizations: The Politics and Processes of Global Governance'.* Boulder, CO: Lynne Rienner Publishers.

Kasarda J.D. and Crenshaw E.M. (1991), 'Third - World Urbanization. Dimensions, Theories and Determinants' *Annual Review of Sociology,* 17: 467 - 501.

Katzenstein P. (1974), *'Corporatism and Change: Austria, Switzerland and the Politics of Industry"* Ithaca, NY: Cornell University Press, 1984; paperback edition 1987.

Kay C. (1989), *'Latin American Theories of Development and Underdevelopment'* London and New York: Routledge, Kegan and Paul.

Kay C. (1991), 'Reflections on the Latin American Contribution to Development Theory' *Development and Change,* 22, 1: 31 - 68.

Kay St. J. (1999), *'Testimony Before the House Committee on Ways and Means Hearing on Social Security Reform Lessons Learned in Other Countries'.* Available at: http://www.house.gov/ways_means/fullcomm/106cong/2-11-99/2-11kay.htm.

Kearny A.T. (2001), 'Measuring Globalization' *Foreign Policy,* at: http://www.foreignpolicy.com/issue_janfeb_2001/atkearney.html.

Kendall P. (2000), *'Interest Rates, Savings and Growth in Guyana'* Economics and Programming Department, Carribean Development Bank, available at: http://www.caribank.org/Staff_Pa.nsf/Kendal-IntRates?OpenPage

Kennedy P. (1989), *'The Rise and Fall of the Great Powers. Economic Change and Military Conflict from 1500 to 2000'* New York: Vintage Books, paperback edition.

Kennedy P. (1993), *'In Vorbereitung auf das 21. Jahrhundert'* Frankfurt a.M.: S. Fischer TB.

Kent G. (1984), *'The political economy of hunger: the silent holocaust'* New York: Praeger.

Kent G. (1991), *'The politics of children's survival'* New York: Praeger..

Kent G. (1995), *'Children in the international political economy'* Houndmills, Basingstoke, Hampshire: Macmillan Press LTD, New York, N.Y.: St. Martin's Press.

Kent N. J. (1990), 'The End of the American Dream: A Break in Political Economy' *Occasional Papers in Political Science, Manoa Campus: University of Hawaii, Department of Political Science,* 3, 3, Jan.: 93 - 107.

Kentor J. D. (1998), 'The Long-Term Effects of Foreign Investment Dependence on Economic Growth, 1940-1990' *American Journal of Sociology,* 103, 4, January: 1024 - 46.

Kentor J. D. (2001), 'The Long Term Effects of Globalization on Income Inequality, Population Growth, and Economic Development' *Social Problems,* 48, no. 4 (2001): 435-455.

Kentor J. D. (2005), 'Transnational Corporate Power. Expansion, Spatial Distribution, and Concentration, 1962 – 1998' in *'The Future of World Society'* (Herkenrath M. et al. (Eds.)) pp. 81 – 101; Sociological Institute, University of Zurich: Intelligent Book Production.

Kentor J. D. and Boswell T. (2003), 'Foreign Capital Dependence and Development: A New Direction' *American sociological review.* 68, no. 2, (2003): 301 (13 pages).

Kentor J. D. and Jang J. S. (2004), 'Yes, There Is a (Growing) Transnational Business Community: A Study of Global Interlocking Directorates 1983-98' *International Sociology* 19, no. 3 (2004): 355-368.

Kentor J. D. and Woo J. (2000), *'Capital and Coercion: The Economic and Military Processes That Have Shaped the World Economy'* New York: Garland Publishing.

Khoury A. Th. (1980), *'Toleranz im Islam'* München: Kaiser und Grünwald.

Khoury A. Th. (1981), *'Gebete des Islams'* Mainz: Matthias Grünewald Verlag, Topos TB.

Khoury A. Th. (1991), *'Was its los in der islamischen Welt? Die Konflikte verstehen'* Freiburg, Basel, Vienna: Herder..

Khoury M. El and Panizza U. (2001), *'Poverty and Social Mobility in Lebanon: A Few Wild Guesses'* Department of Economics, American University of Beirut at http://webfaculty.aub.edu.lb/~ugo/papers/poverty.pdf.

Kick E. L. and Davis B. L. (2001), 'World-System Structure and Change: An Analysis of Global Networks and Economic Growth Across Two Time Periods' *American Behavioral Scientist,* vol. 44, no. 10, pp. 1561-1578.

Kick E. L. et al. (1990), 'Militarization and Infant Mortality in the Third World'. *Journal of Political and Military Sociology,* 18(2):285-305.

Kick E. L. et al. (1995), 'World-System and National Institutional Effects on Infant Mortality in Third World Countries'. *International Third World Studies Journal & Review,* 7:61-67.

Kick E. L., Davis B. L. and Burns T. J. (1998), 'A Cross-National Analysis of Militarization and Well-Being Relationships in Developing Countries.' *Social Science Research,* Volume 27, Number 4, December pp. 351 ff..

Kick E. L., Davis B. L. and Burns T. J. (2000), 'World System Position, National Political Characteristics and Economic Development Outcomes.' *Journal of Political and Military Sociology,* vol. 28, no. 1, pp. 131.

Kiljunen K. (1987), *'Changing patterns in the international division of labour and the implications for Finland'* Brighton, England: Institute of Development Studies at the University of Sussex.

Kiljunen K. (1988), *'The World Bank and the world poverty'* Helsinki: University of Helsinki, Institute of Development Studies.

Kiljunen K. (1992), *'Finland and the new international division of labour. Foreword by Charles P. Kindleberger.'* Houndmills, Basingstoke, Hampshire: Macmillan Press.

Kiljunen K. (2000), *'Global Governance'* Draft. Finnish Parliament.

Kiljunen K. (2003), *'Global Governance'* in *'Globalization: Critical Perspectives'* (Kohler G. and Chaves E. Eds.)), pp. 55 – 92; Hauppauge, N.Y.: Nova Science Publishers.

Kiljunen K. (Ed.)(1984), *'Kampuchea: decade of the genocide: report of a Finnish inquiry commission'* London: Zed Books; Totowa, N.J.: US Distributor, Biblio Distribution Center, 1984.

Kiljunen K. (Ed.)(1989), *'Mini-NIEO: the potential of regional north-south cooperation'* Helsinki: Institute of Development Studies, University of Helsinki.

Kiljunen K. (Ed.)(1990*), 'Region-to-region cooperation between developed and developing countries: the potential for Mini-NIEO.'* Aldershot, Hants, England; Brookfield, Vt., USA: Avebury.

Kiljunen K. and Avakov R. M. (Eds.)(1991), *'World industrial restructuring and north-south cooperation'* Helsinki: University of Helsinki, Institute of Development Studies.

Kiljunen K. et al. (1987), *'Finnish peace making'* [translator, Chris Mann]. Helsinki, Finland: Peace Union of Finland.

Kinder H. and Hilgemann W. (1978) *'The Penguin Atlas of World History'* 2 volumes. London and Harmondsworth: Penguin Reference Books.

Kindleberger Ch. (1996), *'The World Economy and National Finance in Historical Perspectives'* Ann Arbor: University of Michigan Press.

King J. E. (2000), 'Barnett, Kondratiev and the Dynamics of Economic Development: Long Cycles and Industrial Growth in Historical Context' *History of Political Economy,* vol. 32, no. 2, pp. 406-407.

Kirby P. (1981), *'Lessons in liberation: the Church in Latin America'* Dublin (St Saviour's, Dublin 1): Dominican Publications.

Kirby P. (1998), *'Has Ireland a future?'* Cork, Irish Republic: Mercier Press.

Kirby P. (2002), *'Celtic tiger in distress: growth with inequality in Ireland'* Houndmills, Basingstoke, Hampshire; New York: Palgrave.

Kirby P. (2003a), *'Introduction to Latin America: twenty-first century challenges'* London; Thousand Oaks, Cal.: SAGE.

Kirby P. (2003b), *'Macroeconomic success and social vulnerability: lessons for Latin America from the Celtic Tiger'* Santiago, Chile: ECLAC, Special Studies Unit, Executive Secretariat Office.

Kirby P. (2006), *'Vulnerability and Violence. The Impact of Globalization'* London and Ann Arbor, Michigan: Pluto Press.

Klein M. *et al.* (2001), 'Foreign Direct Investment and Poverty Reduction' *Globalization Working Paper* 2613, The World Bank, Washington D.C. at http://econ.worldbank.org/files/2205_wps2613.pdf.

Kleinknecht A. (1987), *'Innovation Patterns in Crisis and Prosperity: Schumpeter's Long Cycle Reconsidered.* London: Macmillan.

Kleinknecht A.; Mandel E.; and Wallerstein I.. (1992), *'New Findings in Long-Wave Research*, Macmillan, London..

Klitgaard R. and Fedderke J. (1995), 'Social Integration and Disintegration: An Exploratory Analysis of Cross - Country Data' *World Development,* 23, 3: 357 - 369.

Knesebeck O. v. d., Dragano, N. and Siegris J. (2005). "Social Capital and Self-Rated Health in 21 European Countries." *GMS Psycho-Social-Medicine* 2(Doc02 (20050223)). http://www.egms.de//pdf/journals/psm/2005-2/psm000011.pdf

Knesebeck O. v. d., Verde, P. and Dragano N. (2006). "Education and Health in 22 European Countries." *Social Science and Medicine* 63(5): 1344-1351. http://www.elsevier.com/wps/find/journaldescription.cws_home/315/description?navopenmenu=1

Knoop T. A. (2004), *'Recessions and Depressions: Understanding Business Cycles.'* New York: Frederic Praeger.

Köhler G. (1975), 'Imperialism as a Level of Analysis in Correlates of War Research', Journal of Conflict Resolution (USA), 10: 48-62. French version: 'L'imperialisme, dimension de l'analyse des aspects correlatifs de la guerre' (1976) *Impact: science et societe* (UNESCO), 28: 47-56.

Köhler G. (1976a), 'An Empirical Table of Structural Violence' (with Norman Alcock) *Journal of Peace Research* (Norway), 13: 343-356 [includes 'plateau curve' of life expectancy with income].

Köhler G. (1976b), 'The Global Contract: An Essay on International Economic Order and Foreign Policy Theory', Alternatives (World Policy Institute, USA), 2: 449-477.

Köhler G. (1978a), 'Disarmament and Global Apartheid' Humanity Calls (New Delhi, India), (June): 9-14, 47-50.

Köhler G. (1978b), 'Global Apartheid', Alternatives (Institute for World Order/World Policy Institute, USA), vol. 4, no. 2 (October), pp. 263-275.

Köhler G. (1980a), 'Structural and Armed Violence in the 20th Century: Magnitudes and Trends' (with William Eckhardt) International Interactions (USA), 8: 347-375.

Köhler G. (1980b), 'Determinants of the British Defense Burden, 1689 - 1977: From Imperialism to the Nuclear Age' (1980) Bulletin of Peace Proposals (Norway), 11: 79-85.

Köhler G. (1981a), 'Approaches to the Study of the Causes of War', UNESCO Yearbook on Peace and Conflict Studies 1980. Paris, France: UNESCO, 1981: 115-127.

Köhler G. (1981b), 'Soviet/Russian Defense Burden, 1862 - 1980: From Czarism to Socialism', Bulletin of Peace Proposals (Norway), 11: 131-140.

Köhler G. (1981c), 'Toward Indicators of Detente: An Extension of the Zurich Content Analysis' in: Daniel Frei, ed., Definitions and Measurements of Detente: East and West Perspectives. Cambridge, USA: Oelschlager, Gunn & Hain, 1981: 39-55.

Köhler G. (1995), 'The Three Meanings of Global Apartheid: Empirical, Normative, Existential', Alternatives (World Policy Institute, USA), 20: 403-423.

Köhler G. (1998a), 'The Structure of Global Money and World Tables of Unequal Exchange', Journal of World-Systems Research 4: 145:168; online: http://csf.colorado.edu/wsystems/jwsr.html.

Köhler G. (1998a), 'Unequal Exchange 1965 - 1995: World Trend and World Tables', World-Systems Archive, Working Papers, online: http://csf.colorado.edu/wsystems/archive/papers/Köhlertoc.htm.

Köhler G. (1999a), 'A Theory of World Income', World-Systems Archive, Working Papers, online: http://csf.colorado.edu/wsystems/archive/papers/Köhler.

Köhler G. (1999b), 'Global Keynesianism and Beyond', *Journal of World-Systems Research*, 5: 225-241, online: http://csf.colorado.edu/wsystems/jwsr.html.

Köhler G. (2005), 'Arab Unemployment as a World-System Problem' in *'Dar al Islam. The Mediterranean, the World System and the Wider Europe'* (Herrmann P. And Tausch A. (Eds.)), pp. 179 – 190, Nova Science Publishers: Hauppauge, New York:

Köhler G. and Tausch A. (2000), *'Global Keynesianism: Unequal exchange and global exploitation'*. Huntington NY, Nova Science. ISBN 1-59033-002-1.

Kohli A. et al. (1984), 'Inequality in the Third World: An Assessment of Competing Explanations.' *Comparative Political Studies,* 17, 3, October, pps. 283-318.

Kondratiev N. D. (1980, posthumously), *'Stalin oder Kondratiev: Endspiel oder Innovation? Ulrich Hedtke. Strittige Fragen der Weltwirtschaft und der Krise: Antwort an unsere Kritiker'* Berlin: Dietz.

Kondratiev N. D. (1984, posthumously), *'Long wave cycle.Translated by Guy Daniels; introd. by Julian M. Snyder'*. New York: Richardson & Snyder.

Kondratiev N. D. (1998, posthumously), *'Works of Nikolai D Kondratiev. Eited by Natalia Makasheva and Warren J. Samuels.'* London; Brookfield, Vt.: Pickering & Chatto.

Korcelli P. (1992), 'International Migrations in Europe: Polish Perspectives for the 1990s' *International Migration Review*, 26, 2, Summer: 292 - 304.

Kornhauser A. and Lazarsfeld P. F. (1935), *'The techniques of market research from the standpoint of a psychologist'*. New York, N. Y., American Management Association.

Korpi W. (1985), 'Economic growth and the welfare state: leaky bucket or irrigation system?' *European Sociological Review*, 1, 2: 97 - 118.

Korpi W. (1996), 'Eurosclerosis and the Sclerosis of Objectivity. On the Role of Values Among Economic - Policy Experts' *Economic Journal*, 106, 439: 1727 - 1746.

Korpi W. and Palme J. (2000), 'Distributive Conflict, Political Mobilization and the Welfare State: Comparative Patterns of Emergence and Retrenchment in Westernized Countries' Swedish Institute for Social Research, Stockholm University, available at: http://www.kub.nl/~fsw_2/home/worschot/rc19/papers/korpi.htm.

Korzeniewicz R. P. and Moran T. P. (1997), 'World Economic Trends in the Distribution of Income, 1965-1992'. *American Journal of Sociology*, 102, 4, January, pps. 1000-1039.

Kothari R. (1986), 'Masses, Classes and the State' *Alternatives*, XI, 2: 167 - 183.

Krahn H. and Gartrell J. W. (1985), 'Effects of Foreign Trade, Government Spending, and World-System Status on Income Distribution.' *Rural Sociology*, 50, 2, pps. 181-192.

Kriz J. (1978), *'Statistik in den Sozialwissenschaften'* Reinbek: rororo studium.

Krzysztofiak M. and Luszniewicz A. (1979), *'Statystyka'* Warsaw: PWE.

Kunzmann P. et al. (1996), „dtv Atlas zur Philosophie' München: Deutscher Taschenbuch-Verlag.

Kuznets S. (1940), 'Schumpeter's Business Cycles", *American Economic Review*, vol 30, June, pp. 157-69.

Kuznets S. (1955), 'Economic Growth and Income Inequality' *The American Economic Review*, 45, 1: 1 - 28.

Kuznets S. (1976), *'Modern Economic Growth: Rate, Structure and Spread'* New Haven, CT: Yale U. Press.

Landesmann M. (1996), *'Emerging Patterns of European Industrial Specialization: Implications for Labour Market Dynamics in Eastern and Western Europe'* Research Reports, 230, Vienna Institute for Comparative Economic Studies.

Landesmann M. and Burgstaller J. (1997), *'Vertical Product Differentiation in EU Markets: the Relative Position of East European Producers'* Research Reports, 234a, Vienna Institute for Comparative Economic Studies.

Landesmann M. and Rosati D. (Eds.)(2004), 'Shaping the new Europe: economic policy challenges of European Union enlargement' Houndmills, Basingstoke, Hampshire; New York, N.Y.: Palgrave Macmillan.

Landesmann M. and Székely I. (Eds.)(1995), *'Industrial restructuring and trade reorientation in Eastern Europe'* Cambridge; New York, NY: Cambridge University Press, 1995..

Landesmann M. et al. (Eds.)(2003), *'Prospects for further (South-)Eastern EU enlargement: from divergence to convergence?'* Wien: Wiener Institut fuer Internationale Wirtschaftsvergleiche.

Lasswell H. D. (1936), *'Politics; who gets what, when, how'*. New York, London: Whittlesey house, McGraw-Hill book Co.

Laxer G. (1993), 'Social Solidarity, Democracy and and Global Capitalism' The 1993 Porter Lecture, Canadian Sociology and Anthropology Association, available at: http://www.socsci.mcmaster.ca/soc/porterlectures/laxer.htm.

Laxer G. (2005), 'US Empire and Popular Sovereignty' in *'The Future of World Society'* (Herkenrath M. et al. (Eds.)) pp. 199 – 229; Sociological Institute, University of Zurich: Intelligent Book Production.

Lecaillon, J. et al. (1994), *'Income Distribution and Economic Development: An Analytical Survey'*. Geneva, Switzerland: International Labor Office.

Lemke D. (2002), *'Regions of War and Peace'* Cambridge: Cambridge University Press.

Lena H. F. and London B. (1993), 'The Political and Economic Determinants of Health Outcomes: A Cross-National Analysis.' *International journal of health services,* vol. 23, no. 3, pp. 585.

Lewis - Beck M. S. (1980), *'Applied Regression. An Introduction'* Beverly Hills: Sage University Paper.

Lewis Sir W.A. (1978), *'The Evolution of the International Economic Order'* Princeton N.J.: Princeton University Press.

Liemt G. van (1992), *'Industry on the move. Causes and consequences of international relocation in the manufacturing industry'* Geneva: International Labor Office.

Lindemann D. (2000), 'Incentives and Design Issues in Pension Reform' The World Bank China Country Office, available at: http://www.worldbank.org.cn/English/content/pension6.shtml.

Lindert P. H, and Williamson J. G. (2001), *'Does Globalization Make World More Unequal?"*, National Bureau of Economic Research, Working Paper No. 8228, April.

Linnemann H. and Sarma A. (1991), 'Economic Transformation in Eastern Europe: Its Genesis, Adjustment Process, and Impact on Developing Countries' *Development and Change,* 22, 1: 69 - 92.

Lipset S.M. (1994), 'The Social Requisites of Democracy Revisited. 1993 Presidential Address' *American Sociological Review,* 59, February: 1 - 22.

Lipton M. (1977), *'Why Poor People Stay Poor: Urban Bias in World Development'* Cambrige, MA: Harvard University Press.

Lizardo O. L. and Collett J. C. (2005). *"Why Biology is not (Religious) Destiny: A Second Look at Gender Differences in Religiosity"*. Annual Meeting of the American Sociological Association, Philadelphia, Pennsylvania, USA. http://www.nd.edu/~olizardo/papers/biorelgend.pdf#search=%22why%20biology%20is%20not%20religious%20destiny%22

Loeffelholz H. D., und G. Köpp (1998), *'Ökonomische Auswirkungen der Zuwanderungen nach Deutschland'* Berlin: Duncker und Humblot.

London B. (1987), 'Structural Determinants of Third World Urban Change: An Ecological and Political Economic Analysis' *American Sociological Review,* 52: 28 - 43.

London B. (1988), 'Dependence, Distorted Development, and Fertility Trends in Non-Core Nations: A Structural Analysis of Cross-National Data.' *American Sociological Review,* 53, 4(August 1988):606-618.

London B. (1990), 'National Politics, International Dependency, and Basic Needs Provision: A Cross-National Analysis'. *Social forces,* 1990, vol. 69, no. 2, pp. 565.

London B. and Robinson T. (1989), 'The Effects of International Dependence on Income Inequality and Political Violence.' *American Sociological Review,* 54, April, pps. 305-308.

London B. and Ross R. J. S. (1995), 'The Political Sociology of Foreign Direct Investment: Global Capitalism and Capital Mobility, 1965 - 1980' *International Journal of Comparative Sociology,* 36, 3 - 4: 198 - 218.

London B. and Smith D. A. (1988), 'Urban Bias, Dependence, and Economic Stagnation in Noncore Nations' *American Sociological Review,* 53: 454 - 463.

London B. and Williams B. A. (1988), 'Multinational Corporate Penetration, Protest, and Basic Needs Provision in Non - Core Nations: A Cross - National Analysis' *Social Forces,* 66, 3: 747 - 773.

London B. and Williams B. A. (1990), 'National Politics, International Investment, and Basic Needs Provisions: A Cross-National Analysis'. *Social Forces,* 69:565-584.

London B., Bradshaw Y. and Kim Y. J. (1993), 'Transnational Economic Linkages, the State, and Dependent Development in South Korea, 1966-1988: A Time-Series Analysis.' *Social Forces,* 72, 2(December 1993):315-345.

Lopez G. A. and Stohl M. (1989), *'Dependence, Development, and State Repression'* Westport, CT: Greenwood Press.

Louçã F. (1997), *'Turbulence in economics: an evolutionary appraisal of cycles and complexity in historical processes'.* Cheltenham, UK; Lyme, US: Edward Elgar.

Louçã F. (1999), 'Nikolai Kondratiev and the Early Consensus and Dissensions about History and Statistics.' *History of political economy,* vol. 31, no. 1, pp. 169.

Louçã F. and Reijnders J. (Eds.)(1999), *'The foundations of long wave theory: models and methodology'* Northampton, Ma.: Edward Elgar Publishing.

Lundberg M. and Squire L. (2001), *'The Simultaneous Evolution of Growth and Inequality'* World Bank Research Working Paper at: http://www.worldbank.org/research/growth/pdfiles/squire.pdf.

Luttwak E. (1999), *'Turbo-Capitalism. Winners and Losers in the Global Economy'* New York: Harper Perennial.

Mackelar L. et al. (2000), *'Globalization and social security'* Paper, presented at the ISSA Conference 'Social security in the global village', Helsinki, 25-27 September 2000, available at: http://www.iiasa.ac.at/Publications/Documents/IR-99-056.pdf.

Maddison, A.. (2000) *The World Economy: A Millennial Perspective.* Paris: Organisation for Economic Cooperation and Development (Development Centre Studies).

Malcolm N. (1995), 'The Case Against 'Europe'' *Foreign Affairs,* March, April: 52 - 68.

Mandel E. (1972), *'Late Capitalism.* London: New Left Books, 1975.

Mandel E. (1973), *'Der Spaetkapitalismus'* Frankfurt a.M.: edition suhrkamp.

Mandel E. (1978), *'The Second Slump: A Marxist Analysis of Recession in the Seventies.* London, England: NLB, 1978 [revised and translated from the 1977 German edition].

Mandel E. (1980), *'Long Waves of Capitalist Development'* Cambridge: at the University Press.

Martin W. and Wallerstein I. (Eds.)(1990), *'Semiperipheral States in the World-Economy'* Westport, CT: Greenwood Press.

Martínez-Herrera, E. and Moualhi D. (2005). "*Actitudes ante las políticas de inmigración (Attitudes in the face of immigration policies)."* In: *"España: sociedad y política en perspectiva comparada".* (L. M. M. Torcal, S. Pérez-Nievas (Eds.)). Valencia, Tirant lo Blanch: 333-357.

Mayhew L. (2001*), 'Disability - global trends and international perspectives'* Department of Geography and Centre for Pensions and Social Insurance, Birbeck College, University of London, available at: http://www.pensions-research.org/papers/default.htm.

McCallum C. (1999), *'Globalisation, Developments and Trends in the New International Division of Labour'* Centre for International Business Studies at South Bank University, London, available at: http://www.sbu.ac.uk/cibs/pdf/19-99.pdf.

McCleary R. M. and Barro R. J. (2006), 'Religion and Economy'. *Journal of Economic Perspectives,* vol. 20, no. 2, pp. 49-72.

McCleary R. M. and Barro R. J. (2006), 'Religion and Political Economy in an International Panel' *Journal for the Scientific Study of Religion,* vol. 45, no. 2, pp. 149-175.

McKinnon R. I. (1973), *'Money and Capital in Economic Development',* Brookings Institution, Washington, D.C.

Meier G.M. and Seers D. (Eds.)(1984), *'Pioneers in Development'* New York and Oxford: Oxford University Press.

Melchior A., Telle, K., and Wiig, H. (2000), '*Globalisation and Inequality: World Income Distribution and Living Standards, 1960-1998*, Royal Norwegian Ministry of Foreign Affairs, Studies on Foreign Policy Issues, Report 6B: 2000. Available at: http://odin.dep.no/archive/udvedlegg/01/01/rev__016.pdf.

Meulemann H. (2006). "Religiosität: Immer noch die Persistenz eines Sonderfalls (Religiosity: Still the persistency of a special case)." *Aus Politik und Zeitgeschichte. Beilage zur Wochenzeitung Das Parlament.* Cologne.

Meulemann H. (2006). *"Empowerment at the work place - An Analysis of the measurement instrument use in the European Social Survey".* European Association for Methodology. Budapest.

Meyer W. H. (1996. 'Human Rights and MNCs: Theory versus Quantitative Analysis'. *Human Rights Quarterly,* 18: 368 – 397.

Microsoft Excel (1992), *'Microsoft Excel. Verzeichnis der Funktionen'* Microsoft Corporation.

Midgal J. S. (2001), *'State in Society: Studying How States and Societies Transform and Constitute One Another '* Cambridge: Cambridge University Press.

Midlarsky M. I. (1998), 'Democracy an Islam: Implications for Civilizational Conflict and the Democratic Peace.' *International studies quarterly,* vol. 42, no. 3, pp. 485.

Midlarsky M. I. (2000), 'Handbook of War Studies II' Ann Arbor: university of Michigan Press.

Milanovic B. (2002), 'True World Income Distribution, 1988 and 1993: First Calculations Based on Household Surveys Alone' *The Economic Journal,* Volume 112, Number 476, January 2002, pp. 51-92.

Milanovic B. (2003a), 'Inequality in the World Economy-By the Numbers'. *Multinational Monitor,* 2003, vol. 24, no. 7/8, pp. 23-29.

Milanovic B. (2003b), 'The Two Faces of Globalization: Against Globalization as We Know It' *World Development,* Volume 31, Number 4, April 2003, pp. 667-683.

Milanovic B. (2005), 'Can We Discern the Effect of Globalization on Income Distribution? Evidence from Household Surveys' *World Bank Economic Review,* 2005, vol. 19, no. 1, pp. 21-44.

Milanovic B. and Squire L. (2005), 'Does tariff liberalization increase wage inequality? Some empirical evidence' *NBER Working Paper Series,* 2005, no. 11046, pp. (entire).

Miller C. D. (1999), 'Research note: How Did Economic Development and Trade Affect Women's Share of the Labor Force in the 1980s?' *Journal of World-Systems Research,* available at: http://jwsr.ucr.edu/index.phpV, 3: 463 – 473.

Miller M. A. L. (1995), *'The Third World in Global Environmental Politics* ' Boulder, CO: Lynne Rienner.

Mills J. (2002), 'A Critical History of Economics: Missed Opportunities' Basingstoke and London: Palgrave Macmillan.

Mittelman J. (1994), 'The Globalization of Social Conflict' in *'Conflicts and New Departures in World Society'* (Bornschier V. and Lengyel P. (Eds.)), pp. 317 - 337, New Brunswick (U.S.A.) and London: Transaction Publishers, World Society Studies, Volume 3.

Moaddel M. (1994), 'Political Conflict in the World Economy: A Cross - national Analysis of Modernization and World - System Theories' *American Sociological Review,* 59, April: 276 - 303.

Moaddel M. (1996), 'The Social Bases and Discursive Context of the Rise of Islamic Fundamentalism: The Cases of Iran and Syria'. *Sociological inquiry,* 1996, vol. 66, no. 3, pp. 330.

Moaddel M. (1998), 'Religion and Women: Islamic Modernism versus Fundamentalism.' *Journal for the scientific study of religion,* vol. 37, no. 1, pp. 108.

Moaddel M. (2004), 'The future of Islam after 9/11' *Futures,* 2004, vol. 36, no. 9, pp. 961-977.

Modelski G. (1983), 'Long Cycles of World Leadership' in *'Contending Approaches to World System Analysis'* (Thompson W.R. (Ed.)), pp. 115 - 139, Beverly Hills: Sage.

Modelski G. (1987), *'Long Cycles in World Politics'* Basingstoke: Macmillan.

Modelski G. (1988a), *'Is America's decline inevitable?'* Wassenaar NL: NIAS, 1988.

Modelski G. (1988b), *'Seapower in global politics, 1494-1993.'* Seattle: University of Washington Press,

Modelski G. (1989), 'Is America's Decline Inevitable?' *The Bridge,* 1989, vol. 19, no. 2, pp. 11.

Modelski G. (1990), 'Is world politics evolutionary learning?' *International organization,* vol. 44, no. 1, pp. 1 ff.

Modelski G. (1995), 'The Evolution of Global Politics' *Journal of World Systems Research,* 1, 7, electronic journal, available on the Internet at http://csf.colorado.edu/wsystems/jwsr.html.

Modelski G. (1996a), 'Evolutionary Paradigm for Global Politics'. *International studies quarterly,* vol. 40, no. 3, pp. 321 ff.

Modelski G. (1996b), *'Portuguese Seapower and the Evolution of Global Politics'* Lecture, delivered to the Academia de Marinha, Lisboa, October 15, 1996; available from the Internet at http://faculty.washington.edu/modelski/MARINHA.html.

Modelski G. (1999), 'From Leadership to Organization: The Evolution of Global Politics' in *'The Future of Global Conflict'* (Bornschier V. and Chase-Dunn Ch. K. (Eds.)), pp. 11 - 39, London, Thousand Oaks and New Delhi: Sage Publications.

Modelski G. (2000a), *'Kondratiev Waves'* Internet publication at 'The Evolutionary World Politics Homepage', http://faculty.washington.edu/modelski/IPEKWAVE.html.

Modelski G. (2000b), *'Time, Calendars, and IR: Evolution of Global Politics in the 21st Century'* Internet publication at 'The 'Evolutionary World Politics Homepage', http://faculty.washington.edu/modelski/time.html.

Modelski G. (2001), 'What causes K-waves?' *Technological Forecasting and Social Change,* Volume 68, Issue 1, September: 75-80.

Modelski G. (2005), 'Long-Term Trends in World Politics' in *'The Future of World Society'* (Herkenrath M. et al. (Eds.)) pp. 39 – 51; Sociological Institute, University of Zurich: Intelligent Book Production.

Modelski G. and Perry, G (1991), 'Democratization in Long Perspective'. *Technological forecasting and social change,* vol. 39, no. 1/2, pp. 23.

Modelski G. and Poznanski, K (1996), 'Evolutionary Paradigms in the Social Sciences'. *International studies quarterly,* vol. 40, no. 3, pp. 315.

Modelski G. and Thompson W. R. (1996), *'Leading Sectors and World Powers: the Coevolution of Global Politics and World Economics'* Columbia, SC: University of South Carolina Press.

Modelski G. and Thompson W. R. (1999), 'The Long and the Short of Global Politics in the Twenty-first Century: An Evolutionary Approach'. *The International Studies Review,* Volume 1, Number 2, 1999, pp. 109.

Modigliani F. (1985), *'Life Cycle, Individual Thrift and the Wealth of Nations'* Nobel Prize Lecture in Economics, available at: http://nobelprize.org/economics/laureates/1985/modigliani-lecture.pdf.

Modigliani F. (1987), *'European economic recovery: a need for new policies?'* Stockholm, Sweden: Industrial Institute for Economic and Social Research: Distribution, Almqvist & Wiksell International.

Modigliani F. and Muralidhar A. (2004), *'Rethinking Pension Reform"* Cambridge, at the University Press.

Modigliani F., Ceprini M.L., and Muralidhar A. (2000), 'A Solution to the Social Security Crisis' Sloan Working paper 4051, available at: http://www.iza.org/index_html?lang=de&mainframe=http%3A//www.iza.org/de/calls_conferences/pension_reform_html.

Moeller St. *et al.* (2003), 'Determinants of Relative poverty in Advanced Capitalist Democracies' *American Sociological Review,* 68, 1, February: 22 – 51.

Moon B.E. and Dixon W.J. (1992), 'Basic Needs and Growth Welfare - Trade Offs' *International Studies Quarterly,* 36, 2: 191 - 212.

Moore M. (2003), *'A World Without Walls: Freedom, Development, Free Trade and Global Governance'* Cambridge: Cambridge University Press.

Morawetz R. (1991), *'Recent foreign direct investment in Eastern Europe: Towards a possible role for the Tripartite Declaration of Principles concerning Multinational Enterprises and Social Policy'* Geneva: International Labor Office, Multinational Enterprises Programme, Working Paper 71.

Morawska E. (2000), *'International Migration and Consolidation of Democracy in East Central Europe: A Problematic Relationship in a Hostorical Perspective'* University of Pennsylvania, emorawsk@as.upenn.edu.

Muenz R. (2006), *"Population Change and the Impact of Demographic Aging: Consequences and Policy Options for Europe"* International Conference on Cultural and Political Conditions for the Reform and Modernisation of Social Models in Europe and the U.S., Vienna, May 19-20, 2006, Institute for Human Sciences, Vienna

Muenz R. (2006), "Population Change and the Impact of Demographic Aging: Consequences and Policy Options for Europe" International Conference on Cultural and Political Conditions for the Reform and Modernisation of Social Models in Europe and the U.S., Vienna, May 19-20, 2006, Institute for Human Sciences, Vienna

Müller Andreas *et al.* (2000), *'Global Capitalism, Liberation Theology, and the Social Sciences: An Analysis of the Contradictions of Modernity at the Turn of the Millenium'* Nova Sciences: Huntington and Commack, New York.

Muller E. N. (1988), 'Democracy, Economic Development, and Income Inequality.' *American Sociological Review,* 54, pps. 868-871.

Muller E. N. (1993), 'Financial Dependence in the Capitalist World Economy and the Distribution of Income Within States.' in *'Development and Underdevelopment: The Political Economy of Inequality"* (Seligson M. A. and Passe-Smith J. T. (Eds.)), pp. 267 – 293 – 39, Boulder CO: Lynne Rienner Publishers.

Muller E. N. (1995), 'Economic Determinants of Democracy.' *American Sociological Review,* 54, pps. 966-982.

Muller E. N. and and Seligson M. A. (1987), 'Inequality and Insurgency.' *American Political Science Review,* 81, pps. 425-449.

Munasinghe M., Miguel: de and Sunkel O. (2001), *'Sustainability of long-term growth: socioeconomic and ecological perspectives'* Cheltenham, UK; Northampton, MA: Edward Elgar.

Mundell R. A. and Clesse A. (Eds.)(2000), *'Euro as a stabilizer in the international economic system'* Boston: Kluwer Academic (Luxembourg Institute for European and International Studies).

Mundell R. A. et. al. (Eds.)(2005), *'International monetary policy after the euro'* Cheltenham, UK; Northampton, MA: Edward Elgar.

Myrdal G. (1972), *'Politisches Manifest ueber die Armut in der Welt'* Frankfurt a.M.: suhrkamp TB.

Myrdal G. (1974), *'Oekonomische Theorie und unterentwickelte Regionen. Weltproblem Armut'* Frankfurt a.M.: Fischer TB.

Myrdal G. (1984), 'International Inequality and Foreign Aid in Retrospect' in *'Pioneers in Development. A World Bank Publication'* (Meier G.M. and Seers D. (Eds.)) pp. 151 - 165. New York and Oxford: Oxford University Press.

Neapolitan J. L. and Schmalleger F. (1997), *'Cross-National Crime: A Research Review and Sourcebook'* Westport, CT: Greenwood Press.

Nederveen-Pieterse J. (1997), 'Equity and Growth Revisited: A Supply-Side Approach to Social Development' *The European Journal of Development Research,* 9, 1, June: 128-149.

Neller K. (2005). "Kooperation und Verweigerung: Eine Non-Response Studie (Co-operation and Refusal: A Non-Response Study)." *ZUMA-Nachrichten* 29(57): 9-36. http://www.gesis.org/Publikationen/Zeitschriften/ZUMA_Nachrichten/documents/pdfs/57/06_Neller.pdf

Neller K. N. (2006). "Die zweite Welle des European Social Survey (ESS) 2004/2005 (The second round of the European Social Survey (ESS) 2004/2005)." *ZA-Information* 58: 92-102.

Neller K. N. and van Deth, J. (2006). "Politisches Engagement in Europa (Political Commitment in Europe)." *Aus Politik und Zeitgeschichte* 30-31: 30-38. http://www.bpb.de/files/HYHZ7V.pdf

Nielsen F. (1995), 'Income Inequality, Development and Dualism: Results from an Unbalanced Cross-National Panel.' *American Sociological Review,* 60, pps. 674-701.

Nielsen F. and Alderson A. (1997), 'The Kuznets Curve and the Great U-Turn: Income Inequality in U.S. Counties, 1970 to 1990.' *American Sociological Review,* 62, 1, February, pps. 12-33.

Nielsen J. S. (1999) *'Towards a European Islam'.* New York: St. Martin's Press.

Nisbet E. C. (2005). "The Engagement Model of Opinion Leadership: Testing Validity within a European Context." *International Journal of Public Opinion Research.* http://ijpor.oxfordjournals.org

Nolan P. D. (1983), 'Status in the World System, Income Inequality and Economic Growth'; *American Journal of Sociology,* 89, 410-419.

Noland M. (2004), *'Religion and economic performance'.* Washington D.C.: The Peterson Institute, available at: http://www.petersoninstitute.org/publications/wp/03-8.pdf

Noland M. (2005), *'Explaining Middle Eastern Authoritarianism'.* Washington D.C., Institute for International Economics, Working Paper Series 05-5 (entire), available at: http://www.iie.com/publications/wp/wp05-5.pdf

Noland M. and Pack H. (2004), *'Islam, Globalization, and Economic Performance in the Middle East'.* International Economics Policy Briefs, Washington D.C., Institute for International Economics, PB 04-4, June (entire), available at: http://www.iie.com/publications/pb/pb04-4.pdf

Nollert M. (1990), 'Social Inequality in the World System: An Assessment' in *'World Society Studies. Volume 1'* (Bornschier V. and Lengyel P. (Eds.)), pp. 17 - 54, Frankfurt and New York: Campus.

Nollert M. (1994a), 'Ressourcenmangel, Soziooekonomische Ungleichheit und Delinquenz: Ein internationaler Vergleich' *Schweizerische Zeitschrift fuer Soziologie,* 20, 1: 127 - 156.

Nollert M. (1994b), 'World Economic Integration and Political Conflict in Latin America' in *'Conflicts and New Departures in World Society'* (Bornschier V. and Lengyel P. (Eds.)), pp. 159 - 179, New Brunswick (U.S.A.) and London: Transaction Publishers, World Society Studies, Volume 3.

Nollert M. (1996), 'Verbandliche Interessenvertretung in der Europaeischen Union: Einflussressourcen und faktische Einflussnahme' *Zeitschrift fuer Politikwissenschaft (vormals Jahrbuch fuer Politik),* 6, 3: 647 - 667.

Nollert M. (2005), 'Transnational Corporate Networks. Theoretical Perspectives, Empirical Evidence, and Prospects' in *'The Future of World Society'* (Herkenrath M. et al. (Eds.)) pp. 103 – 127; Sociological Institute, University of Zurich: Intelligent Book Production.

Nollert M. and Fielder N. (1997), *'Lobbying for a Europe of Big Business: the European Roundtable of Industrialists'* Department of Sociology, University of Zurich, Research paper (Raemistrasse 69, CH-8001, Zurich).

Nolte H. H. (1982), *'Die eine Welt. Abriss der Geschichte des internationalen Systems'* Hannover: Fackeltraeger.

Nolte H. H. (1989), *'Tradition des Rueckstands. West - Ost - Technologietransfer in der Geschichte'* Department of History, University of Hannover, FRG.

Normann G. and Mitchell D. J. (2000*), 'Pension Reform in Sweden: Lessons for American Policymakers'* The Heritage Foundation, Backgrounder, 1381, June 29, 2000, available from http://www.heritage.org/library/backgrounder/bg1381es.html.

Novak M. A. (1987), *'Liberation Theology and the Liberal Society'* Washington D. C.: American Enterprise Institute.

Novak M. A. and Jackson M. P. (1985), *'Latin America, Dependency or Interdependence?'* Washington D. C.: American Enterprise Institute.

Nuscheler F. (1993), 'Nach dem Fall von Mauern und Grenzen in Europa' in *'Die Neuen Mauern. Krisen der Nord - Sued - Beziehungen'* (Datta A. (Ed.)), pp. 13 - 30, Wuppertal: P. Hammer.

Nye J. (2001), 'Globalization and the need for pension reform' *FinanceAsia.com,* 11th July 2001 at: http://www.financeasia.com/articles/4CA32C70-6C1B-11D5-81CE0090277E174B.cfm.

O'Hara P. A. (1994), 'An Institutionalist Review of Long Wave Theories: Schumpeterian Innovation, Modes of Regulation, and Social Structures of Accumulation", *Journal of Economic Issues,* vol 28, no 2, June.

O'Hara P. A. (2000) *'Marx, Veblen and Contemporary Institutional Political Economy: Principles and Unstable Dynamics of Capitalism.* Cheltenham, UK and Northampton, US: Edward Elgar. Pp. 266-291.

O'Hara P. A. (2001), 'Long Waves of Growth and Development", in P.A. O'Hara (ed), *Encyclopedia of Political Economy.* London and New York: Routledge, pp. 673-677. Paper edition..

O'Hara P. A. (2003a), '*Principles of Political Economy: Integrating Themes from the Schools of Heterodoxy.* Working Paper, Global Political Economy Research Unit, Economics Department, Curtin University. http://pohara.homestead.com/files/principles.doc.

O'Hara P. A. (2003b), 'Recent changes to the IMF, WTO and SPD: emerging global mode of regulation or social structure of accumulation for long wave upswing?' *Review of International Political Economy,* Volume 10, Number 3, August 2003, pp. 481-519.

O'Hara P. A. (2004a), 'A New Family-Community Social Structures of Accumulation for Long Wave Upswing in the United States, *Forum for Social Economy,* vol 34, no 2, December.

O'Hara P. A. (2004b), 'Cultural Contradictions of Global Capitalism' *Journal of Economic Issues,* 2004, vol. 38, no. 2, pp. 413-420.

O'Hara P. A. (2005a), 'Contradictions of Neoliberal Globalisation: The Importance of Ideologies and Values in Polical Economy' *Journal of Interdisciplinary Economics,* vol. 16, no. 3, pp. 341-365.

O'Hara P. A. (2005b), *'Growth and Development in the Global Political Economy. Social Structures of Accumulation and Modes of Regulation'* Oxford and New York: Routledge, Taylor and Francis Group.

O'Hara P. A. (Ed.)(2001), *'Encyclopedia of Political Economy,* London and New York: Routledge, Paper edition. 2 vols.

O'Hara P. A. (Ed.)(2004), 'Global political economy and the weath of nations: performance, institutions, problems, and policies' New York: Routledge.

O'Loughlin J.; Ward M. D.; and Shin M. (1998), 'The Diffusion of Democracy, 1946-1994.' *Annals of the Association of American Geographers,* Volume 88, Number 4, December 1998, pp. 545.

O'Neill H. (1997), 'Globalization, Competitiveness and Human Security: Challenges for Development Policy and Institutional Change' *The European Journal of Development Research,* 9, 1, June: 7-37.

Oddone C. N. (2004), *'La participación de España en la Guerra de Irak, consecuencias para el sistema democrático de gobierno'* (coautoría de Granato, L.) en V Jornadas de Reflexión Académica Los desafíos de la democracia: entre la representación y la participación. Sociedad Argentina de Análisis Político y carrera de Ciencia Política de la Universidad de Belgrano. Buenos Aires, 2 y 3 de septiembre de 2004. (Incluido en el CD de las Jornadas. Editorial de Belgrano, ISBN: 987-577-096-0).

Oddone C. N. (2005), *'Escenarios comparados: México, Sudeste Asiático y Argentina. Crisis Financiera Internacional y Mercados emergentes.'* I Congreso Nacional de Relaciones Internacionales "Argentina, Latinoamérica y el Mundo", Universidad Empresarial Siglo I. Córdoba, del 20 al 23 de abril de 2005.

Oddone C. N. (2005), *'Globalización, Desigualdad y Pobreza'.* (coautoría de Granato, L.). Encuentro Internacional sobre Pobreza, Desigualdad y Convergencia. Grupo EUMED, Universidad de Málaga, del 3 al 30 de marzo de 2005. (ISBN: 84-689-0637-9, incluido en el CD de EUMED).

Oddone C. N. (2005), *'La contribución del Marxismo a la Teoría del Estado'* (coautoría de Granato, L.) en II Encuentro Internacional de Economía y Sociedad. Grupo EUMED, Universidad de Málaga, 2 al 20 de febrero de 2004. (ISBN 84-688-6812-4, incluido en CD de EUMED).

Oddone C. N. (2005), *'La Globalización como proceso e ideología: las desigualdades se acrecientan'* (coautoría de Granato, L.) en II Encuentro Virtual Internacional sobre Globalización y Desigualdad Económica. Grupo EUMED, Universidad de Málaga, 1 al 20 de diciembre de 2003. (ISBN 84-609-0004-5, incluido en CD de EUMED).

Oddone C. N. (2005), *'Mercados Emergentes y Crisis Financiera Internacional'.* Malaga: Grupo EUMED, Universidad de Málaga, España. Agosto de 2004. (ISBN 84-688-8059-0).

Oden B. (2004), 'Alternatives Forms of International Governance and Development Cooperation" in in 'Global Governance in the 21st Century: Alternative Perspectives on World Order' (Hettne B. and Oden B. (Eds.)), pp. 184 - 202. Stockholm: Almkvist & Wiksell. Availabla also at: http://www.egdi.gov.se/pdf/study/study2002_2.pdf.

Ogg J. (2005). "Social exclusion and insecurity among older Europeans: the influence of welfare regimes." *Ageing and Society* (25): 1-22.

Olson M. (1982), *'The Rise and Decline of Nations'* New Haven and London: Yale University Press.

Olson M. (1982), *'The Rise and Decline of Nations'* New Haven and London: Yale University Press.

Olson M. (1986), 'A Theory of the Incentives Facing Political Organizations. Neo - Corporatism and the Hegemonic State' *International Political Science Review,* 7, 2, April: 165 - 89.

Olson M. (1986), 'A Theory of the Incentives Facing Political Organizations. Neo - Corporatism and the Hegemonic State' *International Political Science Review,* 7, 2, April: 165 - 89.

Olson M. (1987), 'Ideology and Economic Growth' in *'The Legacy of Reaganomics. Prospects for Long - term Growth'* (Hulten Ch.R. and Sawhill I.V. (Eds.)), pp. 229 - 251, Washington D.C.: The Urban Institute Press.

Olson M. (1987), 'Ideology and Economic Growth' in *'The Legacy of Reaganomics. Prospects for Long - term Growth'* (Hulten Ch.R. and Sawhill I.V. (Eds.)), pp. 229 - 251, Washington D.C.: The Urban Institute Press.

Omran M. (2001), *'Testing for the Signiciant Change in the Egyptian Economy under the Economic Reform Programme Era'* Arab Academy of Science and Technology. Alexandria at: http://www.wider.unu.edu/conference/conference-2001-2/poster%20papers/Omran.pdf.

Opitz P. J. (1988), *'Das Weltfluechtlingsproblem. Ursachen und Folgen'* Munich: C.H. Beck.

Opp K.D. and Schmidt P. (1976), *'Einfuehrung in die Mehrvariablenanalyse. Grundlagen der Formulierung und Pruefung komplexer sozialwissenschaftlicher Aussagen'* Reinbek: rororo studium.

Orenstein M. A. (1996), 'The Failures of Neo - Liberal Social Policy in Central Europe' *Transition,* 28 June 1996.

Orenstein M. A. (2001), *'Mapping the Diffusion of Pension Innivation' Paper presented to the IIASA Conference on the Political Economy of Pension Reform,* available at: http://wbln0018.worldbank.org/HDNet/hddocs.nsf/2d5135ecbf351de6852566a90069b8b6/cc289fc4c077670285256a9c00666690/$FILE/Orenstein.pdf.

Orlowski L. T. (1995), 'Social Safety Nets in Central Europe: Preparation for Accession to the European Union?' *Comparative Economic Studies,* 37, 2, Summer: 29-48.

Orlowski L. T. (1996*), 'Fiscal Consolidation in Central Europe in Preparation for Accession to the European Union'* Center for Social and Economic Research, Bagatela 14, PL-00-585 Warsaw, Studies and Analyses, 77.

Orszag P. R. and Stiglitz J. E. (1999), *'Rethinking Pension Reform: Ten Myths About Social Security Systems'* Presented at the conference on 'New Ideas About Old Age Security' The World Bank, Washington D.C., September 14 - 15: http://www.worldbank.org/knowledge/chiefecon/conferen/papers/rethinking.htm.

Palme J. (2005), *'Why the Scandinavian Experience is Relevant for the Reform of ESM'* Stockholm, Institute for Future Studies (Discussion paper prepared for the UK Presidency, available at http://www.eu2005.gov.uk/servlet/Front?pagename=Open Market/Xcelerate/ShowPage&c=Page&cid=1107293391098&a=KArticle&aid=1119527 321606).

Panitch L. and Leys C. (Eds.)(2002), *'Fighting identities: race, religion and ethnonationalism'* London, U.K. and Merlin; USA: Monthly Review Press.

Parnreiter Ch. (1994), *'Migration und Arbeitsteilung. Auslaenderbeschaeftigung in der Weltwirtschaftskrise'* Vienna: promedia.

Paukert F. (1973), 'Income Distribution at Different Levels of Development: A Survey of the Evidence'. *International Labor Review,* 108, pps. 97-125.

Paul S. S. and Paul J. A. (1996*), 'The World Bank and the Attack on Pensions in the Global South'* Global Action on Aging, New York: http://www.globalaging.org/.

Pedersen L. (1999), *'Newer Islamic movements in western Europe'*. Aldershot, Hants, England; Brookfield, Vt.: Ashgate.

Pepelasis A. and Yotopoulos P. A. (1962), *'Surplus labor in Greek agriculture, 1953-1960'* Athens (Center of Economic Research. Research monograph series, 2).

Perez C. (2003), *'Technological Revolutions and Financial Capital: The Dynamics of Bubbles and Golden Ages'* Aldershot, Hants, England; Brookfield, Vt., USA: E. Elgar Pub. Co.

Perroux F. (1961), *'L'économie du e siècle'* Paris: P.U.F.

Petrella R. (1995), 'Europe between competitive innovation and a new social contract' *International Social Science Journal,* 143: 11 - 23.

Pettersson Th. (2006), *'Religious commitment and socio-poltical orientations: different patterns of compartmentalization among Muslims and Christians?'* Paper, presented at the International Stduies Association Convention, Centre for Multiethnic Research, Uppsala University, Sweden

PEW Research Center for the People and the Press (2006), "The Great Divide: How Westerners and Muslims View Each Other. Europe's Muslims More Moderate" PEW, Washington D.C.: http://pewglobal.org/reports/display.php?ReportID=253 (June 22, 2006)

Pfaller A. (2000), 'Social Democracy in the Globalized Post-Industrial Society' *Politik und Gesellschaft Online,* Friedrich-Ebert-Stiftung, 2, available at: http://www.fes.de/IPG/ipg2_2000/artpfaller.html.

Piore M. (1990), 'Work, labor and action: Work experience in a system of flexible production' in *'Industrial Districts and Inter - Firm Cooperation in Italy'* (Pyke F. *et al.* (Eds.)), pp. 52 - 74, Geneva: International Institute for Labor Studies.

Pipes D. (2002), 'God and Mammon: Does Poverty Cause Militant Islam? *The National Interest,* Winter 2002, available at: http://www.danielpipes.org/article/104

Polany, K. (1979), *'Oekonomie und Gesellschaft'* Frankfurt a.M.: suhrkamp taschenbuch wissenschaft.

Polanyi K. (1957), *'The Great Transformation'* Boston: Beacon.

Polanyi K., Lewis J. Kitchin D. (1972), *'Christianity and the social revolution'* Freeport, N.Y.: Books for Libraries Press..

Pollins B. M. (1996), 'Global Political Order, Economic Change, and Armed Conflict: Coevolving Systems and the Use of Force' *American Political Science Review,* 90, 1: 103 - 117.

Polychronious Ch. (1992), *'Perspectives and Issues in International Political Economy'* New York: Frederic Praeger Publishers.

Poortinga W. (2006). "Social capital: An individual or collective resource for health?" *Social Science & Medicine.* 62(2): 292-302. http://www.sciencedirect.com/science/journal/02779536

Popper Sir K. (1991), 'The Best World We Have Yet Had. George Urban Interviews Sir Karl Popper' *Report on the USSR,* 3, 22, May 31: 20 - 22.

Portillo M. (1999), *'For a Global Britain'* Speech delivered by the Rt. Hon. Michael Portillo, Westminster Hall, available from the Internet at http://www.keele.ac.uk/socs/ks40/port.htm.

Prebisch R. (1981*), 'Capitalismo periférico: crisis y transformación'* México: Fondo de Cultura Económica.

Prebisch R. (1983), 'The crisis of capitalism and international trade' *CEPAL Review,* 20, August: 51 - 74.

Prebisch R. (1984), 'Five Stages in My Thinking on Development' in *'Pioneers in Development. A World Bank Publication'* (Meier G.M. and Seers D. (Eds.)), pp. 175 - 191. New York and Oxford: Oxford University Press.

Prebisch R. (1986), 'The Dynamic Role of the Periphery, ' in: K. Ahooja-Patel, A.G. Drabek and M. Nerfin (eds.), *World Economy in Transition: Essays presented to Surendra Patel.* Oxford, United Kingdom: Pergamon Press, 1986, p. 3-9.

Prebisch R. (1988a), 'Dependence, development, and interdependence, ' in: G. Ranis and T.P. Schultz (eds.), *The State of Development Economics.* Oxford, United Kingdom: Basil Blackwell, 1988.

Prebisch R. (1988b), *'Raúl Prebisch, pensamiento y obra'* Fundación Raúl Prebisch. Buenos Aires, República Argentina: Editorial Tesis.

Prechel H. (1985), 'The Effects of Exports, Public Debt and Development on Income Inequality'. *International Labor Review,* 108, pps. 97-125.

Pryor F. (2006), *'The Economic Impact of Islam on Developing Nations'* As yet unpublished draft, Swarthmore College, Pennsylvania, available at: http://papers.ssrn.com/sol3/papers.cfm?abstract_id=929104

Puchala D. J. (2003), *'Theory and Histroy in International Relations'* London and New York: Routledge.

Quiggin J. (1998*), 'Social Democracy and market reform in Australia and New Zealand'* Department of Economics, James Cook University, available at: http://ecocomm.anu.edu.au/quiggin/JournalArticles98/AustNZ98.html.

Rabasa A. M. et al. (2006), *"The Muslim World after 9/11. Prepared for the United States Air Force".* Rand Corporation, Santa Monica, California, Rand Project Air Force, available at: http://www.rand.org/pubs/research_briefs/2005/RAND_RB151.pdf

Rabasa A. M. et al. (2006), "The Muslim World after 9/11. Prepared for the United States Air Force". Rand Corporation, Santa Monica, California, Rand Project Air Force, available at: http://www.rand.org/pubs/research_briefs/2005/RAND_RB151.pdf

Radzicki M. J. (2003), 'Mr. Hamilton, Mr. Forrester, and a Foundation for Evolutionary Economics' *Journal of Economic Issues,* Vol. 37, 133 - 173.

Raffer K. (1987a), 'Tendencies Towards a 'Neo Listian' World Economy', *Journal für Entwicklungspolitik,* vol.3, n.3, pp.45ff.

Raffer K. (1987b), *'Unequal Exchange and the Evolution of the World System Reconsidering the Impact of Trade on North-South Relations'* London, Basingstoke and New York: Macmillan and Saint Martin's Press..

Raffer K. (1993), 'International financial institutions and accountability: The need for drastic change', in: S.M. Murshed & K. Raffer (eds), *Trade, Transfers, and Development, Problems and Prospects for the Twenty First Century,* Aldershot, Hants, England; Brookfield, Vt., USA: E. Elgar Pub. Co. pp.151ff.

Raffer K. (1995), 'The Impact of the Uruguay Round on Developing Countries', in: F. Breuss (ed), *The World Economy after the Uruguay Round,* Service Fachverlag, Vienna, pp.169ff.

Raffer K. (1996), 'Exportorientierte Entwicklung und Weltmarkt - Das Beispiel der asiatischen 'Tiger", in: E. Binderhofer, I. Getreuer-Kargl, H. Lukas (eds), *Das pazifische Jahrhundert?,* Brandes & Apsel/Südwind, Frankfurt aM/Wien, pp.41ff.

Raffer K. (1997), 'Debt Management and Structural Adjustment: Neglected Issues', in: S.D. GUPTA (ed) *The Political Economy of Globalization*, Kluwer, Boston etc., pp.269ff.

Raffer K. (1998), 'The Tobin Tax: Reviving a Discussion'. *World Development,* Volume 26, Number 3, March pp. 529 ff.

Raffer K. (2003), 'Social Expenditure, Pension Systems, and Neoliberalism' Alternatives. Turkish Journal of International Relations, Volume 2, Number 3&4, Fall&Winter 2003, at http://www.alternativesjournal.net/volume2/number3and4/raffer.pdf.

Raffer K. (2004), 'International Financial Institutions and Financial Accountability Ethics and International Affairs', vol. 18, no. 2, pp. 61-78.

Raffer K. and Murshed S. M. (1993), *'Trade, transfers, and development: problems and prospects for the twenty-first century'* Aldershot, Hants, England; Brookfield, Vt., USA: E. Elgar Pub. Co.

Raffer K. and Salih M. A. M. (Ed.)(1992), *'Least developed and the oil-rich Arab countries: dependence, independence, or patronage?'* New York, N.Y.: St. Martin's Press, 1992..

Raffer K. and Singer H. W. (1996), *'The Foreign Aid Business, Economic Assistance and Development Co-operation*, E.Elgar, Cheltenham [paperback: 1997].

Raffer K. and Singer H. W. (2001), *'Economic North-South divide: six decades of unequal development'* Cheltenham, UK; Northampton, MA: Edward Elgar.

Ragin C. C. and Bradshaw Y. W. (1992), 'International Economic Dependence and Human Misery, 1938-1980: A Global Perspective'. *Sociological perspectives,* vol. 35, no. 2, pp. 217.

Ram R. (1992), 'Intercountry Inequalities in Income and Basic-Needs Indicators: A Recent Perspective.' *World Development,* 20, 6, pps. 899-905.

Ramonet I. (1998), *'Die neuen Herren der Welt. Internationale Politik an der Jahrtausendwende'* Zürich: Rotpunkt-Verlag.

Rao J. M. (1998), 'Development in the time of Globalization' UNDP Working Paper Series, Social Development and Poverty Elimination Division, February 1998, available at http://www.undp.org/poverty/publications/wkpaper/wp2/RAO-Rf1.PDF

Ray J. L. (1983), 'The 'World System' and the Global Political System: A Crucial Relationship?' in *'Foreign Policy and the Modern World - System'* (Mc Gowan P. and Kegley Ch.W. Jr. (Eds.)), pp. 13 - 34, Beverly Hills: Sage.

Reijnders J. (2001), 'Vincent Barnett, Kondratiev and the Dynamics of Economic Development: Long Cycles and Industrial Growth in Historical Context' *Journal of the History of Economic Thought,* vol. 23, no. 3, pp. 385-387.

Rennstich K. J. (2002), 'The new economy, the leadership long cycle and the nineteenth K-wave.' *Review of International Political Economy* 9, no. 1 (2002): 150-182.

Rennstich K. J. (2003), 'The Future of Great Power Rivalries' *Contributions in economics and economic history.* 2, no. 230, (2003): 143-161.

Rennstich K. J. (2005), 'The Future of Hegemony and Global System Leadership' in *'The Future of World Society'* (Herkenrath M. et al. (Eds.)) pp. 53 – 79; Sociological Institute, University of Zurich: Intelligent Book Production.

Reuveny R. and Thompson W. R. (2003), *'Growth, Trade, and Systemic Leadership'* Ann Arbor: University of Michigan Press.

Rex J. (1996), *'Ethnic minorities in the modern nation state: working papers in the theory of multiculturalism and political integration'.* Houndmills, Basingstoke, Hampshire and London: MacMillan Press; New York: St. Martin's Press.

Robinson R. D. (1987), *'Direct Foreign Investment: Costs and Benefits'* New York: Praeger Publishers.

Robinson T.D. and London B. (1991), 'Dependency, Inequality, and Political Violence. A Cross - National Analysis' *Journal of Political and Military Sociology,* 19, 1: 119 - 156.

Rodas-Martini P. (2001*),* '*Has income distribution really worsened in the South? And has income distribution really worsened between the North and the South?'* Background paper for the Human Development Report 2001, available at: http://www.undp.org/hdr2001/.

Rodrik D. (1997), *'Globalization, Social Conflict and Economic Growth'* Harvard University. Available at: http://ksghome.harvard.edu/~.drodrik.academic.ksg/global.PDF.

Rogers R. (1992), 'The Politics of Migration in the Contemporary World' *International Migration,* 30, Special Issue: Migration and Health in the 1990s: 30 - 55.

Rohdes R. A. W. (1996), 'The new governance: governing without government" *Political Studies,* vol. 44, n°4, 1996, pp 652-667.

Roos J. P. (2000), 'The Consequences of the Crisis of the 1990s to the Nordic Welfare State: Finland and Sweden' University of Helsinki, Department of Social Policy, available at: http://www.valt.helsinki.fi/staff/jproos/Nordsocp.htm.

Rosenau J. (1992), 'The United Nations in a Turbulent World, International Peace Academy (Occasional Paper Series), Boulder(CO), Lynne Rienner Pub, 1992, pp87 ff.

Rosenau J. (1995), 'Governance in the Twenty-first Century', in Global Governance, Spring 1995, vol.1, n°1, pp13-42..

Rosenau J. (1997), 'Along the Domestic-Foreign Frontier, Exploring Governance in a Turbulent World, Cambridge University Press, Cambridge, 1997, 467p..

Ross R. J. S. and Trachte K.C. (1990), *'Global Capitalism: The New Leviathan'* Albany: State University of New York Press.

Rostow W. W. (1978) *The World Economy: History and Prospect.* London and Basingstoke: Macmillan.

Rostow W. W. (1980) *Why the Poor get Richer and the Rich Slow Down: Essays in the Marshallian Long Period.* London and Basingstoke: Macmillan..

Rothenbacher F. (2000), 'The Changing Public Sector in Europe: Social Structure, Income and Social Security' Mannheim Center for European Social Research, University of Mannheim, available at: http://www.mzes.uni-mannheim.de/eurodata/newsletter/no8/feature.html.

Rother P. C., Catenaro M. and Schwab G. (2003), *'Ageing and Pensions in the Euro Area. Survey and Projection results'.* World Bank Social Protection Discussion Paper Series, 0307, available at: http://wbln0018.worldbank.org/HDNet/HDDocs.nsf/65538a343139acab85256cb70055e6ed/2b83b260804d9df985256cf00060b044/$FILE/0307.pdf.

Rothgeb J. M. Jr. (1993a), 'A Regional Analysis of the Relationship Between Foreign Investment and Political Conflict in Developing Countries.' *Journal of Political and Military Sociology,* 21, pps. 219-240.

Rothgeb J. M. Jr. (1993b), 'A Regional Analysis of the Relationship Between Foreign Investment and Political Conflict in Developing Countries'. *Journal of Political and Military Sociology,* vol. 21, no. 2, pp. 219 ff.

Rothgeb J. M. Jr. (1996a), 'War, Empire, and Democracy: Three New Examinations of Some Dominant Forces of the Twentieth Century.' *The journal of politics,* 1996, vol. 58, no. 2, pp. 551.

Rothgeb J. M. Jr. (1996b), *'Foreign Investment and Political Conflict in Developing Countries'.* New York: F. Praeger.

Rothgeb J. M. Jr. (1999), 'Testing Mobilization Views of the Relationship Between International Interdependence and Political Conflict in Developing Countries'. *The Social science journal,* 1999, vol. 36, no. 3, pp. 469.

Rothgeb J. M. Jr. (2002), 'Foreign Investments, Privatization, and Political Conflict in Developing Countries' *Journal of Political and Military Sociology,* vol. 30, no. 1, pp. 36-50.

Rothgeb, J. M. Jr. (1995), 'Investment Penetration, Agrarian Change, and Political Conflict in Developing Countries' Studies in Comparative International Development, 30, 4: 46 - 62.

Rothschild K. W. (1944), 'The Small Nation and World Trade' *The Economic Journal,* April: 26 - 40.

Rothschild K. W. (1963), 'Kleinstaat und Integration' *Weltwirtschaftliches Archiv,* 90, 2: 239 - 275.

Rothschild K. W. (1966), *'Marktform, Loehne, Aussenhandel'* Vienna: Europa - Verlag.

Rothschild K. W. (1984), *'Politische Oekonomie in Oesterreich seit 1945'* Roma: Instituto A. Gramsci, 10 - 11.5 (mimeo).

Rothschild K. W. (1985), 'Felix Austria? Zur Evaluierung der Oekonomie und Politik in der Wirtschaftskrise' *Oesterreichische Zeitschrift fuer Politikwissenschaft,* 3: 261 - 274.

Rothschild K. W. (1993a), *'Employment, wages, and income distribution: critical essays in economics'* London; New York: Routledge.

Rothschild K. W. (1993b), *'Ethics and economic theory: ideas, models, dilemmas'* Aldershot, Hants., England; Brookfield, Vt.: E. Elgar.

Rothschild K. W. (1997), *'Some Considerations on the Economics and Politics of the EU and the Maastricht Treaty'* Vienna: quoted from the author's typescript.

Rouban L. (2005). "Europe: La Fracture Sociale - La Culture Sociopolitique des Salaries (The Social Divide in Europe - The Social and Political Worldview of the Workforce)." *Futuribles* 313 (November 2005): 5-26.

Rouban L. (2005). "Public/privé : la culture sociopolitique des salariés en Europe (Public Sector/Private Sector : The Sociopolitical World of European Workers)." Les Cahiers du CEVIPOF 40: 1-162.

Roubini N. and Sala-i-Martin X. (1992), 'Financial Repression and Economic Growth' *Journal of Development Economics,* Vol. 39: 5-30.

Rubinson R. (1976), 'The World - Economy and the Distribution of Income within States: A Cross - National Study' American Sociological Review, 41: 638 - 659.

Rummel R. R. (1994), 'Power, Genocide and Mass Murder' *Journal of Peace Research,* 31, 1: 1 - 10.

Rummel R. R. (1995), 'Democracy, Power, Genocide, and Mass Murder' *The Journal of Conflict Resolution,* 39, 1, March: 3 - 26.

Russell B. (1999), *„Philosophie des Abendlandes. Ihr Zusammenhang mit der politischen und sozialen Entwicklung (A History of Western Philosophy)'* Wien: Europa-Verlag.

Russett B. (1967), *'International Regions and the International System. A Study in Political Ecology'* Westport, Con.: Greenwood Press.

Russett B. (1978), 'The marginal utility of income transfers to the Third World' *International Organization,* 32, 4: 913 - 928.

Russett B. (1983a), 'International Interactions and Processes: The Internal versus External Debate Revisited' in *'Political Science: The State of the Discipline'* (Finifter A. (Ed.)), pp. 541 - 68, Washington D.C.: American Political Science Association.

Russett B. (1983b), 'The Peripheral Economies. Penetration and Economic Distortion, 1970 - 75' in *'Contending Approaches to World System Analysis'* (Thompson W.R. (Ed.)), pp. 79 - 114, Beverly Hills: Sage.

Russett B. (1994), 'The Democratic Peace' in *'Conflicts and New Departures in World Society'* (Bornschier V. and Lengyel P. (Eds.)), pp. 21 - 43, New Brunswick (U.S.A.) and London: Transaction Publishers, World Society Studies, Volume 3.

Russett B. M; Oneal J. R. and Cox M. (2000), 'Clash of Civilizations, or Realism and Liberalism Deja Vu? Some Evidence. *Journal of Peace Research,* vol. 37, no. 5, pp. 583.

Rutkowski M. (1998), *'A New Generation of Pension Reforms Conquers the East - A Taxonomy in Transition Economies'* World Bank Transition Newsletter, available at: http://www.worldbank.org/html/prddr/trans/julaug98/rutkowsk.htm.

Rutkowski M. (1999), *'The Quest for Modern Solutions: Pension Reforms in Transition Economies'* Presentation for the World Bank Conference 'Ten Years After: Transition and Growth in Pst-Communist Countries', Warsaw, poland, October 15-16; paper, available in two parts at http://www.wne.uw.edu.pl/~liberda/additional_materials/liberda/pan_ pension2.html.

Salt J. (1996), *'Current trends in international migration in Europe'* Council of Europe, 6th Conference of European Ministers responsible for migration affairs, MMG - 6 (96) 3 E, Warsaw, 16 - 18 June 1996.

Salt J. *et al.* (1999), *'Assessment of Possible Migration Pressure and Its Labour Market Impact Following EU Enlargement to Central and Eastern Europe'*. Migration Research Unit, Department of Geography, University College, London.

Samuelson P. (1964), 'Theoretical Notes on Trade Problems' *The Review of Economics and Statistics,* Vol. 46, No. 2, 145-154.

Samuelson P. A. (n.d.), *'Summing Up on Business Cycles: Opening Address »,* available at: http://www.bos.frb.org/economic/conf/conf42/con42_02.pdf.

Sapir A. (2005a), ‚Globalisation and the Reform of European Social Models'. Brussels, BRUEGEL Institute (Background document for the presentation at ECOFIN Informal Meeting in Manchester, 9 September 2005), available at: http://www.bruegel.org/ Repositories/Documents/publications/working_papers/SapirPaper080905.pdf .

Sapir A. (2005a), *‚Globalisation and the Reform of European Social Models'*. Brussels, BRUEGEL Institute (Background document for the presentation at ECOFIN Informal Meeting in Manchester, 9 September 2005), available at: http://www.bruegel.org/ Repositories/Documents/publications/working_papers/SapirPaper080905.pdf.

Sapir A. (2005a), ‚Globalisation and the Reform of European Social Models'. Brussels, BRUEGEL Institute (Background document for the presentation at ECOFIN Informal Meeting in Manchester, 9 September 2005), available at: http://www.bruegel.org/ Repositories/Documents/publications/working_papers/SapirPaper080905.pdf .

Sapir A. (2005b), ‚Globalisation and the Reform of European Social Models' Brussels, BRUEGEL Institute, bruegel policy brief, 01, November (restricted).

Sapir A. (2005b), ,Globalisation and the Reform of European Social Models' Brussels, BRUEGEL Institute, *bruegel policy brief,* 01, November (restricted).

Sapir A. (2005b), ,Globalisation and the Reform of European Social Models' Brussels, BRUEGEL Institute, bruegel policy brief, 01, November (restricted).

Sapir A. et al. (2004), *"An agenda for a growing Europe. Making the EU economic system deliver"* available at: http://www.euractiv.com/ndbtext/innovation/sapirreport.pdf

Sapir A. et al. (2004), "An agenda for a growing Europe. Making the EU economic system deliver" available at: http://www.euractiv.com/ndbtext/innovation/sapirreport.pdf

Savage T. M. (2004), 'Europe and Islam: Crescent Waxing, Cultures Clashing' The Washington Quarterly, Summer, 27, 3: 25-50, available at: http://www.twq.com/04summer/docs/04summer_savage.pdfsearch=%22crescent%20waxing%20savage%22

Savage T. M. (2004), 'Europe and Islam: Crescent Waxing, Cultures Clashing' The Washington Quarterly (Summer 2004), 27, 3: 25 – 50. Available at: http://www.twq.com/04summer/docs/04summer_savage.pdf#search=%22savage%20washington%20crescent%20waxing%22

Savage T. M. (2004), 'Europe and Islam: Crescent Waxing, Cultures Clashing' The Washington Quarterly, Summer, 27, 3: 25-50, available at: http://www.twq.com/04summer/docs/04summer_savage.pdf#search=%22crescent%20waxing%20savage%22

Sawada Y. and Yotopoulos P. A. (1999), *'Currency Substitution, Speculation, and Financial Crisis: Theory and Empirical Analysis.'* SIEPR Policy Paper Series No. 99- 5.

Sawada Y. and Yotopoulos P. A. (2002), 'On the Missing Link between Currency Substitution and Crises' *Zagreb International Review of Economics and Business,* vol. 5, no. VOL 2, pp. 83-104.

Scandella L. (1998), *'Le Kondratieff. Essai de théorie des cycles longs économiques et politiques'* Paris: Economica, Economie poche.

Scherman C. G. (2000), *'The Future of Social Security'* Ministry of Social Affairs and Health, Finland, available at: http://www.vn.fi/stm/english/tao/publicat/financing/scherman.htm.

Scheuregger D. and Spier T. (2005). "Working-class authoritarianism und die Wahl rechtspopulistischer Parteien - Eine ländervergleichende Untersuchung für Westeuropa (Working-Class Authoritarianism and the Vote for Right-Wing Populist Parties - A Comparative Analysis for Western Europe)." *Politische Herausforderungen im Verhältnis von Bürgern und Politik - Aktuelle Fragen der Wahl- und Einstellungsforschung,* Mannheim.

Schmidt M. G. (1983), 'The Welfare State and the Economy in Periods of Economic Crisis: A Comparative Study of Twenty - three OECD Nations' *European Journal of Political Research,* 11, 1: 1 - 26.

Schmidt M. G. (1986), 'Politische Bedingungen erfolgreicher Wirtschaftspolitik. Eine vergleichende Analyse westlicher Industrielaender (1960 - 1985), ' *Journal fuer Sozialforschung,* 26, 3: 251 - 273.

Schmitt J. and Zipperer B. (2006), 'Is the U.S. a Good Model for Reducing Social Exclusion in Europe?' Center for Economic and Policy Research, Washington D.C., available at: http://www.cepr.net/publications/social_exclusion_2006_08.pdfsearch=%22Is%20the%20US%20a%20Godd%20Model%20for%20Reducing%20Social%20Exclusion%20in%20Europe%20%22Is%20the%20U.S.%20a%20Good%20Model%20for%20Reducing%20Social%20Exclusion%20in%20Europe%22%22

Schmitt J. and Zipperer B. (2006), 'Is the U.S. a Good Model for Reducing Social Exclusion in Europe?' Center for Economic and Policy Research, Washington D.C., available at: http://www.cepr.net/publications/social_exclusion_2006_08.pdf#search=%22Is%20the%20US%20a%20Godd%20Model%20for%20Reducing%20Social%20Exclusion%20in%20Europe%20%22Is%20the%20U.S.%20a%20Good%20Model%20for%20Reducing%20Social%20Exclusion%20in%20Europe%22%22

Schneider F. and Enste D. (1998), *'Increasing shadow Economies all over the world - fiction or reality? A survey of the global evidence of their size and of their impact from 1970 to 1995'* Working Paper 9819, Department of Econocimcs, University of Linz, published on the Internet http://www.economics.uni-linz.ac.at/Members/Schneider/EnstSchn98.html.

Schnell S.R. and Trappmann T.M. (2006). *"The Effect of the Refusal Avoidance Training Experiment on Final Disposition Codes in ther German ESS 2"*. Konstanz, Center for Quantitative Methods and Survey Research, University of Konstanz. http://www.uni-konstanz.de/struktur/fuf/polfak/trappmann/RATESS2FINAL.pdf

Schultz T. P. (1998), `Inequality in the Distribution of Personal Income in the World: How it is Changing and Why', *Journal of Population Economics*, 11: 3 pp 307-344. Available at: http://www.econ.yale.edu/growth_pdf/cdp784.pdf.

Schulz B. (1999), 'Germany, the USA and Future Intercore Conflict' in *'The Future of Global Conflict'* (Bornschier V. and Chase-Dunn Ch. K. (Eds.)), pp. 226 - 243, London, Thousand Oaks and New Delhi: Sage Publications.

Schumpeter J. A. (1950), '*Capitalism, Socialism and Democracy*. Third Edition. New York & London: Harper & Row, 1975.

Schumpeter J. A. (1969), '*The Theory of Economic Development: An Inquiry into Profits, Capital, Credit, Interest, and the Business Cycle*. London and Oxford: Oxford University Press, 1969. Translated by Redvers Opie.

Schumpeter J. A. (1980), '*Kapitalismus, Sozialismus und Demokratie'* Munich: A. Francke, 5th printing, 1980 ('Capitalism, Socialism and Democracy' New York: Harper and Brothers).

Schumpeter J. A. (1982), *'Business cycles: a theoretical, historical, and statistical analysis of the capitalist process'* Philadelphia: Porcupine Press.

Schwartz H. (2000), 'Social Democracy Going Down or Down Under: Institutions, Internationalized Capital and Indebted States' University of Virginia, Department of Government and Foreign Affairs, available at: http://www.people.virginia.edu/~hms2f/social.html.

Schwartz S. H. and Rubel T. (2005). "Sex differences in value priorities: Cross-cultural and multi-method studies." *Journal of Personality and Social Psychology* 89(6).

Seers D. (Ed.)(1978), *'Underdeveloped Europe'* Hassocks: Harvester Press.

SEF (Stiftung Entwicklung und Frieden) (current issues), ‚*Globale Trends: Fakten, Analysen, Prognosen (edited by I. Hauchler)*. Frankfurt, Germany: Fischer.

Senghaas D. (1985), *'The European experience: a historical critique of development theory"*. Leamington Spa, Warwickshire; Dover, N.H., USA: Berg Publishers.

Senghaas D. (1989), 'Transcending Collective Violence, the Civilizing Process and the Peace Problem' in *'The Quest for Peace'* (Vaerynen R. et al. (Eds.)), pp. 3 - 18, London, Beverly Hills: Sage.

Senghaas D. (1994), *'Wohin driftet die Welt?: uber die Zukunft friedlicher Koexistenz'* Frankfurt am Main: Suhrkamp.

Senghaas D. (2002), *'Clash within civilizations: coming to terms with cultural conflicts'* London; New York: Routledge.

Senghaas D. (Ed.)(1971), *'Kritische Friedensforschung'* Frankfurt a.M.: edition suhrkamp.

Servan-Schreiber (1968), *'The American challenge'*. New York: Atheneum.

Shadid W. A. R. and van Koningsveld P. S. (Eds.)(1996). *'Political participation and identities of Muslims in non-Muslim states'*. Kampen, the Netherlands: Kok Pharos

Shafik N. and Bandyopadhyay S. (1992), *'Economic Growth and Environmental Quality. Time Series and Cross - Country Evidence'* Policy Research Working Papers, WPS, 904, Washington D.C.: The World Bank.

Shandra J. M., London B. and Williamson J. B. (2003), 'Environmental Degradation, Environmental Sustainability, and Overurbanization in the Developing World: A Quantitative, Cross-National Analysis' *Sociological Perspectives,* vol. 46, no. 3, pp. 309-330.

Shandra J. M., Ross R. J. S., London B. (2003), 'Global Capitalism and the Flow of Foreign Direct Investment to Non-Core Nations, 1980-1996: A Quantitative, Cross-National Analysis' *International Journal of Comparative Sociology,* Vol. 44, 199-238.

Shandra J. M.; London B.; Whooley O. P; Williamson J. B. (2004), 'International Nongovernmental Organizations and Carbon Dioxide Emissions in the Developing World: A Quantitative, Cross-National Analysis' *Sociological Inquiry,* Volume 74, Number 4, November, pp. 520-545.

Shandra J. M.; London B.; Williamson J. B. (2003), 'Environmental Degradation, Environmental Sustainability, and Overurbanization in the Developing World: A Quantitative, Cross-National Analysis' *Sociological Perspectives,* 2003, vol. 46, no. 3, pp. 309-330.

Shandra J. M.; Nobles J.; London B.; Williamson J. B. (2004), 'Dependency, democracy, and infant mortality: a quantitative, cross-national analysis of less developed countries.' *Social Science and Medicine,* vol. 59, no. 2, pp. 321-333.

Shandra J. M.; Nobles, J. E.; London B.; Williamson, J. B. (2005), 'Multinational Corporations, Democracy and Child Mortality: A Quantitative, Cross-National Analysis of Developing Countries' *Social Indicators Research,* vol. 73, no. 2, pp. 267-293.

Shandra J., London B, Whooley O. P., et al. (2004), 'International Nongovernmental Organizations and Carbon Dioxide Emissions in the Developing World: A Quantitative, Cross-National Analysis.' *Sociological Inquiry* 74, no. 4 (2004): 520-545.

Sharpe A. (2001), *'Estimates of Relative and Absolute Poverty Rates for the Working Population in Developed Countries'* Ottawa, Ontario, Canada: Centre for the Study of Living Standards, available at: http://www.csls.ca/events/cea01/sharpeilo.pdf

Shaw E. S. (1973), *'Financial Deepening in Economic Development'*. Oxford University Press, 1973.

Shaw T. M. (1994), *'The South at the end of the twentieth century: rethinking the political economy of foreign policy in Africa, Asia, the Caribbean, and Latin America'* New York: St. Martin's Press.

Shaw T. M. (1995), 'Globalization, Regionalisms and the South in the 1990s: Towards a New Political Economy of Development' *The European Journal of Development Research,* 7, 2, Dec.: 257 - 275.

Shen C. and Williamson J. B. (2001), 'Accounting for Cross-National Differences in Infant Mortality Decline (1965-1991) among less Developed Countries: Effects of Women's Status, Economic Dependency, and State Strength' *Social Indicators Research, 53,* no. 3 (2001): 257-288.

Shin M and Ward M. D. (1999), 'Lost in Space: Political Geography and the Defense-Growth Trade-Off.' *The journal of conflict resolution,* vol. 43, no. 6, pp. 793.

Shin M. E. (1975), 'Economic and Social Correlations of Infant Mortality: A Cross-Sectional and Longitudinal Analysis of 63 Countries. *Social Biology,* 22: 315 – 25.

Shin M. E. (2002), 'Income inequality, democracy and health: A global portrait' University of California, Los Angeles, Department of Geography, available at: http://www.colorado.edu/IBS/PEC/gadconf/papers/shin.pdf.

Siebert H. (2000), 'Pay-as-you-go pensions face a bleak future' *Financial Times,* 23 August, available from: http://www.globalaging.org/pension/world/pay-as-you-go.htm.

Siebert, H. (1997) *Weltwirtschaft.* Stuttgart, Germany: Lucius & Lucius.

Silver B. J. (1992), 'Class Struggle and Kondratiev Waves", in Alfred Kleinknecht, Ernest Mandel & Immanuel Wallerstein (eds), *New Findings in Long-Wave Research,* London & New York: Macmillan & St Martins Press, pp. 279-95.

Silver B. J. (1994), 'Cycles of Hegemony and Labor Unrest in the Contemporary World' in *'Conflicts and New Departures in World Society'* (Bornschier V. and Lengyel P. (Eds.)), pp. 339 - 359, New Brunswick (U.S.A.) and London: Transaction Publishers, World Society Studies, Volume 3.

Silverberg G. (2005), *'When is a Wave a Wave? Long Waves as Empirical and Theoretical Constructs from a Complex Systems Perspective'.* Maastricht Economic Research Institute on Innovation and Technology, MERIT Infonomics Research Memorandum series, 016, available at: http://www.merit.unimaas.nl/publications/rm.php?year_id=2005.

Silverberg G. And Soete L. (1994), 'The Economics of growth and technical change: technologies, nations, agents'. Aldershot, Hants., Brookfield, Vt.: E. Elgar.

Simpson M. (1990), 'Political Rights and Income Inequality: A Cross-National Test.' *American Sociological Review,* 55, pps. 682-693.

Singer P. I. (1971), *'Forca de trabalho e emprego no Brasil: 1920-1969. Com a assistencia de Frederico Mazzucchelli nos cálculos e na redacão do anexo metodológico'.* São Paulo, CEBRAP.

Singer P. I. (1971), *'Dinámica de la población y desarrollo'* Mexico D.F.: Ed. Siglo I.

Singer P. I. (1972), *'Milagre brasileiro': causas e consequencias'.* Sao Paulo, CEBRAP.

Singer P. I. (1973), *'Economia política da urbanizacão; [ensaios, por] Paul Singer.'* São Paulo: Editora Brasiliense, 1973..

Singer P. I. (1974), *'Elementos para uma teoria do emprego aplicável a países não desenvolvidos'* São Paulo: CEBRAP: Distributed by Editora Barsiliense.

Singer P. I. (1976), *'Crise do 'milagre': interpretacão crítica da economia brasileira'* Rio de Janeiro: Paz e Terra, 1976..

Singer P. I. (1977), *'Economia política do trabalho: elementos para uma análise histórico-estrutural do emprego e da forca de trabalho no desenvolvimento capitalista'* São Paulo: Editora Hucitec.

Singer P. I. (1981a), *'Dominacão e desigualdade: estrutura de classes e repartição da renda no Brasil'.* Rio de Janeiro, RJ: Paz e Terra.

Singer P. I. (1981b), 'O feminino e o feminismo' in *'Sao Paulo: O povo em movimento'* (Singer P.I. *et al.* (Eds.)), pp. 109 - 142, Petropolis, Rio de Janeiro: Editora Vozes.

Singer P. I. (1986), *'Reparticão da renda: pobres e ricos sob o regime militar'* Rio de Janeiro: J. Zahar.

Singer P. I. (1987), *'Dia da lagarta: democratizacão e conflito distributivo no Brasil do cruzado'* São Paulo, SP: Editora Brasiliense.

Singer P. I. (1988), *'Estado da transicão: política e economia na Nova República'* São Paulo, SP, Brasil: Vértice.

Singer P. I. (1991), *'Formacão da classe operária'* Campinas-SP: Editora da UNICAMP; São Paulo-SP: Atual Editora.

Singer P. I. (1998), *'Utopia militante: repensando o socialismo'* Petrópolis: Editora Vozes.

Singer P. I. (1999a), *'Brasil na crise: perigos e oportunidades'* São Paulo: Editora Contexto.

Singer P. I. (1999b), *'Globalizacão e desemprego: diagnóstico e alternativas'* São Paulo, SP: Editora Contexto.

Singer P. I. et al. (1977), *'Multinacionais: internacionalizacão e crise'*. São Paulo: Editora Brasiliense.

Smith D. A and London B. (1990), 'Convergence in World Urbanization?: A Quantitative Assessment'. *Urban affairs quarterly,* vol. 25, no. 4, pp. 574.

Smith D. A. (1994), 'Uneven Development and the Environment: Toward a World-System Perspective. *Humboldt Journal of Social Relations,* 20(1):151-175.

Smith D. A. (1996), *'Third World Cities in Global Perspective: The Political Economy of Uneven Urbanization'* Boulder, CO: Westview Press.

Smith D. and Wright S. (2000), *'Whose Europe?'* Malden MA: Blackwell.

So A. Y. (1990), *'Social Change and Development. Modernization, Dependency, and World - System Theories'* Newbury Park, CA.: Sage Library of Social Research, 178.

Soete L. (2005), *'Activating Knowledge'* Maastricht, NL: United Nations University (Discussion paper prepared for the UK Presidency, available at http://www.eu2005.gov.uk/servlet/Front?pagename=OpenMarket/Xcelerate/ShowPage&c=Page&cid=1107293391098&a=KArticle&aid=1119527321606).

Soysa I. de (2002), 'Ecoviolence: Shrinking Pie, or Honey Pot?' *Global Environmental Politics,* 2, no. 4 (2002): 1-34.

Soysa I. de (2003), *'Foreign direct investment, democracy, and development: assessing contours, correlates, and concomitants of globalization'* London, New York: Routledge.

Soysa I. de and Gleditsch N. P. (2002), 'The Liberal Globalist Case' in *'Global Governance in the 21st Century: Alternative Perspectives on World Order'* (Hettne B. and Oden B. (Eds.)), pp. 26 – 23. Stockholm: Almkvist & Wiksell. Availabla also at: http://www.egdi.gov.se/pdf/study/study2002_2.pdf.

Soysa I. de and John R. Oneal, J. R. (2000), 'Boon or bane?. Reassessing the productivity of foreign direct investment.' *Journal of Planning Literature,* 14, no. 4 (2000).

Soysa I. de and Neumayer E. (2005), 'False Prophet, or Genuine Savior? Assessing the Effects of Economic Openness on Sustainable Development, 1980-99' *International Organization,* 59, no. 3 (2005): 731-772.

Soysa I. De and Nordas R. (2006), *'Islam's Bloody Innards? Religion and Political Terror, 1980 – 2000'*. As yet unpublished Conference Paper, International Peace Research Institute, Oslo (PRIO), available at: http://www.prio.no/files/file48349_desoysa_nordas_wg3meeting.pdf

Spar D. (1999), 'Foreign Investment and Human Rights' *Challenge,* Vol. 42, 55 - 80.

Spiesberger M. (1998), 'Uebergangsregime zur Abfederung von Differenzen bei EG/EU-Beitritten' *Oesterreichische Zeitschrift fuer Politikwissenschaft,* 27, 4: 407 - 423.

Srubar I. (1994), 'Variants of the Transformation Process in Central Europe. A Comparative Assessment' *Zeitschrift fuer Soziologie,* 23, 3, Juni: 198 - 221.

St. John S. (1999), *'Retirement Policy Issues That We are Not Talking about'* New Zealand Association of Economists Annual Conference, Rotorua, 30th June - 2nd July, available at: http://www.geocities.com/Wellesley/Garden/9441/SusanStJohn/RotoruaConf1999.html.

Stack St and Zimmerman D. (1982), 'The Effect of World Economy on Income Inequality: A Reassessment.' *Sociological Quarterly,* 23(Summer): 345-358..

Stack St. (1978), 'The Effect of Direct Government Involvement in the Economy on the Degree of Income Inequality: A Cross-National Study.' *American Sociological Review,* 43 (December): 880-888..

Stack St. (1980), 'The Political Economy of Income Inequality: A Comparative Analysis.' *Canadian Journal of Political Science,* 13, pps. 273-286.

Stack St. (1998), 'Marriage, Family, and Loneliness: A Cross-National Study.' *Sociological Perspectives,* 41(2): 415-432..

Stacul J., Moutsou Chr. and Kopnina H. (Eds.)(2006); *'Crossing European boundaries: beyond conventional geographical categories'* New York: Berghahn Books

Stalker P. (1994), *'The Work of Strangers: A Survey of international labor migration'* Geneva: International Labor Office.

Stathopoulou, T. (2005). "Aspects of religiosity in Greece and Europe". 28th International Conference of ISSR (International Society for the Sociology of Religion), Zagreb.

Stiftung Entwicklung und Frieden (current issues), *'Globale Trends. Daten zur Weltentwicklung'* Frankfurt a.M.: Fischer Taschenbuch Verlag.

Stiglitz J. (1998), *'The Role of International Financial Institutions in the Current Global Economy'* World Bank, Address to the Chicago Council on Foreign Relations, available at: http://www.gdnet.org/tm-frame.html?http://www.worldbank.org/html/extdr/extme/jssp022798.htm.

Stilwell F. (2000), 'Globalization: How did we get to where we are? (and where can we go now?)' available at: http://www.phaa.net.au/conferences/stilwell.htm.

Stokes R. and Anderson A.. (1990), 'Disarticulation and Human Welfare in Less-Developed Countries.'. *American Sociological Review,* 55, pps. 63-74.

Stouffer S. A. and Lazarsfeld P. F. (1937), *'Research memorandum on the family in the depression.'* New York, N.Y., Social Science Research Council.

Strack M. (2005). "Organizing diverse sets of data with the Schwartz Value Circle". 1st European Association for Survey Research Conference, Barcelona. http://www.psych.uni-goettingen.de/abt/6/personal/strack/files/Strack_2005_EASR.pdf

Streissler E. (2002), *'Exchange Rates and International Finance Markets: An Asset-Theoretic Perspective with Schumpeterian Innovation'* London and New York: Routledge.

Strom St. et al. (Eds)(1998), *‚Econometrics and Economic Theory in the 20th Century: The Ragnar Frisch Centennial Symposium'* Cambridge, Cambridge University Press.

Sunkel O. (1966), 'The Structural Background of Development Problems in Latin America' *Weltwirtschaftliches Archiv,* 97, 1: pp. 22 ff.

Sunkel O. (1973a), 'Transnationale kapitalistische Integration und nationale Desintegration: der Fall Lateinamerika' in *'Imperialismus und strukturelle Gewalt. Analysen ueber abhaengige Reproduktion'* (Senghaas D. (Ed.)), pp. 258 - 315, Frankfurt a.M.: suhrkamp. English version: 'Transnational capitalism and national disintegration in Latin America' *Social and Economic Studies,* 22, 1, March: 132 - 76.

Sunkel O. (1973b), *'El subdesarrollo latinoamericano y la teoria del desarrollo'* Mexico: Siglo Veintiuno Editores, 6a edicion.

Sunkel O. (1978a), 'The Development of Development Thinking' in *'Transnational Capitalism and National Development. New Perspectives on Dependence'* (Villamil J.J. (Ed.)), pp. 19 - 30, Hassocks, Sussex: Harvester Press.

Sunkel O. (1978b), 'Transnationalization and its National Consequences' in *'Transnational Capitalism and National Development. New Perspectives on Dependence'* (Villamil J.J. (Ed.)), pp. 67 - 94, Hassocks, Sussex: Harvester Press.

Sunkel O. (1980), *'Transnacionalizacion y dependencia'* Madrid: Ediciones Cultura Hispanica del Instituto de Cooperacion Iberoamericana.

Sunkel O. (1984), *'Capitalismo transnacional y desintegracion nacional en America Latina'* Buenos Aires, Rep. Argentina: Ediciones Nueva Vision.

Sunkel O. (1990), *'Dimension ambiental en la planificacion del desarrollo.* English The environmental dimension in development planning ' 1st ed. Santiago, Chile: United Nations, Economic Commission for Latin America and the Caribbean.

Sunkel O. (1991*), 'El Desarrollo desde dentro: un enfoque neoestructuralista para la America Latina'* 1. ed. Mexico: Fondo de Cultura Economica.

Sunkel O. (1994), *'Rebuilding capitalism: alternative roads after socialism and dirigisme'* Ann Arbor, Mich.: University of Michigan Press.

Suter Ch. (1992), *'Debt Cycles in the World-Economy: Foreign Loans, Financial Crises, and Debt Settlements, 1820-1990'* Boulder, CO: Westview Press.

Suter Ch. (2005), 'Research on World Society and the Zurich School' in *'The Future of World Society'* (Herkenrath M. et al. (Eds.)) pp. 377 – 383; Sociological Institute, University of Zurich: Intelligent Book Production.

Szentes T. (1988), 'The political economy of underdevelopment'. Budapest: Akadémiai Kiadó

Szentes T. (1989), 'The transformation of the world economy: new directions and new interests'. Tokyo: United Nations University: London: Zed, 1989

Szentes T. (2002), 'Comparative theories and methods of international and development economics: a historical and critical survey.' Budapest: Akadémiai Kiadó, 2002

Szentes T. (2003a), 'The political economy of development globalisation and system transformation. (The political economy of underdevelopment -- revisited)' Budapest: Akadémiai Kiadó, 2003

Szentes T. (2003b), 'World economics' Budapest: Akadémiai Kiadó, 2002-2003.

Tausch A. (1979), *'Armut und Abhaengigkeit. Politik und Oekonomie im peripheren Kapitalismus'.* Studien zur österreichischen und internationalen Politik, Bd. 2 (Eds. P. GERLICH und A. PELINKA) W. Braumueller, Vienna http://www.braumueller.at/

Tausch A. (1986), 'Positions within the Global Order, Patterns of Defense Policies, and National Development: Austria and Pakistan Compared' in *'Security for the Weak Nations. A Multiple Perspective. A Joint Project of Pakistani and Austrian Scholars'* (S. FAROOQ HASNAT/PELINKA A. (Eds.)), Izharsons, Lahore: 245-255.

Tausch A. (1989), 'Armas socialistas, subdesarrollo y violencia estructural en el Tercer Mundo' *Revista Internacional de Sociologia, CSIC, Madrid,* 47, 4: 583-716.

Tausch A. (1989), 'Stable Third World Democracy and the European Model. A Quantitative Essay' in *'Crisis in Development'* (Z. BABLEWSKI and B. HETTNE (Eds.), The European Perspectives Project of the United Nations University, University of Gothenburg, PADRIGU-Papers: 131-161.

Tausch A. (1990), 'Quantitative aspects of a socio-liberal theory of world development'. *Economic Papers, Warsaw School of Economics, Research Institute for Developing Countries,* 23: 64 - 167.

Tausch A. (1991), *'Jenseits der Weltgesellschaftstheorien. Sozialtransformationen und der Paradigmenwechsel in der Entwicklungsforschung'.* (Eds. H. REINWALD, H.A. STEGER) Wilhelm Fink, Muenchen, Beitraege zur Soziologie und Sozialkunde Lateinamerikas (first printing, second printing at Grenzen und Horizonte (Eds. G. AMMON, H. REINWALD, H.A. STEGER) Eberhard, Muenchen)

Tausch A. (1991), *'Russlands Tretmühle. Kapitalistisches Weltsystem, lange Zyklen und die neue Instabilität im Osten'.* Eberhard, Muenchen

Tausch A. (1993), *'Produktivkraft soziale Gerechtigkeit? Europa und die Lektionen des pazifischen Modells'* Munich. Eberhard.

Tausch A. (1993; under collaboration of Fred PRAGER), *'Towards a Socio-Liberal Theory of World Development'.* Basingstoke and New York: Macmillan/St. Martin's Press

Tausch A. (1997), *'Schwierige Heimkehr. Sozialpolitik, Migration, Transformation, und die Osterweiterung der Europaeischen Union'* Munich: Eberhard.

Tausch A. (1998), *'Globalization and European Integration'* Electronic book publication at the World Systems Archive (Coordinator: Christopher K. Chase-Dunn, Johns Hopkins University), http://csf.colorado.edu/wsystems/archive/books/tausch/tauschtoc.htm.

Tausch A. (1998), *‚Transnational Integration and National Disintegration.'* Electronic book publication, World Systems Archive, University of California at Riverside, available at: http://wsarch.ucr.edu/archive/papers/tausch/t1/tausch1.htm and http://wsarch.ucr.edu/archive/papers/tausch/t2/tausch2.htm.

Tausch A. (1999, with Andreas Müller OFM and Paul Zulehner), *"Global Capitalism, Liberation Theology and the Social Sciences. An analysis of the contradictions of modernity at the turn of the millennium"* (with contributions by Samir Amin et. al) Huntington, New York: Nova Science. Paperback edition 2001

Tausch A. (2001), 'Mature Economy' in *'Routledge Encyclopedia of Political Economy'* (Ed. R. J. Barry Jones) Vol. 2, pp. 1007 – 1008. London and New York: Routledge

Tausch A. (2001), *'Sozial- und gesundheitspolitische Aspekte der EU-Erweiterung'* Band 48, Schriftenreihe des Zentrums für europäische Studien, Jean Monnet Lehrstuhl für europäische Studien, Universität Trier http://www.uni-trier.de/zes/bd48.html.

Tausch A. (2001, with Gernot Köhler), *'Global Keynesianism: Unequal exchange and global exploitation'.* Huntington NY, Nova Science. ISBN 1-59033-002-1. Paperback edition 2001

Tausch A. (2001, with Peter Herrmann), *'Globalization and European Integration'.* Huntington NY, Nova Science. ISBN: 1-560729295.

Tausch A. (2002), 'Evropeiskii Sojus i budushaja mirovaja sistema" in *Evropa,* 2(3), 2002: 23 – 62, Warsaw, Polish Institute for International Affairs (in Russian language).

Tausch A. (2002), 'The European Union and the World System'. In: *'The European Union in the World System Perspective'* (The Polish Institute for International Affairs, Ryszard Stemplowski (Ed.)), Warsaw: Collections PISM (Polish Institute for International Affairs): 45 – 93.

Tausch A. (2002), 'The European Union and the World System'. In: *'The European Union in the World System Perspective'* (The Polish Institute for International Affairs, Ryszard Stemplowski (Ed.)), Warsaw: Collections PISM (Polish Institute for International Affairs): 45 – 93..

Tausch A. (2003), (Ed.) *'The Three Pillars of Wisdom? A Reader on Globalization, World Bank Pension Models and Welfare Society'*. Nova Science Hauppauge, New York, 2003

Tausch A. (2003), 'Social Cohesion, Sustainable Development and Turkey's Accession to the European Union'. *Alternatives: Turkish Journal of International Relations,* 2, 1, Spring http://www.alternativesjournal.net/ and http://www.alternativesjournal.net/volume2/number1/tausch.htm.

Tausch A. (2003), 'The European Union: Global Challenge or Global Governance? 14 World System Hypotheses and Two Scenarios on the Future of the Union' in *'Globalization: Critical Perspectives'* (Gernot Kohler and Emilio José Chaves (Editors)), pp. 93 – 197, Hauppauge, New York: Nova Science Publishers.

Tausch A. (2003), 'Jevropejskaja perspektiva: po puti k sosdaniju 'obshtshevo srjedisemnomorskovo doma' i integrirovaniju polozytelnovo potencjala obshestvjennovo razvitija islamskich stran' *Evropa,* 4 (9), 2003: 87 – 109, Warsaw, Polish Institute for International Affairs (in Russian language).

Tausch A. (2004), 'Die EU-Erweiterung und die soziale Konvergenz. Ein 'Working Paper' zur Globalisierung und wachsenden Ungleichheit im neuen und alten Europa' *Studien von Zeitfragen,* ISSN-1619-8417, 38(2): 1 – 185 http://druckversion.studien-von-zeitfragen.net/Soziale%20Konvergenz%20EU-Erweiterung.pdf.

Tausch A. (2004), 'Europa - groß und mächtig?' In *"Solidarität. Gesellschaft, Gemeinschaft und Individuum in Vergangenheit, Gegenwart und Zukunft"* (Michael Rosecker and Bernhard Müller (Eds)) Wiener Neustadt, Austria: Verein Alltag Verlag, ISBN 3--902282-02-9: pp. 98 - 126

Tausch A. (2004), ‚*Soziale und regionale Ungleichgewichte, politische Instabilität und die Notwendigkeit von Pensionsreformen im neuen Europa'* Schriftenreihe des Zentrums für europäische Studien, Universität Trier, Band 56, ISSN 0948-1141 http://www.uni-trier.de/zes/schriftenreihe/056.pdf.

Tausch A. (2004), ‚Towards a European Perspective for the Common Mediterranean House and the Positive Development Capability of Islamic Countries' In , *European Neighbourhood Policy: Political, Economic and Social Issues'* (Fulvio Attina and Rosa Rossi (Eds.) Università degli Studi di Catania Facoltà di Scienze Politiche: 145 – 168. Also available as a Jean Monnet e-book at http://www.fscpo.unict.it/EuroMed/cjmEBOOKSengl.htm.

Tausch A. (2004), ‚Waiting for the Next Tsunami' *Asia Times,* 5, 21 – October 2004: 1 – 5; http://www.atimes.com/atimes/archive/10_20_2004.html.

Tausch A. (2005), ‚Did recent trends in world society make multinational corporations penetration irrelevant? Looking back on Volker Bornschier's development theory in the light of recent evidence'. *Historia Actual On-Line,* 6 (2005), available at http://www.hapress.com/abst.php?a=n06a05.

Tausch A. (2005), ‚Europe, the Muslim Mediterranean and the End of the era of Global Confrontation'. *Alternatives. Turkish Journal of International Relations,* Volume 3, Number 4, Winter 2004, 1-29; available at: http://www.alternativesjournal.net/volume3/number4/arno3.pdf.

Tausch A. (2005), 'Is Islam really a development blockade? 12 predictors of development, including membership in the Organization of Islamic Conference, and their influence on 14 indicators of development in 109 countries of the world with completely available data'. Ankara Center for Turkish Policy Studies, ANKAM, *Insight Turkey,* 7, 1, 2005: 124 - 135. Full PDF version available at http://www.insightturkey.com/tausch2005_multivariate_analysis_world_dev.pdf.

Tausch A. (2005, with Peter Herrmann), *'Dar al Islam. The Mediterranean, the World System and the Wider Europe.* Vol. 1: The "Cultural Enlargement" of the EU and Europe's Identity; Vol. 2: The Chain of Peripheries and the New Wider Europe'. Hauppauge, New York: Nova Science Publishers. Abridged paperback editions 2006 under the title: "The West, Europe and the Muslim World" (Vol. 1) and "Towards a Wider Europe" (Vol. 2)

Tausch A. (2005, with Russell A. Berman) „Yet Another reason They Dislike Us. „Europe is rich, but the United States is richer." *Hoover Digest,* 2005, 1: 69–73

Tausch A. (2006) 'On heroes, villains and statisticians'. *The Vienna Institute Monthly Report,* No. 7, July 2006: 20 - 23. Vienna: The Vienna Institute for International Economic Studies (wiiw)

Tausch A. (2006), *'The City on a Hill? The Latin Americanization of Europe and the Lost Competition with the U.S.A.'* Amsterdam: Rozenberg and Dutch University Press.

Tausch A. (2006), ‚Für Rückkehr der Vernunft in der Türkei-Politik' *Europäische Rundschau,* 34, 1: 121 - 132

Tausch A. (2006, with Almas Heshmati) 'Turkey and the Lisbon process. A short research note on the position of Turkey on a new "Lisbon Strategy Index" (LSI).' Ankara Institute for Turkish Policy Studies, ANKAM, *Insight Turkey,* 8, 2, 2006: 7 – 18.

Tausch A. (2006, with Christian Bischof, Tomaz Kastrun and Karl Mueller), 'Why Europe has to offer a better deal towards its Muslim communities.A quantitative analysis of open international data.' Electronic book, http://ideas.repec.org/b/erv/ebooks/b001.html ; published in the series Entelequia. Revista Interdisciplinar, University of Malaga, Spain, ISBN: 84-690-1558-3, depósito legal en la Biblioteca Nacional de España número de registro: 06/78410.

Tausch A. (2007, forthcoming), 'From the "Washington" towards a "Vienna Consensus"? A quantitative analysis on globalization, development and global governance'. Hauppauge, N.Y.: Nova Science Publishers.

Tausch A. (2007, forthcoming, with Almas Heshmati), 'Roadmap to Bangalore? Globalization, the EU's Lisbon Process and the Structures of Global Inequality' Hauppauge, N.Y.: Nova Science Publishers.

Tausch A. (2007, with Christian Bischof and Karl Mueller) *'Muslim Calvinism'* Amsterdam: Dutch University Press (under review).

Tellis A. J. et al. (2001), *'Measuring National Power in the Postindustrial Age'* Santa Monica, California: The Rand Corporation.

Telo M. and Telr M. (2006), *'Europe: A Civilian Power? European Union, Global Governance, World Order'.* Basingstoke: Palgrave.

The New Economics Foundation (2007), *"Happy Planet Index",* available at http://www.happyplanetindex.org/list.htm

The PEW Research Center for the People and the Press (2006), "The Great Divide: How Westerners and Muslims View Each Other. Europe's Muslims More Moderate" PEW, Washington D.C.: http://pewglobal.org/reports/display.php?ReportID=253 (June 22, 2006)

The World Bank Group (2000), 'Flagship Course in Pension Reform' available at: http://www.worldbank.org/wbi/pensionflagship/.

Therborn G. (1985), *'Arbeitslosigkeit. Strategien und Politikansaetze in OECD - Laendern'* Hamburg: VSA.

Therborn G. (1986), 'Karl Marx Returning. The Welfare State and Neo - Marxist, Corporatist and Statist Theories' *International Political Science Review,* 7, 2, April: 131 - 164.

Thompson W. R. (1983a), 'Cycles, Capabilities and War: An Ecumenical View' in *'Contending Approaches to World System Analysis'* (Thompson W.R. (Ed.)), pp. 141 - 163, Beverly Hills: Sage.

Thompson W. R. (1983b), 'The World - Economy, the Long Cycle, and the Question of World - System Time' in *'Foreign Policy and the Modern World System'* (Mc Gowan P. and Kegley Ch.W.Jr. (Eds.)), pp. 35 - 62, Beverly Hills: Sage.

Thompson W. R. (1999), *'Great Power Rivalries'* Columbus: University of South Carolina Press.

Thompson W. R. (2001), *'Evolutionary Interpretations of World Politics'* London and New York: Routledge.

Thompson W. R. and Modelski G. (1994), 'Long Cycle Critiques and Deja Vu All Over Again: A Rejoinder to Houweling and Siccama.' *International interactions,* 1994, vol. 20, no. 3, pp. 209.

Tibi B. (1973), *„Militär und Sozialismus in der Dritten Welt: allgemeine Theorien und Regionalstudien über arabische Länder'.* Frankfurt am Main: Suhrkamp.

Tibi B. (1981), *'Arab nationalism: a critical enquiry. Edited and translated by Marion Farouk-Sluglett and Peter Sluglett'* London: MacMillan Press, 1981..

Tibi B. (1985), *'Der Islam und das Problem der kulturellen Bewältigung sozialen Wandels'* Frankfurt am Main: Suhrkamp, 1991.

Tibi B. (1990), *'Arab nationalism: a critical enquiry'* New York, N.Y.: St. Martin's Press.

Tibi B. (1992), 'Kreuzzug oder Dialog? Der Westen und die arabo - islamische Welt nach dem Golfkrieg' in *'Kreuzzug oder Dialog. Die Zukunft der Nord - Sued - Beziehungen'* (Matthies V. (Ed.)), pp. 107 - 120, Bonn: J.H.W. Dietz Nachfolger.

Tibi B. (

Tibi B. (1997a), *'Arab nationalism: between Islam and the nation-state'* New York: St. Martin's Press.

Tibi B. (1997b), *'Challenge of fundamentalism: political Islam and the new world disorder'.* Berkeley: University of California Press.

Tibi B. (1997c), *'Conflict and war in the Middle East, 1967-91: regional dynamic and the superpowers. Translated by Clare Krojzl'.* Houndmills, Basingstoke, Hampshire: Macmillan in association with the Center for International Affairs, Harvard University.

Tibi B. (1998a*), 'Conflict and war in the Middle East: from interstate war to new security'* New York: St. Martin's Press.

Tibi B. (1998b), *'Crisis of modern Islam: a preindustrial culture in the scientific-technological age. Translated by Judith von Sivers; foreword by Peter von Sivers'*. Salt Lake City: University of Utah Press.

Tibi B. (2001a), *'Islam between culture and politics'*. New York: Palgrave, in association with the Weatherhead Center for International Affairs, Harvard University.

Tibi B. (2001b), *'Kreuzzug und Djihad. Der Islam und die christliche Welt'*. München: Goldmann Taschenbuchausgabe.

Tibi B. (2002), *'Islamische Zuwanderung: die gescheiterte Integration'* München: Deutsche Verlags-Anstalt.

Till M. (2002), *'Risk of Poverty and Social Exclusion in Europe'* The Interdisciplinary Centre for Comparative Research in the Social Sciences, ICCR, Vienna, available at: http://www.iccr-international.org/impact/docs/till.doc

Tilly Ch. (1992), *'Coercion, Capital, and European States, Ad 990 – 1992'* Malden MA: Blackwell.

Timberlake M. and Kantor J. (1983), 'Economic Growth: A Study of the Less Developed Countries' *Sociological Quarterly*, 24: 489 - 507.

Timberlake M. and Williams K.R. (1984), 'Dependence, Political Exclusion, and Government Repression: Some Cross - National Evidence' *American Sociological Review*, 49: 141 - 46.

Timberlake M. and Williams K.R. (1987), 'Structural Position in the World - System, Inequality and Political Violence' *Journal of Political and Military Sociology*, 15: 1 - 15.

Togan S. (2002), 'Turkey and the EU: The Economics of Accession' Bilkent University, Ankara, available at: http://www.gdnet.org/tm-frame.html?http://www.bilkent.edu.tr/~togan/Turkey_Paper.

Tovias A. (2002), *'The Political Economy of the Partnership in Comparative Perspective'* The Hebrew University of Jerusalem, Department of International Relations, available at: http://ies.berkeley.edu/research/AlfredTovias.pdf.

Trezzini B. and Bornschier V. (2001*)*, *'Social Stratification and Mobility in the World System: Different Approaches and Recent Research'* Department of Sociology, University of Zurich, available at: http://www.suz.unizh.ch/bornschier/publikationen.pdf.

Troll S.J. Chr. (2001*)*, "Muslime in Deutschland. Ziele, Strömungen, Ogranisationen/ Strukturen"
http://www.jesuiten.org/aktuell/jubilaeum/files/jahresthema_2001_troll_1.pdf

Troll S.J. Chr. (2001), "Muslime in Deutschland. Ziele, Strömungen, Ogranisationen/ Strukturen"
http://www.jesuiten.org/aktuell/jubilaeum/files/jahresthema_2001_troll_1.pdf

Tsai P-L. (1995), 'Foreign Direct Investment and Income Inequality: Further Evidence.' *World Development*, 23, 3, pps. 469-483.

Tsoukalis L. (2005), '2005), *'Why we Need a Globalisation and Adjustment Fund'* Athens: Hellenic Foundation for European and Foreign Policy (Discussion paper prepared for the UK Presidency, available at http://www.eu2005.gov.uk/servlet/Front?pagename=OpenMarket/Xcelerate/ShowPage&c=Page&cid=1107293391098&a=KArticle&aid=1119527321606).

Turner J. (2000), 'Social security reform around the world' Public Policy Institute AARP, Washington DC, available at: http://www.pensions-research.org/attachments/march2001/Social%20Security%20around%20the%20world.pdf.

Twomey M. J. (1993), *'Multinational Corporations and the North American Free Trade Agreement'* New York: Frederic Praeger Publishers.

United Kingdom Foreign and Commonwealth Office (2004), "*Draft Report on Young Muslims and Extremism*". UK Foreign and Commonwealth Office/Home Office, available at: http://www.globalsecurity.org/security/library/report/2004/muslimext-uk.htm

United Kingdom Foreign and Commonwealth Office (2004), "Draft Report on Young Muslims and Extremism". UK Foreign and Commonwealth Office/Home Office, available at: http://www.globalsecurity.org/security/library/report/2004/muslimext-uk.htm

United Nations (1995) *International Trade Statistics Yearbook* 1995, 2 Vols..

United Nations (2005) '*United Nations Human Development Report*'. New York and Oxford: Oxford University Press.

United Nations Centre on Transnational Corporations (1983), *'Transnational Corporations in World Development'* New York: United Nations.

United Nations Conference on Trade and Development (current issues), '*World Investment Report.*' New York and Geneva: United Nations.

United Nations Department of Economic and Social Affairs (2004), '*World Economic and Social Survey 2004. International Migration*' New York: United Nations. Available at: http://www.un.org/esa/policy/wess/wess2004files/part2web/part2web.pdf

United Nations Department of Economic and Social Affairs (2004), 'World Economic and Social Survey 2004. International Migration' New York: United Nations. Available at: http://www.un.org/esa/policy/wess/wess2004files/part2web/part2web.pdf

United Nations Development Programme (1998a), '*Overcoming Human Poverty*'. UN New York, UNDP.

United Nations Development Programme (1998b), '*The Shrinking State*' UN New York, UNDP.

United Nations Development Programme (2004), '*Reducing Disaster Risk. A Challenge for Development. A Global Report*'. UNDP Bureau for Crisis Prevention and Recovery, available at: http://www.undp.org/bcpr/disred/documents/publications/rdr/english/rdr_english.pdf.

United Nations Development Programme (2005a), '*Governance Indicators: A users' Guide*'. Oslo and New York, United Nations Development Programme, Oslo Governance Centre, available at: http://www.undp.org/oslocentre/docs04/UserGuide.pdf.

United Nations Development Programme (2005b), '*Overview Existing Framework of Governance Indicators*' available at: Oslo and New York, United Nations Development Programme, Oslo Governance Centre, http://www.undp.org/oslocentre/docsjuly03/Overview%20Existing%20Framework%20of%20Indicators.xls.

United Nations Development Programme (current issues), *'Human Development Report'* New York and Oxford: Oxford University Press.

United Nations Development Programme, Arab Fund for Economic and Social Development (2002), '*Arab Human Development Report 2002. Creating Opportunities for Future Generations*' Cairo and New York: United Nations Development Programme Regional Bureau for Arab States (RBAS).

United Nations Development Programme, Regional Bureau for Europe and the CIS (1999), *'Human Development Report for Central and Eastern Europe and the CIS'* New York: UNDP.

United Nations Economic and Social Council (1993a), *'International Migration Flows among ECE Countries'* New York: United Nations Economic Commission for Europe CES 778, 27 May.

United Nations Economic and Social Council (1993b), *'International Migration Flows Among ECE Countries, 1991'* New York: United Nations, CES/778, 27 May.

United Nations Economic Commission for Europe (1994), *'International Migration: Regional Processes and Responses'* Geneva: United Nations Economic Commission for Europe Economic Studies, 7 (entire).

United Nations Economic Commission for Europe (1996), *'International Migration in Central and Eastern Europe and the Commonwealth of Independent States'* Geneva: United Nations Economic Commission for Europe Economic Studies, 8 (entire).

United Nations Economic Commission for Europe (1998), *'In-Depth Studies on Migration in Central and Eastern Europe: The Case of Poland'* Geneva: United Nations Economic Commission for Europe Economic Studies, 11 (entire).

United Nations Economic Commission for Europe (current issues), *'Economic Survey of Europe'* New York: United Nations.

United Nations Economic Commission for Europe and United Nations Population Fund (1998), *'In-Depth Studies on Migration in Central and Eastern Europe: The Case of Poland'* Geneva: United Nations Economic Commission for Europe, Economic Studies, 11 (entire).

United Nations Economic Commission for Latin America, ECLAC/CEPAL, (2002), *'Globalización y desarrollo".* available at: http://www.eclac.cl/cgi-bin/get Prod.asp?xml=/publicaciones/xml/6/10026/P10026.xml&xsl=/tpl/p9f.xsl&base=/MDG/tp l/top-bottom.xsl.

United States Arms Control and Disarmament Agency (current issues), *'World Military Expenditures and Arms Transfers'* Washington DC.: US Government Printing Office.

United States Central Intelligence Agency, National Foreign Intelligence Board (2001), *'Growing Global Migration and Its Implications for the United States'* Langley, Virginia, National Foreign Intelligence Board, NIE 2001-02D, March 2001, available at: http://www.cia.gov/nic/graphics/migration.pdf.

United States Department of State (curent issues), *'International Drug Control Strategy Report'* Washington D.C.: US Government Printing Office.

United States Department of State (current issues), *'Country Reports on Human Rights Practices'* Washington D.C.: US Government Printing Office.

United States Government (2002), 'The National Security Strategy of the United States of America". The White House, Washington D.C., available at: http://www.state.gov/ documents/organization/15538.pdf.

University of Rotterdam (2007), *'World Database of Happiness - Happiness in Nations'* available at http://www1.eur.nl/fsw/happiness/hap_nat/nat_fp.htm

Vaeyrynen R. (1987), 'Global Power Dynamics and Collective Violence' in *'The Quest for Peace. Transcending Collective Violence and War among Societies, Cultures and States'* (Vaerynen R. *et al.* (Eds.)), pp. 80 - 96, London: Sage.

Vaeyrynen R. (1997), *'Post-Hegemonic and Post-Socialist Regionalism: A Comparison of East Asia and Central Europe'* University of Notre Dame, The Joan B. Kroc Institute Occasional Papers, Internet edition, http://www.nd.edu/.

Van Apeldoom B. (2002), *'Transnational Capitalism and the Struggle over European Integration'* London and New York: Routledge.

Van Rossem R. (1996), 'The World System Paradigms General Theory of Development: A Cross - National Test' *American Sociological Review,* 61, June: 508 - 527.

Vedder R. K. and Gallaway L. E. (1999), *'Unemployment and Jobs in International Perspective'* Joint Economic Committee Study, United States Congress, http://www.house.gov/jec/employ/intern.htm.

Vertovec S. (Ed.)(1998), *'Muslim European youth: reproducing ethnicity, religion, culture'.* Aldershot, England; Brookfield, Vt., USA: Ashgate.

Vertovec S. and Peach C. (Eds.)(1997), *'Islam in Europe: the politics of religion and community'.* New York: St. Martin's Press

Vickrey W. (1996), *'Fifteen Fatal Fallacies of Financial Fundamentalism. A Disquisition on Demand Side Economics'* New York: Columbia University, Web-Site: http://www.columbia.edu/dlc/wp/econ/vickrey.htm.

Wagstaff A. and Watanabe N. (2002), *'Socioeconomic Inequalities in Child Malnutrition in the Developing World'* World Bank Working Papers health and Population at: http://econ.worldbank.org/files/1189_wps2434.pdf.

Walker R. A. (1989), *'The Capitalist Imperative: Territory, Technology and Industrial Growth'.* Oxford: Basil Blackwell..

Walker R. A. (1992), *'The New Social Economy: Reworking the Division of Labor.'* Cambridge, MA: Basil Blackwell..

Walker R. A. (1995), 'Regulation and flexible specialization as theories of capitalist development. Challengers to Marx and Schumpeter?' in: *'Spatial Practices: Critical Explorations in Social/Spatial Theory.'* (Liggett H. and Perry D. (Eds.)) pp. 167-208, London: Sage.

Walker R. A. (1996), 'California's collision of race and class' *Representations,* No. 55, 163-183, Summer. Reprinted: Robert Post and Michael Rogin (eds.), Race and Representation: Affirmative Action. New York: Zone Books, 1998, pp. 281-308.

Walker R. A. (1999a), 'Capital's global turbulence'. *Against the Current* 78, January-February 1999: 29-35.

Walker R. A. (1999b), 'Putting capital in its place: globalization and the prospects for labor'. *Geoforum.* 30/3: 263-84.

Walker R. A. (2004a), *'The Conquest of Bread: 150 Years of California Agribusiness'.* New York: The New Press.

Walker R. A. (2004b), 'The Spectre of Marxism -- The Return of The Limits to Capital'. *Antipode* (June) 36:3.

Wallerstein I. (1974), 'The Modern *World-System 1: Capitalist Agriculture and the Origins of the European World-Economy in the Sixteenth Century'.* New York & London: Academic Press.

Wallerstein I. (1976), 'Semi - Peripheral Countries and the Contemporary World Crisis' *Theory and Society,* 4: 461 - 483.

Wallerstein I. (1978), 'World-System Analysis: Theoretical and Interpretive Issues, ' in: Kaplan, B.H. (ed.), *Social Change in the Capitalist World Economy.* Beverly Hills, USA: SAGE Publishing, p. 219-235.

Wallerstein I. (1979a), *'The Capitalist World Economy'* Cambridge, England: Cambridge University Press.

Wallerstein I. (1979b), 'Underdevelopment and Phase B: Effect of the Seventeenth - Century Stagnation on Core and Periphery of the European World - Economy' in *'The World - System of Capitalism: Past and Present'* (Goldfrank W.L. (Ed.)), pp. 73 - 85, Beverly Hills: Sage.

Wallerstein I. (1980), 'The Modern *World-System II: Mercantilism and the Consolidation of the European World-economy, 1600-1750'.* New York & London: Academic Press.

Wallerstein I. (1982), 'Socialist States: Mercantilist Strategies and Revolutionary Objectives' in *'Ascent and Decline in the World - System'* (Friedman E. (Ed.)), pp. 289 - 300, Beverly Hills: Sage.

Wallerstein I. (1983a), 'Crises: The World Economy, the Movements, and the Ideologies' in *'Crises in the World - System'* (Bergesen A. (Ed.)), pp. 21 - 36, Beverly Hills: Sage.

Wallerstein I. (1983b), *'Historical Capitalism'* London: Verso.

Wallerstein I. (1984), *'Der historische Kapitalismus. Uebersetzt von Uta Lehmann - Grube mit einem Nachwort herausgegeben von Hans Heinrich Nolte'* Westberlin: Argument - Verlag.

Wallerstein I. (1986), "Krise als Uebergang' in *'Dynamik der globalen Krise'* (Amin S. and associates), pp. 4 - 35, Opladen: Westdeutscher Verlag.

Wallerstein I. (1989a), 'The Modern *World-System III: The Second Era of Great Expansion of the Capitalist World-Economy, 1730-1840s'.* New York & London: Academic Press.

Wallerstein I. (1989b), *'The National and the Universal: Canada There Be Such a Thing as World Culture?'.* Fernand Braudel Centre for the Study of Economies, Historical Systems, and Civilizations, Binghamton, New York: Suny Binghamton.

Wallerstein I. (1990), *'America and the World: Today, Yesterday, and Tomorrow'* Fernand Braudel Centre for the Study of Economies, Historical Systems, and Civilizations, Binghamton, New York: Suny Binghamton.

Wallerstein I. (1991a), *'The Concept of National Development, 1917 - 1989: Elegy and Requiem'* Fernand Braudel Centre for the Study of Economies, Historical Systems, and Civilizations, Binghamton, New York: Suny Binghamton.

Wallerstein I. (1991b), *'Who Excludes Whom? or The Collapse of Liberalism and the Dilemmas of Antisystemic Strategy'* Fernand Braudel Centre for the Study of Economies, Historical Systems, and Civilizations, Binghamton, New York: Suny Binghamton.

Wallerstein I. (1997), *'The Rise of East Asia, or The World-System in the Twenty-First Century'* SUNY Binghamton, http://fbc.binghamton.edu/iwrise-htm.

Wallerstein I. (1998), *'Is Japan Rising or Declining?'* Commentary 3, 1, Fernand Braudel Center, Binghamton University.

Wallerstein I. (2000), *'The Essential Wallerstein'* New York: The New Press.

Wallerstein M. (1989), 'Union Organization in Advanced Industrial Democracies' *American Political Science Review,* 83, 2, June: 481 - 501.

Ward K. B. (1984), *'Women in the World-System: Its Impact on Status and Fertility'.* New York: Frederic Praeger.

Warner C. M. and Wenner M. W. (2002), *'Organizing Islam for Politics in Western Europe'*. Hoover Institution, Stanford University, available at http://faculty.washington.edu/tgill/544%20Warner%20Islam%20Europe.pdf

Warner C. M. and Wenner M. W. (2002), 'Organizing Islam for Politics in Western Europe'. Hoover Institution, Stanford University, available at http://faculty.washington.edu/tgill/544%20Warner%20Islam%20Europe.pdf

Weede E. (1985), *'Entwicklungslaender in der Weltgesellschaft'* Opladen: Westdeutscher Verlag.

Weede E. (1986a), 'Catch - up, distributional coalitions and government as determinants of economic growth or decline in industrialized democracies' *The British Journal of Sociology,* 37, 2: 194 - 220.

Weede E. (1986b), 'Verteilungskoalitionen, Staatstaetigkeit und Stagnation' *Politische Vierteljahresschrift,* 27, 2: 222 - 236.

Weede E. (1989), 'Democracy and Inequality Reconsidered.' *American Sociological Review,* 54, pps. 865-868.

Weede E. (1990), *'Wirtschaft, Staat und Gesellschaft'* Tübingen: J.C.B. Mohr.

Weede E. (1992), *'Mensch und Gesellschaft. Soziologie aus der Perspektive des methodoligischen Individualismus'* Tuebingen: J.C.B. Mohr.

Weede E. (1993a), *'Development and underdevelopment: the political economy of inequality'.* Boulder, Colo.: L. Rienner Publishers.

Weede E. (1993b), 'The Impact of Democracy or Repressiveness on the Quality of Life, Income Distribution and Economic Growth Rates.' *International Sociology,* 8, pps. 177-195.

Weede E. (1994), 'Determinanten der Kriegsverhuetung waehrend des Kalten Krieges und danach: Nukleare Abschreckung, Demokratie und Freihandel' *Politische Vierteljahresschrift,* 35, 1: 62 - 84.

Weede E. (1996a), *'Economic development, social order, and world politics with special emphasis on war, freedom, the rise and decline of the West, and the future of East Asia'.* Boulder: L. Rienner Publishers.

Weede E. (1996b), 'Political Regime Type and Variation in Economic Growth Rates' *Constitutional Political Economy,* 7, no. 3 (1996): 167 (10 pages).

Weede E. (1997), 'Income inequality, democracy and growth reconsidered.' *European Journal of Political Economy,* Volume 13, Number 4, December 1997, pp. 751.

Weede E. (1999a), 'Economic development, social order, and world politics'. *Peace Research Abstracts,* 36, no. 3.

Weede E. (1999b), 'Future Hegemonic Rivalry between China and the West?' in *'The Future of Global Conflict'* (Bornschier V. and Chase-Dunn Ch. K. (Eds.)), pp. 244 - 262, London, Thousand Oaks and New Delhi: Sage Publications.

Weede E. (2002), 'Impact of Intelligence and Institutional Improvements on Economic Growth'. *Kyklos,* 55, no. 3 (2002): 361-380.

Weede E. (2003), 'On the Rise and Decline of Two Nations' *International Interactions,* 29, no. 4 (2003): 343-364.

Weede E. (2004a), 'Comparative Economic Development in China and Japan'. *Japanese Journal of Political Science,* 5, no. 1 (2004): 69-90.

Weede E. (2004b), 'Does Human Capital Strongly Affect Economic Growth Rates? Yes, But Only If Assessed Properly' *Comparative Sociology,* 3, no. 2 (2004): 115-134.

Weede E. (2004c), 'On Political Violence and its Avoidance' *Acta Politica,* 39, no. 2 (2004): 152-178.

Weede E. (2004d), 'The Diffusion of Prosperity and Peace by Globalization' *Independent Review,* vol. 9, no. 2, pp. 165-186.

Weede E. (2005), 'Living with the Transatlantic Drift'. *Orbis,* vol. 49, no. 2, pp. 323-335.

Weede E. (2006), 'Is there a contradiction between freedom and Islam? Paper, Department of Sociology, University of Bonn (FRG); available at: http://admin.fnst.org/uploads/896/Weede_engl.pdf

Weede E. and Muller E. N. (1998), 'Rebellion, Violence and Revolution: A Rational Choice Perspective.' *Journal of peace research,* vol. 35, no. 1, pp. 43.

Weede E. and Tiefenbach H. (1981), 'Some Recent Explanations of Income Inequality: An Evaluation and Critique.' *International Studies Quarterly,* 25, 2, June, pps. 255-282.

Weil P. (2005), ‚*A Flexible Framework for a Plural Europe'* Paris: CNRS (Discussion paper prepared for the UK Presidency, available at http://www.eu2005.gov.uk/servlet/Front?pagename=OpenMarket/Xcelerate/ShowPage&c=Page&cid=1107293391098&a=KArticle&aid=1119527321606).

Went R. (2002), *'The Enigma of Globalisation: A Journey to a New Stage of Capitalism'* London and New York: Routledge.

Westerlund D. and Svanberg I. (Eds.) (1999), *'Islam outside the Arab world'*. New York: St. Martin's Press.

Wheelwright T. (2001), 'Developments in the Global Economy and their Effects on Australia' available at: http://www.angelfire.com/ma/rank/tedw.html.

White, Adrian G. (2007), *"A Global Projection of Subjective Well-being: A Challenge to Positive Psychology?"* University of Leicester, School of Psychology, available at: http://www.le.ac.uk/pc/aw57/world/sample.html

Whitehouse E. (2000), *'How Poor are the Old? A Survey of Evidence from 44 Countries'* World Bank Social Protection Discussion Paper Series, 0017, available at: http://wbln0018.worldbank.org/HDNet/hddocs.nsf/0/e28c5467c943aab18525690e006e3649/$FILE/0017.pdf.

Wickrama K. A. S. and Mulford Ch. L. (1996), 'Political Democracy, Economic Development, Disarticulation, and Social Well - Being in Developing Countries' *The Sociological Quarterly,* 37, 3: 375 - 390.

Williamson J. G. (1991), *'Inequality, Poverty, and History'.* Cambridge, MA.: Basil Blackwell.

Williamson J. G. (1996), 'Globalization, Convergence and History' *The Journal of Economic History,* 56, 2: 277 - 306.

Williamson J. G. (1997), 'Globalization and Inequalities, Past and Present' *The World Bank Research Observer,* 12, 2, August: 117-135.

Williamson J. G. (1998a), *'Real Wages and Relative Factor Prices in the Third World 1820 - 1940: The Mediterranean Basin'.* Discussion Paper 1842, Harvard Institute of Economic Research; *http://www.economics.harvard.edu/faculty/jwilliam/papers/.*

Williamson J. G. (1998b), 'Harvard Institute of Economic Research, Internet site (with link-up to the data base on wages in the world periphery 1820-1940): *http://www.economics.harvard.edu/~jwilliam/.*

Wimberley D. W. (1990), 'Investment Dependence and Alternative Explanations of Third World Mortality: A Cross - National Study' *American Sociological Review,* 55: 75 - 91.

Wimberley D. W. (1991), 'Transnational Corporate Investment and Food Consumption in the Third World: A Cross-National Analysis.' *Rural sociology,* 1991, vol. 56, no. 3, pp. 406 ff..

Wimberley D. W. and Bello R. (1992), Effects of Foreign Investment, Exports, and Economic Growth on Third World Food Consumption. *Social Forces,* 70:895-921.

Wimmer A. (2002), *'Nationalist Exclusion and Ethnic Conflict: Shadows of Modernity* ' Cambridge: Cambridge University Press.

Woehlcke M. (1987), *'Umweltzerstoerung in der Dritten Welt'* Munich: C.H. Beck.

Woehlcke M. (1993), *'Der oekologische Nord - Sued - Konflikt'* Munich: C.H. Beck.

Wolf, R.; Weede, and E.; Snyder, J. (1996), 'Democratization and the Danger of War.' *International security,* vol. 20, no. 4, pp. 176.

Wood A. (1994), *'Structural Unemployment in the North: Global Causes, Domestic Cures'* Vienna: Kreisky Commission Symposion, 21 - 22 March.

Woods A. (2000), *'A socialist alternative to the European Union'* Available from the Internet at http://www.newyouth.com/archives/westerneurope/a_socialist_alternative_to_the_e.html.

Woodward A. and Kohli M. (2001), *'Inclusions and Exclusions in European Societies."* London and New York: Routledge.

World Bank (current issues), *'World Development Report'* Washington D.C.: World Bank and Oxford University Press.

World Bank Middle East and North Africa Region (2002), *'Reducing Vulnerability and Inrceasing Opportunity. Social Protection in the Middle East and North Africa'* Washington D.C.: Orientations in Development Series.

World Resources Institute (in collaboration with the United Nations Environmental Programme and United Nations Development Programme), (1998), *'World Resources 1998-1999'.* New York: Oxford University Press.

Yotopoulos P. A. (1966), *'Economic analysis and economic policy'.* Edited by Pan A. Yotopoulos. Contributors: Arthur S. Goldberger [and others]. Athens [Center of Planning and Economic Research] (Center of Planning and Economic Research. Training seminar series, 6).

Yotopoulos P. A. (1967), *'Allocative efficiency in economic development; a cross section analysis of Epirus farming'* Athens [Center of Planning and Economic Research] (Center of Planning and Economic Research. Research monograph series, 18).

Yotopoulos P. A. (1977), *'The population problem and the development solution'* Stanford, Calif.: Food Research Institute, Stanford University, (Food Research Institute studies; v. 16, no. 1).

Yotopoulos P. A. (1984), *'Middle income classes and food crises'* Athens: Centre of Planning and Economic Research, (Papers / Centre of Planning and Economic Research; 5).

Yotopoulos P. A. (1989a), 'Distributions of real income: Within countries and by world income classes'. *The Review of income and wealth,* no. 4, pp. 357 ff..

Yotopoulos P. A. (1989b), 'The (Rip) Tide of Privatization: Lessons from Chile.' *World development,* vol. 17, no. 5, pp. 683 ff..

Yotopoulos P. A. (1989c), 'The meta-production function approach to technological change in world agriculture.' *Journal of development economics,* vol. 31, no. 2, pp. 241 ff..

Yotopoulos P. A. (1996), *'Exchange rate parity for trade and development: theory, tests, and case studies'* Cambridge [England]; New York: Cambridge University Press.

Yotopoulos P. A. (1997a), *'Financial crises and the benefits of mildly repressed exchange rates'* Stockholm: Stockholm School of Economics, Economic Research Institute, (Working paper series in economics and finance; no. 202, October 1997).

Yotopoulos P. A. (1997b), *'Food security, gender and population'* New York, NY: United Nations Population Fund, 'E/850/1997'.

Yotopoulos P. A. (2004), *'The Success of the Euro, Globalization, and the EU Enlargement'* University of Florence, available at: http://www.ceistorvergata.it/conferenze&convegni/mondragone/XVI_papers/paper-yotopoulos2.pdf.

Yotopoulos P. A. and Floro S. L. (1992), 'Income distribution, transaction costs and market fragmentation in informal credit markets.' *Cambridge journal of economics,* 1992, vol. 16, no. 3, pp. 303 ff.

Yotopoulos P. A. and Lin J. Y. (1993), 'Purchasing Power Parities for Taiwan: The Basic Data for 1985 and International Comparisons.' *Journal of economic development,* 1993, vol. 18, no. 1, pp. 7 ff.

Yotopoulos P. A., Nugent J. B. (1976), *'Economics of development: empirical investigations'* New York: Harper & Row.

Yotopoulos P. and Sawada Y. (2005), *'Exchange Rate Misalignment: A New test of Long-Run PPP Based on Cross-Country Data'* CIRJE Discussion Paper CIRJE-F-318, February 2005, Faculty of Economics, University of Tokyo, available at: http://www.e.u-tokyo.ac.jp/cirje/research/dp/2005/2005cf318.pdf.

Yunker J. A. (2000), *'Common Progress: The Case for a World Economic Equalization Program'* New York: Frederic Praeger.

Zaidi A. (2006), 'Poverty of Elderly People in EU25' Policy Brief August 2006, European Centre, Vienna, available at: http://www.euro.centre.org/data/1156245035_36346.pdf#search=%22Zaidi%20A.%20(2006)%2C%20%E2%80%98Poverty%20of%20Elderly%20People%20in%20EU25%E2%80%99%20Policy%20Brief%20August%202006%2C%20European%20Centre%2C%20Vienna%2C%20available%20at%3A%20%22

Zaidi A. et al. (2006), 'Poverty of Elderly People in EU25. Project financed by the European Commission' available at: http://www.csmb.unimo.it/adapt/bdoc/2006/41_06/06_41_44_PENSIONI.pdf#search=%22Zaidi%20A.%20(2006)%2C%20%E2%80%98Poverty%20of%20Elderly%20People%20in%20EU25%E2%80%99%20Policy%20Brief%20August%202006%2C%20European%20Centre%2C%20Vienna%2C%20available%20at%3A%20%22

Zmerli S. (2004). "Politisches Vertrauen und Unterstützung (Political confidence and support)." In *"Deutschland in Europa".* (J. W. van Deth (Ed.)) Wiesbaden, VS Verlag Sozialwissenschaften: 229-255.

Zmerli S. (2006). *"Political confidence in Europe".* International Political Science Association 20th World Congress. Fukuoka, Japan.

INDEX

A

Abdullah, 7, 219
access, 3, 18, 205, 212, 217
accountability, 266
accounting, 1
achievement, 131, 140, 204, 205, 206
activity rate, viii, 1, 28, 36, 44, 46, 51, 53, 54, 55, 56, 57, 58, 59, 60, 61, 63, 104, 117, 121, 136, 153, 160, 161, 162, 163, 164, 165, 187
adjustment, 22
adult literacy, 43, 201, 203
adults, 205
Afghanistan, 15, 90
Africa, 8, 15, 16, 55, 73, 75, 121, 273, 289
age, viii, 1, 3, 11, 13, 20, 28, 36, 44, 46, 51, 53, 54, 55, 56, 57, 58, 59, 60, 61, 63, 66, 68, 104, 106, 116, 121, 136, 150, 160, 161, 162, 163, 164, 165, 186, 205, 247, 282
age of enlightment, 54
ageing population, 237
aggregation, 131, 222
aging, vii, 23, 127, 237
aging society, vii, 127
agrarian, 3
agricultural sector, 18
agriculture, 4, 239, 265, 289
air pollution, 208
Al Jazeera's, 72
Albania, 34, 47, 89, 154, 160, 166, 169, 172, 175, 180, 187, 191
al-fadil, 140
Algeria, 34, 49, 90, 154, 160, 166, 169, 172, 175, 178, 180, 187, 191, 225
al-ijtima', 140
Al-Kindi, 139
Allah, 79

al-Razi's, 139
alternative, 45, 133, 277, 289
alternatives, 141
amphibia, 208
Amsterdam, 183, 222, 226, 235, 240, 242, 280
Andes, 236
Angola, 34, 50, 132, 154, 160, 166, 169, 172, 175, 178, 180, 187, 191
animals, 140
anthropogenic, 208, 209, 210
anti-globalization, 72
appendix, 29, 42, 53, 84, 89, 131
Arab countries, 72, 267
Arab world, 16, 72, 288
Argentina, 21, 23, 28, 34, 47, 154, 160, 166, 169, 172, 175, 178, 180, 187, 191, 263, 266, 277
argument, 10, 19, 21, 25, 68, 71, 132, 139
Aristotelian, 141, 142
Armenia, 34, 48, 154, 160, 166, 169, 172, 175, 180, 187, 191
articulation, 11
Asia, 8, 55, 73, 75, 121, 244, 273, 279
assessment, vii, 202, 217
assumptions, 67, 68, 132
astronomy, 71
Athens, 265, 282, 289
attention, 16, 17, 66, 67, 201, 205, 206
attitudes, 232, 249
augurs, 140
Australia, 15, 21, 28, 34, 47, 116, 132, 137, 154, 160, 166, 169, 172, 175, 178, 180, 187, 191, 232, 234, 266, 288
Austria, ix, 34, 46, 91, 132, 136, 137, 154, 160, 166, 169, 172, 175, 178, 180, 187, 191, 226, 250, 269, 277, 279
authoritarianism, 73, 271
autonomy, 139
availability, 34, 209

avoidance, 72
Azerbaijan, 34, 48, 90, 132, 154, 160, 166, 169, 172, 175, 178, 180, 187, 191

B

backwardness, 9, 10
Bahrain, 34, 50, 90, 154, 160, 166, 169, 172, 175, 180, 187, 191
bananas, 216
Bangladesh, 34, 48, 90, 154, 160, 166, 169, 172, 175, 178, 180, 187, 191, 237
bankers, 23
banks, 22
barriers, 8, 18
Barro-type, 1
basic needs, 52, 68
behavior, 235
Beijing, 224
Belarus, 34, 48, 154, 160, 166, 169, 172, 175, 178, 180, 187, 191
Belgium, 34, 47, 91, 132, 137, 154, 160, 166, 169, 172, 175, 178, 180, 187, 191
beneficial effect, 109
benefits, 18, 21, 290
Benin, 34, 49, 89, 154, 160, 166, 169, 172, 175, 178, 180, 187, 191
Bhagwati, 2, 5, 9, 67, 225
bias, 92, 191, 192, 193, 194, 195, 196
binding, 117
biofuels, 216
biosphere, 216
birth, 201, 203, 205, 226
births, 211
blame, vii, 1, 67, 117, 127
blocks, 3, 4, 7
bloodshed, 139
Bolivia, 21, 28, 34, 47, 154, 160, 166, 169, 172, 175, 178, 180, 187, 191
bonds, 23
Bosnia, ix, 15, 72
Botswana, 34, 49, 154, 160, 166, 169, 172, 175, 181, 187, 191
B-phase, 25
Brazil, 34, 48, 109, 154, 160, 166, 169, 172, 175, 178, 181, 187, 191, 230
breeding, 208
Britain, 228, 265
browser, 219
Brussels, 235, 236, 237, 238, 270, 271
budget surplus, 8
Bulgaria, 34, 48, 91, 138, 154, 160, 166, 169, 172, 175, 178, 181, 187, 191

bureaucracy, 20
bureaucratization, 3
Burkina Faso, 34, 50, 90, 154, 160, 166, 169, 172, 175, 178, 181, 187, 191
business cycle, 4

C

California, 79, 240, 266, 274, 278, 280, 281, 285
Cambodia, 34, 49, 132, 154, 160, 166, 169, 172, 175, 178, 181, 187, 192
Cameroon, 34, 50, 90, 154, 160, 166, 169, 172, 175, 179, 181, 187, 192
Canada, 15, 21, 34, 46, 116, 132, 137, 155, 160, 166, 169, 172, 175, 179, 181, 187, 192, 225, 273, 286
CAP, 212, 213, 214
Cape Town, 246
capital flows, 226
capital intensive, 18
capitalism, 3, 4, 8, 10, 18, 25, 26, 57, 219, 220, 221, 224, 225, 228, 234, 236, 241, 250, 255, 256, 260, 262, 266, 268, 272, 273, 277, 278, 285, 286, 288
carbon, 215, 249, 273
Caribbean, 121, 273, 277
Catholic, 23, 94
causal model, 136
causality, 17
celestial bodies, 140
Central Asia, 15, 16, 21
Central Europe, 21, 223, 228, 237, 259, 264, 276, 285
CES, 284
Ceteris paribus, viii
Chad, 34, 45, 50, 90, 132, 155, 161, 166, 169, 172, 175, 179, 181
Chicago, 220, 244, 276
children, 205, 250
Chile, 21, 22, 28, 34, 47, 155, 161, 166, 169, 172, 175, 179, 181, 187, 192, 252, 277, 289
China, 15, 16, 34, 48, 155, 161, 166, 169, 172, 175, 179, 181, 187, 192, 255, 287
Christianity, 227, 265
Christians, 265
citizenship, 226
civil liberties, 217
civil liberty, viii
civil rights, ix, 35, 89, 91, 93, 94, 96, 97, 98, 101
classes, 32, 274, 289
classical economics, 68
classification, x
CO_2, viii, 1, 28, 35, 44, 46, 51, 53, 54, 55, 56, 57, 58, 59, 60, 61, 63, 104, 106, 117, 121, 136, 151, 152, 160, 161, 162, 163, 164, 165, 186, 216, 243

cohesion, ix, 109
Cold War, 243
collaboration, 278, 289
Colombia, 21, 28, 34, 47, 155, 161, 166, 169, 172, 175, 179, 181, 187, 192
colonization, 68
Columbia University, 206, 208, 209, 250, 285
combined effect, 29, 63, 65, 103, 104, 105
commodity, 62
Commonwealth of Independent States, 284
communism, 21
community, 72, 142, 285
comparative advantage, 133
comparative international price level, 2, 35, 61, 62, 77, 78, 86, 87, 97, 99, 100, 101, 102, 104, 105, 122, 123, 124, 126, 132, 134, 135, 144, 145, 146, 147, 148, 149, 150, 151, 152, 153, 154, 155, 156, 157, 158, 159, 197, 198, 199, 200
comparative research, 16
compatibility, 89
competition, 12, 117
complexity, 256
components, ix, 44, 51, 132, 186, 191, 192, 193, 194, 195, 196, 203, 204, 207, 217
composite, 131, 201, 204
compulsion, 79
concentration, 4, 18, 25, 66, 143, 207, 208, 209
concrete, 131
conductivity, 209
confidence, 290
conflict, ix, 10, 65, 71, 125, 244, 274
conflict resolution, 274
Congress, 244, 285, 290
consensus, 9, 12
constraints, 7
construction, vii, ix
consumption, viii, 1, 18, 28, 36, 44, 51, 53, 54, 55, 56, 57, 58, 59, 60, 61, 63, 66, 104, 106, 117, 121, 136, 151, 160, 161, 162, 163, 164, 165, 186, 210, 211, 213, 216
consumption patterns, 18
contingency, 141
continuity, 232
control, ix, 2, 3, 27, 84, 85, 89, 94, 95, 106, 141
convergence, vii, 12, 18, 107, 120, 132, 232, 244, 254
conversion, 11, 202
conversion rate, 11
corporations, 18
correlation, 52, 81, 131, 184, 185, 186
correlations, 131, 186, 219
corruption, 140, 142

Costa Rica, 34, 46, 155, 161, 166, 169, 172, 175, 181, 188, 192, 216
costs, 22, 60, 109
Council of Europe, 270
counter culture, 72
coverage, 204
credit, 18, 239, 290
credit market, 239, 290
crime, 26, 241
Croatia, 21, 28, 34, 47, 91, 137, 155, 161, 166, 169, 172, 175, 181, 188, 192
crocodile, 23
Cross-Sectional Models, x
cultivation, 141
culture, vii, viii, 4, 7, 10, 53, 57, 71, 72, 81, 89, 269, 282, 285
currency, 11, 133, 202
current account, 3, 4, 10
current account balance, 3, 4, 10
cycles, 256, 271, 272
cyclones, 212
Cyprus, 34, 46, 91, 137, 155, 161, 166, 169, 172, 175, 181, 188, 192
Czech Republic, 34, 48, 91, 138, 155, 161, 166, 169, 172, 175, 179, 181, 188, 192

D

danger, 143
data base, 204, 288
data set, 27, 89
database, 215, 242, 244
death, 55, 66, 104, 106, 121, 139, 141, 143, 211
death rate, 211
deaths, 212
debt, 41, 133
decision makers, 132, 136
defects, 19
defense, 19, 222
deficit, 223
deficits, 3, 4, 55, 106
definition, 11, 32, 72, 205
degrees of freedom, 77, 78, 86, 87, 99, 100, 101, 102, 122, 123, 124, 134, 135, 144, 145, 146, 147, 148, 149, 150, 151, 152, 153, 197, 198, 199, 200
demand, 3, 18, 80, 132, 216
democracy, 7, 8, 13, 26, 35, 89, 91, 92, 93, 94, 95, 96, 246, 273, 274, 275, 287
demographic transition, 26
denial, 205
Denmark, 21, 28, 34, 46, 91, 132, 133, 136, 137, 155, 161, 166, 169, 172, 175, 179, 181, 188, 192
Department of State, 284

dependent variable, viii, 14, 28, 29, 35, 36, 54, 55, 56, 57, 58, 59, 60, 61, 125, 131, 186
deposition, 210
depression, 276
deprivation, 202, 206, 238
deregulation, 230
desire, 72, 203
destruction, 3
devaluation, 132, 133
developed countries, 10, 129, 136, 273
developing countries, 17, 18, 83, 205, 206, 252
developing nations, 17, 18
development level, 12, 20, 27, 35, 36, 41, 75, 76, 84, 85, 92, 94, 95, 96
deviation, 2, 110
devolution, 21
direct investment, 8, 275
discipline, 8
discrimination, 80, 81, 83
disorder, 246, 281
disposable income, 205
distress, 252
distribution, 18, 26, 55, 58, 66, 68, 268, 290
distribution of income, 66
divergence, vii, 254
division, 17, 72, 141, 251
division of labor, 17
doctors, 133
domestic economy, 202
dominance, 68
Dominican Republic, 34, 47, 155, 161, 166, 169, 172, 175, 179, 181, 188, 192
draft, 236, 266
drinking water, 212
droughts, 212

E

earth, 72, 216
East Asia, 13, 222, 285, 286, 287
Eastern Europe, 13, 15, 73, 221, 224, 225, 234, 240, 241, 242, 243, 245, 246, 247, 248, 254, 255, 259, 270, 284
ECOFIN, 270
Ecological footprint, 54, 55, 56, 57, 58, 59, 60, 61, 216
ecological indicators, 61
econometric analysis, 133
economic activity, viii, 1, 28, 36, 44, 46, 51, 53, 54, 55, 56, 57, 58, 59, 60, 61, 63, 104, 117, 121, 136, 153, 160, 161, 162, 163, 164, 165, 187
economic crisis, 23
economic development, viii, 21, 71, 248, 289, 290

economic growth, vii, viii, 1, 5, 8, 12, 16, 17, 20, 25, 26, 28, 31, 36, 43, 44, 46, 51, 53, 54, 55, 56, 57, 58, 59, 60, 61, 63, 66, 67, 68, 92, 104, 106, 107, 108, 109, 117, 121, 127, 131, 133, 136, 147, 148, 160, 161, 162, 163, 164, 165, 186, 201, 219, 223, 224, 235, 287
economic growth rate, 12, 60, 109, 133
economic indicator, 11
economic performance, 13, 223, 261
economic policy, 58, 254, 289
economic resources, 205
economic theory, 269
economics, 20, 68, 71, 92, 132, 223, 224, 236, 239, 256, 259, 267, 269, 272, 277, 288, 289, 290
Ecuador, 34, 48, 155, 161, 166, 169, 172, 176, 179, 181, 188, 192
education, 8, 19, 43, 79, 80, 131, 183, 184, 185, 201, 202, 214, 224, 232, 252
education expenditures, 19
educational attainment, 202
EEA, 79, 91, 137, 209
Egypt, 15, 34, 49, 90, 120, 155, 161, 166, 169, 172, 176, 179, 181, 188, 192
Egyptian, 2, 264
EIA, 213
El Salvador, 21, 28
elderly, 22, 23
elites, 3, 18, 31
emotions, 141
employment, 16, 23, 36, 42, 55, 57, 58, 66, 92
empowerment, viii, ix, 1, 19, 28, 29, 36, 44, 45, 51, 83, 84, 85, 105, 117, 121, 137, 172, 173, 174, 201, 202, 204, 205
energy, viii, 1, 28, 35, 43, 44, 46, 51, 53, 54, 55, 56, 57, 58, 59, 60, 61, 63, 104, 117, 121, 136, 152, 160, 161, 162, 163, 164, 165, 186
engagement, 219
England, 221, 246, 251, 252, 256, 265, 266, 267, 269, 285, 286, 290
enlargement, 237, 245, 254
enrollment, 43, 214
environment, ix, 8, 25, 26, 35, 42, 45, 52, 54, 55, 58, 63, 64, 65, 68, 117, 131, 132, 187, 188, 189, 190, 191, 192, 193, 194, 195, 196, 197, 198
environmental impact, 216
environmental policy, 42
environmental sustainability, viii, 1, 28, 44, 45, 51, 58, 137
environmental sustainability index, viii
environmental sustainability index (ESI-Index), viii
environmentalism, 229
EPC, 235, 236
epicurus, 139

equality, 5, 26, 42, 52, 94
equilibrium, 133, 139, 141
equity, 22
ERD, 2, 12, 28, 35, 41, 58, 61, 77, 78, 86, 87, 97, 99, 100, 101, 102, 104, 105, 116, 117, 120, 122, 123, 124, 134, 135, 144, 145, 146, 147, 148, 149, 150, 151, 152, 153, 154, 155, 156, 157, 158, 159, 197, 198, 199, 200
Erk, 240
eros, 83
ESI, viii, 1, 28, 35, 44, 45, 46, 51, 53, 54, 55, 56, 57, 58, 59, 60, 61, 63, 105, 117, 121, 137, 146, 147, 160, 161, 162, 163, 164, 165, 186
Estonia, 34, 48, 91, 138, 155, 161, 166, 169, 172, 176, 181, 188, 192
Ethiopia, 34, 50, 132, 155, 161, 166, 169, 172, 176, 179, 181, 188, 192
ethnicity, 201, 221, 285
EU enlargement, 248, 254
Euro, ix, 120, 222, 238, 260, 268, 290
Euro-Mediterranean Partnership, 222
Europe, vii, 13, 16, 19, 21, 41, 73, 79, 80, 106, 116, 117, 120, 121, 127, 132, 137, 183, 215, 221, 223, 224, 232, 234, 235, 236, 237, 238, 239, 240, 241, 244, 245, 247, 248, 249, 253, 254, 256, 260, 261, 265, 268, 269, 270, 271, 272, 275, 276, 280, 281, 282, 284, 285, 288, 290
European, vii, 10, 11, 19, 20, 22, 35, 36, 41, 42, 57, 61, 64, 79, 80, 83, 89, 91, 117, 119, 120, 121, 127, 132, 136, 206, 207, 208, 209, 211, 220, 222, 223, 224, 227, 228, 229, 232, 234, 235, 236, 237, 238, 240, 241, 242, 244, 245, 246, 247, 248, 249, 252, 254, 257, 259, 260, 261, 263, 264, 268, 269, 270, 271, 272, 273, 276, 278, 279, 280, 282, 285, 286, 287, 289, 290
European Commission, 11, 22, 42, 79, 206, 211, 220, 237, 238, 242, 247, 290
European Community, 227
European integration, 20
European Monetary Union (EMU), 41, 244
European Parliament, 238
European policy, 41, 117
Eurostat, 11, 28, 41, 117, 132, 133, 234, 235, 238
evidence, 2, 7, 8, 11, 19, 20, 21, 66, 67, 71, 89, 91, 98, 237, 258, 272, 279
evil, 79, 143
evolution, 235
exaggeration, 140
exchange rate, 2, 11, 12, 28, 41, 110, 133, 202, 290
exchange rate deviation index, 2
exchange rates, 11, 12, 133, 202, 290
exclusion, 263, 271, 272
exercise, 52

expenditures, 3, 19
exploitation, 11, 253, 278
exports, 25, 133
exposure, 14, 212, 230
expulsion, 23

F

failure, vii, 41, 127, 132, 215
faith, viii, 35, 36, 72, 79
family, 229, 276
FAO, 209, 210, 211, 212, 220
FDI, 246
fear, 139, 141
feedback, 133
feelings, 79, 80, 141
feet, 122
Fermi, 206
FES, 241
Fiji, 34, 47, 155, 161, 166, 169, 172, 176, 181, 188, 192
film, 71
film industry, 71
finance, 224, 232, 237, 290
financial crises, 133
financial institutions, 266
financial markets, 12, 232
financing, 21, 244, 271
Finland, 21, 34, 46, 91, 132, 136, 137, 155, 161, 166, 169, 172, 176, 179, 181, 188, 192, 205, 251, 252, 268, 271
firms, 8, 213
First World, 10
fishing, 216
fluctuations, 10
food, 3, 216, 289
footprint, viii, 1, 28, 35, 44, 51, 136, 144, 145, 210, 215, 216
forecasting, 259
foreign assistance, 3
foreign banks, 22
foreign direct investment, 8, 95, 259, 275
foreign investment, 4, 12, 18
foreign policy, 273
forests, 133
forgetfulness, 142
fossil fuels, 216
fragmentation, 290
France, 8, 10, 34, 46, 91, 132, 137, 155, 161, 166, 169, 172, 176, 179, 181, 188, 192, 253
free trade, 120
freedom, viii, 1, 2, 12, 13, 26, 27, 28, 35, 44, 51, 58, 61, 66, 77, 78, 86, 87, 91, 95, 98, 99, 100, 101,

102, 104, 105, 106, 116, 121, 122, 123, 124, 132, 134, 135, 136, 137, 139, 144, 145, 146, 147, 148, 149, 150, 151, 152, 153, 154, 155, 156, 157, 158, 159, 197, 198, 199, 200, 217, 287, 288
freedoms, 217
freshwater, 210
fuel, 208
fulfillment, 89
funding, 21, 215
funds, 20

G

Gabon, 34, 49, 90, 155, 161, 166, 169, 172, 176, 181, 188, 192
gasoline, 212
GDP, viii, ix, 1, 2, 8, 11, 12, 20, 27, 28, 35, 36, 37, 38, 39, 40, 41, 43, 44, 46, 51, 53, 54, 55, 56, 57, 58, 59, 60, 61, 63, 76, 77, 78, 83, 84, 86, 87, 95, 96, 97, 99, 100, 101, 102, 104, 105, 117, 121, 122, 123, 124, 133, 134, 135, 136, 144, 145, 146, 147, 148, 149, 150, 151, 152, 153, 154, 155, 156, 157, 158, 159, 160, 161, 162, 163, 164, 165, 186, 197, 198, 199, 200, 201, 202, 203, 214, 215
GDP per capita, 41, 57, 95, 96, 201, 202, 203
gender, viii, ix, 1, 5, 7, 19, 26, 29, 42, 45, 51, 52, 54, 57, 66, 81, 83, 84, 85, 86, 94, 95, 117, 131, 132, 172, 173, 174, 187, 188, 189, 190, 191, 192, 193, 194, 195, 196, 198, 199, 201, 202, 204, 205, 206, 290
gender development index, viii, 1, 28, 36, 44, 45, 51, 105, 121, 137
gender disparity, 202, 205, 206
gender empowerment, viii
gender equality, ix, 7, 26, 42, 45, 51, 94, 131, 132, 187, 188, 189, 190, 191, 192, 193, 194, 195, 196, 198, 199
gender inequality, 1, 95, 204, 205
generation, 140
Geneva, 206, 223, 226, 248, 255, 259, 265, 276, 283, 284
genocide, 251
geography, 1, 92, 95, 239
Georgia, 34, 48, 155, 161, 166, 169, 172, 176, 179, 181, 188, 193, 229
Germany, 34, 46, 91, 132, 137, 155, 161, 167, 170, 173, 176, 179, 181, 188, 193, 214, 234, 272, 274
gestures, 23
gift, 139
global economy, 12, 23, 216
global Lisbon index, ix
global Lisbon process, vii, ix, 41, 42, 43, 46, 132, 134, 136, 186

global markets, vii, 127
global networks, 229
global trends, 257
global village, 230, 240, 244, 256
globalization, vii, ix, 2, 8, 9, 12, 26, 35, 55, 56, 58, 60, 65, 66, 67, 84, 92, 95, 110, 120, 125, 127, 128, 130, 132, 219, 220, 221, 226, 227, 230, 231, 233, 236, 239, 242, 243, 245, 246, 250, 251, 252, 255, 256, 257, 258, 261, 262, 263, 267, 268, 273, 275, 276, 278, 279, 280, 285, 288, 290
GNP, 2, 27, 35, 58, 59, 77, 78, 86, 87, 97, 99, 100, 101, 102, 104, 105, 116, 122, 123, 124, 134, 135, 144, 145, 146, 147, 148, 149, 150, 151, 152, 153, 154, 155, 156, 157, 158, 159, 197, 198, 199, 200
God, 139, 140, 265
goods and services, 215
governance, 213, 237, 238, 244, 268, 280
government, 11, 13, 18, 23, 41, 61, 73, 132, 201, 268, 287
government intervention, 13
graph, 27, 45, 103, 136
gratifications, 139
Greece, 34, 47, 91, 132, 137, 156, 162, 167, 170, 173, 176, 179, 181, 188, 193, 276
Greenland, 15
groundwater, 209
groups, 18, 206
growth, ix, 3, 5, 10, 11, 12, 13, 17, 19, 20, 21, 26, 36, 42, 45, 52, 66, 67, 68, 109, 131, 132, 137, 187, 188, 189, 190, 191, 192, 193, 194, 195, 196, 197, 219, 233, 235, 236, 237, 244, 252, 254, 256, 260, 272, 274, 287
growth dynamics, 235
growth theory, 66
Guatemala, 34, 48, 156, 162, 167, 170, 173, 176, 179, 181, 188, 193
guidance, 139
Guinea, 34, 49, 50, 90, 156, 162, 167, 170, 173, 176, 179, 181, 188, 193
gut, 249
Guyana, 15, 34, 46, 89, 156, 162, 167, 170, 173, 176, 181, 188, 193, 250

H

Haiti, 34, 50, 156, 162, 167, 170, 173, 176, 179, 181, 188, 193
happiness, ix, 53, 63, 71, 72, 79, 80, 139, 140, 141, 142, 284
Happy Planet Index, viii, 1, 28, 35, 44, 45, 46, 51, 54, 55, 56, 57, 58, 59, 60, 61, 105, 117, 121, 137, 145, 169, 170, 171, 186, 215, 216, 281
Happy Planet Indicators, 28

Harvard, 224, 239, 243, 247, 255, 268, 281, 282, 288
Hawaii, 31, 219, 250
HDI, 43, 46, 53, 54, 55, 56, 57, 58, 59, 60, 61, 63, 104, 109, 110, 117, 121, 131, 146, 160, 161, 162, 163, 164, 165, 186, 201, 202, 203, 204, 205, 206
HEA, 211
health, 8, 32, 71, 141, 201, 202, 255, 265, 274, 285
health services, 255
heart, 140
hegemony, 222
Heritage Foundation, 27, 262
heterogeneity, 42
hip, viii, ix, 71
Holy Scriptures, ix, 72
Honduras, 34, 48, 156, 162, 167, 170, 173, 176, 179, 181, 188, 193
host, 12, 128
human capital, 19, 121
human condition, 5, 13, 16
human development, viii, 19, 26, 36, 53, 55, 57, 60, 61, 66, 131, 201, 202, 203, 204, 205
human development index, viii, 1, 28, 36, 44, 45, 51, 53, 60, 61, 66, 131, 137, 201, 202, 203, 204
human development report, 7, 19, 29, 202, 203, 204, 206, 268, 283, 284
human needs, ix, 19, 31, 32, 33, 36, 42, 45, 51, 66, 68, 131, 132, 187, 188, 189, 190, 191, 192, 193, 194, 195, 196, 199, 200
human poverty index, 205
human resource development, 7
human rights, viii, ix, 1, 19, 26, 35, 42, 45, 51, 53, 56, 57, 58, 61, 63, 64, 65, 89, 91, 93, 99, 131, 132, 187, 188, 189, 190, 191, 192, 193, 194, 195, 196, 200
humane, 23
humanity, 141, 216
Hungary, 21, 28, 34, 47, 91, 137, 156, 162, 167, 170, 173, 176, 179, 181, 188, 193, 248
hypothesis, 117, 125, 249

I

ICT, 246
id, 235, 266, 274
identification, 142
identity, 245
ideology, 72
imagery, 143
imagination, 140, 142
imbalances, 3, 4, 25, 26
imitation, 72
immigration, 232, 257
implementation, 42
imports, 3, 25, 215
impurities, 72
in transition, 227, 233
incentives, 18
inclusion, 13, 95
income, viii, 1, 3, 5, 9, 12, 16, 17, 18, 20, 22, 23, 25, 26, 28, 36, 44, 46, 51, 53, 54, 55, 56, 57, 58, 59, 60, 61, 63, 66, 67, 75, 92, 104, 106, 109, 110, 117, 121, 131, 136, 151, 160, 161, 162, 163, 164, 165, 186, 201, 202, 204, 205, 206, 230, 239, 247, 253, 268, 269, 270, 289
income distribution, 3, 9, 16, 17, 18, 66, 109, 268, 269
income inequality, 17, 18, 25, 26, 67, 230, 239
income support, 247
income transfers, 270
incomes, 12, 27, 57, 94, 237
incompatibility, 89, 125
independence, 267
independent variable, 2, 27, 34, 63, 131
India, 34, 48, 132, 156, 162, 167, 170, 173, 176, 179, 181, 188, 193, 237, 253
indicators, ix, 1, 7, 11, 12, 19, 25, 26, 28, 29, 41, 42, 58, 61, 63, 65, 71, 72, 84, 95, 106, 109, 110, 117, 131, 202, 203, 204, 205, 216, 280
indices, 43, 131, 201, 202, 203, 204, 206, 219
indigenous, 18
Indonesia, 34, 48, 90, 156, 162, 167, 170, 173, 176, 179, 181, 188, 193
industrial restructuring, 10, 252
industrial revolution, 240
industrialization, 4, 18
industry, 4, 71, 255
inefficiency, 133
inequality, 1, 8, 12, 17, 18, 20, 25, 26, 219, 222, 241, 252, 258, 274, 287
inequity, 18
infant mortality, 68, 273
infectious disease, 211
infectious diseases, 211
information age, 210, 213
innovation, 214, 252, 253, 262, 265, 271, 274, 276
insecurity, 263
insertion, 9
institutionalisation, 229
institutions, 229, 230, 262
instruction, 80
insurance, 230
integration, 92, 143, 231, 267
intellect, 140
intelligence, 19
intensity, 42, 125
interaction, 31, 94

interactions, 133, 222, 281
Inter-American Development Bank, 226
interdependence, 266
interest rates, 8
Intergovernmental Panel on Climate Change, 209
international communication, 3
international division of labor, 10, 13
international migration, 121, 270
International Monetary Fund (IMF), 22, 233, 262
international trade, 266
internet, 41, 219, 228, 231, 235, 237, 238, 246, 258, 259, 265, 272, 285, 288, 289
interpretation, 72, 85, 98, 240
intervention, 13
investment, 10, 18, 21, 25, 36, 42
investors, 18
Iran, 7, 34, 49, 90, 120, 156, 162, 167, 170, 173, 176, 179, 181, 188, 193, 258
Iraq, 15, 90
Ireland, 21, 34, 46, 91, 132, 136, 137, 156, 162, 167, 170, 173, 176, 181, 188, 193, 252
IRR, 211
irrational, 139
irrigation, 211, 254
Islam, vii, ix, 1, 7, 56, 62, 71, 72, 81, 83, 84, 85, 89, 91, 92, 93, 94, 95, 121, 123, 124, 125, 127, 143, 222, 223, 236, 239, 241, 245, 246, 251, 253, 257, 258, 261, 265, 266, 271, 275, 280, 281, 282, 285, 287, 288
Islamic, viii, 7, 34, 49, 72, 89, 90, 142, 156, 162, 173, 179, 181, 188, 193, 238, 258, 265, 279, 280
Islamic movements, 265
Islamic world, 143
isolation, 142
Israel, 11, 34, 47, 67, 72, 109, 132, 137, 156, 162, 167, 170, 173, 176, 179, 181, 188, 193, 234
Italy, 21, 34, 46, 91, 132, 137, 156, 162, 167, 170, 173, 176, 179, 181, 188, 193, 206, 229, 265

J

Jamaica, 34, 47, 156, 162, 167, 170, 173, 176, 181, 189, 193
Japan, 20, 34, 46, 132, 137, 156, 162, 167, 170, 173, 176, 179, 181, 189, 193, 205, 286, 287, 290
Jihadi, 72
jobs, ix, 10, 42, 187, 188, 189, 190, 191, 192, 193, 194, 195, 196, 197
Jordan, 34, 48, 90, 156, 162, 167, 170, 173, 176, 179, 181, 189, 193
justice, 5, 22, 36, 141

K

kahins, 140
Kazakhstan, 21, 28, 34, 49, 90, 156, 162, 167, 170, 173, 176, 179, 181, 189, 193
Kenya, 34, 50, 156, 162, 167, 170, 173, 176, 179, 181, 189, 193
Keynesian, 13, 21, 233
Keynesians, 13
knowledge-based economy, 42
Kondratieff cycle, 25
Korea, 34, 47, 156, 162, 167, 170, 173, 176, 179, 182, 189, 193
Kuwait, 90, 202, 225
Kuznets curve, 109, 237, 261
Kyrgyzstan, 34, 48, 90, 132, 157, 162, 167, 170, 173, 176, 182, 189, 193

L

labor, 3, 18, 23, 42, 55, 56, 120, 205, 248, 251, 265, 276, 285
labor force, 3, 18, 55, 205
labor markets, 120
land, 18, 46, 208, 209, 210, 211, 212, 216
land use, 216
landlocked countries, 97
landlocked country, 27, 36, 54
language, 22, 72, 142, 143, 219, 278, 279
Laos, 167, 170, 176
Latin America, 15, 16, 21, 22, 23, 55, 66, 68, 73, 83, 121, 226, 241, 248, 250, 252, 261, 262, 273, 276, 277, 280, 284
Latin American countries, 22
Latvia, 34, 47, 91, 137, 157, 163, 167, 170, 173, 176, 182, 189, 194
laws, 18
LEA, 242
lead, ix, 21, 23, 66, 133, 142
leadership, 267
learning, 235, 258
learning process, 235
Lebanon, 34, 49, 90, 132, 157, 163, 167, 170, 173, 176, 182, 189, 194, 251
less developed countries (LDCs), 230, 238, 240, 249, 282
liberalism, 72
liberalization, 8, 60, 233, 258
liberation, 9, 226, 252
liberty, viii, 1, 28, 44, 46, 51, 53, 54, 55, 56, 57, 58, 59, 60, 61, 63, 104, 106, 116, 121, 136, 149, 150, 166, 167, 168, 187

Libya, 15, 89, 90
life expectancy, viii, 1, 28, 32, 33, 36, 43, 44, 45, 46, 51, 53, 54, 55, 56, 57, 58, 59, 60, 61, 63, 66, 68, 104, 106, 117, 121, 137, 148, 160, 161, 162, 163, 164, 165, 186, 201, 203, 204, 216, 253
life satisfaction, viii, ix, 1, 28, 36, 44, 45, 51, 53, 54, 55, 56, 57, 58, 59, 60, 61, 63, 71, 73, 75, 78, 79, 105, 106, 117, 121, 137, 144, 169, 170, 171, 186, 215, 216
linear function, 20, 92
links, 31, 136
Lisbon Process Indicators (LPIs), 131, 187
Lisbon strategy, 42, 132, 280
literacy, 19, 43, 201, 205
literature, 2, 5, 7, 9, 10, 11, 13, 14, 16, 17, 20, 31, 55, 58, 65, 66, 67, 95
Lithuania, 34, 47, 91, 137, 157, 163, 167, 170, 173, 176, 182, 189, 194
living conditions, vii
living standards, 202
London, 6, 14, 25, 26, 55, 65, 66, 68, 69, 219, 220, 221, 222, 223, 224, 225, 226, 227, 228, 229, 230, 231, 232, 234, 235, 236, 240, 242, 243, 244, 246, 248, 249, 250, 251, 252, 254, 255, 256, 257, 258, 261, 262, 263, 264, 266, 267, 268, 269, 270, 272, 273, 274, 275, 276, 277, 278, 281, 284, 285, 286, 287, 288, 289
longevity, 201, 205
Los Angeles, 274
LTD, 250

M

Maastricht criteria, 41
Maastricht Treaty, 269
Macedonia, 91
malaise, 10
Malaysia, 34, 48, 90, 157, 163, 167, 170, 173, 177, 179, 182, 189, 194
Mali, 34, 49, 89, 157, 163, 167, 170, 173, 177, 179, 182, 189, 194
mammal, 208
management, 211
manufactured goods, 18
manufacturing, 18, 255
marginal utility, 270
marginalization, 56
market, 8, 11, 22, 42, 55, 56, 68, 72, 73, 254, 266, 290
market economy, 68
market failure, 22
markets, 2, 4, 12, 18, 92, 133, 237
Marx, 228, 262, 281, 285

Marxism, 285
Marxist, 17, 256, 281
Marxists, 133
Maryland, 213
Massachusetts, 235
maturity effects, 20, 27, 56, 57
Mauritania, 34, 49, 90, 157, 163, 167, 170, 173, 177, 182, 189, 194
Mauritius, 34, 46, 157, 163, 167, 170, 173, 177, 182, 189, 194
measurement, 58, 257
measures, 12, 19, 21, 42, 52, 131, 141, 201, 204, 205, 215, 216, 217
media, 3, 71, 201, 219
median, 205
medicine, 71
Mediterranean, 220, 222, 234, 237, 238, 245, 253, 279, 280, 288
membership, vii, viii, 2, 7, 20, 27, 36, 58, 67, 77, 78, 86, 87, 97, 99, 100, 101, 102, 104, 105, 106, 109, 117, 120, 121, 122, 123, 124, 126, 132, 134, 135, 144, 145, 146, 147, 148, 149, 150, 151, 152, 153, 154, 155, 156, 157, 158, 159, 197, 198, 199, 200, 280
memory, 71, 142
men, 139, 204, 205
messages, 27
Mexico, 21, 28, 34, 47, 133, 157, 163, 167, 170, 173, 177, 179, 182, 189, 194, 230, 238, 243, 274, 277
Microsoft, 257
Middle Ages, 53
Middle East, 56, 62, 244, 249, 261, 281, 289
middle income, 31, 92
migration, vii, ix, 121, 122, 127, 226, 228, 232, 245, 270, 276, 284
militant, 265
military, 3, 19, 22, 202
military order, 235
millennium, 14, 215, 239
mining, 4
Minnesota, 222
minorities, 232, 267
minority, 72
MIT, 223
mobility, 18
models, vii, 20, 60, 97, 109, 127, 256, 269
modern society, 79
modernity, 62, 125, 278
modernization, vii, 56, 57, 62, 92, 97, 127, 129, 132
Moldova, 34, 48, 132, 157, 163, 167, 170, 173, 177, 182, 189, 194
monetary policy, 260
money, 68

money income, 68
Mongolia, 34, 47, 157, 163, 167, 170, 173, 177, 182, 189, 194
monograph, 265, 289
monopoly, 3
Montana, 219
Montenegro, 15
moral hazard, 22
Morocco, 7, 34, 48, 90, 157, 163, 167, 170, 173, 177, 179, 182, 189, 194
mortality, 66, 211
mortality rate, 211
movement, 23, 72
Mozambique, 34, 49, 90, 157, 163, 167, 170, 173, 177, 179, 182, 189, 194
multicultural, 137
multiculturalism, 267
multidimensional, 35
multinational corporations, 279
multinational enterprises, 248
multiple regression, 35, 63, 66, 79, 80, 86, 92, 103, 121, 125
multiplicity, 141
multivariate, 7, 75, 92, 99, 117, 280
Muslim, vii, viii, ix, 2, 4, 7, 27, 31, 35, 36, 53, 57, 62, 71, 72, 73, 75, 80, 81, 83, 84, 85, 89, 92, 93, 94, 95, 96, 97, 106, 107, 110, 116, 117, 119, 120, 125, 127, 132, 139, 183, 266, 273, 280, 285
Muslim factor, 53
Muslim state, 273
Muslim states, 273
Muslims, viii, ix, 1, 27, 53, 54, 58, 71, 72, 75, 77, 78, 79, 80, 84, 85, 86, 87, 97, 98, 99, 100, 101, 102, 104, 105, 116, 122, 123, 124, 125, 134, 135, 144, 145, 146, 147, 148, 149, 150, 151, 152, 153, 154, 155, 156, 157, 158, 159, 183, 184, 185, 197, 198, 199, 200, 235, 236, 265, 273, 281, 283
Myanmar, 8

neglect, 11, 20
negligence, 7
neo-liberal, 5, 9, 10, 12, 13, 19, 23, 60, 61, 64, 66, 67, 68, 73, 92, 95, 117, 118, 119, 120, 132, 262
neoliberalism, 121
neo-liberalism, 68
Nepal, 34, 48, 132, 157, 163, 167, 170, 173, 177, 179, 182, 189, 194
net migration, 36, 121, 122, 178, 179, 180
Netherlands, 21, 28, 34, 46, 91, 132, 136, 137, 157, 163, 167, 170, 173, 177, 179, 182, 189, 194, 273
neuroses, 139
New England, 240
New Orleans, 222
New South Wales, 234
New York, 23, 220, 221, 222, 223, 224, 225, 226, 227, 228, 229, 230, 231, 232, 233, 234, 235, 236, 237, 238, 239, 240, 241, 243, 244, 245, 246, 248, 249, 250, 251, 252, 253, 254, 255, 256, 257, 260, 261, 262, 264, 265, 266, 267, 268, 269, 272, 273, 274, 275, 276, 278, 279, 280, 281, 282, 283, 284, 285, 286, 288, 289, 290
New Zealand, 34, 46, 132, 137, 157, 163, 167, 170, 173, 177, 182, 189, 194, 266, 276
NGOs, 201
Nigeria, 34, 50, 90, 125, 157, 163, 167, 171, 173, 177, 179, 182, 189, 194
Nobel Prize, 259
non-linear, ix, 33, 95, 96, 121, 124, 125
non-Muslims, 80
North Africa, 222, 244, 289
North American Free Trade Agreement, 283
North Korea, 15
Norway, 34, 46, 91, 132, 136, 137, 157, 163, 167, 171, 173, 177, 182, 189, 194, 253
Notre Dame, 285
nurses, 133

N

nafs, 140
Namibia, 34, 49, 157, 163, 167, 170, 173, 177, 182, 189, 194
nation, 2, 17, 23, 25, 267, 281
national income, 18, 202, 205
national security strategy, 284
nationalism, 264, 281
nationality, 235
NATO, 235, 243
natural resources, 3, 18
navigation, 71
negative relation, viii, ix, 71

O

oil, 267
Oklahoma, 247
old age, 23, 247
older people, 22
Oman, 90
OPEC, 94
openness, 1, 2, 8, 12, 13, 35, 67
optimism, 53
optimists, 20
orbit, 89, 91, 125
organization, 18, 143, 215, 258, 284

Organization for Economic Cooperation and Development (OECD), 137, 205, 206, 207, 208, 209, 210, 211, 215, 225, 230, 232, 271, 281
Organization of the Islamic Conference (OIC), viii
organizations, 212, 214
orientation, 92
Orthodox, 71
Ottawa, 273
ownership, 18
oxygen, 209
Ozone, 215

P

Pacific, 121
pain, 141
Pakistan, 34, 49, 90, 158, 163, 168, 171, 174, 177, 179, 182, 189, 195, 201, 277
Pakistani, 277
Panama, 34, 47, 158, 163, 168, 171, 174, 177, 182, 189, 195
Papua New Guinea, 34, 48, 158, 164, 168, 171, 174, 177, 179, 182, 189, 195
Paraguay, 34, 48, 158, 164, 168, 171, 174, 177, 180, 182, 189, 195
Paris, 221, 224, 225, 232, 237, 248, 253, 256, 265, 271, 288
Parliament, 251
partnership, vii, 235, 236
PAYGO, 21
pension, vii, ix, 2, 20, 21, 22, 23, 28, 35, 36, 58, 60, 65, 67, 75, 77, 78, 84, 85, 86, 87, 97, 99, 100, 101, 102, 104, 105, 109, 110, 117, 122, 123, 124, 127, 132, 134, 135, 144, 145, 146, 147, 148, 149, 150, 151, 152, 153, 154, 155, 156, 157, 158, 159, 197, 198, 199, 200, 226, 240, 247, 259, 262, 274
pension reforms, ix, 2, 21, 22, 58, 60, 65, 67, 75, 84, 85, 110, 127, 132, 226
pensioners, 22, 23
pensions, 21, 22, 23, 232, 257, 274, 282
per capita income, 56
performance, ix, 19, 21, 36, 41, 42, 55, 56, 57, 60, 89, 92, 93, 94, 95, 96, 97, 98, 99, 100, 101, 102, 262
performers, 83, 89
periphery, 3, 4, 9, 10, 11, 12, 14, 20, 25, 31, 68, 75, 83, 95, 121, 132, 133, 288
personal, 21, 23, 80, 143
personality, 141
personality traits, 141
Peru, 21, 28, 34, 48, 158, 164, 168, 171, 174, 177, 180, 182, 189, 195
pessimism, 57

pessimists, 57
Philippines, 34, 47, 158, 164, 168, 171, 174, 177, 180, 182, 189, 195
philosophers, 53, 139, 140
philosophy, ix, 53, 71, 140, 142
physical health, 141
planning, 206, 277
Plato, 143
pleasure, 142, 143
pleasures, 139
plurality, 141
Poland, 21, 28, 34, 47, 91, 137, 158, 164, 168, 171, 174, 177, 180, 182, 190, 195, 205, 245, 284
polarization, 9, 55, 60
police, 23
policy choice, 201, 202
policy makers, 201
policy making, 110
political participation, 201
political parties, 23
political power, 71
political rights violations, viii, 1, 28, 44, 51, 53, 104, 106, 121, 136
political stability, 26
politics, 220, 228, 238, 240, 244, 250, 258, 269, 282, 285, 287
poor, 8, 9, 10, 12, 20, 68, 205, 206
population, viii, ix, 1, 18, 27, 31, 32, 35, 36, 53, 54, 55, 58, 71, 72, 75, 77, 78, 84, 85, 86, 87, 92, 93, 95, 96, 97, 98, 99, 100, 101, 102, 104, 105, 106, 107, 110, 116, 122, 123, 125, 131, 132, 134, 135, 144, 145, 146, 147, 148, 149, 150, 151, 152, 153, 154, 155, 156, 157, 158, 159, 178, 179, 180, 197, 198, 199, 200, 204, 207, 208, 210, 212, 216, 220, 289, 290
population density, 55
population growth, 220
Portugal, 34, 47, 91, 132, 137, 158, 164, 168, 171, 174, 177, 180, 182, 190, 195, 243
potential realizations, 31, 32, 33
poverty, 10, 19, 20, 23, 25, 31, 42, 67, 68, 79, 80, 184, 185, 201, 202, 205, 206, 222, 232, 233, 235, 250, 251, 259, 267
poverty alleviation, 206
poverty line, 205
poverty rate, 42
poverty reduction, 68
power, ix, 2, 11, 17, 18, 21, 84, 85, 140, 142, 202, 205, 226, 237
power sharing, ix, 85
PPS, 11, 41
predictors, 7, 53, 58, 109, 131, 132, 280
premature death, 32

pressure, 23
PRI, 213, 214
price levels, vii, viii, ix, 11, 12, 28, 36, 41, 58, 61, 65, 73, 75, 76, 84, 85, 97, 109, 116, 117, 118, 119, 127, 132, 202
price mechanism, 35
prices, 60, 110, 133, 137
private property, 217
private sector, 214
privatization, 19, 21, 23
probability, 68, 77, 78, 86, 87, 99, 100, 101, 102, 122, 123, 124, 134, 135, 144, 145, 146, 147, 148, 149, 150, 151, 152, 153, 197, 198, 199, 200, 205
producers, 11
production, 3, 18, 68, 213, 265, 289
production function, 289
productivity, 4, 23, 41, 275
profit, 18
profits, 4, 18, 23
program, 72
promote, 72
prophets, 140
prosperity, 23, 42
proxy, 110, 201
psychologist, 22, 254
public education, 19
public expenditures, 8, 19
public opinion, 23
public pension, 237
public policy, 223
purchasing power, 11, 12, 96, 125, 133, 202

Q

Qatar, 90
quality of life, 238
quantitative research, 5, 66
questioning, 97
quotas, 8

R

race, 110, 137, 138, 264, 285
range, 20
rating scale, 217, 244
ratings, 217
raw materials, 25, 215
readership, 80
reading, ix, 72, 221
real income, 289
reality, vii, 28, 41, 56, 65, 83, 127, 141, 272
reasoning, 12, 140

recall, 3, 31, 68
reconcile, 125, 141
reconciliation, 35
recovery, 259
recycling, 210
redistribution, 12, 18, 67, 249
reduction, 53, 54, 60, 68
reforms, 3, 21, 22, 42, 60, 75
regenerate, 216
regional, 42, 203, 252, 281
regionalism, 248
regression, 3, 4, 36, 77, 78, 87, 93, 97, 102, 122, 123, 124, 132, 135, 153, 200
regression equation, 36
regulation, 262
regulations, 8
relationship, ix, 11, 17, 18, 31, 68, 71, 81, 91, 95, 131, 140, 143
relationships, ix, 5, 75, 92, 110, 143
relevance, 133
religion, 27, 71, 72, 79, 81, 142, 184, 186, 258, 264, 285
religiosity, 276
renewable energy, 213
rent, 4
repression, 65
reputation, 133
research design, viii, 19, 59, 75
residuals, 31, 77, 78, 87, 97, 102, 122, 123, 124, 135, 153, 200
resources, 73, 133, 216
respiratory, 211
restructuring, 254
retirees, 23
returns, 8
revolutionary, 286
rice, 117, 119
Rio de Janeiro, 274, 275
risk, 42
Romania, 34, 47, 89, 91, 138, 158, 164, 168, 171, 174, 177, 180, 182, 190, 195
Rome, 220, 225
ruh, 140
rule of law, 217
Russia, 168, 171, 177, 242
Rwanda, 34, 49, 158, 164, 168, 171, 174, 177, 180, 182, 190, 195

S

safety, 79
Salafism, 72
salvation, 140

sample, 27, 79, 80, 132, 288
satisfaction, ix, 19, 32, 36, 51, 57, 75, 76, 79, 131, 132, 187, 188, 189, 190, 191, 192, 193, 194, 195, 196, 199, 200, 216
Saudi Arabia, 34, 50, 72, 89, 90, 158, 164, 168, 171, 174, 177, 180, 182, 190, 195
savings, ix, 3, 12, 58, 65, 66, 67, 85, 97, 125, 132
Scandinavia, 13
scepticism, 60
schema, 11, 41
school, 11, 19, 25, 66, 72, 203
school enrollment, 19
schooling, 19
science, 7, 28, 56, 71, 132, 212, 253, 265, 269
scores, 27, 91, 216, 217
search, 72, 121, 220, 235, 255, 271, 272, 290
Second World, 246
Secretary of Defense, 16
security, 23, 139, 247, 248, 256, 281, 282, 283, 289, 290
Senegal, 34, 49, 89, 158, 164, 168, 171, 174, 177, 180, 182, 190, 195
Serbia, 15
series, viii, ix, 11, 28, 29, 34, 41, 89, 91, 125, 203, 204, 223, 265, 274, 280, 289, 290
shares, viii, ix, 19, 23, 55, 85, 95, 96, 106, 125, 132, 204, 205
shy, 54
Sierra Leone, 90
sign, 13, 80, 183, 185
signs, 106
simulation, 226
Singapore, 8, 27, 34, 48, 132, 158, 164, 168, 171, 174, 177, 182, 190, 195
skills, 205
Slovakia, 34, 47, 91, 137, 158, 164, 168, 171, 174, 177, 180, 182, 190, 195
smuggling, 22
social change, 259
social cohesion, 8, 19, 42, 57, 60, 104, 107, 108, 109, 121, 187, 188, 189, 190, 191, 192, 193, 194, 195, 196, 197
social contract, 265
social development, 220
social exclusion, 19, 55, 205
social group, 206
social indicator, viii, 1, 28, 44, 51, 65, 137
social inequalities, 67
social injustices, 66
social justice, 8, 19
social market economy, viii, 1, 28, 35, 43, 44, 46, 51, 53, 54, 55, 56, 57, 58, 59, 60, 61, 63, 104, 117, 121, 136, 152, 160, 161, 162, 163, 164, 165, 186

social movements, 240
social order, 31, 287
social policy, 22, 42, 230
social relations, 4
social relationships, 4
social sciences, 66
social security, 23, 232, 230, 240, 244, 250, 256, 259, 264, 268, 271
social structure, 32, 262
social welfare, 21
socialism, ix, 84, 85, 277
society, viii, ix, 11, 17, 19, 20, 23, 31, 32, 57, 58, 66, 71, 79, 84, 85, 95, 125, 140, 142, 143, 227, 279
solidarity, 22, 232
Somalia, 15, 89, 90
soul, 139, 140, 141
South Africa, 34, 49, 91, 158, 164, 168, 171, 174, 177, 180, 182, 190, 195
South Carolina, 259, 281
South Korea, 256
South Pacific, 211
Southeast Asia, 15, 16
Spain, 34, 47, 91, 132, 137, 158, 164, 168, 171, 174, 177, 180, 182, 190, 195, 244, 280
Spatial Models, x
specialization, 4, 285
species, 143, 208, 216
spirit, ix, 140
spirituality, 80
Sri Lanka, 34, 47, 158, 164, 168, 171, 174, 177, 180, 182, 190, 195
stability, 14, 25
stages, 20
standard error, 77, 78, 80, 87, 93, 102, 122, 123, 124, 135, 153, 183, 184, 185, 200
standard of living, 201, 202, 205
standards, vii, 32, 71
state intervention, ix, 2, 27, 35, 36, 58, 61, 65, 77, 78, 84, 85, 86, 87, 98, 99, 100, 101, 102, 104, 105, 116, 121, 122, 123, 124, 134, 135, 144, 145, 146, 147, 148, 149, 150, 151, 152, 153, 154, 155, 156, 157, 158, 159, 197, 198, 199, 200
statistical analysis, 272
statistics, 19, 29, 81, 184, 185, 186, 201, 202, 203, 238
stock, 23, 36
store of value, 132
strategies, 8, 18, 117, 132, 136
stratification, 17
strength, 13, 79
stress, 7, 10, 211
strikes, 23
substitution, 132, 133

Sudan, 89, 90
suffering, 19, 133
sugar, 133
sulfur, 210
summaries, 53
supernatural, 140
supply, 80
Suriname, 15, 89
surplus, 18
survival, 59, 68, 250
sustainability, 35, 58, 65, 117
sustainability index, 35, 58, 65, 117
sustainable development, vii, 127
Sweden, 21, 28, 34, 46, 91, 132, 133, 136, 137, 158, 164, 168, 171, 174, 177, 180, 182, 190, 195, 259, 262, 265, 268
Switzerland, ix, 21, 28, 34, 46, 91, 132, 136, 137, 158, 164, 168, 171, 174, 177, 180, 182, 190, 195, 206, 250, 255
symbols, 18
sympathy, 23
Syria, 89, 90, 168, 171, 177, 258
systems, 2, 4, 10, 21, 23, 65, 66, 133, 231, 237, 240, 247

T

Taiwan, 230, 232, 290
Tajikistan, 34, 49, 90, 159, 164, 168, 171, 174, 177, 182, 190, 195
talent, 23
Tanzania, 34, 49, 159, 164, 168, 171, 174, 177, 180, 182, 190, 195
targets, vii, 13, 41, 110, 117, 127
tariff, 258
tariffs, 8
tax rates, 8
TBP, 215
teachers, 139
technical change, 274
technological change, 289
technology, 3, 212
television, 23
temperance, 139
territory, 208, 217
terrorist, 7
terrorist attack, 7
tertiary sector, 4
Texas, 219
Thailand, 34, 47, 159, 165, 168, 171, 174, 177, 180, 183, 190, 196

theory, 2, 4, 9, 10, 11, 12, 17, 31, 55, 60, 66, 67, 94, 132, 133, 202, 235, 246, 256, 267, 272, 278, 279, 290
thinking, vii, 53, 66, 72, 139
Third World, 31, 67, 229, 230, 236, 240, 243, 244, 246, 247, 249, 251, 253, 255, 258, 270, 275, 278, 288, 289
time lags, 42
time series, 133, 203, 219
Togo, 34, 50, 90, 159, 165, 168, 171, 174, 177, 183, 190, 196
Tokyo, 219, 238, 243, 277, 290
total energy, 213
tourism, 228
trade, 4, 8, 11, 12, 13, 22, 23, 25, 33, 36, 42, 53, 66, 72, 73, 75, 83, 84, 92, 93, 94, 95, 125, 133, 230, 248, 254, 290
trade union, 22, 23
trade-off, 13, 33, 36, 42, 53, 66, 72, 73, 75, 83, 84, 92, 93, 95, 125
trading, 3
tradition, 18, 31, 133
trajectory, 4, 7
transaction costs, 290
transformation, 13, 120, 143, 248, 277
transformations, 228
transition, ix, 2, 3, 27, 35, 36, 56, 67, 77, 78, 84, 85, 86, 87, 97, 98, 99, 100, 101, 102, 104, 105, 110, 117, 121, 122, 123, 124, 134, 135, 144, 145, 146, 147, 148, 149, 150, 151, 152, 153, 154, 155, 156, 157, 158, 159, 197, 198, 199, 200, 225, 247
transition countries, 247
transition country, 27
transition economies, ix, 84, 85, 97, 121
translation, 79, 240
transnational corporations, 18
transparency, 217, 246
transport, 42, 55
treaties, 8
treatment effect models, x
trees, 216
trend, 96, 203, 204
triggers, 133
Trinidad and Tobago, 34, 47, 159, 165, 168, 171, 174, 183, 190, 196
trust, 217
turbulence, 285
Turkey, vii, ix, 7, 34, 48, 72, 89, 90, 91, 120, 133, 138, 159, 165, 168, 171, 174, 178, 180, 183, 190, 196, 223, 237, 279, 280, 282
Turkmenistan, 89, 90

U

Uganda, 34, 49, 90, 159, 165, 168, 171, 174, 178, 180, 183, 190, 196
underprivileged, 25
unemployment, viii, ix, 1, 4, 18, 22, 28, 29, 36, 42, 44, 51, 54, 72, 73, 74, 75, 76, 77, 105, 106, 117, 121, 137, 166, 167, 168, 186, 205, 219
unemployment rate, 42, 75
UNESCO, 203, 214, 253
UNFCCC, 209, 215
unhappiness, 71, 73, 139, 142
UNICEF, 212, 233
uniform, 8
unions, 22
United Arab Emirates, 90
United Kingdom, 20, 21, 28, 34, 47, 91, 132, 133, 137, 159, 165, 168, 171, 174, 178, 180, 183, 190, 196, 205, 239, 241, 247, 256, 260, 262, 264, 266, 267, 275, 282, 283, 288
United Nations (UN), viii, 1, 16, 19, 28, 29, 36, 43, 44, 51, 68, 75, 83, 121, 137, 178, 201, 203, 206, 207, 208, 209, 210, 211, 212, 214, 215, 219, 220, 233, 238, 244, 246, 248, 268, 275, 277, 278, 283, 284, 289, 290
United Nations Development Programme, 13, 19, 83, 212, 283, 284, 289
United Nations Environmental Programme (UNEP), 209, 212, 289
United States, ix, 20, 34, 47, 66, 89, 117, 119, 120, 132, 136, 137, 159, 165, 168, 171, 174, 178, 180, 183, 190, 196, 210, 221, 225, 244, 245, 246, 249, 262, 266, 280, 284, 285
Universal Declaration of Human Rights, 217
unselfconscious, 139
urbanisation, 36
urbanization, ix, 3, 55, 67, 84, 85, 97, 109, 110, 121, 127, 133
urbanization ratio, 2, 35, 55, 77, 78, 86, 87, 97, 98, 99, 100, 101, 102, 104, 105, 117, 122, 123, 124, 134, 135, 144, 145, 146, 147, 148, 149, 150, 151, 152, 153, 154, 155, 156, 157, 158, 159, 197, 198, 199, 200
Uruguay, 21, 22, 28, 34, 46, 159, 165, 168, 171, 174, 178, 183, 190, 196, 202, 248, 266
Uruguay Round, 248, 266
users, 283
USSR, 15, 121, 265
Utah, 230, 282
Uzbekistan, 34, 49, 89, 90, 159, 165, 168, 171, 174, 178, 180, 183, 190, 196

V

Valencia, 257
values, 14, 15, 16, 17, 26, 27, 33, 34, 44, 51, 53, 57, 63, 73, 75, 77, 78, 87, 89, 102, 106, 119, 120, 121, 122, 123, 124, 132, 135, 153, 200, 204
variable, viii, ix, 1, 7, 12, 19, 20, 27, 60, 63, 75, 84, 104, 105, 106, 121, 141
variables, viii, ix, 1, 14, 19, 26, 28, 29, 34, 42, 54, 60, 66, 80, 81, 85, 89, 92, 95, 103, 106, 118, 132, 186, 204, 205, 212
variance, 97, 98, 109, 131
VAT, 183
Venezuela, 34, 48, 159, 165, 168, 171, 174, 178, 180, 183, 190, 196
victimization, 23
Vietnam, 168, 171, 178
violence, viii, 31, 32, 33, 34, 67
Virginia, 272, 284
virtuous world, 140
vision, 20, 42, 72, 79
visualization, 84
vocabulary, 72
voice, 20
vulnerability, 31, 67, 252

W

wages, 4, 11, 219, 269, 288
Wahhabism, 72
Wall Street Journal, 27, 224
war, 281, 287
War on Terror, 249
Warsaw, 242, 254, 264, 270, 278, 279
Washington, 8, 21, 68, 72, 224, 226, 229, 240, 243, 244, 246, 247, 252, 257, 258, 261, 262, 264, 265, 270, 271, 272, 273, 280, 281, 282, 284, 289
Washington Consensus, 8, 68
wealth, 18, 23, 203, 289
web, 231
websites, 90
welfare, 21, 136, 254, 263
welfare state, 254
well-being, 5, 8, 19, 25, 26, 216
Western countries, 84
Western Europe, 3, 15, 106, 221, 254, 271, 287
White House, 284
winning, 23
women, ix, 55, 56, 84, 85, 92, 204, 205
work ethic, 21
workers, 18, 22, 41

World Bank, vii, ix, 7, 8, 11, 21, 22, 28, 35, 36, 60, 65, 67, 84, 85, 97, 109, 110, 127, 132, 203, 210, 211, 212, 213, 219, 224, 225, 229, 234, 236, 247, 251, 252, 255, 256, 258, 260, 264, 266, 268, 270, 273, 276, 279, 281, 285, 288, 289
World Development Report, 250, 289
World Economic Forum, 206, 211, 213, 214
World Health Organization (WHO), 207, 208, 211, 212
World Trade Organization, 211
World War, 10
writing, 67
WTO, 8, 262

Y

Yemen, 34, 49, 90, 159, 165, 168, 171, 174, 178, 180, 183, 190, 196
Yugoslavia, 121

Z

Zimbabwe, 34, 50, 159, 165, 168, 171, 174, 178, 180, 183, 190, 196